Issues, Advocacy, and Leadership in Early Education

SECOND EDITION

Mary A. Jensen
State University of New York–Geneseo

Mary Anne Hannibal
Indiana University of Pennsylvania

Allyn and Bacon
Boston ■ London ■ Toronto ■ Sydney ■ Tokyo ■ Singapore

Vice President, Editor in Chief, Education:
  Paul A. Smith
Editorial Assistant: Bridget Keane
Marketing Manager: Brad Parkins
Editorial-Production Administrator: Annette Joseph
Editorial-Production Coordinator: Susan Freese

Editorial-Production Service: TKM Productions, Inc.
Electronic Composition: Cabot Computer Services
Composition Buyer: Linda Cox
Manufacturing Buyer: Suzanne Lareau
Cover Administrator: Jenny Hart
Cover Designer: Brian Gogolin

Copyright © 2000, 1990 by Allyn & Bacon
A Pearson Education Company
160 Gould Street
Needham Heights, MA 02494
Internet: www.abacon.com

A previous edition was published under the title *Issues and Advocacy in Early Education,* by Mary A. Jensen and Zelda W. Chevalier.

Between the time website information is gathered and then published, it is not unusual for some sites to have closed. Also, the transcription of URLs can result in unintended typographical errors. The publisher would appreciate being notified of any problems with URLs so that they may be corrected in subsequent editions. Thank you.

Library of Congress Cataloging-in-Publication Data

Issues, advocacy, and leadership in early education / [edited by] Mary
  A. Jensen, Mary Anne Hannibal.
      p.   cm.
    Rev. ed. of: Issues and advocacy in early education. c1990.
    Includes bibliographical references and index.
    ISBN 0-205-30811-2
    1. Early childhood education—United States.   2. Child care—
United States.   I. Jensen, Mary A.   II. Hannibal, Mary Anne
Zeitler.   III. Issues and advocacy in early education.
  LB1140.22.I87   2000
  372.21—dc21
                                                        99-35057
                                                        CIP

Printed in the United States of America

10 9 8 7 6 5 4 3 2 1   04 03 02 01 00 99

Photo Credits: pages 5, 6, 17, 71, 111, 167: Will Faller; page 25: Amy Miller/NAEYC; page 78: John Jensen; page 122: Mary Jensen; page 153: Jacques Chevalier; page 207: Florence Sharp.

■ Contents

Preface   ix

■ *Chapter 1*   **Introduction   1**

Demographic Trends in Early Childhood Education   1

Advocacy and Leadership:
New Professional Challenges   3

Characteristics of Effective Advocates and Leaders   6

Strategies for Developing Advocacy Knowledge,
Skills, and Dispositions   7

A Current Events Portfolio   8

Framework for an On-site Study of an Early
Childhood Program   8

Looking Ahead   11

References and Suggested Readings   11

■ *Chapter 2*   **Gender Identity, Gender Role,
and Sex Education   14**

■ Girls Can Be Bull Riders, Too!   16
  Karyn Wellhousen

■ Healthy Sexuality Development in Young Children   22
  Donna Couchenour and Kent Chrisman

■ Teachers and Parents Define Diversity in an Oregon
  Preschool Cooperative—Democracy at Work   28
  Jennifer Lakey

  Ask Yourself: Identifying Issues for Advocacy   37

  Advocacy and Leadership Strategies   39

  References and Suggested Readings   42

■ *Chapter 3*   **Media and Technology   44**

■ Peggy Charren: The Mother of Children's Television   46
   Lauryn Axelrod

■ AAP Addresses TV Programming for Children
   under Age 2   48
   American Academy of Pediatrics

■ Television Violence: Content, Context,
   and Consequences   49
   Amy Aidman

■ Shaping TV for Kids   52
   Richard Louv

■ Your Children Are Talking to Strangers   53
   PC World Magazine

   Ask Yourself: Identifying Issues for Advocacy   55

   Advocacy and Leadership Strategies   56

   References and Suggested Readings   59

■ *Chapter 4*   **Child Health and
                    Child Health Risks   61**

■ Poverty and Brain Development
   in Early Childhood   63
   Larry Aber and Julian Palmer

■ Healthy Habitats for Children   66
   Ruth A. Wilson

■ Healthy Child Care America:
   A Blueprint for Action   70
   U.S. Department of Health and Human Services

■ Multiple Voices for Advocacy: The Story of WIC
   (Special Supplemental Nutrition Program for
   Women, Infants, and Children)   73
   Mary A. Jensen

   Ask Yourself: Identifying Issues for Advocacy   81

   Advocacy and Leadership Strategies   82

   References and Suggested Readings   84

■ *Chapter 5* **Abuse, Neglect, and Violence in
Children's Lives   86**

■ The Effects of Violence on Children's Lives   88
Concerned Educators Allied for a Safe Environment

■ CAN Reflections on 20 Years of Searching   89
James Garbarino

■ Recognizing Child Abuse and Neglect   92
Derry Koralek

Ask Yourself: Identifying Issues for Advocacy   98

Advocacy and Leadership Strategies   100

References and Suggested Readings   102

■ *Chapter 6* **Diversity and Equity   104**

■ Empowering Children to Create a Caring Culture
in a World of Differences   107
Louise Derman-Sparks

■ Teaching Young Children about Native Americans   114
Debbie Reese

■ The Bilingual Education Debate   117
Laurel Shaper Walters

■ The Impact of Changing Roles on Relationships
between Professionals in Inclusive Programs for
Young Children   121
*Joan Lieber, Paula J. Beckman, Marci J. Hanson, Susan
Janko, Jules M. Marquart, Eva Horn, and Samuel L. Odom*

Ask Yourself: Identifying Issues for Advocacy   130

Advocacy and Leadership Strategies   133

References and Suggested Readings   137

■ *Chapter 7*   **The Family:
Parenting Education and Family
Involvement in Education   139**

■ On Our Changing Family Values:
A Conversation with David Elkind   141
Marge Scherer

■ Partners in Learning: How Schools Can
Support Family Involvement in Education   146
Family Involvement Partnership for Learning

■ Father/Male Involvement in Early
Childhood Programs   148
Brent A. McBride and Thomas R. Rane

■ Portrait of a Head Start Parent   151
Glenna Zeak

■ Backing Away Helpfully: Some Roles
Teachers Shouldn't Fill   153
Penny Hauser-Cram

■ The Changing Face of Parenting Education   156
Sharon L. Kagan

Ask Yourself: Identifying Issues for Advocacy   158

Advocacy and Leadership Strategies   159

References and Suggested Readings   162

■ *Chapter 8*   **Developmentally Appropriate
and Educationally
Worthwhile Practice   164**

■ Developmentally Appropriate Interpretation
with Preschool Children   166
Ruth A. Wilson

■ Developmentally Appropriate Practice
Is for Everyone   170
Rosalind Charlesworth

■ Paradise Lost   178
David Ruenzel

Ask Yourself: Identifying Issues for Advocacy   185

Advocacy and Leadership Strategies   188

References and Suggested Readings   189

■ *Chapter 9*   **Quality in Child Care and Early Education   193**

■ Quality in Child Care Centers   195
    National Center for Early Development and Learning

■ Yale Study Faults Child Care in All 50 States   199
    Linda Jacobson

■ Who Cares for the Children? Denmark's Unique
Public Child-Care Model   201
    Valerie Polakow

■ National Campaign Calls for Worthy Wages
for Child Care   209
    Joy Shioshita

Ask Yourself: Identifying Issues for Advocacy   211

Advocacy and Leadership Strategies   212

References and Suggested Readings   216

Appendices   219

■ *1* Websites and Website Links   220

■ *2* Advocacy Tips   220

■ *3* Writing Advocacy Letters   221

■ *4* Working with the Media   222

■ *5* Visiting Public Officials   224

■ *6* Planning a Visit to Child Care Centers
for Legislators   225

■ *7* Developing a Policy Briefing Paper   226

■ *8* Guidelines for an Informal Debate   229

■ *9* Four Steps to Selecting a Child
Care Provider   235

■ *10* Facts about Child Care in America   236

■ *11* The Rights of the Child: Summary of the
         United Nations' Convention   238

■ *12* Are There Signs of Child Abuse and Neglect?
         (Are There Signs That a Family May Be
         in Trouble?)   239

■ *13* Diversity in the Classroom: A Checklist   241

■ *14* Books Related to Ethnic Diversity   243

Index   244

■ *Preface*

Audience and Purpose

This book has been written primarily for early childhood teachers and administrators at both the preservice and inservice levels of professional development. The text also will interest educators who seek a better understanding of current issues in early education and who want to become more active as advocates for children.

This second edition of *Issues, Advocacy, and Leadership in Early Education* is designed to involve readers in reflecting on current issues in early childhood and in assuming an advocacy role. Research today can help us understand the factors that influence young children's learning and brain development. At the same time, changing population demographics and broader social trends place increasing demands on educators who are trying to meet the educational needs of young children. To meet these needs, educators need to gain access to today's broader knowledge base and resources and find new avenues for becoming involved and making a difference in young children's lives.

This book includes topics now recognized to be important determinants of children's well-being and development but generally only touched upon superficially in other textbooks or not addressed at all. To stimulate deeper thinking about alternative positions and perspectives, varied viewpoints, cases, and research studies are presented. The values underlying these different views are closely examined and compared to core values that have formed the basis for professional decisions made in early childhood education. This book takes the reader one step further. Because of changes in educational issues and resources, educators now require more than an understanding of or an ability to debate various positions. Rather, educators need to become advocates and leaders for young children by interacting and becoming involved with others in their school, professional, and civic communities.

Overall, our goals are to (1) extend the knowledge of current issues (e.g., brain development research, welfare reform, state expansion of prekindergarten programs and children's health insurance programs, before- and after-school programs, "ready to learn" initiatives, and the increasing influences of media and technology on children and their

families); (2) expand the use of information resources to include community inquiries, the Internet, and interdisciplinary studies; (3) further involve professional and community organizations; and (4) support leadership development in early education.

Coverage and Features

During the past 20 years, grass-roots advocacy efforts among early childhood personnel have shown a dramatic increase. No longer are policy experts the only ones to testify at hearings or to address governmental representatives and the public concerning current issues in the field. At the same time, the knowledge base for issues in the field of early childhood education has mushroomed. Flourishing research related to young children has led to a need to review these contributions and select those that have meaning and value for the early childhood teacher and administrator. We have chosen articles based on their relevance to issues confronting people today in the field of early childhood education, their emphasis on values underlying particular actions or positions, and their clarity, liveliness, and brevity. In some sections of the book, we present positions that illustrate contrasting viewpoints in order to engage the critical-thinking skills of the reader and to show that different views on a controversial issue need to be considered.

Chapter 1 of *Issues, Advocacy, and Leadership in Early Education* serves as an introduction and description of the approach to issues and advocacy used in the development of this book. Chapters 2 through 9 range in content from issues most evident to the public through mass media coverage to issues given less media coverage but embedded in the policies and operation of early childhood programs and related organizations or institutions in society. Each of these chapters provides intensive treatment of a particular topic and may be read independently of other sections. However, some chapters cover related topics and are grouped together. The order of subject matter is based on student reactions to the topics and their comprehension of the issues.

Chapter 2 launches the examination of critical issues with a topic receiving much media attention in our culture: sex. Its relevance for early education is explored in terms of gender identity and gender-role development as well as sex education. Chapter 3 reviews ideas and evidence concerning the impact of television and media use on young children's development. Chapter 4 examines factors affecting child health and effective health advocacy strategies and intervention programs. Also related to child health are the issues of abuse, neglect, and violence, which are examined in Chapter 5. Chapter 6 addresses the issues of diversity and equity in the education of young children. Chapter 7 considers topics related to the role of parents in early education. Chapter 8 explores issues related to providing developmentally appropriate and worthwhile learning experiences in early education programs. From a concern about developmentally appropriate and worthwhile practice, a focus on quality in early education programs follows naturally in Chapter 9. The issues explored include the availability of quality programs, funding, balancing the needs of children with those of parents, constructing appropriate and coordinated service models for early care and education, and strengthening the professional status and salaries of early education personnel. Finally, Appendices 1 through 14 offer strategy guidelines and fact sheets for advocacy and inquiry activities.

This book provides an abundance of case examples, exercises, and discussion questions to involve the reader in developing his or her knowledge, skills, and dispositions for child advocacy. In order to facilitate this integration and make this text easy to use, we have included the following features:

- *Vignettes,* presented at the beginning of each chapter, describe predicaments faced by early childhood teachers and child advocates. These vignettes may serve as a basis for initial discussion of key issues for the chapter topic.
- *Previews* help the reader develop a framework for the readings and content of each chapter.
- *Ask Yourself* sections, part of the material following readings at the end of each chapter, pose questions for self-reflection or group discussion. These questions will help the reader identify the

various issues, values, and positions to pursue in advocacy activities.

- *Advocacy and Leadership Strategies,* also found at the chapter end, suggest activities that will help the reader (1) relate viewpoints and reported evidence to personal experiences, (2) examine the values underlying various positions, and (3) develop advocacy and leadership skills and dispositions.
- *References and Suggested Readings,* the final section of each chapter, list some additional sources of information for the topic discussed.

Acknowledgments

Many people have helped us write this book. Our appreciation is extended to our students at the State University of New York–Geneseo, who made invaluable contributions to the development of the advocacy involvement activities. Zelda Chevalier, former colleague and coauthor, helped to envision and develop the first edition. We also wish to acknowledge the support of the College Planning Council at the State University of New York–Geneseo in providing a Summer Curriculum Development Grant to help advance our work on this book.

In addition, we thank the following reviewers for their comments and suggestions regarding this new edition: Virginia Durgan Erion, Central Washington University; Carol Foster, Georgia State University; Jean Kueker, Our Lady of the Lake University; and Maureen Murphy, University of Utah. We also thank those individuals who reviewed the first edition: Susan Ferrante, North Shore Community College, Lynn, Massachusetts; Margie Kitano, New Mexico State University; Susan Trostle, University of Rhode Island; and Carol Vukelich, University of Delaware.

Finally, we gratefully acknowledge the efforts of the editorial and production staff at Allyn and Bacon as well as Lynda Griffiths at TKM Productions, whose assistance greatly facilitated our work. Together, they coordinated and guided the project and readily provided advice and support.

■ *Chapter 1*

■ Introduction

Demographic Trends in Early Childhood Education

In the past 35 years, the number of children being served by early childhood education programs has surged. Today, before they enter first grade, most young children receive some type of care and education from individuals other than their parents (West, Wright, & Germino Hausken, 1995). The types of care and education available outside young children's homes have also changed. In the 1950s, most early childhood programs were either kindergartens or half-day nursery-school programs serving middle-class children. Today, the field of early childhood education encompasses not only kindergartens and parent-funded nursery schools but also an array of privately and publicly funded programs (e.g., Head Start, early intervention programs, home-based programs, child-care centers, family child-care homes, prekindergarten programs, and after- and before-school programs). The present need for expanded, high-quality child care and early education services grew out of demographic trends for young children in the United States in the past 35 years. These trends reflect two significant shifts for children in our society: family economic resources and racial and ethnic diversity.

Increasingly, children are living in families of poverty or wealth. Overall, about 5 million, or 23 percent, of young children under the age of 6 live in poverty (National Center for Children in Poverty, 1998). Contributing to this level of poverty has been an increase in the number of young children living in mother-only families (Hernandez, 1995). At the same time, we have witnessed an increasing number of U.S. children living in families of wealth and a shrinking number living in middle-class families. Contributing to this increase has been a growing number of dual-earner families. By 1990, nearly 40 percent of children, ages birth to 5, lived in dual-earner families (Hernandez, 1995).

1

Another way in which the population being served is changing is by becoming increasingly diverse. In 1990, approximately 30 percent of preschool-aged children were minorities (U.S. Government Accounting Office, 1993). Projections suggest that this percentage will continue to grow so that by 2040, minorities will account for about 55 percent of all children (Hernandez, 1995). Also, if the poverty status of minority children continues, we can anticipate a greater increase in the number of children living in poverty in U.S. society.

Children's participation patterns in early care and education programs also vary by family income and ethnicity. Among young children living in families with incomes of $10,000 or less in 1995, only 50 percent participated in some type of nonparental care and education, whereas 77 percent of young children living in wealthy families with incomes exceeding $75,000 participated in such arrangements (West et al., 1995). Among preschool-aged children, only 35 percent of those living in poor or near-poor families in 1993 participated in preschool programs, compared to 45 percent for children living in middle- and high-income families (U.S. Government Accounting Office, 1993). Children's participation patterns also vary by ethnicity. In 1995, the participation rate was 46 percent for Hispanic children, 62 percent for White children, and 66 percent for African American children. The type of care used also varies. White and African American children were more likely to attend centers (33 percent) than were Hispanic children (17 percent). Additionally, African American children were more likely than the other two groups to receive care from a relative in a home (31 percent) (West et al., 1995). (For further elaboration on these trends, see Appendix 10 in this book and the Child Care Bureau link of the Department of Health and Human Services website—Appendix 1.)

These population and participation trends as well as increased child-care needs resulting from welfare reform suggest that three major challenges are facing early childhood education:

1. To meet the increasing needs of dual-earner families and single-parent working families for full-day programs

   (In 1994, about half of all preprimary enrollees attended full-day programs, compared to about one-fifth of them in 1970 [Snyder & Hoffman, 1995].)

2. To finance a system of high-quality care and education, accessible to low- and middle-income families as well as high-income families

   (Along with increased costs of more full-day programs, we can anticipate from current trends that child-care costs will rise. In 1986, a preschool family spent approximately $64 per week on child care; by 1993, this figure in constant dollars had risen to $79. Recent research, however, documents that 80 percent of child-care participants are enrolled in child-care settings of poor or mediocre quality [Kagan & Cohen, 1997]. Also, low staff salaries have hindered efforts to hire well-prepared staff and have led to high staff turnover rates, thus decreasing the overall quality of available early education programs.)

3. To develop relationships within family, community, and peer cultures that support the education and care of young children from diverse backgrounds

(Family engagement in important emergent literacy activities—for example, reading aloud to young children on a regular basis—varies by family characteristics, such as economic status, ethnicity, family structure, and mother's education. We must find ways to support and work with diverse families in early childhood programs and with other community leaders. To enhance the opportunities of all children, we need to recognize the importance of children's education and care and celebrate their learning in multiple settings [e.g., Berndt & Ladd, 1989; Bronfenbrenner, 1986; Harris, 1998; National Education Goals Panel, 1997].)

Advocacy and Leadership:
New Professional Challenges

A commonly observed characteristic of early childhood teachers is their warm delight in young children. Practicing and prospective teachers work with children because they enjoy them and are concerned for their welfare. In assuming this role, teachers undertake to share with parents responsibility for helping children realize their full potential (Buchmann, 1986). This responsibility has expanded as we have learned more from research about brain development. With new evidence from brain-scanning research, we know that warm and responsive care and enriched home and school environments during the early years of life can profoundly affect the development of children's mental capacities (Hotz & Marquis, 1996; Newberger, 1997; Shore, 1997).

Recent social, political, and economic developments in our society also are challenging traditional images of the early childhood practitioner (Bronfenbrenner, 1986; Carnegie Task Force on Meeting the Needs of Young Children, 1994). Whereas conventional role definitions have been grounded in practices of early education and child care, today's practitioners are increasingly being faced with the need to become involved in public-interest issues that impinge directly on their primary role obligations to the children in their care (Hostetler, 1981; Whitebook & Almy, 1986). For example, today's practitioner is required by law to report cases of suspected child abuse and may be involved with providing court-ordered services for abused children; therefore, social policies related to child abuse and neglect affect the practices of the early childhood teacher. Today's teachers also are acutely aware that, apart from parents, they are the most prominent agents who can act on behalf of children and protect children's rights. Thus, early childhood practitioners find themselves extending their concerns for children beyond immediate interactions within the classroom to seeking improvements in the responsiveness and relevance of social policies and services (Melton, 1983; National Education Goals Panel, 1997).

Other changes in our economy and society, such as welfare reform, have impressed on early childhood practitioners the need to advocate for families as well as for children (U.S. Government Accounting Office, 1998). Economic and social changes have brought about less stable communities and shifts in family makeup that have tended to isolate families and put additional strains on the family unit. Child advocacy is particularly important today in providing and bolstering support systems that help children cope with emotional needs. Supporting the family unit as well as helping children meet their full potential are primary goals of early childhood programs (Bredekamp & Copple, 1997; Melton, 1983).

The drive to become more involved in advocacy efforts on behalf of young children has been intensified in recent years by calls to advocate for improvement in the welfare and quality of early childhood personnel (Kagan & Cohen, 1997). The occupation is plagued by low morale brought on by low wages, minimum employee benefits, and poor working conditions (Almy, 1985; Whitebook & Almy, 1986). Both for self-interest and for interest in the well-being of children, the role of the early childhood practitioner is being reconceptualized and restructured from one governed by parochial interests to one that acknowledges the direct and indirect linkages between quality child care, occupational welfare, and events in the public arena (Jorde-Bloom, 1986; Silin, 1985; Washington, 1996; Whitebook, Howes, Darrah, & Friedman, 1982).

To meet the advocacy challenge, some early childhood practitioners have taken a proactive stance. Their activities range from pursuing needed services for individuals and their families to seeking changes in procedures, laws, and resources that affect groups of families and children. In the process of effecting change, they have acquired the systematic knowledge and expertise needed to influence the decisions of legislators, agencies, and organizations whose mission it is to develop policies and legislation that protect the rights and needs of young children (Edelman, 1998; Forgione, 1980; Kilmer, 1980).

Accompanying this quiet revolution in child advocacy (Jorde, 1986) have been efforts by early childhood personnel to professionalize the occupation (Almy, 1985; Feeney, 1985; Hostetler & Klugman, 1982; Katz, 1984; Raines, 1983; Washington, 1996). A critical step in this venture is clarifying and obtaining consensus on the beliefs and values of practitioners in order to establish a professional code of ethics (Feeney & Kipnis, 1989). The construction of such a set of ethical principles provides an external framework for critical reflection and supports use of advanced professional knowledge in making judgments about positions and courses of action.

If the thrust toward advocacy and professionalization is to be expanded, preservice and inservice teachers will be asked to acquire the requisite knowledge and skills needed to deal with problem issues. They must also be willing to expend the additional time and energy needed to effect change. Important to this enterprise is the task of overcoming feelings of powerlessness and anxiety about anticipated and unanticipated consequences (Jensen, 1986; Lombardi, 1986; Markus & Nurius, 1986). Put another way, if people perceive themselves as ineffective and conjure up possible calamities, they will be reluctant to attempt actions that exceed their ability to cope with unpredictable situations (Bandura, 1977).

In contrast, people who judge themselves adept in coping with potential threats are not deterred from entering into unknown territory (Bandura, 1977). The history of early education, in particular, documents how many practitioners and other interested parties have been instrumental in effecting the adoption of policies and programs that protect child and family welfare (Osborn, 1980). Whether their courage stemmed from motives of altruism or self-interest, these trailblazers of the past and those presently engaged in advocacy efforts provide a model for emulation.

All of us have "possible selves"—what we would like to become and what we are afraid of becoming (Markus & Nurius, 1986). We can remain part of the advocacy problem, bogged down in helplessness and disillusionment, or we can become part of the solution by coming to grips with substantive issues in the field and obtaining, concurrently, the skills and dispositions needed to become effective

The time is right for action.

advocates. Once again, early education has captured the public interest. Today, there is an unprecedented demand for child care by trained, qualified personnel. The time is right for action.

Characteristics of Effective Advocates and Leaders

Learning how to become an effective advocate means obtaining information about advocacy issues, employing the skills needed to carry out the task, and developing and strengthening one's disposition to assume an advocacy role. For purposes of explication, these general goals can be redefined as specific attributes and skills (Dinham & Stritter, 1986), which represent outcomes that the reader will achieve as he or she engages in the inquiry, leadership, and advocacy strategies to be discussed in this book. These intended outcomes include the following:

1. *Cognitive attributes,* which relate to the information base contained in this book and in suggested resources which become transformed for use in both analytical and intuitive reasoning

2. *Attitudinal attributes,* which reflect the values and ethics used to guide choice, argument, rationalization, and action and include the motivation and the disposition to engage in resolution of ethical problems and moral dilemmas

Effective advocates develop their knowledge of child advocacy issues and strategies and strengthen their dispositions to assume advocacy rules.

3. *Psychosocial attributes*, which underpin one's sensitivity to interpersonal relations when communicating with colleagues, clients, and members of the public

4. *Socialization attributes*, which reflect the gradual internalization of professional values and commitment to the role of advocate

5. *Learning skills*, which are needed to keep informed of events and changes in the field, to decide what needs to be learned and where to obtain information, and to know when learning has been accomplished.

These attributes and skills, in one combination or another, are brought into play through participation in activities incorporated in this book.

Strategies for Developing Advocacy Knowledge, Skills, and Dispositions

Suggestions for developing prospective advocates' knowledge of current child advocacy issues and strategies as well as strengthening their dispositions to assume advocacy roles come from several sources (Allen, 1983; Cahill, 1986; Deloria & Brookins, 1982; Fink & Sponseller, 1977; Jensen, 1986; Kilmer, 1980; New York State Child Care Coordinating Council, n.d.; Whitebook & Ginsburg, 1984; Zigler & Finn, 1981). These suggestions can be grouped in the following categories:

1. Issue debates

2. Issue interviews, advocacy speakers, and community discussion panels

3. Role-play or simulation exercises

4. On-site program studies

5. Advocacy journals, current events portfolios, public information displays and media materials, advocacy letters, legislative visits, position and briefing papers, testimony, and parent/community education activities

6. Professional organization contacts, networking, lobbying coalitions, and task forces

Most of these suggestions are incorporated as activities within this book. Taken together, these activities provide a solid foundation from which to take further steps in planning strategies and taking concrete actions to improve conditions for children, families, and early childhood practitioners in our society. The remainder of this chapter, however, will describe two options that can be linked to various chapters and used as ongoing strategies: a current events portfolio and an on-site program study.

A Current Events Portfolio

A current events (or What's in the News?) portfolio is an accumulation of at least 12 articles or reports from newspapers, news magazines, websites, or family magazines (e.g., *Working Mother* or *Parenting*) related to current issues concerning the welfare of young children. These articles must be collected over an extended period of time, come from different sources (record source, date, and page numbers for each article), and relate to topics in this book. In addition, this portfolio contains a reflection paper, which is written after all the articles have been collected and assembled. Details about this paper can be found at the end of Chapter 9.

Framework for an On-Site Study of an Early Childhood Program

The purpose of an on-site program study is to understand better how advocacy issues are recognized or interpreted in a particular early childhood program. Any licensed or state-accredited program that serves children from birth to age 8 can be the focus of this study. As you participate in this study, just as in other inquiries, maintaining high standards of professionalism and confidentiality is important.

Arrange for Your Visits

Well before you would like to visit, you must call or write to the program director or school administrator to make an appointment to observe. Make sure that this person knows that you will be observing several times and that you would like some of his or her time for an interview. Tell the person (1) why you want to visit, (2) what dates and times are good for you (have several alternatives and be sure to consider the program's daily schedule), and (3) what you would like to do (i.e., observe the program and spend about 30 minutes interviewing the director/administrator or head teacher). If you make these arrangements, then ask if any publicity material on the program could be sent to you before your visit so that you may become acquainted with the program.

Prepare for Your Visits

By being prepared, you can gather a great deal of useful information during your classroom visits. You will need to prepare by reviewing readings, presentations, and discussions on early childhood issues and program components, guidelines, and regulations as well as any materials that have been sent to you. Review the accreditation standards by the National Association for the Education of Young Children (NAEYC, 1991) and developmentally appropriate practice guidelines

(Bredekamp & Copple, 1997) for the appropriate age range(s). Prior to your visit, draft a list of questions that you might ask the director/administrator. Immediately following your observations, modify your list based on these observations and take your final draft of these questions with you to the interview. You also might want to have on hand copies of the NAEYC's developmentally appropriate practice guidelines and accreditation standards during the interview as well as during your observations.

Make Your Classroom Observations

Call the center or school the day before your first visit to reconfirm your appointment. Arrive promptly (call the center if you will be detained). You will need to observe several times to get an accurate feel for what is happening in a classroom and to check the reliability of your observational findings. Keep in mind that it is important to maintain a low profile as an observer. Try not to get involved (verbally, physically, or visually) with adults or children. Be sure to introduce yourself to the teacher and ask what she or he wants you to do while you are observing. Assume a comfortable manner and engage briefly in any spontaneous conversation initiated by children or teachers. Otherwise, do not initiate a conversation with the teachers during class time.

Try to observe the following situations and times:

1. Early in the day when the children are first arriving (and possibly leaving their parents)
2. Snack or meal time
3. An organized or teacher-guided activity
4. Free-choice or free-play time
5. When the children are going down for their naps (if a full-day child-care program)
6. Late in the day when the children are departing

Using a small notebook, write notes or running records of the actions and words of the children and their teachers in these situations.

Also make activity scans or records (Klass, 1986) that focus on some important aspects of the room, such as the following:

1. *Use of space.* Note the physical arrangement and purposes of space and materials. (Include a floor plan of the facility and note the provisioning for free-play or child-selected activities.)
2. *Use of time.* Note how routines and transitions are handled, as well as the scheduling and balancing of activities.
3. *Teacher interactions.* If there is more than one teacher and/or aide in the room, note the differences in their interactions with the children and how they interact with each other.

4. *Children's interactions.* Note if the children's interactions are extended or momentary with each other and with adults.

5. *Teacher's activities when not interacting with the children.* Note the specific tasks the teacher does when the children are otherwise occupied.

Interview the Administrator or Teacher

Have your questions ready, along with paper and pen to jot down answers. (If the interviewee agrees, you also may audiotape the interview and then transcribe it at a later date.) This is your opportunity to ask about observed behaviors, activities, or events that you found puzzling or contrary to what you have learned or believe about teaching young children, and to ask how child advocacy issues are addressed, if at all, in program policy. You also may use this opportunity to gain information about the following:

1. Program philosophy and goals for children (How do these young children learn? What educational goals are emphasized in this program? What social values or beliefs are stressed in the education of these children? What are the roles of the teacher, family, and community in the lives and education of these children?)

2. Basic descriptive information (history, location, number of families and children served, fee structure, and type of program)

3. Staffing patterns, staff qualifications, and staff administrative policies (staff wages, fringe benefits, release time, turnover, orientation, inservice training or professional development opportunities, and evaluation)

4. Health and safety policies and services (including transportation of children)

5. Nutrition and food service policies

6. Policies and provisions for inclusion of children with disabilities

7. Policies and provisions for staff/parent interaction and family involvement

8. Screening and assessment of children's development and learning

9. Evaluation of the entire program (licensing as well as other means of evaluation)

Write a Final Report

Your final report analyzes and synthesizes your program observations, interview responses, and any printed information received. In general, your analysis and synthesis should be impartial, open-minded, and professional. Quotes or ideas from printed program materials must be cited, as should any other sources used. Basic components of this report are as follows:

1. Cover Page

2. Table of Contents

3. Brief Description of Field Study Methods Used (describing your initial contact, schedule, length of time for study, and strategies used—that is, how you proceeded with the inquiry, what recording techniques you used, and what you did as an observer and an interviewer)

4. Description of the Center

5. Analysis and Synthesis of Observations (referring to a professional knowledge base [readings] in your discussion of findings, and supporting your opinions with examples from observation notes)

6. Other Program Policies and Early Education Issues (discussing other issues not covered in previous sections—such as gender-role stereotyping, sex education policies, child abuse or neglect, or television viewing)

7. Summary of Your Overall Impressions

8. Thank-You Letter to the Center

9. Reference List

10. Appendices (including publicity materials or forms from the program and your observation and interview process notes)

Looking Ahead

To advocate effectively for children, their families, and the teaching profession is one of the greatest leadership challenges facing early childhood teachers and administrators today. The material in this book will be a resource that teachers and administrators find stimulating and useful when seeking to meet this challenge.

References and Suggested Readings

Allen, K. E. (1983, January). Public policy report: Children, the Congress, and you. *Young Children, 38,* 71–75.

Almy, M. (1985, September). New challenges for teacher education: Facing political and economic realities. *Young Children, 40,* 10–11.

Bandura, A. (1977). *Social learning theory.* Englewood Cliffs, NJ: Prentice-Hall.

Berndt, T. J., & Ladd, G. W. (1989). *Peer relationships in child development.* Somerset, NJ: Wiley.

Bredekamp, S., & Copple, C. (Eds.). (1997). *Developmentally appropriate practice in early childhood programs* (rev. ed.). Washington, DC: National Association for the Education of Young Children.

Bronfenbrenner, U. (1986). Ecology of the family as a context for human development: Research perspectives. *Developmental Psychology, 22,* 723–742.

Buchmann, M. (1986). Role over person: Morality and authenticity in teaching. *Teachers College Record, 87,* 529–543.

Cahill, B. F. (1986). Training volunteers as child advocates. *Child Welfare, 65,* 545–553.

Carnegie Task Force on Meeting the Needs of Young Children. (1994). *Starting points: Meeting the needs of our youngest children.* New York: Carnegie Corporation of New York.

Deloria, D., & Brookins, G. K. (1982). The evaluation report: A weak link to policy. In J. R. Travers and R. J. Light (Eds.), *Learning from experience: Evaluating early childhood demonstration programs* (pp. 254–271). Washington, DC: National Academy Press.

Dinham, S. M., & Stritter, F. T. (1986). Research on professional education. In M. C. Wittrock (Ed.), *Handbook of research on teaching* (3rd ed., pp. 952–970). New York: Macmillan.

Edelman, M. W. (1998, December). A voice for children: Protect our children. *CDF Reports* [Online], 1 page. Available: www.childrensdefense.org/voice.html

Feeney, S. (1985, November). *Professional ethics in early childhood education.* Seminar presented at the Annual Conference of the National Association for the Education of Young Children, New Orleans.

Feeney, S., & Kipnis, K. (1989). Code of ethical conduct and statement of commitment. *Young Children, 45* (1), 24–29.

Fink, J., & Sponseller, D. (1977, March). Practicing for child advocacy. *Young Children, 32,* 49–54.

Forgione, P. D. (1980). Early childhood policy-making. *Education and Urban Society, 12,* 227–239.

Harris, J. R. (1998). *The nurture assumption: Why children turn out the way they do.* New York: Free Press.

Hernandez, D. J. (1995). Changing demographics: Past and future demands for early childhood programs. *Future of Children, 5* (3), 145–160.

Hostetler, L. (1981, March). Child advocacy: Your professional responsibility? *Young Children, 36,* 3–8.

Hostetler, L., & Klugman, E. (1982, September). Early childhood job titles: One step toward professional status. *Young Children, 37,* 13–22.

Hotz, R. L., & Marquis, J. (1996, October 13–16). The brain . . . A work in progress. *Los Angeles Times* [Online], 11 pages. Available: www.latimes.com/HOME/NEWS/SCIENCE/REPORTS/THEBRAIN/thebrain/

Jensen, M. A. (1986, November). *Preparing early childhood teachers to become advocates: A new challenge for teacher education.* Paper presented at the Annual Conference of the National Association for the Education of Young Children, Washington, DC. (ERIC Document Reproduction Service No. ED 275 456)

Jorde, P. (1986). Early childhood education: Issues and trends. *The Educational Forum, 50,* 172–181.

Jorde-Bloom, P. (1986). Teacher job satisfaction: A framework for analysis. *Early Childhood Research Quarterly, 1,* 167–183.

Kagan, S. L., & Cohen, N. E. (1997). *Not by chance: Creating an early care and education system for America's children.* Executive summary, the Quality 2000 Initiative. New Haven, CT: Bush Center in Child Development and Social Policy, Yale University.

Katz, L. G. (1984, July). The professional early childhood teacher. *Young Children, 39,* 3–10.

Kilmer, S. (1980). Early childhood specialists as policy makers. *Education and Urban Society, 12,* 241–251.

Klass, C. S. (1986). *The autonomous child.* New York: Falmer Press.

Lombardi, J. (1986, May). Public policy report. Training for public policy and advocacy: An emerging topic in teacher education. *Young Children, 41,* 65–69.

Markus, H., & Nurius, P. (1986). Possible selves. *American Psychologist, 41,* 954–969.

Melton, G. B. (1983). *Child advocacy: Psychological issues and interventions.* New York: Plenum Press.

National Association for the Education of Young Children. (1991). *Accreditation criteria and procedures of the National Academy of Early Childhood Programs.* Washington, DC: Author.

National Center for Children in Poverty. (1998). Home page. Available: www. cpmcnet.columbia.edu/dept/nccp/

National Education Goals Panel. (1997). *Special early childhood report 1997.* Washington, DC: U.S. Government Printing Office.

New York State Child Care Coordinating Council. (n.d.). *Lobbying techniques.* White Plains, NY: Day Care Council of Westchester.

Newberger, J. J. (1997). New brain development research—A wonderful window of opportunity to build public support for early childhood education! *Young Children, 52* (4), 4–9.

Osborn, D. K. (1980). *Early childhood education in historical perspective.* Athens, GA: Educational Associates.

Raines, S. C. (1983). Developing professionalism: Shared responsibility. *Childhood Education, 59,*151–153.

Shore, R. (1997). *Rethinking the brain: New insights into early development.* New York: Families and Work Institute.

Silin, J. G. (1985, March). Authority as knowledge: A problem of professionalization. *Young Children, 40,* 41–46.

Snyder, T. D., & Hoffman, C. M. (1995). *Digest of Educational Statistics 1995.* Washington, DC: U.S. Government Printing Office.

U.S. Government Accounting Office. (1993). *Poor preschool-aged children: Numbers increase but most not in school.* Briefing Report to the Chairman, Subcommittee on Children, Family, Drugs, and Alcoholism, Committee of Labor and Human Resources, U.S. Senate. Washington, DC: U.S. General Accounting Office.

U.S. Government Accounting Office. (1998). *Welfare reform: States' efforts to expand child care programs.* Report to the Ranking Minority Member, Subcommittee on Children and Families, Committee on Labor and Human Resources, U.S. Senate. Washington, DC: U.S. General Accounting Office.

Washington, V. (1996). Professional development in context: Leadership at the borders of our democratic, pluralistic society. *Young Children, 51* (6), 30–34.

West, J., Wright, D., & Germino Hausken, E. (1995). *Child care and early education program participation of infants, toddlers, and preschoolers.* Washington, DC: U.S. Department of Education, National Center for Education Statistics.

Whitebook, M., & Almy, M. (1986, September). NAEYC's commitment to good programs for young children: Then and now, a developmental crisis at 60? *Young Children, 41,* 37–40.

Whitebook, M., & Ginsburg, G. (Eds.). (1984). *Beyond "just working with kids": Preparing early childhood teachers to advocate for themselves and others.* Berkeley, CA: Child Care Employee Project. (ERIC Document Reproduction Service ED 255 299)

Whitebook, M., Howes, C., Darrah, R., & Friedman, J. (1982). Caring for the caregivers: Staff burnout in child care. In L. G. Katz (Ed.), *Current topics in early childhood education* (Vol. 4, pp. 211–235). Norwood, NJ: Ablex.

Zigler, E., & Finn, M. (1981, May). From problem to solution: Changing public policy as it affects children and families. *Young Children, 37,* 31–58.

■ *Chapter 2*

■ Gender Identity,
■ Gender Role, and
■ Sex Education

A Real Boy?

Karen Dodson was observing her son from the observation booth at Sugar Plum Preschool. As she watched free-play, she noticed her son, Seth, happily occupied with a group of girls in the housekeeping corner. All were busy decking themselves out in ruffly dresses and high heels. Once dressed, they pretended to apply makeup and nail polish. Then the children grabbed purses and pretended to go shopping with their babies. Although the group looked adorable, doubts about this activity began to creep into Mrs. Dodson's mind: Does Seth's enjoyment of this type of activity mean that he will become a sissy? What will my husband say when I tell him what happened today? Should I ask the teacher to steer Seth toward the other boys who are playing "boys'" games?

Questions

1. Should Seth's mother be concerned about her son's behavior? Why or why not?

2. From Seth's perspective, why do you think his behavior makes sense to him?

3. How would you, as a teacher, respond to this mother's concerns? (Option: Role-play a conference incorporating the mother's concerns and the teacher's attempt to convince the mother that the behavior is acceptable [see Cahill & Adams, 1997].)

4. Suppose Seth's father, a police officer, comes in for Open House and sees Seth in the housekeeping area. He approaches you and says, "Don't let Seth play there." How would you respond?

5. What would you do if one of the other boys in the class called out to Seth, "Mr. Skirt, Mr. Skirt, better watch out or you'll get hurt!"?

▪ Preview

How do children learn to figure out appropriate behaviors for boys and girls in our society? How do they come to understand the birth of babies and their own beginnings? A quick flipping of the television dial is enough to reveal that messages related to sex and sex-role behaviors bombard most young children on a daily basis. What messages do parents and teachers convey about gender identity, gender role, and reproduction? What is the role of the teacher in relation to forming concepts of gender identity, gender role, and reproduction? Should young children be protected from exposure to some messages or experiences? At what point do parents' values and their rights to privacy become an issue?

In this chapter, Karyn Wellhousen discusses using children's literature as a classroom resource for discussing and learning about a variety of gender roles and gender fairness. Another disputed issue in our society is what educational practices are best in the area of sex education. Donna Couchenour and Kent Chrisman offer a comprehensive set of developmental guidelines for curriculum decisions and point out issues that teachers often need to consider in making those decisions. Finally, Jennifer Lakey reports on how parents in one cooperative nursery school responded to the presentation of a book about a gay family. She then explains how a parent committee and the staff worked toward a compromise.

Girls Can Be Bull Riders, Too!

Supporting Children's Understanding of Gender Roles through Children's Literature

Karyn Wellhousen

■ ■ ■

The children listen intently as their kindergarten teacher reads *White Dynamite and Curly Kid*. As she reads the last page and shows the final illustration, the children are surprised to find that Lucky, the main character, who appears to be a boy throughout the story, is really a girl who had pigtails hidden beneath her cowboy hat. The children react to the surprise with a variety of comments.

Sonia: How did Lucky turn into a girl?
Valerie: He's a girl? (Smiling) I mean, I thought Lucky was a boy.
Shane: My dad has a ponytail and he's not a girl!
Christopher: Lucky wants to be a bull rider like her dad, but girls can't be bull riders because bulls are bigger and stronger than girls.

These reactions to the story illustrate the different levels of understanding young children can have about gender, including gender identification, gender constancy, and gender-role stereotyping. As children mature cognitively and have experiences in regard to gender, their thinking about gender roles changes.

The first level of understanding that children have concerning gender is gender identity, the recognition of being either male or female. By the age of three, most children are able to correctly identify themselves as boy or girl (Santrock 1995).

Next, children begin to label the people around them according to their gender. However, their understanding of what constitutes gender is still unclear at this stage, and young children use external characteristics, such as hair length, clothing, names, and toy choices, to classify others' gender. Sonia's comment, "How did Lucky turn into a girl?" reflects

her rudimentary understanding of gender. She used the external characteristic of hair length and style as the criteria for labeling the character. In her mind, Lucky was a boy throughout the story while the cowboy hat was worn but, when the pigtails appeared, she changed into a girl.

Gender constancy develops around age six or seven when children begin to understand that their sex is determined by their anatomy and it cannot be changed at will or by altering external appearance (Berk 1994). Valerie is in the early stages of understanding that gender is constant. This is apparent by her initial comment, "He's a girl?" and then, realizing her mistake, rephrasing the comment, which showed her surprise that the character who appeared to be a boy was actually a girl throughout the entire story. Shane demonstrated his understanding of gender constancy by pointing out emphatically that gender is not dependent on hairstyle because his father (whom he knows to be male) wears his hair in a ponytail.

Once children have achieved gender constancy, they rigidly organize information from their world on the basis of gender, which results in gender-role stereotyping (Kohlberg 1966). Classifying behaviors into the category of either boy or girl can influence choices in toys, playmates, activities, color preference, and clothing styles. Information used by children to determine behaviors that are appropriate to males and females comes from a variety of sources, including families (Fagot 1982; Huston 1983; Lamb 1986; Katz 1987; Fagot, Leinback, & O'Boyle 1992), peers (Maccoby & Jacklin 1987; Maccoby 1990, 1992), media (Shepard-Look 1982; Durkin 1985; Santrock 1993), teachers (Sadker & Sadker 1994), children's books (Collins, Ingoldsby, & Dellman 1984;

Karyn Wellhousen. (1996). Girls can be bull riders, too! *Young Children, 51* (5), 79–83. Reprinted with permission from the National Association for the Education of Young Children.

16

Allen, Allen, & Sigler 1993), and instructional materials (Scott & Schau 1985). Children at this stage of understanding believe that everyone should behave in a particular way based on their gender. This rigidity in thinking is illustrated by Christopher, who presented the argument that girls can't be bull riders because bulls are bigger and stronger than girls.

A great deal of learning about gender is taking place between the ages of three and eight, which explains the range of comments the children made when they discovered Lucky's true gender identity. This period in which children are sorting out their understanding of gender and what it means to be male or female can be confusing.

Children need adults who can help them understand that gender identity is based on anatomy, not external characteristics, and that it is constant and unchanging. Most important, they need adults to gently challenge their gender-role stereotypes and encourage them to go beyond gender-role constraints (Derman-Sparks & A.B.C. Task Force 1989). Ignoring or perpetuating children's gender stereotypes has a documented negative effect on children, especially in the area of self-esteem and self-worth (Wellesley College Center for Research on Women 1992; Sadker & Sadker 1994).

A considerable part of meaningful learning about gender roles occurs informally as children comment, question, and discuss aspects of gender they do not fully understand. Teachers can initiate and support these discussions by presenting boys, girls, men, and women in a variety of roles that will stimulate conversation among children.

An ideal classroom resource for learning about the various roles of males and females is children's literature. Children's literature provides a wealth of information from which children can develop healthy attitudes about a variety of subjects (Lamme & McKinley 1992; McGuire 1993), including gender roles (Derman-Sparks & A.B.C. Task Force 1989). Children's literature can introduce or reinforce the idea of gender fairness through the personalities, interests, and actions of various characters. To prepare for using children's literature, teachers can generate a classroom library of quality books that depict characters of both genders in a variety of roles. They also learn to guide discussions to support children's learning.

Generating a Classroom Library

The first step for teachers in generating a classroom library with books representing a variety of gender roles is to review the books they have already. Teachers should use general guidelines for choosing quality children's books (Lynch-Brown & Tomlinson 1993; Beatty 1994) as well as guidelines especially designed to identify bias in children's literature, such as "Ten Quick Ways to Analyze Children's Books for Sexism and Racism" (Council on Interracial Books for Children 1980). According to the Council on Interracial Books for Children, teachers should pay

Are early play behaviors important for sex-role development?

special attention to story lines, language, and illustrations. Achievements of females should be due to their abilities and initiative rather than to beauty or a sweet, compliant nature. Books should depict women using strength, wit, and ability for the good of others, as opposed to usual depiction of these qualities for evil purposes. Male characters should be portrayed as nurturing, caring, and sensitive as well as assured and confident.

Consider the language used in books. Gender-biased language that implies exclusion of women from careers and making contributions to society or the exclusion of men from nontraditional jobs and caregiving roles is not appropriate. Teachers should keep and make available to children the books in their collection that depict men, women, boys, and girls fairly. The value and use of books that demean or ridicule characters because of their gender should be carefully considered. Derman-Sparks and the A.B.C. Task Force (1989) suggest that these types of materials may be saved and used occasionally as nonexamples in a planned lesson about fair and unfair treatment of individuals. This should be done carefully and deliberately so children clearly receive the message the teacher is trying to present.

In making new selections, teachers should look for books which promote gender fairness. There are a variety of ways children's books accomplish this, from sending an obvious message to the reader to creating just a discreet signal. Some themes which promote gender equity include nontraditional pursuits of boys and girls, nontraditional jobs for men and women, and females who take the initiative. Examples and brief descriptions of books reflecting these themes follow.

Nontraditional Pursuits of Boys and Girls

The Girl Who Wore Snakes by Angela Johnson, with paintings by James E. Ransome. 1993. New York: Orchard Books. Suggested ages 4–8.

Ali discovers she has an uncommon love for snakes. She particularly enjoys wearing snakes around her arms, neck, and ankles. Her parents wonder why she loves snakes rather than more traditional pets. Her friends and teacher wonder why she likes them at all. Ali begins to think that she is the only one who sees the beauty in her snakes. Then one day when Ali takes a trip to visit relatives, she finds that a love for snakes creates a special connection between herself and her aunt. The strength of this story is Ali's unusual love for snakes and the ease in which she handles them. Also, her positive attitude toward snakes contrasts with the negative feelings of other characters.

Sheila Rae, the Brave by Kevin Henkes. 1987. New York: Puffin/Penguin USA. Suggested ages 3–7.

Sheila Rae is a feisty mouse who appears to let nothing frighten her. Her little sister Louise marvels at Sheila Rae's bravery. Things that would frighten many children, such as the dark, big dogs, monsters, and her principal, simply give Sheila Rae the opportunity to show her courage. But one day, while taking a new route home from school, Sheila Rae gets in a precarious predicament that frightens even her. Young Louise comes to Sheila Rae's rescue and gets her home safely. Now both Sheila Rae and Louise proudly declare themselves fearless and brave.

Cowboy Dreams by Dayal Kaur Khalsa. 1990. New York: Clarkson N. Potter. Suggested ages 5–8.

A young girl dreams of being a cowboy and wishes for a horse so that her dream can come true. She studies famous paintings of cowboys on horses, goes to western movies, rides the mechanical horse in front of the five-and-dime, and even rides a pretend horse she made on the basement banister. She buys a raffle ticket to win a horse and makes detailed plans on how to convert the garage to a stable. There is no question in this character's mind that being a girl will in anyway interfere with her dream of being a cowboy.

White Dynamite and Curly Kid by Bill Martin Jr. and John Archambault, with illustrations by Ted Rand. 1986. New York: Henry Holt. Suggested ages 4–7.

Curly Kid is a rough, tough, bull riding cowboy and the father of Lucky. Lucky hopes to grow up to be just like this rodeo cowboy. Lucky does most of the talking in this story and uses a cowboy accent and vocabulary. As Lucky watches Curly Kid "twisting like a corkscrew" while bull riding, the little wrangler tries to stay calm by thinking of all the far-away places that rodeo riders travel. It's no surprise that Curly Kid scores a 97 for his bull ride, but when he takes off Lucky's cowboy hat, everyone will be surprised when two long pigtails drop out and that Lucky is a girl. Children enjoy going back through the book, page by page, to determine how the illustrator kept them from knowing Lucky's true identity.

William's Doll by Charlotte Zolotow, with pictures by William Pène Du Bois. 1972. San Francisco: Harper-Collins. Suggested ages 3–6.

William, who wants a doll, is told it will make him a sissy. His father buys him a basketball and a train track but refuses to buy him a doll. William's grandmother sees the importance of this toy for both boys and girls and gives a strong rationale for allowing and encouraging boys to play with dolls. William's love for his doll, as well as the interest he maintains in traditional male toys, provides a good balance. This book is ideal for stimulating a discussion about nontraditional roles for boys.

Wilfrid Gordon McDonald Partridge by Mem Fox, illustrated by Julie Vivas. 1985. Brooklyn, NY: Kane/Miller. Suggested ages 5–8.

Wilfrid Gordon McDonald Partridge lives next door to a nursing home and loves to visit there. He finds all the people interesting but especially Miss Nancy Alison Delacourt Cooper who has lost her memory. Wilfrid Gordon finds a creative, caring way to give Miss Nancy back her memory. He demonstrates genuine concern for older adults and is confident that he has the capabilities to make their lives richer. This book demonstrates children's capabilities for making significant contributions to others' well-being as well as the ability of boys to be sensitive, nurturing, and caring.

Nontraditional Jobs for Men and Women

The Daddies Boat by Lucia Monfried, with illustrations by Michele Chessare. 1990. New York: Puffin/Penguin USA. Suggested ages 3–7.

The Daddies Boat carries working fathers to and from the island where families live in beach houses for the summer. The clever illustrations lead the reader to believe that this young storyteller is making special preparations with her mother, including shopping, cooking, and setting the table, for the arrival of her father on the Daddies Boat. However, as the boat draws nearer, the working parent becomes visible and the reader realizes that in this family, it is the mother who commutes from the island each week. As in *White Dynamite and Curly Kid*, the readers will find themselves looking back through the book to see how they were misled.

Mommies at Work by Eve Merriam, illustrated by Eugenie Fernandes. 1989. New York: Little Simon. Suggested ages 3–7.

Although this book begins by describing and accurately illustrating the many traditional tasks assumed by mothers, such as bathing children, tying shoelaces, and finding missing items, it also shows the many jobs mothers have outside the home, including television director, bridge builder, and factory worker stitching baseball gloves. Fernandes pictures various ethnic groups in his illustrations. Children will be eager to discuss their own mothers and the jobs they have in and out of the home.

Females Who Take the Initiative

Calico and Tin Horns by Candace Christiansen, with paintings by Thomas Locker. 1992. New York: Dial. Suggested ages 6–8.

This story of young Hannah, set just after the American Revolution, is based on the unjust treatment of war veterans who farmed the land along the Hudson River Valley in New York state. Hannah's family farmed land that had been promised to them by wealthy landowners. When the landowners refused to keep their promise and forced the farmers to give up a share of their crops, the farmers rebelled. Hannah knew that everyone in her family was in on a secret plan, but no one would tell her what it was. Hannah watched, listened, and paid close attention to the new and strange things happening around her, such as the way nearby farm families would blow the dinner horn when it wasn't dinnertime and how her father and brother would take off, wearing disguises, on their horses. One day when Hannah is alone and realizes their farm is in danger, she bravely blows the dinner horn to alert nearby farmers. Due to her intelligence and bravery, Hannah saves the day.

Sweet Clara and the Freedom Quilt by Deborah Hopkinson, with paintings by James Ransome. 1993. New York: Alfred A. Knopf. Suggested ages 6–8.

Clara, a young slave girl, worked as a seamstress. Clara heard about the Underground Railroad and learned it was a system to help free slaves, used by those against slavery. Clara was determined to be free but knew that she needed a map to follow to get to the Underground Railroad. Clara saved small scraps of fabric and sewed a special quilt, using the information from other slaves about the lay of the land, rivers, and other landmarks that would lead her to the Underground Railroad. Her ingenuity, patience, and skill enabled her and many others to escape slavery.

Amazing Grace by Mary Hoffman, with pictures by Caroline Binch. 1991. New York: Dial. Suggested ages 4–8.

Grace loves acting out stories—real stories out of books, stories her grandmother tells, or stories from her own head—and always she gives herself the best part. One day her teacher announces auditions for the school play *Peter Pan*. When Grace tells everyone she wants to try out for the main role, she is met with opposition from peers who tell her that she can't play the part because Peter Pan is not a girl and Peter Pan is not Black. With the help of her understanding grandmother, Grace decides that nothing will stop her from playing any role she chooses. Grace practices diligently for the role of Peter Pan. When she auditions, the decision is unanimous. This determined young girl shows readers that factors such as ethnicity or gender should not be considered barriers to playing any role in life one chooses.

Guiding Children's Discussions

After reading books with characters in nontraditional gender roles, leading children's discussions is crucial to their understanding gender identity and gender constancy and to children's development of healthy, gender-fair attitudes. Teachers can encourage discussion by asking divergent or open-ended questions. Divergent questions have no one right answer and, therefore, are capable of provoking discussion among the group. Teachers can plan two or three thought-provoking questions to ask during reading or at the conclusion of a book to help children understand the story's message.

For example, in the opening scenario the teacher may ask, "What did you think when you learned that Lucky in *White Dynamite and Curly Kid* was a girl?" While reading *Amazing Grace*, the teacher could ask, "How do you think Grace felt when her friends told her she couldn't be Peter Pan?" Questions of this nature will encourage children to respond honestly and openly about their impressions of the characters and their situations.

Children's impromptu reactions to books also provide opportunities for launching a meaningful discussion on gender roles. Teachers must be prepared for children's comments, some of which will portray gender bias. When children respond to books or characters with gender-biased comments, such as "That could never happen; girls can't be cowboys" or "Only boys who are sissies play with dolls," teachers should resist overreacting in a negative manner. Instead, she may ask the children to explain their comments or open up the discussion to the class by asking if anyone thinks differently. Also, the teacher may model presenting another point of view by giving examples that refute the attitude expressed, such as "I'm a woman and I once rode a bull" or "I know a famous football player who used to play with dolls as a child." Children's attitudes and comments should be

respected, yet gender bias should always be gently challenged.

Conclusion

Teachers today have many responsibilities to children. One of the most important is to make each child feel capable and confident in [his or her] abilities. Teachers can promote children's understanding of gender and attitudes of gender fairness by sharing with children books that depict characters in non-traditional gender roles. Discussing characters and their actions is crucial to supporting children's understanding of gender and getting across the message of gender fairness. By allowing children to express their feelings and ideas, teachers can plan responses to help them understand gender roles and to reinforce gender fairness.

REFERENCES

Allen, A. M., D. N. Allen, & C. Sigler. 1993. Changes in sex-role stereotyping in Caldecott Medal Award Picture Books 1938–1988. *Journal of Research in Higher Education* 7 (2): 67–73.

Beatty, J. 1994. *Picture book storytelling: Literature activities for young children*. Fort Worth, TX: Harcourt Brace.

Berk, L. 1994. *Infants and children: Prenatal through middle childhood*. Boston: Allyn & Bacon.

Collins, L. J., B. Ingoldsby, and M. M. Dellman. 1984. Sex-role stereotyping in children's literature: A change from the past. *Childhood Education* 60 (4): 278–81.

Council on Interracial Books for Children. 1980. Ten quick ways to analyze children's books for sexism and racism. In *Guidelines for selecting bias-free textbooks and storybooks*, 24–26. New York: Author.

Derman-Sparks, L., & the A.B.C. Task Force. 1989. *Anti-bias curriculum: Tools for empowering young children*. Washington, DC: NAEYC.

Durkin, K. 1985. Television and sex-role acquisition: 1. *British Journal of Social Psychology* 24: 101–13.

Fagot, B. I. 1982. Adults as socializing agents. In *Review of human development*, eds. T. Field, A. Huston, H. Quay, L. Troll, & G. Finely, 304–15. New York: Wiley.

Fagot, B. I., M. D. Leinbach, & C. O'Boyle. 1992. Gender labeling, gender stereotyping, and parenting behaviors. *Developmental Psychology* 28: 225–30.

Huston, A. C. 1983. Sex-typing. In *Handbook of Child Psychology*, 4th ed., vol. 4, ed. P. H. Mussen, 387–467. New York: Wiley.

Katz, P. A. 1987. Variations in family constellations: Effects on gender schemata. *New Directions* 38: 39–56.

Kohlberg, L. 1966. A cognitive-developmental analysis of children's sex-role concepts and attitudes. In *The development of sex differences*, ed. E. E. Maccoby, 82–173. Stanford, CA: Stanford University Press.

Lamb, M. E. 1986. *The father's role: Applied perspectives.* New York: Wiley.

Lamme, L. L., & L. McKinley. 1992. Creating a caring classroom with children's literature. *Young Children* 48 (1): 65–71.

Lynch-Brown, C., & C. Tomlinson. 1993. *Essentials of children's literature.* Boston: Allyn & Bacon.

Maccoby, E. E. 1990. Gender and relationships: A developmental account. *American Psychologist* 45 (4): 513–20.

Maccoby, E. E. 1992. The role of parents in the socialization of children: An historical overview. *Developmental Psychology* 28: 1006–17.

Maccoby, E. E., & C. N. Jacklin. 1987. Gender segregation in childhood. In *Advances in child development and behavior,* ed. H. Reese, vol. 20, 239–87. New York: Academic Press.

McGuire, S. L. 1993. Promoting positive attitudes toward aging: Literature for young children. *Childhood Education* 69 (4): 204–10.

Sadker, M., & D. Sadker. 1994. *Failing at fairness: How America's schools cheat girls.* New York: Charles Scribner's Sons.

Santrock, J. W. 1995. *Children.* Madison, WI: Brown & Benchmark.

Scott, K. P., & C. C. Schau. 1985. Sex equity and sex bias in instructional materials. In *Handbook for achieving sex equity through education,* ed. S. Klein, 218–32. Baltimore, MD: Johns Hopkins University Press.

Shepard-Look, D. 1982. Sex differentiation and the development of sex roles. In *Handbook of Developmental Psychology,* ed. B. Wolman, 403–33. Englewood Cliffs, NJ: Prentice-Hall.

Wellesley College Center for Research on Women. 1992. *How schools shortchange girls: The AAUW report.* Washington, DC: American Association of University Women Educational Foundation.

FOR FURTHER READING

Cunningham, B. 1994. Portraying fathers and other men in the curriculum. *Young Children* 49 (6): 4–13.

George, F. 1990. Checklist for a non-sexist classroom. *Young Children* 45 (2): 10–11.

Powlitsha, K. 1995. Research in review. Gender segregation among children: Understanding the "Cootie phenomenon." *Young Children* 50 (4): 61–68.

Sheldon, A. 1990. Kings are royaler than queens: Language and socialization. *Young Children* 45 (2): 4–9.

■ *Karyn Wellhousen, Ph.D., is assistant professor of early childhood education at the University of New Orleans. She has taught, conducted research, written, and consulted in the area of promoting gender equity in the classroom.*

Healthy Sexuality Development in Young Children

Donna Couchenour and Kent Chrisman

■ ■ ■

Lathesha, a first grader whose parents have shared information about reproduction in response to her questions, asks her father, "What is sex, anyway?"

Jon, a two-year-old, keeps his hand on his penis as the caregiver reads a story to a small group of children.

Suzannah, a three-year-old, tells her preschool teacher that her baby brother has a "weenie," but she doesn't.

Adults who work or live with young children often report discomfort when they think about, discuss, or respond to situations such as these, all of which relate to children's natural curiosity about their sexuality. Some people may find it difficult to reconcile the presence of innocence and sexuality in the same young being. For others, their culture emphasizes propriety or modesty (Wilson, 1991).

Children's candid questions and observations, combined with their gradual discovery of sexuality, make it impossible to ignore this important area. The purpose of this article is to describe typical sexuality development in young children and to discuss some ways that adults can influence healthy attitudes and behaviors regarding human sexuality.

Typical Sexuality Development

Adults often become more comfortable with this topic when they think of *sexuality* as encompassing all areas of children's development. Sexuality includes, but is not limited to, behavior. Healthy sexuality is fostered most effectively by those who view children's sexuality as part of who children are—their basic identity—rather than what they do (Lively & Lively, 1991).

Early educators and families share the responsibility to foster healthy sexuality (Brick et al., 1989). This development begins early. Physical sexual characteristics are established at conception. Cultural influences on children's sexuality, direct and indirect, are in place at birth. "Sexuality in the broadest sense encompasses an individual's personal growth in all its dimensions including the ways a person relates to others. We are all sexual beings" (Lively & Lively, 1991, p, 20).

Physical Development

Attitudes and policies in our society may not always reflect what is known about typical human sexual development. Respectfully sharing information and concerns can help assure that families and caregivers promote children's healthy development.

Expectant parents often first see their child's physical characteristics during a sonogram. Through their early years, children's images of themselves as sexual beings focuses on visible body parts and functions. When infants explore their own bodies and discover fingers and toes, adults rejoice. Rarely, though, is an infant's discovery of genitalia greeted with the same enthusiasm. If spoken about at all,

Donna Couchenour & Kent Chrisman. (1996). Healthy sexuality development in young children. *Dimensions of Early Childhood, 24* (4), 30–36. Reprinted with permission from Dimensions of Early Childhood, Southern Early Childhood Association, 7107 West 12th Street, Suite 102, Little Rock, AR 72204 1-800-305-7322.

families may voice concern about a baby's touching "that area."

Diapering and toileting routines are ideal times to express healthy attitudes about *body functions* and sexuality in young children. Even though elimination is separate from sexuality, the genital area is in view when diapering or toileting. Adult feelings about body functions are communicated through words, voice inflection, facial expressions, and body language.

When diapering babies, Gerber recommends that caregivers talk about what they are doing: "Now I am going to change your diaper. I'll take this diaper off and clean your bottom and then I'll give you a new diaper" (n.d.). As children learn to use a potty, and later when they toilet themselves, adults provide matter-of-fact health information about wiping, flushing, and washing hands. Treating biological functions as natural and normal creates a healthy environment of acceptance.

Other kinds of attention to anatomical differences remain controversial. Some adults provide young children with correct terms for all parts of their bodies: *penis* and *vulva* are offered in much the same manner as *elbow* and *knee;* others use slang labels. Some people avoid naming these body parts until children ask. Even though toys with male and female body parts (anatomically correct dolls and play animals, Barbie™) have been available for years, some adults see no need for such detail.

Babies explore their bodies just as they explore everything else, and in the process usually discover that touching their genitals feels good. Some masturbation throughout childhood is common. Briggs (1970) notes that babies at first experience a "generalized pleasant sensation" and "not the intensely exciting feeling of the mature adult." Young children also enjoy touching their own genitals. Because a male touches his penis for elimination, he is especially likely to notice the pleasant sensation. Boys are attentive to an erect penis as well, as illustrated by the four-year-old who told his mother, "It won't stay down." When children are under too much pressure or have few satisfactory social relationships, masturbation may relieve tension (Briggs, 1970). Adults may occasionally need to remind a few children that masturbation is not public behavior, but it is equally important to offer loving families, healthy self-images, friendships, and opportunities to engage in interesting activities.

Social Development

Sexual development in the social dimension is observed through *gender role typing* and in children's relationships. Culture, conversations, and interactions have considerable impact on children's perceptions about gender roles. Sometimes children's limited experiences result in incomplete information. Sylvia's mother is a medical doctor, but when Sylvia was three-and-one-half years old, she stated that "girls can't be doctors." Adults may intentionally or inadvertently call on "strong boys" to help move an object and tell little girls how pretty they look. Share accurate and current information about gender roles so that children understand their choices.

Children's play is important for social relationships, but misunderstanding and fear may lead to a variety of concerns. One father became upset when he found his six-year-old son wearing a dress while playing in the family living center at his child care program. It is important for adults to clearly recognize the differences between *gender identity, orientation,* and *roles* (Wilson, 1991). Playing dress-up in early childhood is not equivalent to adult cross-dressing or homosexuality.

Children may use dolls to represent sexual activity or to act out the birth process. It is not unusual for young children to engage in sex play, such as to show or touch one another's genitals. Jocelyn, a preschool teacher, matter-of-factly told two four-year-olds who were exploring each other's bodies, "Please pull up your pants now and choose a learning center. Blocks and puzzles are available." In handling such situations, "Adults should calmly set limits about sex play and redirect inappropriate behavior to another activity" (Kostelnik, Stein, Whiren, & Soderman, 1993, p. 310).

Sometimes primary-age children engage in indirect but hostile sexual behaviors. Aggressive behaviors do not demonstrate healthy sexual development and must be addressed seriously.

Emotional Development

Early positive relationships form the foundation for later expression of affection. Empathy is critical to the formation of healthy adult sexual relationships; it is learned as children build trust with adults. Pleasant touching from loving adults provides young children with warm expressions of caring. Holding, patting, and bathing infants all show physical tenderness.

Respect for all people is a critical dimension of healthy self-esteem. Adults model respect for others and discuss human differences and similarities with children. Creating an environment of acceptance of children's varying interests, talents, and abilities regardless of gender sets the stage for good mental health (Greenberg, 1991).

Citing ideas from *Anti-Bias Curriculum* (Derman-Sparks & the A.B.C. Task Force, 1989), Wilson writes, "The earlier parents and educators begin to consciously plan the messages we give young children, the greater the likelihood we will encourage their sense of themselves as lovable, capable, and responsible sexual beings, and the greater the possibility that children will approach diversity among human beings with comfort and empathy" (1991, pp. 5–6).

Cognitive Development

Early understanding of facts and values about sexuality is influenced by children's cognitive development, learning style, and culture. For young children, the most powerful influences are likely to be within the family. Family members of varying ages enable young children to observe a variety of human relationships.

Cultural information about sexuality is communicated through religious institutions, television, music, pictures, videos, computer images, and community interactions. Although these influences are not as powerful as the family during early childhood, they certainly gain influence as children grow older.

Young children typically first identify themselves as a girl or boy—their *gender identity*—based on clothing or other externals. Preschooler Nicole called her friend Amanda a boy. Nicole's mother said, "Amanda is a girl." Nicole responded, "But Amanda didn't have a barrette in her hair." In these situations, adults explain that a person's identification as male or female is based on the presence of a penis or vulva—not by hair style or clothing.

Children's curiosity is valued by those who understand its importance for thinking and learning. Preschool children express curiosity about their own bodies and bodies that look different. Because a mother holds her children close, they touch or ask about her breasts. Rather than hushing questions, this is a teachable moment about parts of the female body and their function.

Keep in mind that children before and during Piaget's preoperational stage (approximately ages two to seven years) may have limited understanding about global concepts related to sexuality. Paley notes that a kindergarten-age child "has become aware of the thinking required by the adult world but is not committed to its burden of rigid consistency" (1981, p. 81). She quotes a child who mentions that babies are fed by mothers' breasts, after which another adds, "And he knows just what to do. He sucks it like a real nipple and there's sort of milk in there."

Children are curious about where babies come from, and their ideas generally fall into four categories (Lansdown & Walker, 1991):

Geographical. A baby grows inside the mother and comes out when it's time.

Manufactured. A baby exists outside the mother and is somehow placed into the mother, but not by sexual means.

Agricultural. Miniature fully formed babies exist in either the sperm or ovum.

Realistic. A generally accurate idea about human reproduction.

Many families and teachers use discussion about real experiences with babies—pets, siblings—to help children understand *reproduction.* Some first ask the child to explain the term, and then use this information as a starting place for discussing facts and values. Be careful not to limit information to sexual *behavior* when responding to questions.

When Answering Children's Questions about Sexuality:

- *Find out more about the children's questions by asking what they think or what they have already heard about the topic.*
- *Check out the children's understanding before and after answering their questions.*
- *Be honest with information and with your level of comfort.*
- *Avoid technical language and jargon; use correct terms, making sure the child understands the meaning. (Wilson, 1991, pp. 34–35)*

Initiating Discussions about Sexuality

Even if questions have not been asked aloud, most children wonder where babies came from and how they got there. Some children are by nature reserved and rarely ask questions. Others interpret adult discomfort with the subject to mean that they should not ask such questions. Paley quotes one child who expressed it well: "I know something about sperm but I don't think it's polite" (1981, p. 77).

Adults who objectively observe children will pick up signals about the time to address sexuality. For example, when a baby touches her genitals, a parent says, "You're touching your vulva," or when a toddler points to his penis, a teacher can provide the correct term for the child.

Children deserve an accurate explanation of reproduction.

Children in the primary grades are often more reserved. They may be modest about their bodies and assume that no one else wants to discuss the topic. Seven- or eight-year-olds may have had plenty of experience with being hushed about sex. On the other hand, with so much exposure to sex in the media, children often get a great deal of inaccurate and/or inappropriate information.

Clemens (1983) describes how and when she introduces sexuality education to four-year-olds, building upon all areas of their development. She considers *physical development* and uses Mister Rogers' song: "Everybody's fancy, Everybody's fine, Your body's fancy, And so is mine." *Social development* is discussed in a chant at circle time: "What is Maurice?" "Maurice is a boy." "What was Maurice when he was born?" "He was a baby boy." "What will Maurice be when he grows up?" "He'll be a man" (p. 53). *Emotions* are considered when she asks children to make a list of people they can kiss without asking first. Then the children practice asking others if they may kiss or hug them. Children are encouraged to respond genuinely with "Yes, please" or "No, thank you." Clemens teaches about human reproduction and notes that because *thinking* is different for preschoolers, "sexual intercourse is not the sexy subject for them" (p. 52).

Parents of a six-year-old wrote to Ann Landers for advice about what to say to their child who walked into their bedroom while they were having intercourse. Although she gave some useful advice about locking the door in the future, she also said that the parents need not mention anything since the child has not asked any questions. A better response would be to relate values about sex as an expression of love, as well as to emphasize the need for adult privacy.

Best Practices in Early Childhood Education

Obtaining information about the best educational practices in the area of healthy sexuality is difficult. Teacher preparation programs typically introduce human sexuality during the study of adolescent development, rather than implementing a more effective approach that would enable students to define values about sexuality, gain knowledge about young children's sexuality development, and learn and practice answering children's questions (Wilson, 1991). Comments from experienced and novice early childhood educators reveal differing perspectives: "Our district has strict policies about sex education." "It's the family's responsibility." "I'm not sure about the best way to respond to children's sexual words or behaviors."

Another challenge to early childhood educators is the lack of a cohesive theory of sexuality development. Despite Piaget's influence on early childhood education, Vygotsky's increasing applications for social-cultural development and literacy, and the Reggio Emilia contributions on the importance of the learning environment, none of these conceptual frameworks incorporates sexuality development.

Adults who understand that sexuality is related to all other areas of development can integrate children's learning experiences and see them as part of developing the whole child. The recommended practices on page 26 are adapted from Bredekamp (1987) for each of Wilson's (1991) developmental expectations.

Parent involvement in early education is an important link between family and school (Koblinsky, Atkinson, & Davis, 1986), so adults keep each other advised about children's growth in all areas. Wilson (1991) suggests these strategies:

- Create an advisory board that includes families to review and approve content and resources.
- Hold a family orientation meeting (and follow-ups, as needed) to share materials and information about healthy sexuality development in young children.
- Provide options for families. Invite them to attend sessions with children. Offer a conference before and/or after information is presented in

Matching Children's Sexuality Development with Best Teaching Practices

Developmental Expectations	Recommended Practices
Infants and Toddlers	
Explore body parts, including genitals	Adults express healthy, accepting attitudes about children's bodies
Develop positive or negative attitude about own body	Adults are attentive to infants during routines such as diaper changing and explain what is happening Caregivers consistently respond to infants to keep them comfortable so they learn security
Experience genital pleasure	Adults express healthy, accepting attitudes about children's body functions
Encouragement to develop male or female identity	Adults praise accomplishments and help children to feel competent; parents are primary source of affection and care
Learn expected behaviors by gender	Adults respect children's developing preferences as a healthy indicator of self-esteem; caregivers plan for active and quiet play for all children
Preschoolers	
Aware of and curious about gender and body differences	Adults use children's natural curiosity to make sense of their world
Masturbate unless taught not to	Adults facilitate the development of self-control, use redirection, and have expectations which match child's developing capabilities
Engage in various forms of sex play	Adults use redirection and have age-appropriate expectations of child's behavior; interactions are designed to promote positive self-esteem; adults design the play environments so supervision of children is possible at all times
Establish firm belief that they are either male or female	Adults facilitate opportunities to develop positive social skills; adults provide opportunities for children to gain understanding about themselves through observing and interacting with others
Enjoy bathroom humor	Adults use positive guidance techniques and have expectations which match child's development
Repeat curse words	Adults facilitate the development of self-control in children by using positive guidance such as modeling appropriate language
Curious about from where they came	Adults use children's natural curiosity to make sense of their world; adults help children to understand themselves through interacting with other people
Kindergarten and Primary Children	
Continue sex play and masturbation	Adults promote self-control through problem solving and redirection; adults try to prevent overstimulation and understimulation based on child's development; adults change activity centers frequently so children have new things to do
Curiosity about pregnancy and birth	Adults build on children's internal motivation to make sense of the world; teachers and parents are partners in the educational process
Strong same-sex friendships	Adults facilitate the development of social skills at all times; adults ensure times with a close friend; adults model and expect acceptance and appreciation of differences and similarities
Strong interest in stereotyped gender roles	Adults plan and implement activities and materials to enrich the lives of all children
Have a basic sexual orientation	Adults view each child as a unique person; adults facilitate positive self-esteem
Choose gender-stereotypical activities	Adults provide a variety of activity choices, with children helping to select some topics; adults guide children's involvement in projects by extending their ideas and challenging their thinking
Tease and call names	Adults promote prosocial behavior and facilitate the development of social skills; adults set clear limits and involve children in establishing rules for the classroom community or the home

the classroom. Give parents the choice to "opt their children out" of certain activities.

- Create assignments that children and families can complete together.
- Send home an evaluation form so families can give input about their perception of the program.
- Offer parenting programs related to sexual development of children.

Ethical considerations are always very important for professionals. Best practices in early childhood education emphasize regard for others, respecting self and others, forming meaningful relationships, acceptance of differences, and empathy. Teachers who model and support these attributes, and who form positive relationships with family members, will influence children's healthy sexuality development. As Nancy, a teacher, stated, "I influence my first graders' sexual development without even saying the word sex."

REFERENCES

Bredekamp, S. (Ed.) (1987). *Developmentally appropriate practice in early childhood programs serving children from birth through age 8.* Washington, DC: National Association for the Education of Young Children.

Brick, P., Davis, N., Fischel, M., Lupo, T., MacVicar, A., & Marshall, J. (1989). *Bodies, birth & babies: Sexuality education in early childhood programs.* Hackensack, NJ: The Center for Family Life Education, Planned Parenthood of Bergen County, Inc.

Briggs D. C. (1970). *Your child's self-esteem: The key to his life.* Garden City, NY: Doubleday.

Clemens, S. (1983). *The sun's not broken, a cloud's just in the way: On child centered teaching.* Mt. Rainier, MD: Gryphon House.

Derman-Sparks, L., & the A.B.C. Task Force. (1989). *Antibias curriculum: Tools for empowering young children.* Washington, DC: National Association for the Education of Young Children.

Gerber, M. (Primary contributor). (n.d.). *Seeing infants with new eyes* [Videocassette]. Washington, DC: National Association for the Education of Young Children.

Greenberg, P. (1991). *Character development: Encouraging self-esteem & self-discipline in infants, toddlers, & two-year-olds.* Washington, DC: National Association for the Education of Young Children.

Koblinsky, S., Atkinson, J., & Davis, S. (1986). Sex education with young children. In J. B. McCracken (Ed.), *Reducing stress in young children's lives.* Washington, DC: National Association for the Education of Young Children.

Kostelnik, M. J., Stein, L. C., Whiren, A. P., & Soderman, A. K. (1993). *Guiding children's social development* (2nd ed.). Albany, NY: Delmar.

Lansdown, R., & Walker, M. (1991). *Your child's development from birth through adolescence: A complete guide for parents.* New York: Alfred A. Knopf.

Lively, V., & Lively, E. (1991). *Sexual development of young children.* Albany, NY: Delmar.

Paley, V. G. (1981). *Wally's stories: Conversations in the kindergarten.* Cambridge, MA: Harvard University Press.

Wilson, P. M. (1991). *When sex is the subject: Attitudes and answers for young children.* Santa Cruz, CA: Network Publications.

- *Donna Couchenour, Ph.D., is an associate professor of early childhood education in the Department of Teacher Education at Shippensburg University of Pennsylvania.*

- *Kent Chrisman, Ed.D., is an assistant professor of early childhood education in the Department of Teacher Education and Director of the Rowland School for Young Children at Shippensburg University of Pennsylvania.*

Teachers and Parents Define Diversity in an Oregon Preschool Cooperative— Democracy at Work

Jennifer Lakey

It's a lovely late summer evening in the Northwest. September often brings the year's best weather, and 1992 is no exception.

Two months from now, Oregonians will vote on Ballot Measure 9, the anti-gay-rights measure sponsored by a local ultraconservative group. The newspapers carry stories on the activities of gay rights groups and the activities of anti-gay groups, about individuals who've suffered discrimination, and on the myriad ways in which the controversy touches our lives. The issue will continue to heat up through October.

In a church basement a group of parents gathers to begin a new year at Multnomah Playschool Cooperative, as parents have gathered there each year since 1948. As the co-op president, I welcome the parents and begin orientation. After I complete the dry business of presenting school policies, teacher Linda Skibinski describes the school's program—this time her 13th year in a row. She gives extra time to explaining how she will incorporate antibias education into the curriculum on an expanded scale. She describes many new practices; one is the addition of families headed by gay and lesbian parents to her unit highlighting various family structures. Neither Linda nor anyone present has any idea how this expansion will ultimately divide the school and bring about lasting change.

Our School's Antibias Focus

Until the events of 1992, at Multnomah Playschool we fancied ourselves enlightened practitioners of antibias education. Name-calling was taboo; children were encouraged to practice negotiation skills and to make deals to resolve conflicts. Classroom mate-rials and teacher-led discussions stimulated their perceptions of similarities and differences. Our multicultural dolls had long been taking communal baths, with children noting the varying skin colors. Classroom pictures and books showed various cultures; we cooked latkes and tortillas; we made batiks and Chinese rubbings. We'd done away with the visit from Santa Claus at the annual Christmas party out of respect for all religious beliefs represented at our school, and the party itself was renamed Winterfest.

In 1993 Linda produced a wider variety of posters for our walls, showing families in all colors and configurations. These would share space with our children's artwork. With the assistance of the diversity committee (then called the Antibias Committee), she purchased plastic sushi and tacos to add to our present store of corn and hamburgers and also added to the diversity of our doll collection. Besides assorted skin tones, we had doll-size eyeglasses, crutches, and a wheelchair. Brown, black, and flesh-colored paint sat alongside red, blue, yellow, and green, and brown and black playdough joined the ranks of primary-colored playdough. And our library grew by several new titles; one was *Daddy's Roommate* by Michael Willhoite.

Linda held up a copy of *Daddy's Roommate* at orientation. She described what she had learned through Pacific Oaks College in a summer course called Anti-Bias Issues Level II:

I learned that while I had included families of different races, families with differently abled members, and divorced and adoptive families, I had overlooked a significant portion of our population—the one-tenth of our families who, according to research, are headed by homosexual parents. I learned that children from these families suffer a loss of self-esteem when classrooms offer positive models of every kind of family structure but their own. I learned that by elementary school they are teased and bullied by their peers and often lie to peers and peers' parents about their families so as not to be excluded socially.

Linda asked us to visualize a child being harassed in the elementary school bathroom. "What kind of preschool had such bullies attended?" she asked. "Had they been allowed to name-call? Had they been taught to respect all kinds of family structures?"

Where Widening the Focus Led Us

The parents had listened quietly at the orientation. No one questioned me or Linda or commented either that night or in the days and weeks afterward. That was a surprise, not only because the topic of gay lifestyles might be expected to provoke comment but also because of the inquisitive, involved nature of the parents who come to Multnomah Playschool.

Family involvement is the cornerstone of our school, which is a parent cooperative serving three- to five-year-olds. Our 16-member board, composed of parents, develops policy in consultation with the teacher. Parents have a standing invitation to attend board meetings. A combination of tuition and fundraising (another parent responsibility) provides our financing. Parents help in the classroom on a regular basis, clean the school, and share day-to-day operation, including transportation for field trips or special outings. Besides being the oldest co-op in the state, we earned accreditation from the National Academy of Early Childhood Programs in 1990 and have since renewed it. By its very nature, our school requires members who are willing and able to give a substantial amount of their time to the school and who have a high degree of interest in their children's development.

For whatever reason, the mention of *Daddy's Roommate* passed into the orientation minutes without fanfare, and the school year began as usual. The diversity committee, formed only the previous spring, had begun meeting during the summer and continued to meet with very scattered attendance. Committee members developed an antibias policy statement, and it was added to our school handbook along with the rest of our new policies. The committee began planning a presentation for the next all-member meeting. It was to be an introduction to antibias curriculum in general, without particular emphasis on same-sex families. At this meeting Linda again displayed for everyone's perusal all the new curriculum materials, including *Daddy's Roommate*. Parents viewed the video *The ABCs of Anti-Bias Curriculum* produced by Pacific Oaks College, then followed with small-group discussion on the possible origins of bias.

As the year progressed, small but significant changes were tried out. We introduced nontraditional music and activities to our Winterfest celebration. In the classroom Linda put into practice the curriculum changes she had described at orientation and incorporated new ideas from parents. One particularly rewarding project involved children bringing family photos from home, pasting them on construction paper, and dictating their thoughts to Linda. A richly diverse family album for each of our three classes resulted; the albums were dog-eared by the end of the year!

Getting Down to Curriculum Specifics

In March, Linda began the unit on family structures, noting in her monthly letter to parents that she would be reading *Daddy's Roommate* during the second week. She invited parents to call her with questions. One parent called to announce that her child would be kept home that day. A divorced couple new to the school that year met with Linda and told her how pleased they were. They had been waiting since orientation for this. The mom confided she was a lesbian and enthusiastically arranged to parent-help the day Linda would read the book.

The second week of March, Linda distributed her lesson plan, which included one reading of *Daddy's Roommate* to each class. Quite suddenly, there was an outcry among some vocal parents. They were indignant that they'd received no warning, angry that the book was being "snuck" into the curriculum. There was talk of boycotting school on the day Linda would read *Daddy's Roommate*.

The first class to hear the story was the afternoon prekindergarten. Two parents kept their children home because of the book. Later, when Linda read it to the class of three-year-olds, again two children were kept home. The mother of a third child telephoned to reassure Linda that she supported her reading the book, but her son really was ill. In both classes the reading was uneventful. The children focused on two aspects of the story: the fact that the boy's parents were divorced and that when he had nightmares, he got to sleep with the grownups.

On the day the four-year-olds' class met, the lesbian mom arrived along with the other parent-helper, a Mormon dad who had taken the morning off and brought his collection of musical instruments to share with the children. But only five children (out of 18 enrolled) came to school; one of the children's parents shared her irritation at receiving a phone call that morning urging her to join in a trip to the zoo instead of bringing her child to class.

It was an emotional morning for the adults. The Mormon dad consoled the lesbian mom, who wondered if the absent children would have been allowed to attend her daughter's recent birthday party had they known her own orientation.

Letters Home to Parents as Preparation

That same week Linda sent two articles home. One was from *Young Children,* titled "Penny's Question: I Will Have a Child in My Class with Two Moms— What Do You Know about This?" by Elaine Wickens (1993). The other was "With Liberty and Justice for All: Exploring Homophobia" by Oregonian Sara Packer (1992). The articles infuriated some parents who were already upset. Two stated outright that they felt like they were being accused of homophobia.

Also, that week the board was scheduled to meet. All board meetings are open to the entire membership, but usually only board members attend. This night (luckily our hostess had a large living room) at least half the school showed up, with parents and even a grandparent squeezed in together.

Parameters for Discussion

After introductions I set parameters for discussion, explaining that each person should have an opportunity to express an opinion while no one should be allowed to dominate the discussion. I asked all those who wished to speak to limit themselves to five minutes. Each speaker would be guaranteed *no interruptions* and, when finished, would wait until all others had a turn before speaking a second time. In the interest of reserving time for other business, I set a one-hour limit on the topic of *Daddy's Roommate.* We agreed that if we had not resolved our differences by that time, we should at least have made a plan for doing so. Linda then read aloud the book in case some parents hadn't yet heard it.

A timekeeper was chosen and discussion began. But after 20 minutes these normally restrained parents were overtaken by their emotions and, ignoring the parameters, moved the discussion's tone from a thoughtful, intellectual approach to a loud, distrustful one.

Tempers flared and some parents repeatedly brought up what they described as the "surprise addition" of *Daddy's Roommate* to the lesson plan. Others accused the diversity committee of sneaking the new antibias policy into the school handbook. Typical comments were, "It's not developmentally appropriate" or "They have so much on their little minds already—why do we need to bring up sex?" or "My junior-high schoolers can barely understand this; how is a three-year-old supposed to understand it?"

On the more thoughtful side, some parents asked, "What alternatives are there for families who've been taught that homosexuality is a sin?" Other parents made thinly veiled accusations of bigotry and homophobia. They charged that we had narrow-minded parents in our midst who could only see the issue in terms of sex, when it was really about teaching children that *different* doesn't mean *bad.* We also listened to some moving accounts of personal experience with homosexual bias involving friends and relatives.

A Committee of Advisers

Two hours later, everyone had certainly had a chance to express herself or himself. But simply sharing our concerns had brought us no closer to a solution. Rather, we were left with two camps, and they had squared off. Out of the fracas of the meeting, however, I succeeded in appointing a committee of parents, the Curriculum Advisory Committee, headed by a parent who had experience in conflict resolution. Two parents opposed to material on same-sex families were on the committee, plus a parent with a viewpoint somewhere in the middle, and lastly another parent and the committee head who both supported the material. I purposely selected five people for two reasons: (1) in case they needed to vote among themselves, they wouldn't be evenly divided; and (2) three seemed too small a number to be representative of the school, and seven seemed too many to be efficient. The committee's mission was to identify specific areas of concern for parents and propose solutions. These actions would provide a starting point from which we hoped to reach a consensus.

Exchanging and Considering Our Views Further

Two months remained until school would close for summer. We believed this would allow us plenty of time to exchange views, consider each others' ideas in an unhurried manner, and develop a fair and thoughtful solution. Our monthly newsletter was due out in a few days, and I took the opportunity to write a few paragraphs encouraging parents to look upon the situation as a chance to grow, not as an unnecessary and destructive squabble:

By now we're all aware of the current controversy sparked by the reading of Daddy's Roommate *in our school. Its use in the classroom has engendered spirited discussion as well as brought up the larger question of the range and depth of our diversity curriculum. Views from one end of the spectrum to the other have been expressed, and these views are strongly held. No one need be reminded that this is truly a test of the cooperative spirit of our organization.*

This spirit makes room for every opinion to be heard, and opportunities for this have been provided and will continue. We are also obliged to determine the majority opinion and put this into practice. Ultimately, a vote by the entire membership will be taken, and this will occur before the year-end.

Until we reach a resolution, it's wise to be patient with ourselves and with our fellow co-op members no matter the difference in views. Developing our diversity curriculum can be viewed as a work-in-progress, and we are learning as we go. When breaking new ground, I suppose we must expect to find a few rocks.

But I truly believe that debating new ideas is healthy for our school, and I know each of us brings our best intentions, for our children and for the school, to bear upon this matter. Each step we take in this process, however small, represents progress.

I suppose I hoped that such a message would help parents accept the fact that the issue was planted firmly in our midst and that we would benefit from devoting some serious thought to its solution. I did at first presume that, like me, everyone else saw that the topic's highly controversial nature meant we *must* work toward compromise, that a fair compromise must be our goal. It turned out I was wrong. Most people *were* working toward compromise; some, however, wanted to eliminate all mention of gay and lesbian families, while others sought a revolution of our curriculum. We did not yet have a common goal.

Our Committee Takes on the Issues

The first action of the Curriculum Advisory Committee addressed the problem of establishing a common goal. The group called a schoolwide meeting which about half of the parents attended. Again the atmosphere was emotionally charged. Resentment ran high among parents who felt they were being labeled as bigots. The committee head, Walter Peck, suggested that the group focus on three tasks:

- Defining the impressions parents have of the book *Daddy's Roommate* and more generally with the inclusion of gay and lesbian family structures in the school's curriculum;
- Identifying guiding principles, or school philosophy that could be applied to the problem to help shape acceptable solutions; and
- Identifying concrete curriculum suggestions that would deal directly with the identified problems while staying true to the guiding principles developed by the group.

The meeting provided parents with an opportunity to reiterate their concerns and see them duly recorded (see "Parent Comments toward Establishing a Common Goal" on p. 32). We also were able to identify some common ground and translate negative emotion into ideas for positive action.

At the close of the meeting, Walter volunteered to type the minutes and distribute them to all co-op members. The rest of the school needed to see the minutes of this meeting, but a vocal group of parents present would not permit the distribution, wishing to review the final version of the minutes first. They didn't completely trust the advisory committee, suspicious that some committee members had an agenda to push through a pro-gay curriculum.

Walter held back the minutes as requested even though this delayed their distribution by a week or more. Right away, parents unable to attend the meeting protested at having to wait to see the minutes. They were being denied access to the information and rightly felt left out of the resolution process. We realized that we must devise a procedure for gathering opinions and ideas from *all* the parents *and* make sure they all were getting the same information. During spring break I met with Linda and Walter, and we developed a step-by-step procedure for resolving the issue. I sent copies to the board members prior to formally presenting it to all parents at the next general meeting.

According to the procedure developed, I was responsible for assembling an information packet to ensure that each family had a complete, up-to-date picture of the situation and for distributing it within a week. Each family was asked to read the packet thoroughly and write a response in the packet to the ideas they could support and those they could not. Responses would remain anonymous unless families wished to identify themselves. The packet would

Parent Comments toward Establishing a Common Goal

1. Defining the Problems

Problem statements were recorded as they were raised and do not reflect group consensus in all cases.

A. There was a sense that *Daddy's Roommate* initiated exposure to sexuality. The fact that it involved two homosexual men was a particular concern for some; others were concerned that, regardless of the orientation, exposure to sexuality is premature at this time.

B. *Daddy's Roommate* was not viewed as age appropriate for preschool-age children.

C. Our focus should not be on "lifestyle" but rather "family structure." Vocabulary is important. Rather than describing individuals as gay or lesbian, our focus should be "two moms" or "two dads."

D. There was inadequate discussion and education with parents and teacher before this issue was addressed in the classroom.

E. Parents are reading too much into the message of *Daddy's Roommate*. Children do not glean notions about sexuality/homosexuality from the story, as do adults. Instead, the messages they hear are about families, divorce, and a child knowing he is loved and feeling OK about himself.

F. Discussions and handouts provided *after* the issue left some families feeling like they had been unfairly labeled as homophobic and discriminatory.

G. Omission of a particular family structure from our curriculum, whether divorced, racially mixed, or gay and lesbian, can leave a child feeling isolated [because] his or her home life is not acknowledged.

2. Identifying Guiding Principles

The purpose of identifying guiding principles was to establish some foundation values that could be applied to the problems we identified. Ideally, the outcome provides solutions we can all support or live with.

Unlike the discussion of problems above, the group was generally in agreement on the list of guiding principles we generated.

A. It is important/acceptable for our curriculum to represent the full diversity of family structures children may experience directly or be exposed to through friendships and associations with other children

B. We want to encourage our children to respect the human differences they will encounter in life.

C. At the preschool level, information and education specific to sexuality is the responsibility and right of parents.

D. All Multnomah Playschool students should experience support and validation during their school experience.

E. Parental decisions concerning preschool students need to be respected by the school community.

3. Developing Solutions

During this part of the meeting, we tried to come up with concrete curriculum ideas or resources. We used the guiding principles as a sort of litmus test.

A. Place posters in the classroom that reflect the full range of different family structures. Attach no labels.

B. Maintain *Daddy's Roommate* as a resource for individual children or families; do not read [it] to entire classes.

C. Avoid labels (gay, lesbian, heterosexual). Describe people in terms of a child's family structure (two moms, two dads, mom and dad, two people who love each other). Attach no value judgment.

D. Develop a book that describes (validates) the families of Multnomah Playschool students, using pictures and stories.

E. Encourage students to describe and talk about their families during group time.

F. Explore other curriculum ideas suggested by Louise Derman-Sparks in NAEYC's book *Anti-Bias Curriculum: Tools for Empowering Young Children.*

G. Look for other books for the classroom that describe gay and lesbian family structures in the context of a presentation of many different kinds of families.

H. Utilize the first general meeting of the year to give a more detailed overview of the school's curriculum; don't invite a guest speaker to this first meeting.

Source: Curriculum Advisory Committee meeting notes, 17 March 1993, Multnomah Playschool Cooperative, Oregon.

serve as a tool for gauging the views of our school community.

After one week, the committee would collect the packets and compile the responses. They would use the information to draft a list of ways to present (or not present) material on gay and lesbian families in the classroom. With board approval this list would become our official written ballot for conducting a formal vote.

At our general meeting the proposal was presented in the form of a timeline. Everyone agreed to the plan after adding a step (holding a second vote if needed). With less than a week to compile the packet, I immediately went to work. Each packet included these materials:

- Background on the development of our diversity curriculum, going back a little more than a year;
- Our teacher's philosophy, the reasons behind it, and ways she would implement that philosophy in the classroom;
- A series of three stories crafted by Linda as a more comfortable alternative to *Daddy's Roommate* and centered on a little koala named Hank who is adopted by two male koalas, with the suggestion that cuddly puppets accompany the reading of the stories;
- A copy of Louise Derman-Sparks's letter endorsing the koala stories (Linda had sent her copies);
- Approved minutes from the committee meeting of March 17; and
- Position statements from any family wishing to present one.

Parents Respond and a Voting Plan Is Prepared

Parents submitted position statements on both sides of the issue in fairly equal numbers. The range of perspectives clearly showed that this issue meant different things to different people, that the discussion was not and never had been merely an analysis of curriculum. One paper stated that children wouldn't understand the varying needs or priorities that might lead people to develop their lifestyles and this couldn't be adequately explained in the classroom. Another statement asserted the right of parents to decide what is appropriate for their children, to pass this on to their children without judgment, and to keep such decisions in the home, not the school.

One family felt that children would ask about sexuality when they were ready to hear about it and that discussion of any such topic in school would undermine parents' control over how they would instruct their children. The family further declared that deciding the issue in a truly fair manner would require a discussion and vote at the start of each school year, allowing each new membership to decide a course of action for itself. Another family felt the controversy was too damaging to school morale and wondered if the benefits of a discussion of gay and lesbian lifestyles were worth the mistrustful undercurrent the discussion had caused in the school.

In support of the antibias curriculum were such comments as

During the board discussion, the meaning of Daddy's Roommate *kept slipping into value judgments about the father's homosexuality; but if you go back to the book, you'll see the focus is not on any evaluation of the men but on the boy's feeling of still having fun, being loved, and having "normal" life experiences. . . . I wish to emphasize the choice to let children be aware and feel safe to ask questions because the alternatives—denial, silence— will only create shame.*

and

As a parent of preschool-age children I want to provide my kids with a fundamental appreciation for diversity as well as an understanding of prejudice. I want my children to be able to recognize biased behavior on their own. I want them to have heard words they can use to respond to this biased behavior. If some kids on the playground are making fun of another child because of his parents, I want my child to be able to say, "Hey, that's not right!" . . . What we are doing at Multnomah Playschool with our diversity curriculum is being proactive. Teach the children before they learn it on the playground from children who have yet to learn about respecting diversity. . . . Leaving the gay lifestyle out of our diversity curriculum is prejudice. If you really want to teach your children that the gay lifestyle is just another family structure, then let them hear it from you!

Comments Shape the Ballot for Choosing a Plan

When the packets came back in with parents' comments, the committee faced a massive pile of paper. The group valiantly sifted through the responses and presented a sample ballot at the next board meeting (see "Ballot and the Vote Results" on p. 34).

Discussion of the ballot content bogged down repeatedly; items were cut out only to be stuck back in. Hours later we approved something similar to what we had started with—a graded list of four curriculum plans with the first allowing the reading of *Daddy's Roommate* along with the use of related

Ballot and the Vote Results: Four Plans for Multnomah Playschool Antibias Curriculum

Instructions: Each family is asked to cast two weighted votes on their ballot. Families with two children in the school will receive two ballots. Ballots should be placed in the ballot box no later than Thursday, April 29. A quorum will be based on the number of returned ballots.

- Mark a "5" by the ballot item (A, B, C, or D) that *best* fits your family's view on the issue.
- Mark a "3" by a different ballot item (A, B, C, or D) that your family could support as a *compromise* solution.

A second ballot will be administered if no ballot item receives a majority of the total weighted votes. The two choices with the highest total scores on the first ballot would appear on the second ballot.

Tally	Plans
_90_	**A.** Gay and lesbian family structures are included in the curriculum; terms "gay" and "lesbian" can be used in stories and other curriculum. Read *Daddy's Roommate* to classes. Stories such as Linda's koala series are used. Posters of many different family configurations, including gay and lesbian couples, are hung in the classroom; no labels attached. Teachable moments are taken advantage of to discourage bias and encourage respect for diversity. Children continue to use family photos to create a book of school families.
_111_	**B.** Gay and lesbian family structures are included in the curriculum—described as "two moms" and "two dads"; no parent- or teacher-initiated use of "lesbian" and "gay" labels. Do not read *Daddy's Roommate* to classes; retain it as a resource for parents. Stories such as Linda's koala series are used. Posters of many different family configurations, including "two moms" and "two dads," are hung in the classroom; no labels attached. Teachable moments are taken advantage of to discourage bias and encourage respect for diversity. Children continue to use family photos to create a book of school families.

Tally	Plans
_69_	**C.** No teacher- or parent-initiated discussion of family structures with "two moms" or "two dads"; no koala stories, no books that include pictures or text that refer to "two moms" or "two dads." Posters of many different family configurations, including "two moms" and "two dads," are hung in the classroom; no labels attached. Retain *Daddy's Roommate* as a resource for parents. Children continue to use family photos to create a book of school families.
_35_	**D.** Remove all references (posters, stories, etc.) to family structures with "two moms" and "two dads." Retain *Daddy's Roommate* as a resource for parents. Children continue to use family photos to create a book of school families.

materials according to the teacher's discretion and the last disallowing all mention of gay and lesbian lifestyles. The second and third plans represented two methods of compromise.

In a proposed point system for tallying votes, members were to choose *two* preferred plans, assigning five points to their first choice and three points to their second choice. The plan with the most points would win.

The ballot's inclusive style, listing four plans instead of only two polar views, permitted the committee to consider both radical and moderate positions by members, in keeping with the school's aim to allow all views to be heard. The tally method was designed to seek out the middle ground that allowed the most comfort for the most people—the first choice permitting voters to choose their ideal solution, the second requiring them to identify a plan they could live with. In effect, the ballot forced people to make room for compromise.

Tallying Becomes an Issue

A protracted debate over the tally method followed the discussion of the four plans themselves, reflecting a resistance to compromise among some individuals and groups. Some suggested we mark only one plan, which was likely to produce a runoff and drag out the process further. Others proposed ranking the plans from one to four. Realizing the board was not going to agree based on the discussion, I asked for a vote by the membership. So we voted on how to vote! The majority chose the originally proposed method of tallying.

The Vote and Outcome

The vote got underway right after the ballot's approval. To everyone's amazement and consternation, the ballot box was tampered with and a re-vote became necessary. This time the ballots were numbered and printed on red paper. When the committee finished the final tally, the school had opted for compromise and chosen curriculum plan B (see "Ballot and the Vote Results"), which replaced *Daddy's Roommate* with the koala stories but retained the rest of our antibias curriculum for full implementation. This would include using photos of same-sex families on the walls and Linda's freedom to use the teachable moment if the topic of alternative families came up at school (although not to initiate conversation using the words "gay" or "lesbian" but instead to say "two moms," "two dads," or "partners"). As a whole, the school voted to trust Linda's judgment. How could we bring our children there otherwise?

Among the four choices of plans on the ballot, curriculum plan B received 37% of the vote. Plan A, the most liberal in its allowing the reading of *Daddy's Roommate*, received 30%. Together, these two plans garnered two-thirds of the vote, illustrating the presence of a sizable silent majority.

Conclusions

In retrospect, it is clear that large meetings were useful primarily for clarifying problems and giving us a starting point in the resolution process. Beyond that, talk tended to volley between loud minorities, shutting out voices of compromise. Open discourse never produced agreement, nor did it provide an accurate assessment of each family's position. Even under the calmest circumstances, not everyone is comfortable speaking up. Using a tool such as the information packet permitted us to move forward because, within the confines of a written forum, people were able to express themselves clearly and thoughtfully without the accompanying emotion that, publicly expressed, often hindered mutual understanding. The ballot itself was a design masterstroke, allowing for the emergence of the much sought-after gray area of compromise.

Assembling a representative committee also helped simplify the process since the committee functioned as a microcosm of the school. We were fortunate in having in our midst a parent with group problem-solving experience, who willingly headed the committee. In the absence of such a skilled person, seeking an experienced adviser from outside the school would be useful and could provide a neutral voice. Our committee head, although skilled, was not viewed as neutral.

Traditionally, on all issues, the president's job is to maintain a neutral position and function as a facilitator. On this issue, upholding that tradition was particularly important and difficult. I focused on creating an atmosphere of mutual patience and the feeling that we would all have a chance to be heard, keeping members informed, and maintaining open channels of communication so the school could continue to function. I did have an opinion, however, and toward the end of this experience I had trouble subordinating it. This could be another reason for considering the services of a consultant, even if only for one or two meetings.

When the school settled down, some families, as we anticipated, left the program. They were unhappy with the results, unhappy with the process, or just turned off by the whole discussion. There's an inevitable sense of loss since many families were good friends before the issue started; in some cases friendships were permanently broken. The loss is offset, however, by the many new friendships that continue to spring up as the school welcomes new members and we rebuild our feeling of unity and cohesiveness.

A Look to the Future

The pendulum of conflict now has swung the other way, perhaps in response to the struggles of that spring. The following year, parents overflowed with ideas to bring our small community together: a Valentine dance, an auction, potlucks, and parties. Prospective members are briefed very specifically on our diversity curriculum to avoid surprises, and we continue to move forward. Our new logo, silk-screened on t-shirts, sweatshirts, and aprons, pictures a boy and girl joining hands and the words "Welcoming families of all shapes and colors." We have refined our antibias policy (see "Multnomah Playschool Antibias Policy" below) and continue to explore options for increasing diversity at the school. One policy enables the membership chair to use her own discretion, within fair and reasonable bounds, to bring diversity to the school.

Some of our potlucks have doubled as fundraisers, and with the proceeds we have purchased "persona doll" bodies (see Derman-Sparks & A.B.C. Task Force 1989, 16). A parent who is a professional artist painted on beautiful faces; another who is an accomplished seamstress designed and made their attire. Linda gave each doll a name, age, and family story; the classroom group times in which a doll is used always produce lively discussions among the children. "Hunter" is a special favorite, not so much because she has two moms but because at three-and-a-half she often gets into the same behaviors the children themselves are working on. She is frequently advised by the children who've just behaved the same way: "She could say, 'Let's take turns'" or "I'd tell her spitting might get somebody sick!"

Multnomah Playschool Antibias Policy

Multnomah Playschool is committed to promoting and celebrating the diversity that occurs in our school, community, and world. We choose to take an active role in counteracting biases. We value diversity and aim to provide opportunities for understanding how and why we differ from one another, as well as how and why we are alike. We will provide an environment welcoming to all people, regardless of gender, race, age, culture, ability, and family configuration. As part of the curriculum we will

1. provide toys, games, books, stories, and visual materials that depict peoples of all races, cultures, ages, abilities, gender, religion, and lifestyle in a positive and nonstereotypical manner;

2. present activities, including songs, music, and cooking projects, that describe diversity and explore the similarities and differences among us all;

3. encourage our families to share their own traditions, cultures, and lifestyles with our school;

4. present antibias information in our newsletters and at our general meetings;

5. provide a forum, in an antibias committee, in which parents can discuss issues around bias in a safe and supportive manner; and

6. elect a board member to serve as diversity/equity coordinator. (This person will function as a liaison between the teacher, antibias committee, parents, and school board. This job will include assisting the teacher in obtaining antibias materials and presenting antibias information to parents via the newsletter and general meetings.)

Our most inspiring project, perhaps, has been the construction of a beautiful quilt, designed and sewn with the help of artist-in-residence Jeanette Meyer. The children made a batik in vibrant earth tones, then used it to construct a border with a miniature nine-patch design. Each child decorated a figure cut of Ultrasuede that was available in a number of flesh tones. The doll-size people, joined hand-to-hand, form a large circle of friends against an azure, hand-dyed background. While working on this project, children talked about the many ways quilts warm the heart as well as the body, and they shared stories of favorite quilts at home. This beautiful piece of art now hangs inside our school entrance and welcomes, with no words necessary, families of all "shapes" and colors.

REFERENCES

Derman-Sparks, L., & A.B.C. Task Force. 1989. *Anti-bias curriculum: Tools for empowering young children*. Washington, DC: NAEYC.

Packer, S. 1993. With liberty and justice for all: Exploring homophobia. *OAEYC Bulletin* 28 (4): 9.

Wickens, E. 1993. Penny's question: "I will have a child in my class with two moms—What do you know about this?" *Young Children* 48 (3): 25–28.

■ *Jennifer Lakey, B.A., writes reviews of children's literature for Writers' NW. She served four years on the board of her children's preschool cooperative and volunteers extensively in the public schools, heading a Junior Great Books program for kindergarten and first grade.*

■ Ask Yourself

Identifying Issues for Advocacy

1. Discuss the differences, if any, you have noticed in how people respond to boy babies and girl babies.

2. What behavioral and temperamental differences have been found for boys and girls (Eisenberg, Martin, & Fabes, 1996; Honig, 1983; Maccoby, 1980; Pollack, 1998)? How are these differences significant or insignificant? Should teachers adjust their curriculum and classroom routines to accommodate these gender differences (e.g., for a class of 10 boys and 5 girls)? Explain your answer.

3. Why do you think teachers tend to give boys who display socially aggressive behaviors a lot of attention? In contrast, why do you think teachers tend to reinforce socially submissive or spectator behaviors in girls (AAUW, 1995, 1997; Phillips, 1998; Sadker & Sadker, 1994; Sommers, 1995)? If teachers give girls less attention than they do boys or often silence their voices in the classroom, why do girls usually outperform boys in grades?

4. Should books that depict females in a demeaning manner (i.e., in a manner similar to racist books) be removed from preschool library corners? Explain your answer. In Iowa, a picture book, *The Pumpkin Patch*, was taken off the shelves because a character declared, "Boys can make jack-o'-lanterns better than girls" (Zepezauer, 1981). Do you consider this action to be censorship or careful screening of young children's picture books for sexist bias?

Why? Are young children able to critically listen to and view picture books for sexist bias (Patt & McBride, 1993; Williams, Vernon, Williams, & Malecha, 1987)? Explain your answer.

5. In some preschool programs, boys will spend most of their free-play time in the block and carpentry areas, and girls will tend to move into the housekeeping and cooking areas (Cameron, Eisenberg, & Tyson, 1985). During free-play, should a preschool teacher attempt to draw both boys and girls into all activity areas of the classroom (e.g., housekeeping, blocks, manipulatives, art, music, sand/water play, library, cooking, and carpentry)? Or is this forcing boys and girls to participate in an activity? Why or why not?

6. View the videocassette "Anti-Bias Curriculum" (Louise Derman-Sparks, Pacific Oaks Bookstore, 5 Westmoreland Place, Pasadena, CA 91103) or the videocassette "It's Elementary: Talking about Gay Issues in School" (Debra Chasnoff and Helen Cohen, Women's Education Media Inc., New Day Films, Hohokus, NJ). Identify evidence of antisexist or nonsexist classroom practices and discuss the value of these practices for children.

7. Why should parents be involved from the very start in program policies related to sex education? What is the importance of their role in sex education? Why is the early childhood period an important time to start sex education? Does NAEYC offer guidelines for sex education in early childhood programs? If so, what are they? If not, should they (see Planned Parenthood Federation of America, 1993, 1996; Rothbaum, Grauer, & Rubin, 1997; Sexuality Information and Education Council of the United States, 1998)?

8. How should a preschool teacher handle questions about where babies come from (see Bernstein, 1976)? What is the value of simple responses and correct terminology? Why do adults often give inaccurate responses to young children, and what values or attitudes might this type of response represent (see Koblinsky, Atkinson, & Davis, 1980; Planned Parenthood Federation of America, 1993)?

9. Should preschool, kindergarten, or primary teachers discuss body differences with young children? Why or why not? As a preschool teacher, would you favor having an open arrangement in the bathroom, or should dividers be required between boys' and girls' toilets (Cohen, 1996)? Why? Should dolls be anatomically correct? Why or why not? Should books depicting naked children be available in the classroom (see, for example, Maurice Sendak's *In the Night Kitchen*)? Why or why not? If anatomically correct language is not included in the written program or school district health curriculum, should a teacher use these terms? Why or why not?

10. How should teachers respond to young children's use of obscene words, or "bathroom language," in the preschool or kindergarten classroom (see Koblinsky et al., 1980)?

11. You have been noticing that one boy in your preschool group tends to masturbate during nap and occasionally while listening to a story during circle time. You mention this behavior to his mother during a conference. She responds that she has noticed similar behavior at home during naps or while watching TV, and that she asked Tommy if anything was bothering him. He said, "No." When asked why he did this, he replied, "Because it feels good." His mother expresses concern to you about this response. What do you say (see Rothbaum et al., 1997)?

12. Are healthy images of males and females portrayed in television programs aimed at young children? Give some examples to support your answer.

13. During circle time, a girl in your preschool class offers, "I'm going to a movie with my mommy and daddy." Another 3-year-old girl quips, "I don't have a mommy and a daddy. I have a mommy and a donor." How would you respond (see Hanson & Gilkerson, 1996)?

■ Advocacy and Leadership Strategies

1. After reading the Wellhousen article, examine five or six picture books in the children's collection of a local library. Include in your selection two books published before 1975. (Or examine the picture books displayed in the library corner of a classroom where you are conducting a field study—also see Appendix 13.) Using the following criteria, look for evidence of sex bias in the books you screen. Also consider if differences exist among books with recent and older publication dates.

   Criteria to Consider When Selecting Children's Books: Sexism
   These criteria may help you to decide if a children's book is sexist. But remember that a book's *overall* messages (the combination of plot, illustrations, words, and characterization) is most important, not simply the inclusion of characters representing sexist stereotypes. In other words, do not throw away *Goldilocks and the Three Bears*. Finally, use your own discretion in book selection by considering what is best for your group of children.

   a. *Look for balance in characterization and illustrations.* Does the group of books you are examining include an equal number of male and female main characters? If not, could the balance of main characters be changed without altering the messages of the stories? Is the number of illustrations of males and females similar? If not, could the balance of illustrations be changed without altering the messages of the stories?

b. *Look for assumptions about social behavior.* Are girls depicted more often than boys as spotless, slim, pretty, demure, inactive, submissive, tearful, helpless or receiving help, and engaging in quiet play? Are boys shown more often than girls in physically active play, being competitive, showing independence, taking initiative, being inventive, solving problems, taking risks, being brave, being strong, receiving recognition, and helping or protecting the opposite sex? Do women more often than men in the books show tenderness toward children and scold children? Do men more often than women in the books play with children, teach children, and take children on outings? Does the book downgrade or make fun of characters who display social behaviors traditionally associated with the opposite sex? Does acceptance depend on traditional boy/girl behavior? Are achievements of girls based on their good looks or on their own initiative and intelligence?

c. *Look for assumptions about occupations.* Are adult males shown more often than adult females as breadwinners or providers? Are adult males shown more often than adult females in prestigious, highly paid jobs? Are adult males shown in more varied job positions than adult females? Are adult females shown more often than adult males as homemakers and shoppers? Are adult females shown more often than adult males in service positions?

d. *Look for gender-biased language.* Watch for "loaded" words and phrases (such as *sissy, tomboy, ladylike, manly, honey, boys will be boys,* etc.). Derogative adjectives and offhand remarks have subtle effects on a child's self-image and self-esteem.

e. *Look for antisexist messages.* Does the book let both boys and girls know they have many options open to them? Does the book confront gender-biased language or behavior and thus encourage the listener to act against or to value action against injustices resulting from sexism?

Books to Consider for Review (also see Wellhousen)

Bauer, M. D. (1995). *When I go camping with Grandma.* Mahwah, NJ: BridgeWater Books.

Beim, J. (1955). *Country school.* New York: William Morrow.

Brisson, P. (1994). *Wanda's roses.* Honesdale, PA: Boyds Mills Press.

Cooney, B. (1996). *Eleanor.* New York: Viking.

Darrow, W. (1970). *I'm glad I'm a boy! I'm glad I'm a girl!* New York: Simon & Schuster.

Eichler, M. (1971). *Martin's father.* Chapel Hill, NC: Lollipop Power.

Fine, A. (1989). *Bill's new frock.* London: Mammoth Books.

Graham, B. (1988). *Crusher is coming.* New York: Viking Kestrel.

Greenfield, E. (1991). *Daddy and I.* New York: Black Butterfly Books.

Hoban, L. (1976). *Arthur's pen pal.* New York: Harper & Row.

Kunhardt, D. (1961). *Billy the barber.* New York: Viking Press.

Leaf, M. (1938). *The story of Ferdinand.* New York: Viking Press.

Lyon, G. E. (1994). *Mama is a miner.* New York: Orchard Books.

Newman, L. (1989). *Heather has two mommies.* Boston: Alyson Wonderland.

Quinlan, P. (1987). *My daddy takes care of me.* Toronto: Annick Press.

Ringgold, F. (1993). *Dinner at Aunt Connie's house.* New York: Hyperion.

Seignobosc, F. (1957). *What do you want to be?* New York: Charles Scribner's Sons.

Skutch, R. (1995). *Who's in a family?* Berkeley, CA: Tricycle Press.

Stamm, C. (1990). *Three strong women: A tall tale from Japan.* New York: Viking.

Uchida, Y. (1993). *The bracelet.* New York: Philomel.

Willhoite, M. (1990). *Daddy's roommate.* Boston: Alyson Wonderland.

Yolen, J. (1992). *Letting Swift River go.* Boston: Little, Brown.

2. Visit the greeting card section of a local store. Examine and analyze the birthday and get-well cards (aimed at children) for their gender-role messages.

3. Visit a local toy store. Are the aisles organized by gender? Analyze the gender-role messages suggested by displayed toys.

4. Contact a local hospital. Interview a representative about the hospital's sibling programs, birth attendance policies, and postpartum programs for mothers. For example, does the hospital provide information or programs for siblings? Does it allow the father to make videotapes of the birth process or does it allow siblings to attend the birth? Based on these responses, what seems to be the hospital's stance toward birth and family relationships?

5. In a small group, review several of the following books about conception, birth, and babies. Is information presented clearly, accurately, and sensitively? Explain. Which would be most appropriate for young children? Why? Which would be good additions to a parent library and which would be good additions to a classroom library? Why? Do you feel that any of the books would be inappropriate for parents or teachers to use with young children? Why or why not? As an outcome of your review, prepare a list of recommended books for a classroom library and one for a parent library. Be prepared to justify your choices.

Books about Conception, Birth, and Babies

Banish, R. (1988). *Let me tell you about my baby.* New York: Harper & Row.

Bernstein, A. C. (1994). *Flight of the stork* (rev. ed.). Indianapolis, IN: Perspectives Press.

Bighall, J. (1998). *My new baby sister.* London: Minivera Press.

Brooks, R. B. (1983). *So that's how I was born!* New York: Simon & Schuster.

Chocolate, D. M. N. (1995). *On the day I was born.* New York: Scholastic.

Cole, B. (1993). *Mommy laid an egg!: Or where do babies come from?* San Francisco: Chronicle Books.

Cole, J. (1994). *How you were born* (rev. ed.). New York: Mulberry.

Cole, J. (1998). *The new baby at your house* (rev. ed.). New York: Morrow Junior Books.

Collman, B. J. (1995). *Kid's book to welcome a new baby* (rev. ed.). St. Paul, MN: Marlor Press.

Girard, L. (1983). *You were born on your very first birthday.* Niles, IL: Albert Whitman.

Gordon, S., & Gordon, J. (1992). *Did the sun shine before you were born?* Buffalo, NY: Prometheus Books.

Green, J. (1998). *Our new baby.* Brookfield, VT: Copper Beach Books.

Herzig, A. C., & Mali, J. L. (1980). *Oh, boy! Babies!* Boston: Little, Brown.

Jam, T. (1998). *This new baby.* Toronto: Douglas & McIntyre.

Kitzinger, S. (1992). *Being born.* New York: Putnam & Grosset.

Lasky, K. (1987). *A baby for Max.* New York: Aladdin Books.

Lewis, D. S. (1995). *When you were a baby.* Atlanta, GA: Peachtree.

Lively, V., & Lively, E. (1991). *Sexual development of young children.* Albany, NY: Delmar.

Mayle, P. (1997). *Where did I come from?* Secaucus, NJ: Carol Publishing.

Meredith, S., Stitt, S., & Chen, K. K. (1991). *Where do babies come from?* Tulsa, OK: EDC Publishing.

Powell, T. (1995). *Hi! I am the new baby.* Norval, ONT: Moulin.

Pringle, L. P. (1997). *Everybody has a bellybutton.* Honesdale, PA: Caroline House, Boyds Mills Press.

Rogers, F. (1985). *The new baby.* New York: G. P. Putnam's Sons.

Ross, K. (1988). *When you were a baby.* New York: Random House.

Royston, A. (1996). *Where do babies come from?* Toronto: Macmillan Canada.

Sheffield, M. (1983). *Where do babies come from?* New York: Knopf.

Wilson, P. M. (1991). *When sex is the subject: Attitudes and answers for young children.* Santa Cruz, CA: ETR Associates.

6. Organize a book club of four to five people (fellow students, worksite colleagues, or community members), and read and discuss one of the following books:

Phillips, L. (1998). *The girls report: What we know and need to know about growing up female.* New York: The National Council for Research on Women. Summary available: www.ncrw.org/research/girls_report.html

Pollack, W. (1998). *Real boys.* New York: Random House.

■ References and Suggested Readings

AAUW. (1995). *How schools shortchange girls: The AAUW report.* Washington, DC: American Association of University Women.

AAUW. (1997). *Gender and race on the campus and in the school: Beyond affirmative action* (Symposium proceedings). Washington, DC: American Association of University Women.

AAUW. (1998). *Separated by sex: A critical look at single-sex education for girls.* Washington, DC: American Association of University Women.

Bernstein, A. C. (1976, September). How children learn about sex and birth. *Psychology Today,* 31–35.

Cahill, B., & Adams, E. (1997). An exploratory study of early childhood teachers' attitudes toward gender roles. *Sex Roles, 36* (7/8), 517–529.

Cameron, E., Eisenberg, N., & Tyson, K. (1985). The relations between sex-typed play and preschoolers' social behavior. *Sex Roles, 12* (5/6), 601–615.

Cohen, D. L. (1996). "Potty-gate" bill requires bathroom dividers. *Education Week, 15* (21), 14.

Crawford, S. H. (1996). *Beyond dolls and guns: 101 ways to help children avoid gender bias.* Portsmouth, NH: Heinemann.

Derman-Sparks, L., & the A.B.C. Task Force. (1989). *Anti-bias curriculum: Tools for empowering young children.* Washington, DC: National Association for the Education of Young Children.

Eisenberg, N., Martin, C. L., & Fabes, R. A. (1996). Gender development and gender effects. In D. C. Berliner & R. C. Calfee (Eds.), *Handbook of educational psychology* (pp. 358–396). New York: Simon & Schuster.

Hanson, M. F., & Gilkerson, D. (1996). Children born from artificial reproductive technology: Implications for children, parents, and caregivers. *Early Childhood Education Journal, 23*, 131–134.

Hardesty, C., Wenk, D., & Morgan, C. S. (1995). Paternal involvement and the development of gender expectations in sons and daughters. *Young & Society, 28*, 283–297.

Honig, A. S. (1983). Sex role socialization in early childhood. *Young Children, 38* (6), 57–70.

Koblinsky, S., Atkinson, J., & Davis, S. (1980). Sex education with young children. *Young Children, 36* (1), 21–31.

Maccoby, E. E. (1980). *Social development: Psychological growth and the parent-child relationship*. New York: Harcourt Brace Jovanovich.

Myra Sadker Advocates. (1998). What you can do on Myra Sadker Day: 100+ ideas! [Online]. Available: www/sadker.org/ideas.htm

Patt, M. B., & McBride, B. A. (1993, April). *Gender equity in picture books in preschool classrooms: An exploratory study*. Paper presented at the annual meeting of the American Educational Research Association, Atlanta, GA. (ERIC Document Reproduction Service No. ED 362 298)

Phillips, L. (1998). *The girls report: What we know and need to know about growing up female*. New York: The National Council for Research on Women. Summary available: www.ncrw.org/research/girls_report.html

Planned Parenthood Federation of America. (1993). Human sexuality: What children should know and when they should know it. [Online]. Available: www.plannedparenthod.org/Library/sexualityeducation/whatchildrenshould.htm

Planned Parenthood Federation of America. (1996). How to be a good parent. [Online]. Available: www.plannedparenthod.org/GUIDESPARENT/SexGuideShow.htm

Pollack, W. (1998). *Real boys*. New York: Random House.

Rothbaum, F., Grauer, A., & Rubin, D. J. (1997, September). Becoming sexual: Differences between child and adult sexuality. *Young Children, 50* (6), 22–28.

Sadker, M., & Sadker, D. (1994). *Failing at fairness: How America's schools shortchange girls*. New York: Charles Scribner's Sons.

Sexuality Information and Education Council of the United States. (1998). SIECUS parents area, [Online]. Available: www.siecus.org/parent/pare0001.html

Sommers, C. H. (1995, July 17). Capitol Hill's girl trouble: The flawed study behind the Gender Equity Act. *Washington Post*, p. C1.

Spillane, C., & Cowley, M. (1996). *Books for boys and girls today: An annotated bibliography of non-sexist books for infants, toddlers, and preschoolers*. Wellesley, MA: Wellesley College, Center for Research on Women.

Williams, J. A., Vernon, J. A., Williams, M. C., & Malecha, K. (1987). Sex role socialization in picture books: An update. *Social Science Quarterly, 68* (1), 148–156.

Zepezauer, F. S. (1981). Treading through the feminist minefield. *Phi Delta Kappan, 63*, 268–272.

■ *Chapter 3*

■ Media and Technology

Television as Curriculum?

Ever since your center's television set broke down, your staff seems to have done nothing but gripe about its loss. Particularly at issue are those transition times in the early morning and late afternoon.

When the day is just getting underway, the children straggle in, so only a few staff are needed. Yet, between setting up, doing health checks, greeting parents, and serving breakfast, it is difficult to monitor the children adequately. Inevitably, the first ones to arrive are the most lively. Unless closely supervised, these children tend to get out of hand, and the day begins on a negative note. You also have heard some parents complain about "wildness."

Things are not much better at the end of the day. Both staff and children have had it! They tend to be irritable and cranky. Fatigued parents faced with a tearful, grumpy child on their hands have been muttering, "Oh, no, not again!"

Clearly something needs to be done and done fast. Should you, against your better judgment, replace the television?

Questions

1. Should television be used in a child-care center? Why or why not?

2. If television is used, should children watch only educational programs? State your reasons.

3. If television is not used, what activities could be substituted?

■ Preview

There is a proliferation of media and technology geared toward young children. Certain television channels are devoted entirely to children's programming, television programs geared toward infants and toddlers are becoming popular, children as young as 2 years old have video collections and can operate a VCR, computer programs and CD-ROMs are marketed for toddlers and preschoolers, and an increasing number of young children can access the Internet. What impact does this exposure to media and technology have on young children? What is being done to ensure quality television programming for children and to safeguard children from violence and exploitation in all forms of media and technology?

This chapter begins with an article by Lauryn Axelrod about Peggy Charren, one of the original advocates for quality children's television. Since Ms. Charren began her work, there have been many positive changes in television for young children. Recently, though, television programming produced for infants and toddlers has been introduced, the appropriateness of which is questioned by the American Academy of Pediatrics in the second article. And, as Amy Aidman points out, children's exposure to violent television content is a continuing issue that we must address. Richard Louv, another advocate for quality children's programming, discusses how we need to shape television for today's children. Finally, we must consider the influence of other types of media on young children, such as the Internet. The final article in this chapter, from *PC World Magazine,* presents several points to be considered as young children surf the Net. As technology continues to advance rapidly, you will want to update this chapter by considering current issues being discussed about young children and computers, Internet access, video games, and recent television programs and videos produced for young children.

Peggy Charren

The Mother of Children's Television

Lauryn Axelrod

■ ■ ■

Peggy Charren doesn't see herself as a TV watch-dog and never has. But this 69-year-old grandmother and recipient of the Presidential Medal of Freedom has been an active and effective children's television advocate for more than 30 years. Her crusades for better children's television have resulted in major legislation and industry change and she's not through yet.

Why Can't Children's TV Be Better?

In the pre-cable, pre-VCR 1960's, Charren, the mother of two young daughters, was frustrated by the lack of quality children's television programming available for her kids. With a background as a children's book fair organizer and a love of children's books, she thought that children's television should be more like a good children's library.

So in 1968, Charren founded Action for Children's Television (ACT) as a three-year effort designed to get broadcasters and legislators to pay more attention to the needs of children, at the time one of the largest yet most underrepresented television viewing audiences. But unlike some other media critics, Charren was always a strong supporter of the First Amendment; she was never interested in the censorship of television, but rather the potential of television to teach.

"ACT never tried to get bad programs off the air," Charren explains. "Only to get more good programs on."

Working for Change

In the early years, ACT received a tremendous amount of publicity as a grassroots organization of housewives and mothers struggling against the Goliath television industry. Large organizations such as the National PTA, the National Association of Pediatrics, religious and labor groups stood behind ACT and formed a coalition that eventually caught the attention of lawmakers, the FCC and the TV industry.

The result was what Charren refers to as "The Golden Age of Children's Television," and a number of high quality children's programs, like ABC's *After-School Specials* and NBC's *Little House on the Prairie*, poured into the living rooms of America.

When many of these shows were canceled in the early '80's, Charren and ACT went into high gear and filed complaints with the FCC and the legislature. With the support of Rep. Edward Markey, D-Mass., the landmark Children's Television Act of 1990 was shepherded into law. The law mandates that broadcasters provide a certain amount of programming *specifically designed* to educate children every day.

Unfortunately, the TV industry didn't respond as well as Charren hoped. Most networks didn't create new educational children's programs, claiming that existing programs, like *The Jetsons*, were educational and fulfilled the law. Charren kept pushing and as a result, starting in September 1997, broadcasters are required to provide at least *three hours* of specifically designed educational children's programming each week.

Keeping Watch

ACT closed its doors in 1992 and the legislative effort to oversee its implementation is now continued by the Center for Media Education, but Charren remains a vocal advocate for children's television. She keeps a watchful eye on how well broadcasters are

Lauryn Axelrod. (1997, Winter). The mother of children's TV. *Smart TV*, pp. 28–29. Reprinted by permission of the author and publisher.

complying with the new three-hour children's programming minimum and, although she believes there have been improvements in children's television over the years, she is quick to say that the real potential for children's programming has not been fully realized.

"The industry needs to recognize that the marketplace isn't always the best way to measure quality when it comes to children's programming," she says.

Charren would like to see the TV industry develop more dramatic and historical programming for children and increase programming for children between the ages of 7–12, for whom there aren't enough high quality shows.

From her position as the foremost guardian of children's television, Charren vows to continue to speak up for television's most vulnerable and neglected young audience members.

"I want to make sure that my grandchildren and their children have as many quality programs and choices on their screens as possible," says Charren. "That's what good television is all about."

■ *Lauryn Axelrod is a documentary filmmaker, a media educator, and the author of* TV-Proof Your Kids: A Parents' Guide to Safe and Healthy Viewing.

Reprinted with permission from Smart TV Magazine. *For a free sample issue, call 888-884-3226 or order through the Smart TV website at www.smarttvmag.com/smarttvmag/ index.htm*

AAP Addresses TV Programming for Children under Age 2

American Academy of Pediatrics

■ ■ ■

Recent new programming for children younger than age 2 has prompted the American Academy of Pediatrics (AAP) to reaffirm its stance that the early years are a crucial period in a child's development. According to recent research on early brain development, it is during the first three years that a child's brain can be positively influenced by environmental factors, such as interactions between parents, other adults and children. Active communication, reading, listening to music or playing are paramount in a child's development.

The AAP is concerned about the language and developmental impact of television programming intended for children younger than age 2. The AAP strongly opposes programming that targets children younger than age 2, which also may be designed to market products.

The AAP calls for additional research to determine possible negative consequences of television on early childhood development. The benefits of parent-child interactions are not in dispute, but any positive effect of television on infants and toddlers is still open to question. Until more research is conducted, pediatricians recommend that parents should focus on positive interaction with children under age 2 rather than allowing them to watch television.

For children older than age 2, the AAP recommends that total television time be limited to no more than 1 to 2 hours per day. Such programming should be developmentally based, pro-social and non-violent in nature and should reinforce language and social skills.

■ *The American Academy of Pediatrics is an organization of 53,000 primary care pediatricians, pediatric medical subspecialists and pediatric surgical specialists dedicated to the health, safety and well-being of infants, children, adolescents and young adults.*

American Academy of Pediatrics. (1998, June). AAP addresses TV programming for children under age 2 (Press release). [Online]. Available: <www.aap.org/advocacy/archives/juntele.htm>. Reprinted by permission.

Television Violence

Content, Context, and Consequences

Amy Aidman

■ ■ ■

Social science research conducted over the past 40 years supports the conclusion that viewing violent television programming has negative consequences for children, and the research suggests three areas in which watching violent television programs can impact young viewers:

1. Media violence can encourage children to learn aggressive behavior and attitudes.
2. Media violence can cultivate fearful or pessimistic attitudes in children about the non-television world.
3. Media violence can desensitize children to real-world and fantasy violence.

According to Eron (1992), "(T)here can no longer be any doubt that heavy exposure to televised violence is one of the causes of aggressive behavior, crime, and violence in society. The evidence comes from both the laboratory and real-life studies. Television violence affects youngsters of all ages, of both genders, at all socio-economic levels and all levels of intelligence. The effect is not limited to children who are already disposed to being aggressive and is not restricted to this country" (p. 1).

This digest reports recent findings on violent television content, highlights the recently developed television ratings system, and offers suggestions for parental guidance and mediation of children's viewing of television programs.

Not All Violence Is Equal

The National Television Violence Study (NTVS) is the largest study of media content ever undertaken. It is a three-year study that assesses the amount, nature,

and context of violence in entertainment programming, examines the effectiveness of ratings and advisories, and reviews televised anti-violence educational initiatives. The study, which began in 1994 and is funded by the National Cable Television Association, defines television violence as "any overt depiction of the use of physical force—or credible threat of physical force—intended to physically harm an animate being or group of beings. Violence also includes certain depictions of physically harmful consequences against an animate being or group that occur as a result of unseen violent means" (National Television Violence Study, Executive Summary, 1996, p. ix).

Not all violence is equal, however. While some violent content can convey an anti-violence message, it is typical to sanitize, glamorize, or even glorify violence on U.S. television. According to the National Television Violence Study (Federman, 1997), only 4% of programs coded had a strong anti-violence theme in the 1995–96 season. In the two years of the study that have been reported, 58% (1994–95) and 61% (1995–96) of programs coded contained some violence.

Certain plot elements in portrayals of violence are considered high risk for children and should be evaluated by parents when judging possible program effects for children. Characterizations in which the perpetrator is attractive are especially problematic because viewers may identify with such a character. Other high-risk factors include showing violence as being justified, going unpunished, and having minimal consequences to the victim. Realistic violence is also among the high-risk plot elements.

NTVS findings from 1995–96 indicate that these high-risk plot elements abound in U.S. broadcast and

Amy Aidman. (1997). *Television violence: Content, context, and consequences.* ERIC Digest. Champaign, IL: ERIC Clearinghouse on Elementary and Early Childhood Education. (ERIC Document Reproduction Service No. ED 414 078)

49

cable television. Of all violent acts, 40% were committed by attractive characters, and 75% of violent actions went unpenalized and the perpetrators showed no remorse. In 37% of the programs, the "bad guys" were not punished, and more than half of all violent incidents did not show the suffering of the victim.

Based on reviews of social science research, it is possible to predict some effects of violent viewing in conjunction with specific plot elements:

Aggressive behavior. Learning to use aggressive behavior is predicted to increase when the perpetrator is attractive, the violence is justified, weapons are present, the violence is graphic or extensive, the violence is realistic, the violence is rewarded, or the violence is presented in a humorous fashion. Conversely, the learning of aggression is inhibited by portrayals that show that violence is unjustified, show perpetrators of violence punished, or show the painful results of violence.

Fearful attitudes. The effects of fearful attitudes about the real world may be increased by a number of features, including attractive victims of violence; unjustified violence; graphic, extensive, or realistic violence; and rewards to the perpetrator of violence. According to the work of George Gerbner and his colleagues (1980), heavy viewers of violent content believe their world is meaner, scarier, and more dangerous than their lighter-viewing counterparts. When violence is punished on television, the expected effect is a decrease in fearful attitudes about the real world.

Desensitization. Desensitization to violence refers to the idea of increased toleration of violence. It is predicted from exposure to extensive or graphic portrayals and humorous portrayals of violence and is of particular concern as a long-term effect for heavy viewers of violent content. Some of the most violent programs are children's animated series in which violence is routinely intended to be funny, and realistic consequences of violence are not shown.

Viewer Differences

Just as not all violence is equal, there are distinctions to be made among viewers. Characteristics such as age, experience, cognitive development, and temperament should be considered as individual factors that can interact with the viewing of violent content. Very young children, for example, have an understanding of fantasy and reality different from that of older children and adults. They may be more frightened by fantasy violence because they do not fully understand that it is not real. When parents consider their children's viewing, both age and individual differences should be taken into account.

Using Television Ratings as Guidelines

As a result of the Telecommunications Act of 1996, a ratings system has been developed by the television industry in collaboration with child advocacy organizations. It is currently in use by some of the networks. Eventually ratings will also be used in conjunction with the V-chip, a device that can be programmed to electronically block selected programming. Beginning in 1998, new television sets are to include V-chip technology.

Ratings categories are based on a combination of age-related and content factors as listed below. These ratings may help parents determine what they consider appropriate for their children to watch. However, it is important to consider that ratings may make programs appear more attractive to some children, possibly creating a "forbidden fruit" appeal. Furthermore, critics point out the potentially problematic nature of having the television industry rate its own programs, and these critics support the development of alternative rating systems by non-industry groups.

TV-Y:	All Children
TV-Y7:	Directed to Older Children
TV-G:	General Audience
TV-PG:	Parental Guidance Suggested
TV-14:	Parents Strongly Cautioned
TV-MA:	Mature Audience Only

A content advisory for fantasy violence, *FV,* may be added to the *TV-Y7* rating. Several content codes may be added to the *TV-PG, TV-14,* and *TV-MA* ratings. These are *V* for intense violence; *S* for intense sexual situations; *L* for strong, coarse language; and *D* for intensely suggestive dialogue.

Beyond Ratings: What Can Parents Do?

Parents can be effective in reducing the negative effects of viewing television in general and violent television in particular.

1. *Watch television with your child.* Not only does watching television with children provide par-

ents with information about what children are seeing, but active discussion and explanation of television programs can increase children's comprehension of content, reduce stereotypical thinking, and increase prosocial behavior.

2. *Turn the program off.* If a portrayal is upsetting, simply turn off the television and discuss your reason for doing so with your child.

3. *Limit viewing.* Set an amount of time for daily or weekly viewing (suggested maximum limit is 2 hours per day), and select programs that are appropriate for the child's age.

4. *Use television program guides or a VCR.* Television program guides can be used to plan and discuss viewing with your child. A VCR is useful for screening programs, building a video library for children, pausing to discuss points, and fast-forwarding through commercials.

5. *Encourage children to be critical of messages they encounter when watching television.* Talking about TV violence gives children alternative ways to think about it. Parents can point out differences between fantasy and reality in depictions of violence. They can also help children understand that in real life, violence is not funny. Discussion of issues underlying what is on the screen can help children to become critical viewers.

REFERENCES

Boyatzis, Chris J. (1997). Of Power Rangers and V-chips. *Young Children, 52*(8), 74–79.

Center for Media Literacy [Homepage of the Center for Media Literacy], [Online]. (1997). Available: http://www.medialit.org/index.html [1997, November 4].

Eron, L. D. (1992). The impact of televised violence. Testimony on behalf of the American Psychological Association before the Senate Committee on Governmental Affairs, *Congressional Record,* June 18, 1992.

Federman, J. (Ed.). (1997). *National Television Violence Study: Vol. 2. Executive summary.* Santa Barbara: University of California, Center for Communication & Social Policy.

Gerbner, George, & Gross, Larry. (1980). The violent face of television and its lessons. In Edward L. Palmer & Aimee Dorr (Eds.), *Children and the faces of television: Teaching, violence, selling* (pp. 149–162). New York: Academic Press.

Levine, Madeline. (1996). *Viewing violence: How media violence affects your child's and adolescent's development.* New York: Doubleday. ED 402 085.

Molitor, Fred, & Hirsch, Kenneth W. (1994). Children's toleration of real-life aggression after exposure to media violence: A replication of the Drabman and Thomas studies. *Child Study Journal, 24*(3), 191–207. EJ 496 752.

National Television Violence Study, Executive Summary, 1994–95. (1996). Studio City, CA: MediaScope, Inc.

Paik, Haejung, & Comstock, George. (1994). The effects of television violence on antisocial behavior: A meta-analysis. *Communication Research, 21*(4), 516–546. EJ 487 681.

S.1383, Children's Protection from Violent Programming Act of 1993; S.973, Television Report Card Act of 1993; and S.943, Children's Television Violence Protection Act of 1993. Hearing before the Committee on Commerce, Science, and Transportation. United States Senate, 103d Cong., 1st Sess. Congress of the U.S. (1993). ED 386 658.

Singer, Dorothy G.; Singer, Jerome L.; & Zuckerman, Diana M. (1990). *A parent's guide: Use TV to your child's advantage.* Reston, VA: Acropolis Books.

Smith, Marilyn E. (1993). *Television violence and behavior: A research summary.* ERIC Digest. Syracuse, NY: ERIC Clearinghouse on Information and Technology. ED 366 329.

The TV Parental Guidelines [Homepage of the TV Parental Guidelines Monitoring Board], [Online]. Available: http://www.tvguidelines.org [1997, November 4].

Shaping TV for Kids

Richard Louv

■ ■ ■

In the future, the television industry, particularly the networks, will be forced to work harder to attract young viewers. This is partly because of TV fragmentation (100 cable channels competing for the same viewer). Another factor is the likelihood that school hours will be longer (cutting into afternoon TV time) and more demanding. While we will see more electronics in the classroom, the screen that will dominate won't be the TV screen but the computer screen.

Ralph Whitehead, professor of communications at the University of Massachusetts, Amherst, points to the growing upscale-downscale split in the TV audience. The American middle class is diverging into two main groups—one more educated and affluent than the middle class has ever been, the other drifting slowly toward less education and poverty. For upscale children, he says, "watching TV will be as declasse as smoking cigarettes." That sounds like hyperbole, but upscale children may well prefer to spend more of their time on computers or the coming interactive technologies, which will integrate computers and video. "If the twenty-one inch, low-definition generic TV set continues to display a flat, two-dimensional, mass-produced show like *The Smurfs*, then television will become the KMart of the new electronic marketplace," says Whitehead.

The question television executives should be asking is: What kind of shows will attract the upscale young viewers, with disposable income, and help bring the downscale audience up to scale? The most important element in such programming is that it should be more *reality-based*. Many of us sense that

our children are growing up in an imitation society, an electronic bubble in which most of life's references are from television. Paradoxically, TV could encourage kids and parents to turn off the TV and *do something*.

For example, baby boomers love *This Old House* or similar programs that show how to remodel or build houses. How about *This Old Treehouse?*

How about more kids shows about other hands-on experiences, such as fixing or customizing cars, art, fishing, or hiking?

Or story lines that show kids interacting with adults in the neighborhood, learning from them, getting help from them? (Ward Cleaver may never have removed his tie, but you did have a sense of place in the Beaver's neighborhood.) Or parents talking to other parents and to neighbors? "For two decades Americans wondered if Walter Cronkite had legs; for nearly a decade we have wondered if the Cosbys have neighbors," says Whitehead. Except for the grandparents, is there a community of support for this family, or did they raise their kids alone? To be a good parent or good neighbor today can be an act of quiet heroism, but that kind of heroism is seldom seen on TV. Mainly we get exploding Ninja warriors.

The most powerful forces in the television industry are on the side of the failing status quo. Of course, many people in the TV industry do want to change. They need all the encouragement and lobbying they can get from parents and other Americans who care about children.

■ *Richard Louv is the author of several books about children and family life, including* The Web of Life *(Conari Press). He is also senior editor of KidsCampaigns* [www.kidscampaigns.org].

Richard Louv. (1998). Shaping TV for kids. [Online]. <www.benton.org>. Reprinted by permission of the author.

Your Children Are Talking to Strangers

PC World Magazine

■ ■ ■

Ever since households with children started gaining access to the Web, parents and child-protection groups have been fretting about the issue of adult content and trying to devise products and schemes for shielding kids from inappropriate material. No less than ten filtering options are available, counting Microsoft's recent entry into the market with Microsoft Plus for Kids.

Now, I don't want my children stumbling across lurid pictures in their online wanderings any more than the next parent, but there's another issue that concerns me even more: the many attempts to collect from my kids personal information about our family. For example, I know of few children (or adults) who have "happened" onto pornographic Web sites, but just about everyone I know has landed on a site that asked for personal information in exchange for letting them join in the fun or take advantage of the site's services. As adults, we know that such information will be used to sell us products and services later on, but most kids have no clue. They just want the stuff.

Consider this scenario: Mom and Dad are in another room, and Mary is clicking away in the Fun Zone of the Toys "R" Us Web site when she comes across a great offer—a personalized electronic birthday card. All she has to do is enter her e-mail address, date of birth, and gender. There's no disclaimer about what else might be done with the information, no word of caution to check with Mom or Dad before giving it out. It's a seemingly innocent offer. How many kids will pass that up? Mary types in the information, and pretty soon her parents start receiving solicitations for toy products.

Offers of free gifts, screen savers, software updates, and chances to win a great prize abound in cyberspace. Here are just a few examples of the creative ways in which companies collect information from kids online:

- Children can send a personal letter to their favorite Street Shark (www.wid.com/sharks) just by typing in their message and passing along their name, e-mail address, and hometown. There's no on-screen notice indicating what this information will be used for or advising children to ask their parents for permission.
- Kids wishing to play at the KidsCom site (www.kidscom.com) must first register by providing their full name, birth date, gender, favorite TV show, and more.
- In the Drop Zone section of the Pepsi site (www.pepsi.com), visitors are encouraged to provide their full name, e-mail address, and telephone number: "Share with us the information we ask from you below and you will automatically hold the key to participating in our great contests and sweepstakes, chat areas, special events and everything else we like to call The Pepsi World Experience."

Those are tough offers for kids to refuse.

In spring of 1996, the Center for Media Education, a national electronic-media watchdog group, released Web of Deception: Threats to Children from Online Marketing, a report documenting the many ways that businesses use the Internet and online services to collect personal information and market their products to children. The group called for the Federal Trade Commission to review online marketing practices and to establish guidelines that would prevent the gathering of personal data from children.

But despite the initial furor that the CME report produced—the FTC held hearings, and several industry groups promised to review questionable sites—more than one year after the report's release not much has changed, according to Shelly Pasnik, director of children's policy for the CME and one of the report's authors.

If anything, the situation is more grave than when her organization first documented the abuses. "We're just as concerned today as when we issued the report—even more so," says Pasnik, noting that companies that took a wait-and-see approach to Web development in 1996 have now joined the online bandwagon. As a result, it's hard to find a toy-store chain, an action-figure producer, a cereal maker, or any other kid-product marketer that isn't online.

Hey, Kid, Want Some Candy?

Using the lure of well-known product mascots like Snap, Crackle, and Pop or Tony the Tiger, plus offers of free interactive games and other "gifts," companies are attracting children as young as preschool age to their new playgrounds on the Web. Certainly, marketing to kids is nothing new: Any parents who have ever watched Saturday-morning television or taken their children grocery shopping can see the impact that a single cartoon character or toy surprise can have on a young child. But however enticing they may be, commercials are still just that—a break from regular programming to sell a product. Online, these come-ons have a particularly strong influence and appear in many disguises: Kids can send cards, draw pictures, print out images of their favorite characters, even listen to sound clips from the latest animated hit. These activities aren't interrupting their online fun—they are the online fun.

So when 12-year-old Kim saw the banner in Yahooligans (the children's version of the popular Yahoo search engine) for a Lucky Charms Scavenger Hunt, she thought, "Cool. This will be fun." Enticed by the promise of a diploma for finding all the hidden marshmallows, she and a friend spent nearly an hour engrossed in the activity, without ever realizing that the game they were playing was just slick advertising.

Marketing to kids is big business. According to Dr. James McNeal, a leading children's marketing expert at Texas A&M University, children ages 4 through 12 had a direct influence on $170 billion in sales of products and services in 1995—and indirectly influenced twice that amount. Teens spend nearly $100 billion a year.

Although TV still gets the big bucks, many companies are looking to the Web as the next great advertising medium. "This is a medium for advertisers that is unprecedented," notes an advertising director for Saatchi & Saatchi. "There's probably no other product or service that we can think of that is like it in terms of kids' interest." The large advertising agency has an entire group, in fact, focusing exclusively on children's online habits and the best way to market to them.

What's the big attraction? First, there's the lack of regulations in the online world. In television, product mascots are prohibited from hosting full-length programs: You won't see a half-hour cartoon hosted by Tony the Tiger or Toucan Sam. No such prohibitions exist online.

As part of its Action for Children in Cyberspace project, the CME advocates that no personal information be collected from children online, that all advertising and promotions be clearly marked and kept separate from content areas, that children's areas not be linked directly to advertising sites, that no online interaction take place between children and product mascots, and that microtargeting of and direct-response marketing to children be prohibited.

Unfortunately, as of now the FTC does not seem inclined to adopt such regulations. Instead, the commission has opted to hold more hearings and to study the matter further.

In the meantime, it looks like we parents are on our own. And so are our kids.

Web Smarts:
How You Can Do Your Part

Few parents can sit with their children every minute they're online—particularly as kids approach the teenage years. But here are some steps you can take to protect your children's privacy and help make them smarter consumers. A full brochure, downloadable in Adobe Acrobat format, is available from the Center for Media Education (tap.epn.org/cme/adfct.pdf).

- Advise your children never to give out their name, e-mail address, or physical location without first asking your permission. Make sure they realize that this rule applies to individuals who might request such information as well as to cereal-box characters or their favorite action heroes.
- Send e-mail to the Federal Trade Commission (www.ftc.gov) detailing your concerns and urging action on the behalf of children.

- Complain to companies whose deceptive practices target your kids.
- Spend time with your children online. Tour new sites together, so you can help them distinguish advertising- and marketing-driven sites from those with purely editorial or educational content.
- Find out your children's school policy regarding commercial Internet sites.

Ask Yourself

Identifying Issues for Advocacy

1. What is the average number of hours per day that preschool children watch television or videos (see the Children's Television Act Tool Kit at www.tap.epn.org/cme/ctatool/fguide.html)?

2. What are the positive and/or negative effects of television, videos, and video games on young children (see Kohn, 1998; Levin, 1998; Pipher, 1996)?

3. Is the child who does not view television deprived of information about the larger world? Why or why not?

4. What kinds of television shows and videos are worthwhile and appropriate for young children? Inappropriate? What information is available to help parents decide which shows and movies are acceptable for young children? (Search the websites listed at the end of this chapter and in Appendix 1.)

5. How does television viewing affect children's play? Is children's play with media-linked toys a cause for concern? Why or why not? How can early childhood teachers deal with the aggressive actions that a child imitates from observing violence in the media (see Levin, 1998)?

6. After reading this chapter, search the Web to identify the current issues surrounding television and computer technology that early childhood advocates need to address.

7. When should a child's computer education begin? How should the computer be introduced to young children? Is there appropriate software for toddlers and preschoolers (see Healy, 1998; Coalition for Quality Children's Media at www.cqcm.org/kidsfirst)?

8. Research the topic of children's television programming in countries other than the United States. Are there regulations governing children's programming and/or advocacy organizations monitoring the appropriateness of programs for children?

9. Do the children at your field site watch television or videos? Are there computers in the center or classroom? Inquire about the school's policy concerning both television and video viewing and the use of computers and computer software.

■ Advocacy and Leadership Strategies

1. Design and distribute a parent information brochure on television viewing that contains the following: family activities for television viewing, tips for dealing with media violence and inappropriate programming for young children, websites for parents about children's television and videos, recommended age-appropriate television programs and videos, and suggestions on how parents can be advocates for quality children's programming.

2. Compare commercial on-line computer services as to the parent controls they offer. Also inquire about the local library's and elementary schools' policies concerning children on-line (i.e., filters, adult supervision, and age limits). Gather information from the Surfsmart website (www.surfsmart.com) and the Center for Media Education's Campaign to Protect Children from Harmful Cyber-Advertising (www.tap.epn.org/cme) and write a parent letter discussing your findings and suggesting Internet safety guidelines.

3. Interview the children's liaison at a local commercial television station, review the station's Children's Television Act files, and discuss the following: the Children's Educational/Informational Television Report, how the station is meeting the requirements of the Children's Television Act, and what feedback the station is receiving from the public. See www.tap.epn.org/cme/ctatool/ fguide.html for background information. Using the report card at this website, evaluate the educational merits of the three hours of educational programming the station airs and note if the E/I logo is used in the newspaper TV listings. Offer feedback, in letter form, to both the network and the FCC. (See Appendix 3 for suggestions on writing the advocacy letter.)

4. Review a wide range of computer software designed for toddlers and preschoolers. Which software would you recommend to parents? Why? Which would you not recommend? Why? Would you have any of the programs in your preschool classroom? Why or why not? Write to one manufacturer and give your critique of its software for toddlers and preschoolers. (The following websites contain software for preschool children: <www.broderbund.com> <www.edmark.com> and <www.humongous.com>. Your local library or media store may also provide the opportunity to preview software.)

5. Read *The Shelter of Each Other* by Mary Pipher (1996). Relate her observations both to this chapter and to Chapter 7 in this book. Present a review and summary to your class. Submit a review of this book, or a similar book of your choice, to your early childhood association affiliate newsletter. (See Appendix 4 on submitting articles for publication.)

6. Organize a book discussion group composed of parents and/or teachers and discuss *Remote Control Childhood? Combating the Hazards of Media Culture* by Diane E. Levin (1998). Lead the group to form an action plan and report on your project to the class. (See Appendix 2 for points to consider when designing your action plan.)

7. There are now educational television networks for children only (e.g., NOGGINS in the United States and Treehouse TV in Canada). Each member of the class videotape one hour of programming on one of these networks and one hour of programming aired for preschool-aged children on a major network. Then view and evaluate the programs using the television program evaluation form in Figure 3.1. Your study would be enhanced by watching these programs with a preschool-aged child and recording his or her reactions and comments. Compare and share your findings. After completing your study of these programs, do one of the following activities:

    a. Write a letter to the editor or television critic of the local newspaper about your findings and the appropriateness of the programs for young children (see Appendix 4). Your input may lead the newspaper editor or critic to write a column on your positive or negative comments about a TV program for children.

    b. Many programs have a website, which includes advertisements geared toward young children. Refer to the Center for Media Education's guidelines on cyber-advertising <www.tap.epn.org/cme>. Then visit the website of one of the programs you reviewed. Present to the class a report on this program website and your evaluation of it. Also note and comment on the developmental appropriateness of learning activities suggested on the site.

    c. Evaluate the commercials during the two hours of programming by responding to the following questions with yes or no responses and descriptive statements. Write to a product sponsor and express your views (positive or negative) on the appropriateness of the commercials for young children.

        (1) Is the size of the product made clear?

        (2) Is a child or adult shown doing something unsafe?

        (3) Does the ad promote poor eating habits?

        (4) Does the ad promote sexist or racist attitudes or behaviors?

        (5) Are children shown using a product not intended for children?

        (6) Are children shown using a product in a way that the average child could not?

        (7) Does the ad suggest that a child will be superior to friends or more popular if he or she owns a given product?

■ **FIGURE 3.1** Television Program Evaluation Form

Program _____ Evaluator _____

I. Rate a commercial children's TV program viewed against the following positive and negative characteristics to help you decide whether or not you would recommend the program be viewed by preschool children. Add comments to clarify rating. Enter a check in the last column if the characteristic is not applicable.

Characteristic	Positive		Negative	N.A.
A. Content fits the interests of the intended audience.	Content relates to children's interests and experiences.	←——————→ 4 3 2 1 0 Comments:	Not relevant; children lose interest in content quickly.	
B. If an entertainment show, the tone is appropriate.	Wholesome, exciting, and/or humorous.	←——————→ 4 3 2 1 0 Comments:	Gruesome, violent, and/ or antisocial behavior.	
C. It aids the child in self-understanding and/or understanding of others.	Deals with problems relevant to young children. Supports positive relationships with others.	←——————→ 4 3 2 1 0 Comments:	Problems are not relevant to young children. Promotes incorrect ideas about people and their characteristics.	
D. It promotes positive social values.	Fair play, kindness, honesty, empathy.	←——————→ 4 3 2 1 0 Comments:	Crime, cheating, lying, hurting.	
E. It promotes and encourages constructive play and activities.	Promotes and encourages behavior such as constructive fantasy play, working with others, an interest in appropriate play materials (such as books or paint) or further inquiry and problem solving.	←——————→ 4 3 2 1 0 Comments:	Shows details of criminal activities; inappropriate materials being used; or extremely competitive or very aggressive behavior.	
F. The program production is high quality.	Production has high-quality script, music, artwork, sets, sound effects, photography, and acting.	←——————→ 4 3 2 1 0 Comments:	Production is sloppy; artwork or sets are poorly done; cartoons are oversimplified and unattractive; acting and/or voice dubbing is poor; action is hard to follow, too fast, or too slow.	
G. Program is free of prejudice and fair in treatment of different groups of people.	Nonsexist and nonracist. Equality and understanding are promoted. All ages, races, cultures, handicapping conditions, and sexes are presented fairly and honestly.	←——————→ 4 3 2 1 0 Comments:	Unfair to any age, race, sex, culture, or handicapping condition. Presents unrealistic stereotypes, or omits different ages, races, cultures, handicapping conditions, and sexes.	
H. If program presents them, emergent reading, math, and writing skills/concepts are age appropriate and well presented.	Concepts presented clearly, repeated in a variety of formats, and illustrated concretely.	←——————→ 4 3 2 1 0 Comments:	Concepts/skills beyond the preschool child's level; presentation misleading and confusing.	

Source: Adapted from *Understanding Child Development,* 2nd ed., by R. Charlesworth, 1987, Albany, NY: Delmar.

     (8) Does the ad suggest that an adult who buys a product for a child is better or more caring than one who does not?

     (9) Do program hosts or characters appear in commercials within their own programs?*

8. View PBS's *Teletubbies* and *Preschool Power* (or other recent additions to their preschool programming) and then contact your local public broadcasting station. Inquire about their plans for children's programming in the future, the Ready to Learn Service, the Family Education Company, the ChildCare Partnership, and the station's need for volunteers. Report on your findings to the class or arrange for a representative from the station to speak to a parent and/or teacher group. Organize and/or involve classmates or friends in a volunteer effort that will benefit the station. You may also organize a debate on the appropriateness of television programming for infants and toddlers. (See Appendix 8 for guidelines on organizing and conducting the debate.)

9. View five current G-rated movies and note if they contain violence and/or mature content inappropriate for children less than 7 years of age. Mothers Offended by the Media (MOM) is requesting that the Motion Picture Association of America institute a G-6 rating, indicating the movie is appropriate for children under age 7. Investigate the status of this campaign (founder: J. Sears, P.O. Box 382, Southampton, MA 01073, phone: 413-536-9282). Also interview ticket sellers at a local cineplex. Ask if they observe parents taking young children to only G-rated movies. If there is a video arcade at the cineplex, observe the types of games preschool-aged children are playing or watching. Do the arcade games contain violence and/or mature content? Summarize your observations and develop an advocacy project based on your findings. (See Appendix 2 for advocacy tips.)

10. Read the summary of the United Nations' Rights of the Child (Appendix 11). As a class, discuss the eleventh right: Children have the right to access to information and material from a diversity of national and international sources. Relate your readings and research from this chapter to your discussion.

■ References and Suggested Readings

Axelrod, L. (1997). *TV-proof your kids.* Secaucus, NJ: Carol Publishing, Citadel Press.

Collins, M., & Kimmel, M. (Eds.). (1996). *Mister Rogers Neighborhood—Children, TV and Fred Rogers.* Pittsburgh, PA: University of Pittsburgh Press.

Source: Items (1) through (9) are adapted from Children's Advertising Review Unit, National Advertising Division Council of Better Business Bureaus, Inc., 845 Third Avenue, New York, New York, 212/754-1353.

DeGaetano, G., & Bander, K. (1996). *Screen smarts: A family guide to media literacy.* Boston: Houghton Mifflin.

Fox, R. F. (1996). *Harvesting minds: How TV commercials control kids.* Westport, CT: Praeger.

Healy, J. (1998). *Failure to connect: How computers affect our children's minds—For better and worse.* New York: Simon and Schuster.

Kline, S. (1993). *Out of the garden: Toys and children's culture in the age of TV marketing.* London: Verso.

Kohn, A. (1998). *What to look for in a classroom . . . And other essays.* San Francisco: Jossey-Bass.

Levin, D. (1998). *Remote control childhood? Combating the hazards of media culture.* Washington, DC: National Association for the Education of Young Children.

Macbeth, T. (Ed.). (1996). *Tuning in to young viewers' social science perspectives on TV.* Thousand Oaks, CA: Sage.

Murphy, J., & Tucker, K. (1996). *Stay tuned! Raising media-savvy kids in the age of the channel-surfing couch potato.* New York: Doubleday.

Pipher, M. (1996). *The shelter of each other: Rebuilding our families.* New York: Ballantine Books.

Media Websites

Center for Media Education: www.cme.org

Child Internet Safety: www.safekids.com

Children's Advocacy Group: www.childrennow.org

Children's Television Workshop: www.ctw.org

Coalition for Quality Children's Media: www.cqcm.org/kidsfirst

Kid Safe Sites: www.cwa.co.nz/eduweb/edu/worlded/kidsafe.html

National Coalition on Television Violence: www.nctvv.org

National Institute of Media and the Family: www.mediaandthefamily.org

Chapter 4

Child Health and
Child Health Risks

No Freebie Food?

Dear Editor:

I would like to comment on your editorial concerning the need for government food programs such as Women, Infants, and Children (WIC). To me, it's just another giveaway welfare program. So what if the food supplement is restricted to foods rich in protein and vitamins! What guarantee is there that the babies will get the nourishment they need? From what I have seen of these people, the mothers and their boyfriends will eat the food.

My husband and I have worked hard for everything we own. We scrimped and saved to buy our own home, to clothe and feed our children, and to send them to college. Why should we pay taxes to support people who were not even born here? Answer me that!

Signed,
Not a Bleeding Heart

Questions

1. In your opinion, what is the value of spending tax dollars on supplemental food programs such as WIC, the Child and Adult Care Food Program, Food Stamps, or the School Lunch Program?

2. Based on your observations and experiences, what are the pros and cons of the programs mentioned in question 1?

■ Preview

In recent years, research evidence has led policy makers to place increased emphasis on the interrelatedness of child health and readiness to learn (e.g., see the most recent volume of the National Educational Goals Report). As Larry Aber and Julian Palmer point out, health risk factors such as inadequate nutrition, maternal substance abuse, maternal depression, exposure to environmental toxins, early trauma or abuse, and quality of daily care can influence a child's brain development. The second reading in this chapter, written by Ruth A. Wilson, examines more closely some of these environmental risk factors and the implications for action that can be drawn from the evidence. To energize and support coordinated community efforts to improve children's health, the U.S. Department of Health and Human Services has launched a Healthy Child Care America Campaign and has set out a 10-point blueprint to guide action. Finally, Mary A. Jensen examines the history and development of a highly successful federal child nutrition program: WIC (Special Supplemental Nutrition Program for Women, Infants and Children). The WIC story offers a compelling example of how advocates have used diverse advocacy strategies to secure funding.

Poverty and Brain Development in Early Childhood

Larry Aber and Julian Palmer

■ ■ ■

Overview

Researchers have gathered new evidence on the importance of the first years of life for children's emotional and intellectual development (Shore, 1997). Unfortunately, millions of American children are poor during these crucial years. Almost one in four (24 percent) of America's children under age three lived in poverty in 1995. These 2.8 million poor children face a greater risk of impaired brain development due to their exposure to a number of risk factors associated with poverty. Many poor young children are resilient and able to overcome tremendous obstacles but poverty poses serious threats to children's brain development. Recent advances in the study of brain development show a sensitive period when the brain is most able to respond to and grow from exposure to environmental stimulation. This window of optimal brain development is from the prenatal period to the first years of a child's life. While all children are potentially vulnerable to a number of risk factors which can impede brain development during this sensitive period, a disproportionate number of children in poverty are actually exposed to such risk factors. These risk factors can influence the brain through multiple pathways [as shown on the next page].

The Impact of Poverty on Brain Development: Multiple Pathways

Inadequate Nutrition

Children deprived of proper nutrition during the brain's most formative years score much lower on tests of vocabulary, reading comprehension, arithmetic, and general knowledge. The more severe the poverty a child faces, the lower his or her nutritional level is likely to be (Brown & Pollitt, 1996). Malnutrition causes social withdrawal, delayed motor skills development, and delayed physical growth, leading to lower expectations from parents/teachers and less environmental probing.

Substance Abuse

Doctors have known for years the harmful effects of nicotine, alcohol, and drugs both during and after pregnancy. Research has demonstrated that much of their impact on children stems from poor brain development, centered around stunted neurons in the brain and a lack of brain cells in crucial developmental stages, causing serious neurological disorders (Mayes, 1996).

Maternal Depression

Many children whose mothers suffer from depression lack healthy brain development. It is vital for children to be stimulated by their environment during the first years of life. Mothers who are suffering from depression are less able to provide the positive responses needed by babies, less likely to interact with their babies, and often fail to respond to their infants' emotional needs. These deficits lead to babies who are more withdrawn, less active, and have shorter attention spans (Belle, 1990).

Exposure to Environmental Toxins

Exposure to neurotoxins such as lead causes brain damage and stunts the growth of the brain. One

Poverty and Brain Development in Early Childhood by Larry Aber and Julian Palmer and published by the National Center for Children in Poverty (NCCP), Joseph L. Mailman School of Public Health of Columbia University, 154 Haven Avenue, New York, NY 10032. Phone: (212) 304-7100, Fax: (212) 544-4200, or e-mail: <nccp@columbia.edu>. Reprinted by permission of the publisher.

The Impact of Poverty on Brain Development:
Multiple Pathways

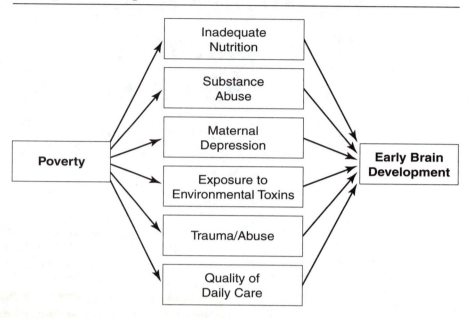

American child in six has toxic levels of lead in his or her blood; and 55 percent of African American children living in poverty have toxic levels of lead in their blood. Each year 400,000 newborns are delivered with toxic levels of lead in their blood that came from their environment (National Health/Education Consortium, 1991).

Trauma/Abuse

Experiences of trauma or abuse during the first years of life result in extreme anxiety, depression, and/or the inability to form healthy attachments to others. While physical abuse is the most noticeable, emotional and mental trauma are also damaging. Another troubling effect of early trauma is that it leads to a significantly higher propensity for violence later in life. The stressors that face poor families cause much more trauma for their children (Brooks-Gunn, Klebanov, Liaw & Duncan, 1995).

Quality of Daily Care

Daily interaction plays an important role in a child's emotional and mental development. While the brain is forming and "learning" how to develop, consistent positive interaction is needed to ensure proper brain activity. Poor day care hinders a child's brain activity and impedes development by discouraging interaction and limiting environmental stimulation. Compared to those who were not in day care, studies show that high quality day care can in fact enhance the intellectual development of poor children

(Burchinal, Lee & Ramey, 1989; Cost, Quality & Child Outcome team, et al., 1995).

What Can Be Done?

Reduce the Poverty Rate

Given the importance of the first years of life to the development of the brain and to the ability of children to reach their full potential, it is particularly important to reduce children's exposure to critical risk factors during early childhood. There are many important programs and services which can improve the life chances of children in poverty. Also, it is critically important to attack child poverty directly. Poverty is a primary risk factor which increases the likelihood that young children will be exposed to multiple risk factors. These additional risk factors can have important negative effects on children's brain development. Any comprehensive strategy to promote early childhood brain development must therefore include strategies to reduce the poverty rate for young children.

Every other major Western industrialized nation has been more successful in preventing the incidence of child poverty and thereby decreasing the risks to healthy brain development. The United States can learn from these countries and develop new public- and private-sector strategies to reduce the child poverty rate that are consistent with its national values and economic means (Danziger, Smeeding & Rainwater, 1995).

REFERENCES

Belle, D. (1990). Poverty and women's mental health. *American Psychologist, 45*(3), pp. 385–389.

Brooks-Gunn, J.; Klebanov, P.; Liaw, F.; & Duncan, G. (1995). Toward an understanding of the effects of poverty upon children. In Fitzgerald, H. E.; Lester, B. M.; & Zuckerman, B. (Eds.). *Children of poverty: Research, health, and policy issues.* New York, NY: Garland Publishing, Inc.

Brown, L. & Pollitt, E. (1996). Malnutrition, poverty and intellectual development. *Scientific American, 274*(2), pp. 38–43.

Burchinal, M.; Lee M.; & Ramey, C. (1989). Type of day care and preschool intellectual development in disadvantaged children. *Child Development, 60*(1), pp. 128–137.

Cost, Quality, and Child Outcome Study Team; Helburn, S.; Culkin, M.; Morris, J.; Mocan, N.; Howes, C.; Phillipsen, L.; Bryant, D.; Clifford, R.; Cryer, D.; Peisner-Feinberg, E.; Burchinal, M.; Kagan, S.; & Rustici, J. (1995). *Cost, quality, and child outcomes in child care centers.* Denver, CO: University of Colorado at Denver, Department of Economics.

Danziger, S.; Smeeding, T.; & Rainwater, L. (1995). *The Western welfare state in the 1990s: Toward a new model of anti-poverty policy for families with children* (Luxembourg Income Study (LIS) Working Paper No. 128). Syracuse, NY: Syracuse University, Maxwell School of Citizenship and Public Affairs.

Mayes, L. (1996). Early experience and the developing brain: The model of prenatal cocaine exposure. Paper presented at the invitational conference: "Brain Development in Young Children: New Frontiers for Research, Policy, and Practice," The University of Chicago, June 12–14.

Shore, R. (1997). *Rethinking the brain: New insights into early development.* New York, NY: Families and Work Institute.

The National Health/Education Consortium. (1991). Healthy brain development. *The National Health/Education Consortium Report,* January, pp. 4–5.

See also: *Public policy: A new bottom line: To measure poverty, look at the children.* Opinion Article published in the *Boston Globe,* Sunday, September 29, 1996.

Healthy Habitats for Children

Ruth A. Wilson

■ ■ ■

Environmental Justice Issues

The ecology movement means more than just a concern for parks, rivers, and forests. It's also a concern for people and how they're affected by environmentally related decisions and practices. While the early years of environmentalism did not always encompass the needs of human beings, an emerging awareness of the interrelationship between environmental violation of the earth and environmental violation of its human inhabitants is leading to an expanded definition of the environment.

Environmentalists working from this new definition are now becoming involved in issues relating to "endangered urban habitats, childhood lead poisoning, energy and transportation, facility siting, equal protection, and a host of other issues related to where people live, work, and play" (Bullard, 1994, p. 35). A major contribution of this definition is that it adds a human face to the environmental field.

This new direction in environmentalism is being referred to as the *environmental justice movement* and represents one of the strongest new forces to emerge in the field in many years. *Environmental justice* refers to the fair or equitable treatment of people of all races, cultures and incomes with respect to the development, implementation, and enforcement of environmental laws, regulations, programs, and policies. Fair or equitable treatment means that no racial, ethnic, or socioeconomic group should bear a disproportionate share of the negative environmental consequences resulting from the operation of industrial, municipal, and commercial enterprises. As Carol Browner, the EPA's administrator, stated (quoted by Johnson, 1995), "All Americans deserve clean air, pure water, land that is safe to live on, food that is safe to eat. All Americans deserve to be protected from pollution—not just those who can afford to live in the cleanest, safest communities (p. 2)." Such, however, is not the case. While we all live

on the same earth, we do not all breathe the same air, drink the same water, nor play in the same soil.

While a sense of justice calls for the right of all people to live in areas free from ecological destruction, many young children continue to live in physical environments that are detrimental to their health, growth, and overall development. Current statistics indicate, for example, that two in five Americans live in areas where the air is dangerous to breathe (Browner, 1995). In addition to air pollution, other factors contributing to the ecological destruction of the neighborhoods in which many children live include congestion, excessive noise, solid wastes, and toxic chemicals.

The children who suffer the most from environmental degradation tend to be those living in low-income and racial minority communities (i.e., poor people and people of color) (Blahna & Toch, 1993; Collin, 1993; Ember, 1992). Children living in these communities experience higher-than-average exposure to toxic pollutants, largely because three out of every four toxic-waste dumps that fail to comply with EPA (Environmental Protection Agency) regulations are in black or Hispanic neighborhoods (Environmental Protection Agency, 1992).

Most families living in low-income and environmentally degraded communities do so not by choice, but because they lack the mobility to escape such areas (Rogue, 1993). The situation becomes worse once the presence of a toxic threat is known. Residents then become trapped in their homes. Their economic situation doesn't allow for a variety of options as to where they live, and their political situation doesn't give them the clout to keep their communities safe from becoming "dumping grounds" for the rest of society's wastes (Collin, 1993). Because environmental harms tend to follow the path of least resistance, disenfranchised communities (i.e., com-

Ruth A. Wilson. (1996). Healthy habitats for children. *Early Childhood Education Journal, 23*(4), 235–238. Reprinted by permission of the author and publisher.

munities without the power to exercise their rights) usually end up with the toxic-waste problems.

Health-Related Implications

Children and families pay a high price for living in areas of environmental degradation, in that people living in such areas are more likely than the general population to suffer from a number of different health and learning problems. Health problems linked to exposure to high levels of toxic wastes and other forms of environmental degradation include a higher incidence of infant mortality, miscarriages, deformed fetuses, cancer, respiratory illnesses, childhood leukemia, and immune deficiency (Adeola, 1994). Children exposed to environmental hazards are also at greater risk of mental disorders, mental retardation, and other forms of learning disabilities.

While environmental hazards affect people of all ages, young children are at greater risk from environmental contaminants than adults (Kane, 1985). The reason is that children breathe more rapidly than adults, their skin is more permeable, they engage in more hand-to-mouth activities, their immune systems are less developed, and they absorb a greater proportion of many substances from their intestinal tract and lungs. Additionally, their bodies are in the process of rapid growth and development and, thus, are more vulnerable to disruptions of the process with potentially serious long-term effects. In addition to the increased exposure to environmental toxins, many families living in low-income communities also have inadequate medical care and lack proper access to information regarding the potential health consequences of environmental contaminants.

One of the major environmental health issues affecting young children is exposure to lead poisoning. While the toxicity of lead has been known for hundreds of years, the use of lead in the United States increased significantly up through the late 1970s (Gottlieb, 1993). Lead-based paints on walls, furniture, and even baby cribs were putting many young children at great risk of lead poisoning. Even though by 1940 the paint industry had begun replacing lead with other pigments, many children living in low-income communities are still being exposed to dangerous levels of lead.

When too much lead builds up in the body, a condition called *lead poisoning* results. Lead poisoning often leads to brain damage and mental retardation. The primary way children become lead-poisoned is by eating dust, oil, or paint chips containing lead. Lead-based paint chips taste slightly sweet and are thus appealing to many children. The children most at risk of lead poisoning are those living in low-income urban areas. Many homes or apartments in such areas still have lead-based paint on indoor and outdoor surfaces, and these surfaces are often in a deteriorating condition, in which the paint chips or peels away. In some inner-city communities, one out of two children risks permanent mental impairment due to excessive lead exposure (Ember, 1992).

Exposure to smog and other types of air pollution is another health hazard often affecting children living in poor urban areas. Such exposure puts children at greater risk of asthma and other respiratory illnesses. Children with such illnesses experience not only the distress of their condition but often curtailed physical activity and missed days of school as well.

Another dangerous compound that has drawn much attention in recent years is dioxin, a by-product of incinerators and paper manufacturing. While it's believed that dioxin is now carried by almost everyone on earth, the amount varies greatly from individual to individual. Children living close to incinerators and paper-manufacturing facilities are the most affected.

Other children often affected by environmental toxins are children of migrant farm workers. According to statistics supplied by the Campaign on Human Rights Violations, 300,000 Hispanic farm laborers suffer each year from illnesses related to pesticides.

Because exposure to environmental health hazards does not usually present an immediate health crisis, it is sometimes overlooked as a threat to young children. Such thinking, however, is dangerous. The long-term effects on human health and development can be devastating. Environmentalists, educators, social-policy makers, and the general public need to recognize that "the protection of human and natural communities cannot be viewed as being mutually exclusive" (Chavis, 1992, p. 38) and need to direct their efforts accordingly.

Educational Implications and Suggestions

Many educators and other professionals working with young children are not aware of the issues related to environmental equity. While they may have heard of NIMBY ("not-in-my-back-yard") politics regarding toxic-waste disposal, they may not be aware of the extent of the damage done to children living in disenfranchised communities. Yet a first step toward solving the problem involves awareness and concern. It also involves an understanding of and a commitment to the concept of *collective responsibility* (i.e., we all have a responsibility to eliminate, reduce, or control pollution and to care for the health and welfare of people in all communities).

The concept of collective responsibility also suggests that people of all classes and colors must come together to fight pollution and ensure safe environments for young children. The "not-in-my-back-yard" attitude does not make the problem go away—someone still suffers. The struggle for the environment and social justice requires a collaborative approach and one that is based on caring. "Environmental problem solving must become a collaborative effort, not only by scientists and engineers, but also by public health specialists, social scientists, politicians, and community members" (Harding & Holdren, 1993, p. 1991). We need to come together as a society of caring people "in which all members respect, identify with, and appreciate each other" (Bartoli, 1995, p. 192).

Early childhood educators, too, should be aware of the issues related to environmental degradation and should become advocates for the children most at risk. At the least, early childhood educators should be aware of the possible sources of developmental and learning problems exhibited by many children exposed to environmental contamination and should seek to provide special monitoring and intervention services for them. They should also provide appropriate information to parents regarding potential health and safety concerns in their homes and neighborhood communities.

It is also incumbent on educators and other members of the community to ensure that the school environment itself will be free of environmental contaminants. Environmental assessments of the school and the surrounding area should be made annually and should include attention to health, safety, and comfort factors affecting children, visitors to the school, teachers, and other school personnel.

The safety of how children get to and from school should also be considered. The social-environmental conditions of some neighborhoods make it unsafe for children to walk to school. Children living in neighborhoods where drug trafficking and other forms of crime present real dangers should be bused to school, even if the distance from home to school is no more than a few blocks.

One suggestion for increasing community awareness of environmental quality issues and engaging support for appropriate interventions is to work with the early-intervention local collaborative group (LCG) or local interagency coordinating council (ICC). The passage of Public Law 99-457 (Education for All Handicapped Children Act Amendments of 1986) called for the establishment of interagency councils at the federal, state, and local levels to facilitate ongoing coordination of the community agency services providing educational, therapeutic, medical, and social services to young children with disabilities and those at risk of developmental delays. These interagency councils are designed to provide a forum for the discussion of issues related to the needs and problems of young children with special needs or at risk of developmental delays. Most communities throughout the United States now have some form of an early-intervention local collaborative group. Identifying and combating environmental assaults on young children should be an important part of the agenda of such groups.

Another suggestion is that communities establish and maintain information systems that identify and track children exposed to environmental pollutants. This initiative could be linked with other information systems already in place, which typically focus on such risk factors as prematurity, teen pregnancies, and a family history of health-related conditions. Such a tracking system could lead to the early identification of and intervention for the special health and/or educational needs of young children exposed to various types of environmental hazards.

Conclusion

It's no longer a secret that industrial America has been dumping its waste and hazardous facilities in low-income and minority communities. The people in such communities are often too poor and powerless to stop it. The effect of this dumping is the creation of life-threatening situations for many young children, who are the true victims of environmental carelessness.

While teachers acting alone may not be able to prevent young children's exposure to many environmental hazards, they can, through community networking, raise the level of awareness and concern and can foster an attitude of collective responsibility regarding the quality of the physical environments in which young children live. Individual and community efforts to care for and/or save the environment should focus, not only on the natural environment, but on human-social environments as well. There is no doubt that reforms in how we relate to the environment are urgently needed. Such reforms, however, should be designed to help meet social as well as environmental goals (Blahna & Toch, 1993). As outlined in the "Principles of Environmental Justice" (1991), the education of present and future generations should emphasize both social and environmental issues. Such education should be based on the understanding that every living thing, especially our young children is entitled to a healthy habitat.

Young children are politically without a voice. Their stories and their needs can be heard only if caring adults take the initiative to work on their behalf. A poster carried by one of the delegates to the UN Fourth World Conference on Women provides a good example of the kind of message that the public needs to hear. A child's smiling face looks out from the poster. A question above the picture reads, "What would you like to be when you grow up?" The one-word answer, "Alive," calls for a careful scrutiny of our political and social priorities.

Resources

For more information about environmental justice issues and environmental hazards to young children, the following resources are suggested. Additional resources can also be found in the reference list.

Child Neglect in Rich Nations
S. A. Hewlett
New York: United Nations Children's Fund, 1993

Children's Environmental Health Network
5900 Hollis Street, Suite E
Emeryville, CA 94608
(510) 540-3657

Environmental Hazards to Young Children
Dorothy Noyes Kane
Phoenix: Oryx Press, 1985

"Lead Poisoning and Your Children"
EPA Pamphlet No. 800-B-92-0002, 1992

Office of Environmental Justice
U.S. Environmental Protection Agency
401 M Street, SW
Washington, DC 20460

Race, Poverty, and the Environment
A newsletter of the Urban Habitat Program
Earth Island Institute
300 Broadway, Suite 28
San Francisco, CA 94133

Raising Children Toxic Free
H. L. Needleman and P. J. Landrigan
New York: Farrar, Strauss & Giroux, 1994

Safe Schools
Environmental and Occupational Health Sciences
    Institute
681 Frelinghuysen Road

P.O. Box 1179
Piscataway, NJ 08855-1179
(908) 932-0110

Toxic Struggles
R. Hofrichter (Ed.)
Philadelphia, PA: Temple University Press, 1993

Toxic Waste and Race in the U.S.
United Church of Christ Commission for Racial
    Justice
700 Prospect
Cleveland, OH 44115

REFERENCES

Adeola, F. O. (1994). Environmental hazards, health, and racial inequity in hazardous waste distribution. *Environment and Behavior, 26*(1), 99–126.

Bartoli, J. S. (1995). *Unequal opportunity.* New York: Teachers College Press.

Blahna, D. J., & Toch, M. F. (1993). Environmental reporting in ethnic magazines: Implications for incorporating minority concerns. *Journal of Environmental Education, 24*(2), 22–29.

Browner, C. M. (1995). Why environmental education? *EPA Journal, 21*(2), 6–8.

Bullard, R. D. (1994, Spring). Grassroots flowering. *The Amicus Journal,* pp. 32–37.

Chavis, B. F. (1992, September–October). Race, justice and the environment. *Nature Conservancy,* p. 38.

Collin, R. W. (1993). Environmental equity and the need for government intervention: Two proposals. *Environment, 35*(9), 41–43.

Ember, L. R. (1992, March 30). House subcommittee blasts EPA's Environmental Equity Report. *E & EN,* pp. 13–15.

Environmental Protection Agency. (1992). *Environmental equity: Reducing risk for all communities.* Washington, DC: Author.

Gottlieb, R. (1993). *Forcing the spring.* Washington, DC: Island Press.

Harding, A. K., & Holdren, G. R. (1993). Environmental equity and the environmental professional. *Environment, Science, Technology, 27*(10), 1990–1993.

Johnson, G. (1995, April 16). "Environmental racism" draws lawyers to city neighborhoods. *The Blade,* Toledo, OH, pp. 1–2 (Section B).

Kane, D. N. (1985). *Environmental hazards to young children.* Phoenix: Oryx Press.

Principles of Environmental Justice. (1991). Washington, DC: First National People of Color Environmental Leadership Summit.

Rogue, J. A. (1993). Environmental equity: Reducing risk for all communities. *Environment, 35*(5), 25–28.

■ *Ruth A. Wilson is an associate professor in Early Childhood Special Education and Environmental Education at Bowling Green State University in Ohio. Dr. Wilson's research focuses primarily on young children and their relationship with the natural environment.*

Healthy Child Care America

A Blueprint for Action

U.S. Department of Health and Human Services

■ ■ ■

In communities across the nation, innovative projects are forging new ground to ensure that the millions of children attending child care are in healthy, safe environments. Their efforts are part of the *Healthy Child Care America Campaign,* launched by the U.S. Department of Health and Human Services' Child Care Bureau and Maternal and Child Health Bureau to bridge the public health and early childhood communities. Linking health care providers, child care providers, and families makes good sense—for maximizing resources, for developing comprehensive and coordinated services, and most important, for nurturing children.

The campaign revolves around the Blueprint for Action—10 steps that communities can take to either expand existing private and public services and resources or to create new services and resources that link families, health care, and child care. Communities are encouraged to launch their own Healthy Child Care campaigns, building on the blueprint yet focusing on locally determined priorities and goals. Begin by assessing existing child care and health care services, needs, and resources. Then choose to take action in all 10 areas, or focus your efforts on areas of particular interest.

1. Promote safe, healthy, and developmentally appropriate child care environments for all families.

Responsive caregiving must take place within a setting that is consistently safe and supportive. In a safe, nurturing, highly interactive setting—whether this is a family home or a center—children feel confident to fully explore and experience their environ-

ment, free from injury or harm. Safe, secure transportation of children to and from the setting also should be ensured. Families should receive information about quality so they can make informed child care choices.

2. Increase immunization rates and preventive services for children in child care settings.

Although immunizations have dramatically reduced the incidence of many infectious diseases, we have recently witnessed outbreaks of serious infection because too many of our young children have not been fully immunized. Only 53% of all two-year-old children nationally have been immunized; in licensed child care facilities, however, 94% of the children have been immunized—demonstrating the critical contribution of child care settings as an access point for children's health services. To increase immunization rates, both families and providers should receive information on resources.

3. Assist families in accessing key public and private health and social service programs.

Millions of young children from low-income working families lack health insurance and could benefit from assistance programs such as Medicaid and the Special Supplemental Nutrition Program for Women, Infants, and Children (WIC). Since children of working parents are likely to be cared for in some type of early childhood setting, child care providers can help families learn about Medicaid and WIC

Adapted from U.S. Department of Health and Human Services. (1996). *Healthy Child Care America: A blueprint for action.* Washington, DC: U.S. Government Printing Office. In *Young Children, 51* (5), 57–58.

benefits, as well as other federal and state assistance programs.

4. Promote and increase comprehensive access to health screenings.

Many young children have undetected health conditions that, if untreated, could result in serious injury or illness. Child care programs can provide a key access point for conducting health and dental screening, including evaluation and referrals for con-

ditions such as lead poisoning, impaired vision or hearing, and baby bottle tooth decay. Developmental screenings also are important components of comprehensive services. Recognizing and treating potentially harmful conditions earlier rather than later is not only more effective and less costly but can prevent future problems.

5. Conduct health and safety education and promotion programs for children, families, and child care providers.

Promoting the safety and the healthy growth and development of our children is a responsibility shared by all. Health care and child care providers working closely together can share information and training with staff and parents on issues such as immunization, injury prevention, physical fitness, and recognition of illnesses and developmental difficulties. Child care providers, in partnership with others, also can provide information on preventing deaths and injuries caused by car crashes, drownings, fires, suffocation, poisoning, and falls. When children learn early the importance of personal hygiene practices such as brushing their teeth or washing their hands properly, and safety practices such as what to do in case of a fire, these lessons can lead to good health and safety habits that last a lifetime.

While participating in a school breakfast program, a young boy examines a cereal box.

6. **Strengthen and improve nutrition services in child care.**

Nutrition education and health promotion programs help to inform families and providers of the nutritional needs of all young children. When young children share nourishing meals and snacks together, they grow healthier, think more clearly, explore their world eagerly, develop language and social skills, and feel comforted and cared for. The developmental, cultural, and emotional needs of children should be considered in menu planning.

7. **Provide training for and ongoing consultation with child care providers and families in the areas of social and emotional health.**

Child care programs can promote healthy social and emotional development by informing and guiding child care providers and families in ways that encourage sensitive and age-appropriate care. They also can contribute to early identification of children and intervention with children who reflect the ill effects of exposure to violence, substance abuse, child abuse and neglect, or other emotional and behavioral problems. It is important to make more mental health services available to child care communities so that families and child care providers can take advantage of opportunities to enhance the social and emotional health of children.

8. **Expand and provide ongoing support to child care providers and families caring for children with special health needs.**

Passage of the Americans with Disabilities Act in 1992 has significantly strengthened access to child care for children with special health needs for developmental disabilities. Child care providers and families need ongoing training, technical assistance, mentoring, and consultation to care for children with special needs, ranging from helping children with asthma or diabetes to assisting children in wheelchairs or those with developmental delays or disabilities. Providers and families also need information and resources concerning how the Americans with Dis-

abilities Act will impact child care programs in such areas as inclusion of children with special needs in programs, eligibility for services, and removal of barriers in facilities.

9. **Use child care health consultants to help develop and maintain healthy child care.**

Health care providers can play a vital role in the training of child care staff, as well as in the licensing, monitoring, and evaluation of child care facilities. Child care health consultants can provide guidance and assistance on a range of issues affecting the health and safety of children. These can be as fundamental as helping staff determine ideal placement for eating areas and diaper-changing tables in facilities, or as technical as performing on-site assessments of hygiene and safety practices and assisting in developing licensing standards. Trained child care providers who are informed about preventive health care and safety practices and resources can promote the healthy development of children and reduce illness and injury in child care settings.

10. **Assess and promote the health, training, and work environment of child care providers.**

A healthy child care setting and continuing education in the health and safety of children and staff can help providers in meeting day-to-day challenges. Avoiding back injuries, reducing risk of infectious disease, and scheduling adequate rest breaks can enhance job satisfaction and the overall well-being of child care providers. Healthy staff provide the best care for children.

FOR FURTHER INFORMATION

The Child Care Bureau, Administration on Children, Youth and Family, will provide information, coordination, and technical assistance for the Healthy Child Care America Campaign. For additional information, please contact the Child Care Bureau, 200 Independence Avenue, Room 320-F, Washington, DC 20201. Phone: (202) 690-5641. Fax: (202) 690-5600.

Multiple Voices for Advocacy

The Story of WIC
(Special Supplemental Nutrition Program
for Women, Infants, and Children)

Mary A. Jensen

■ ■ ■

Views differ on the extent to which governmental agencies should provide nutritional assistance to people in the United States. In a land of plenty, competitive food prices, and numerous charitable groups, some people contend that adequate nutrition is readily available to all. Others point to the large number of children living in poverty in our country and the nutritional risks associated with poverty.

A key governmental response to concern about adequate child nutrition has been the WIC (Special Supplemental Nutrition Program for Women, Infants and Children) Program. WIC is a federally funded program that provides nutritional foods and nutrition education to women who are pregnant or breastfeeding or who have recently delivered a baby, and to infants and children up to the age of 5. To be eligible, participants must establish nutritional need through a medical exam and must meet income guidelines.

The WIC program is a classic example of how advocacy can dramatically affect policy decisions and program expansion, even in times of fiscal restraint. WIC began in 1972 as a $20 million pilot program aimed at a few thousand participants. Twenty-five years later, it was serving approximately 7.4 million participants and had a budget of more than $3.7 billion (Food and Nutrition Service, 1998b). This dramatic expansion cannot be attributed to any single cause or to the isolated efforts of a few. Many forces coalesced and contributed to the establishment and growth of WIC: prevalent social values and beliefs, political climate, economic conditions, media attention, constituency letter writing, opportune research findings, court decisions, and "umbrella" legislative packages. Also, diverse voices at many levels shaped the present WIC program: farm interests, antipoverty groups, antihunger groups, social service pro-

viders, lawmakers, judges, administrators in the Department of Agriculture, evaluators, health clinics, child advocacy groups, public interest law firms, and so on. The interactive dynamics of this process involved numerous decisions by a broad array of people who had various agendas and value systems. To understand the establishment and expansion of WIC, we must consider the political, social, and economic contexts of decision making and the complex interactions among and shifting influences of various forces and alliances (Hayes, 1982). This article traces and examines the changing issues and various forms of advocacy in the history of the WIC program.

Setting the Stage for the WIC Program

Several federal initiatives, begun in the mid-1930s, set precedents for today's child nutrition programs. During the Roosevelt administration, the U.S. Department of Agriculture (USDA) offered grants for a number of school lunch programs, reaching up to 400,000 children by 1941. The USDA also piloted a Food Stamp program in Rochester, New York, that eventually spread to other parts of the country, reaching about 4 million people (Nelson, 1982). During the 1940s, Congress did not continue support for the Food Stamp program, but did pass the National School Lunch Act (P.L. 79-396) in 1946, making the program a permanent piece of legislation. To receive monies and commodities under this act, the lunch programs were required to (1) meet USDA nutritional standards; (2) be nonprofit; (3) be available to all children, offering free or reduced rate lunches to the needy; and (4) provide some matching funds (Committee on Education and Labor, 1987).

Another nutritional assistance program that affects today's children is the Food Stamp Program.

Roughly half of the program's participants are children (Oliveira, 1998b). The Kennedy administration revived the program as a series of pilot projects in 1961. In 1964, Congress passed the Food Stamp Act (amended in 1977, P.L. 95-113), giving legitimacy to guidelines established by the Kennedy administration for the pilot programs. During the late 1960s, concerns grew about the lack of participation among the poorest of the poor. After some eligibility reforms and a downward swing in the economy, participation rates leaped upward. (The number of participants was 2.9 million in 1969 and 18.9 million in 1975.) But by the mid-1970s, the public began to voice the opinion that Food Stamps were too easy to obtain and that lax eligibility review led to cheating and fraud. Although Food Stamps can be used to purchase almost any food item, some thought that participants should not be using tax dollars to buy steaks. These voices began to dominate in the 1980s, leading to a series of changes in eligibility and benefit regulations as well as to spending cuts in fiscal year 1982 (Berry, 1984).

A third federal nutrition program that has set precedents for WIC and that reaches many young children is the Child Care Food Program (CCFP), now the Child and Adult Care Food Program (CACFP). This program began in 1968 as a pilot program under the National School Lunch Act. It expanded and in 1978 became a permanent piece of legislation (P.L. 95-627). CACFP provides federal reimbursement for meals and snacks to nonprofit child-care centers (or to child-care centers where at least 25 percent of the child care is subsidized by Title XX Social Services monies) and to child-care homes. To be eligible, centers or homes must be licensed or approved by federal, state, or local standards. Reimbursement rates are based on individual family income and are similar to those for school lunches and breakfasts (Oliveira, 1998b). Also like the school lunch program, food served in child-care centers or homes has to meet USDA nutritional requirements (Committee on Agriculture, Nutrition, and Forestry, 1983). Like WIC, this program has grown dramatically, perhaps as a result of the growing numbers of mothers in the work force and the growing need for child care. In 1997, 98 percent of the participants were children (Oliveira, 1998a). (For a comparison of funding and participation levels in these four major child nutrition programs, see the table below.)

The Supplemental Food Program: A Precursor of WIC

Reminiscent of values espoused during the Roosevelt administration, the Johnson administration promised to build a Great Society through domestic legislation. Spending for the Vietnam War, however, curtailed Lyndon Johnson's plans. By the mid-1960s, nutritional aid to poor families was being provided by the revival of the Food Stamp Program. Also, the comprehensive Child Nutrition Act of 1966 provided food for children in school or institutional settings. Neither of these efforts proved to be sufficient, however. In 1967 and 1968, the astonishing extent of hunger in the United States was discovered by the media, researchers, government officials, and the public. CBS televised its much acclaimed documentary, "Hunger in America." Researchers published

Federal Appropriations and Selected Participation Figures (in Millions) in Four Major Nutrition Programs Serving Children, Fiscal Years 1983–1995

Program	$ in FY 1983 (participation)	$ in FY 1986 (participation)	$ in FY 1989 (participation)	$ in FY 1992 (participation)	$ in FY 1995 (participation)
WIC	1,123.1 (2.3)	1,580.5 (3.3)	1,910.9 (4.1)	2,596.7 (5.4)	3,430.6 (6.9)
Child and Adult Care Food Program[*]	329.6 (.92)	465.7 (1.10)	670.3 (1.37)	1,065.1 (1.87)	1,411.2 (2.36)
National School Lunch Program	2,401.7 (23.4)	2,714.3 (24.3)	3,005.6 (24.8)	3,586.5 (25.1)	4,466.8 (25.7)
Food Stamp Program	11,862.5 (21.6)	11,693.7 (19.4)	12,932.3 (18.8)	22,462.4 (25.4)	24,621.0 (26.6)

Sources: Committee on Education and Labor, 1987; Food and Nutrition Service, 1998a; National Agricultural Statistics Service, 1993, 1996, 1998.
[*]In 1988, eligible adults were included in the program.

Hunger, U.S.A. and *Your Daily Bread.* Both charged the government with ineptitude in meeting the needs of the poor. Senate hearings were held on malnutrition in Mississippi. Among those who testified was Robert Coles of Harvard University, well known for his work in Mississippi with poor children. At the hearings, he raised the question of possible permanent physical damage in infants and young children caused by malnutrition. The public also generated political pressure through the 1968 Poor People's Campaign and their march on Washington (Nelson, 1982).

In response, the Johnson administration initiated regulations for a $15 million Supplemental Food Program (SFP) that supplied commodity food packages to pregnant and postpartum women, infants, and young children. The legal authority for creation of this program came from an act in 1935 for commodity distribution to low-income groups. Now known as the Commodity Supplemental Food Program, this program continues to operate under the Food and Nutrition Service, but participation has dropped since the start of the WIC program (Committee on Agriculture, Nutrition, and Forestry, 1983).

At the beginning of his administration in 1969, Richard Nixon showed interest in the congressional hearings on hunger, particularly testimony regarding relationships between malnutrition and prenatal brain damage or infant retardation. Plans were made to expand the Supplemental Food Program (SFP), but SFP suffered two major setbacks. First a study of the local program in Washington, DC, indicated that distribution of commodity parcels accounted for 35 percent of program costs, transportation problems of participants reduced parcel pickup to 60 percent, and all family members ate the foods. These findings led to a decision by the Food and Nutrition Service to either consolidate the Supplemental Food Program with the Food Stamp Program or to transform SFP into a voucher program. In 1970, the Food and Nutrition Service started a pilot voucher program for low-income, pregnant women and infants in five areas of the country. The women received booklets of $.25 coupons for milk, infant formula, and baby cereal. While pregnant, women received $5 coupon booklets each month. After giving birth, they received $10 coupon booklets each month for one year. Those referred by local health clinics as well as welfare recipients were eligible for the program.

A second major setback for SFP came when evaluator David Call found that the pilot voucher program failed to significantly increase the quantity of formula or milk intakes or the nutrient intakes in infants and that it did not increase the milk intakes

of women. With the results of this second study in hand, the Food and Nutrition Service, persuaded that the Supplemental Food Program was ineffective, was prepared to abandon the program. Politics, however, slowed the process down. Constituents and congressional representatives still were expressing concerns about hunger among pregnant women and infants. Moreover, research was accumulating that confirmed a relationship between nutrition and mental development. It was this growing body of research as well as the political climate that spawned the WIC Program (Nelson, 1982). (See the table on the next page for an overview of key events and advocacy strategies in the initiation of WIC.)

Establishment and Early Expansion of the WIC Program

In 1972, during Senate hearings on the child nutrition bill, Hubert Humphrey introduced an amended bill with a $20 million annual provision for a Special Supplemental Food Program for Women, Infants, and Children (WIC). This proposal was distinct in that it more closely linked food assistance with health care. Unlike previous programs, WIC included: (1) a medical examination and referral rather than income as the chief criterion for eligibility, (2) children up to the age of 4, and (3) vouchers for specific foods medically known to be essential for proper nutrition (i.e., protein and vitamins in iron-fortified formula or cereal, fruit juice, milk, cheese, eggs, or vegetable juices). In hearings and a subsequent Senate floor fight, Humphrey dramatized his case with photographs and x-rays of malnourished infants and their underdeveloped brains and with research testimony on the effects of infant malnutrition. When challenged by the conclusions of the Call evaluation, he refuted the methodology of Call's study and pointed out that Call's study did not include medical data. In the end, the child nutrition bill was amended to include a two-year experimental program subject to a medical evaluation prior to reconsideration of any extension. The bill passed both houses of Congress with a veto-proof majority (Nelson, 1982).

In 1973, several advocacy efforts focused attention on the new WIC program. Having been persuaded that the Supplemental Food Program was ineffective, the USDA and the Food and Nutrition Service reluctantly began to execute the WIC program (Nelson, 1982). By March, efforts to design the program were under way (Committee on Agriculture, Nutrition, and Forestry, 1983). But during the spring, *Redbook* magazine published a provocative article by Virginia Hardman called "How to Save Babies for Two Dimes a Day." Her article chronicled

Time Line of Key Events and Advocacy Strategies in the Creation and Expansion of WIC

1966	1967	1968	1970	1971	1972
Child Nutrition Act passed	Senate expert testimony on malnutrition and physical development; TV documentary: "Hunger in America"; research reports on U.S. hunger	Poor People's Campaign and March; Supplemental Food Program (SFP) created	1st negative evaluation: distribution system; pilot voucher program for SFP created	2nd negative evaluation: pilot voucher program; public outcry about hunger persists; research on malnutrition and mental development accumulates	Photos, x-rays, and research testimony on mental development support creation of $20 million WIC program with provision for medical evaluation in Child Nutrition Act

1973	1976	1977	1978	1979
Article in *Redbook* and letter writing; class action suit against USDA for spending slowdown	Class action suit against USDA for spending slowdown (1974–1975); lobbying coalitions formed; 1st medical evaluation = positive	2nd medical evaluation = positive, but calls for more stress on nutrition education	P.L. 95-627 requires states to spend $ on nutrition education	Funding reaches $712.3 million

personal observations of and conversations about efforts at St. Judes Hospital in Memphis to help large numbers of malnourished children. Descriptive accounts supported by photographs of children over time, statistics, medical testimony, and a personal appeal from actor Danny Thomas created a powerful message. The author urged readers to write to Earl Butz, Secretary of Agriculture, to persuade him to end delays in feeding hungry children and to write to their congressional representatives for a copy of the bill containing provisions for WIC. The public responded. About the same time, the Food Research and Action Center, a public interest law firm, learned that the USDA planned to implement WIC in 1973 with only a limited amount of the $40 million allocated for 1973–74 (i.e., $5–6 million). Seeing the potential of WIC as a major feeding program, the firm filed a class action suit on behalf of the beneficiaries to speed up implementation of WIC, charging that funds had been unused or misspent in terms of congressional intent. The suit called for all authorized funds ($40 million) to be spent by the end of June 1974. The effect of this strategy was to double the program's size. In June, the court ordered USDA to publish regulations by July 1973, and in August, ordered USDA to spend all allocated funds by July 1974 (Nelson, 1982).

By the end of 1974, WIC was operating at around $100 million. And in 1975, carryover from 1974 was added to the $100 million allocated. Despite a veto by President Ford, Congress then allocated $250 million annually for WIC over the three-year period of 1976–79 and extended eligibility to include children up to age five. But another USDA slowdown in spending during 1974–75 and USDA's attempt to spread annual spending for 1976 over five quarters rather than four—after changes in federal fiscal year dates—led to another class action being filed. In June 1976, the judge ordered the USDA to spend $687.5 million on the WIC program by September 1978 and to submit quarterly reports on WIC spending and development (Committee on Agriculture, Nutrition, and Forestry, 1983; Nelson, 1982).

Delayed for over a year, the first medical evaluation of WIC (Endozien, Switzer, & Bryan, 1976) was completed and released by the USDA in July 1976. Although the U.S. General Accounting Office had raised questions about the value of results from human nutrition evaluations, these long awaited results were critical for WIC funding deliberations. And unexpectedly, the results of the Endozien study indicated that except for eggs, food intake of all participants increased, and for infants, physical growth and hemoglobin levels increased while anemia decreased. The researchers concluded that the WIC program was a clear-cut success. The methodology and conclusions of the study, however, received much criticism. About the same time, the USDA released another WIC study that noted an increase in health clinic visits for WIC participants, but questioned the value of the nutritional counseling component (Nelson, 1982).

In 1977, the Centers for Disease Control (CDC) in Atlanta completed a third evaluation of WIC for USDA's Food and Nutrition Service. Sensitive to criticism of the Endozien study, CDC carefully noted the delimitations of their study and findings. Children who entered the program were found to have a high prevalence of anemia, delay in linear growth, or excessive weight gain. After a year in the WIC program, these children evidenced improved hematocrit/hemoglobin levels (anemia), gains in weight-to-length ratios and linear growth, and decreases in overweight. Also, the proportion of infants entering the program with low birth weight decreased. Other findings led CDC to recommend that more stress be placed on nutrition education as an adjunct to food assistance (Nelson, 1982). A governmental response to this suggestion came in November 1978 with the passage of P.L. 95-627, which requires states to spend at least one-sixth of their administrative funds on nutrition education activities (Stansfield, 1984).

Although originally proposed as a way to prevent expansion of WIC, the USDA evaluations basically confirmed the convictions of WIC supporters. By 1978 and 1979, funding for the WIC program had become a mother-and-apple-pie issue. Congressional representatives were reluctant to vote against additional funding for an apparently effective program aimed at feeding low-income, pregnant women and babies (Nelson, 1982). In 1978, WIC funding reached $527.3 million, and for 1979, funding rose to $712.3 million (Committee on Agriculture, Nutrition, and Forestry, 1983).

The successes and cost benefits of WIC have been documented many times. For example, a 1979 study by the Harvard School of Public Health concluded that as much as $3 was saved on neonatal/infant medical care for every $1 spent on prenatal care in the WIC program. Nevertheless, WIC evaluation studies continue to encounter skepticism and resistance from some policy makers. For example, a five-year, $5 million study by David Rush found numerous positive outcomes for WIC, but disputes arose when USDA delayed its release, omitted Rush's favorable summaries, and substituted their own compendium of results ("U.S. Accused of Altering Study," 1986). In his study of WIC, Rush found improve-

ments in length of gestation, iron intake for infants, and women's use of prenatal care and their weight gain during pregnancy. He also found that WIC participants spent less on foods away from home and more on WIC-type foods than did the control group. However, WIC participation had no effect on the mother's intent to breast-feed, rate of breastfeeding, or use of tobacco or alcohol. He recommended improvements be made in the health education component of WIC (Committee on Agriculture, Nutrition, and Forestry, 1985).

Perhaps in response, the U.S. Department of Agriculture along with the U.S. Department of Health and Human Services formed, in 1990, a consortium of health-related organizations and agencies, including WIC, to raise awareness of and support for breastfeeding. A year later, the Institute of Medicine published its landmark review of research on breastfeeding, which underscored the importance of the consortium's efforts. One result for WIC has been that in six years, the percentage of WIC mothers breastfeeding at birth has grown from 34 percent to 47 percent. Building on this success, WIC launched the National Breastfeeding Promotion Project in 1997. Using social marketing research strategies, a social marketing firm helped to develop pamphlets, posters, public service announcements, provider kits, and training materials based on WIC recipients' concerns about breastfeeding. Promotional materials also emphasized the importance of community support for breastfeeding (Watkins, 1997). What has been the most effective strategy in this project, however, has been peer counseling (English, 1998). Another health education strategy for WIC has been an effort to expand recipients' awareness and use of nutritious foods though the WIC Farmers' Market Program. This program, established in 1992, provides WIC participants with additional coupons that can be used to purchase fresh produce at local farmers' markets.

A number of studies have focused on the effects of WIC on anemic children. Perhaps the most comprehensive was one reported in the *Journal of the American Medical Association* (Centers for Disease Control, 1986). In 1974, CDC established the Pediatric Nutrition Surveillance System to monitor growth and anemia prevalence in low-income children enrolled in programs such as WIC in six selected states. Between 1975 and 1985, CDC found a 60 percent decline in prevalence of anemia which, given the magnitude and consistency of the difference, they primarily attributed to WIC. This conclusion is impressive because anemia can adversely affect intellectual development. The major factors contributing

WIC preschoolers improve their intake of 10 of 15 basic nutrients.

to this decline in anemia among WIC children appear to be breastfeeding during early infancy and using iron-fortified formula (Owen & Owen, 1997).

Other studies have found that prenatal participation in WIC is associated with substantial savings in medical care costs for women and their babies (Buescher, Larson, Nelson, & Lenihan, 1993; Devaney, Bilheimer, & Schore, 1992). In addition, researchers (Rose, Habicht, & Devaney, 1998) have documented that WIC preschoolers improve their intake of 10 of 15 basic nutrients.

Adequacy of Regulations and Effectiveness of State and Local Management

Current discussions of the merits of WIC tend to focus more on regulatory or management needs than on funding needs. Concerns have been raised about the adequacy of local systems for determining eligibility, targeting benefits to the most needy, monitoring vendors, and the participation of ineligible individuals (Committee on Agriculture, Nutrition, and Forestry, 1985; Greenstein, 1998). According to an investigation of the WIC operations in five states by the General Accounting Office (1985), income documentation is nonexistent in many local files and procedures for verifying income documentation are not always adequate. Problems, however, can arise with income determination. For example, when a teenage parent lives with her parents because she

can't afford or can't manage to live alone, should her parents' income be used in determining eligibility (English, 1987)?

Another concern in determining eligibility has been the lack of uniformity and imprecise application of nutritional risk criteria in various states. Variations have occurred in the diseases and conditions included on state referral forms. In response to this concern, the National Association of WIC Directors (NAWD) and the Food and Nutrition Service (FNS) have developed a new national policy on nutrition risk criteria. This policy was based on an independent review of nutrition risk criteria conducted by the Institute of Medicine of the National Academy of Sciences (Vogel, 1998). It also establishes a representative collaborative that will facilitate the ongoing development and review of appropriate nutrition risk criteria and will promote their consistent application. Another question has been the more frequent use of inadequate dietary pattern than of medical factors as a nutritional risk criterion. Some contend that many Americans have poor diets and that assessments of dietary patterns using 24-hour recall interviews are unreliable. Others point out that inadequate diet is authorized in WIC legislation as a risk criterion. This dispute, in part, reflects different views of the purposes of WIC. Although WIC was established as a preventive program, much emphasis has been placed on cases of children whose health has improved as a result of WIC participation rather than on helping at-risk children before health deteriorates. The USDA, however, is making efforts to improve methods of assessing inadequate dietary patterns (General Accounting Office, 1985).

A third concern has been lack of local targeting given the limited WIC funds available. By 1985, seven service priority categories had been established in WIC regulations. Participants classified as high-risk included pregnant and breast-feeding women, and infants referred for medical conditions rather than for inadequate dietary patterns. WIC legislation, however, does not mandate targeting. And program policies have not encouraged targeting benefits to those at highest risk except at year's end when the maximum caseload has been reached and additional funding has become uncertain (Committee on Agriculture, Nutrition and Forestry, 1984, 1985; General Accounting Office, 1985). To monitor state and local targeting performance more carefully, recent USDA regulatory changes require WIC programs to report semiannually caseloads and numbers of participants served in each of the seven priority categories (General Accounting Office, 1985). This information may allow USDA in the future to reward states that do a better job of targeting and to allocate to them the unspent funds of less productive states. Some states are presently rewarding local programs for targeting. For example, New York offers local programs a "bounty" for cases in the top-risk category (English, 1987).

A fourth management issue has been adequacy of vendor monitoring and vendor regulation and the related issue of cost containment. A number of states have adopted strategies to assure proper use of WIC vouchers. California has instituted a training program for vendors or grocers to improve understanding of which foods can be purchased with WIC checks (Serrano, 1986). Other states such as Texas and Illinois maintain aggressive monitoring schemes to assure that vendors do not overcharge WIC customers, exchange WIC vouchers for unauthorized foods, or trade vouchers for cash. Surprise visits are made to stores to check on prices, stock, and receipts, and sometimes investigators will pose as WIC recipients and attempt to make illegal purchases. If violations are found, vendors will be dropped from both WIC and Food Stamp Programs (English, 1987; Greenstein, 1998; Rhodes, 1983). Computerized vouchers or Electronic Benefit Transfer (EBT) also are being used in some states to monitor vendors and WIC purchases (Stansfield, 1984). Expansion of EBT to all states and elimination of paper WIC checks could substantially reduce overcharging and other vendor abuses. To accelerate this effort, reauthorization legislation could contain incentives for state agencies to allocate more administrative monies to the development and use of management information systems, including EBT (Greenstein, 1998). Savings from curbing vendor fraud and barring higher-priced stores from entry into WIC could be used to provide these incentives.

In the early 1990s, however, the Food and Nutrition Service did propose regulations to curb vendor fraud and restrict higher-priced stores from participation in WIC. But the retail food industry mounted intense opposition, and the proposal was withdrawn before Congress even considered it. Retailers were strongly opposed to regulations restricting their participation in WIC based on the prices they charged. Nevertheless, strong national vendor regulations could save WIC substantial amounts of money, as is now the case in the state of Texas (Greenstein, 1998). Of course, WIC already has instituted one of the federal government's most successful cost-containment strategies: the infant formula rebate system. By contracting with infant formula manufacturers, state agencies or multistate consortia have been able to negotiate purchase rebates, which have allowed them to serve more people. In fiscal year 1996, state agencies or consortia spent about $620 million on infant formula and received rebates totaling nearly $1.2 billion, which equals 31 percent of their total food expenditures (National Association of WIC Directors, 1998).

Finally, lack of end-of-year funding flexibility has been a management problem for WIC programs. At the end of each fiscal year, only 1 percent of unspent grant funds can be carried over to the next year (National Association of WIC Directors, 1998). Moreover, programs are never certain if they suddenly will be allocated additional unspent funds from other programs or if rebate revenues or food prices will change. This budget management policy causes disruption of sound program planning. Congress has been urged by the National Association of WIC Directors and by the General Accounting Office to allow carryovers of funds not to exceed 3 percent at the end of the year, but Congress has not adopted this recommendation (Committee on Agriculture, Nutrition, and Forestry, 1984, 1985).

In the course of its development, WIC has garnered broad support from many quarters. Although not permanently authorized in legislation as an entitlement program, WIC seems to be here to stay and is considered to be one of the federal government's most cost-effective programs (Committee on Education and Labor, 1987). Advocacy strategies that have fostered development of this program have taken many forms: congressional testimony, television documentaries, letter writing campaigns, displays of photos and x-rays, magazine articles, class action suits, newspaper articles, developmental research, evaluation studies, and formation of lobbying coalitions. Perhaps WIC can serve as a model of advocacy orchestration for other child advocacy efforts. In any case, WIC supporters can claim much success in their advocacy efforts as they have faced continuing challenges and new issues.

REFERENCES

Berry, J. M. (1984). *Feeding hungry people: Rule-making in the Food Stamp Program.* New Brunswick, NJ: Rutgers University Press.

Buescher, P. A., Larson, L. C., Nelson, M. D., & Lenihan, A. J. (1993). Prenatal WIC participation can reduce low birth weight and newborn medical costs: A cost-benefit analysis of WIC participation in North Carolina. *Journal of the American Dietetic Association, 93,* 163–166.

Centers for Disease Control. (1977, December). *Analysis of nutrition indices for selected WIC participants.* Atlanta: Author.

Centers for Disease Control. (1986, October 24–31). Declining anemia prevalence among children enrolled in public nutrition and health program, Selected states, 1975–1985. *Journal of the American Medical Association, 256,* 2165.

Committee on Agriculture, Nutrition, and Forestry. (1983). *Child nutrition programs: Description, history, issues, and options* (S. Prt. 98-15). Washington, DC: U.S. Government Printing Office.

Committee on Agriculture, Nutrition, and Forestry. (1984, March 15/April 9). *Evaluation and reauthorization of the Special Supplemental Food Program for Women, Infants, and Children (WIC)* (S. Hrg. 98-985). Washington, DC: U.S. Government Printing Office.

Committee on Agriculture, Nutrition, and Forestry. (1985, June 17). *Reauthorization of WIC, the Commodity Supplemental Food Program and the Temporary Emergency Food Assistance Program* (S. Hrg. 99-401). Washington, DC: U.S. Government Printing Office.

Committee on Education and Labor. (1987, October 7). *The Chairman's report on children in America: A strategy for the 100th Congress, A guide to federal programs that affect children* (Vol. II). (H. R. Serial No. 100-0). Washington, DC: U.S. Government Printing Office.

Devaney, B., Bilheimer, L., & Schore, J. (1992). Medicaid costs and birth outcomes: The effects of prenatal WIC participation and the use of prenatal care. *Journal of Policy Analysis and Management, 11,* 573–592.

Endozien, J. C., Switzer, B. R., & Bryan, R. B. (1976, July). *Medical evaluation of the Special Supplemental Food Program for Women, Infants, and Children (WIC)* (6 vols.). Chapel Hill, NC: University of North Carolina, School of Public health.

English, C. (1987, October). Personal communication.

English, C. (1998, November). Personal communication.

Food and Nutrition Service. (1998a). *Annual historical review of FNS programs: Fiscal year 1996.* Washington, DC: U.S. Department of Agriculture.

Food and Nutrition Service. (1998b). Questions and answers on WIC: The Special Supplemental Nutrition Program for Women, Infants, and Children. [Online]. Available: www.usda.gov/fcs/ogapi/wicunf~1.htm

General Accounting Office. (1985). *Need to foster optimal use of resources in the Special Supplemental Food Program for Women, Infants, and Children* (WIC). Report to the Secretary of Agriculture. Washington, DC: Author.

Greenstein, R. (1998). *Strengthening WIC program integrity.* Washington, DC: Center on Budget and Policy Priorities.

Hardman, V. M. (1973, April). How to save babies for two dimes a day. *Redbook,* 68, 70, 72–75.

Hayes, C. D. (1982). *Making policies for children: A study of the federal process.* Washington, DC: National Academy Press.

Institute of Medicine. (1991). *Nutrition during lactation.* Washington, DC: National Academy Press.

National Agricultural Statistics Service. (1993). *Agricultural statistics 1993.* Washington, DC: Government Printing Office.

National Agricultural Statistics Service. (1996). *Agricultural statistics 1995–96.* Washington, DC: Government Printing Office.

National Agricultural Statistics Service. (1998). *Agricultural statistics 1998.* Washington, DC: Government Printing Office.

National Association of WIC Directors. (1998). *NAWD's four-star approach for WIC in the 21st century.* Washington, DC: National Association of WIC Directors.

Nelson, J. R. (1982). The Special Supplemental Food Program for Women, Infants, and Children. In C. D. Hayes (Ed.), *Making policies for children: A study of the federal process* (pp. 85–150). Washington, DC: National Academy Press.

Oliveira, V. (1998a). Spending on food-assistance programs decreased in 1997. *FoodReview, 21* (1), 16–22.

Oliveira, V. (1998b). Welfare reform affects USDA's food-assistance programs. *FoodReview, 21* (1), 8–15.

Owen, A. L., & Owen, G. M. (1997). Twenty years of WIC: A review of some effects of the program. *Journal of the American Dietetic Association, 97,* 777–782.

Rhodes, R. J. (1983, April). How Texas works with WIC vendors. *Food and Nutrition,* 6–7.

Rose, D., Habicht, J., & Devaney, B. (1998). Household participation in the Food Stamp and WIC programs increases the nutrient intakes of preschool children. *The Journal of Nutrition, 128,* 548–555.

Serrano, T. (1986, July). Special effort in California helps grocers understand WIC. *Food and Nutrition,* 14–15.

Stansfield, C. M. (1984, January). WIC celebrates its tenth anniversary. *Food and Nutrition,* 2–8.

U.S. accused of altering study of food program. (1986, January 30). *New York Times,* 9.

Vogel, R. J. (1998). WIC Policy Memorandum 98-9: Nutrition risk criteria. [Online]. Available: www.usda.gov/fcs/wic/nrpol3.htm

Watkins, S. R. (1997). USDA looks toward the new millennium. [Online]. Available: www.fns.usda.gov/fncs/shirley/speeches/support/sw971113.htm

■ Ask Yourself

Identifying Issues for Advocacy

1. According to recent research on brain development, how is the brain developing in the first years of life? How do emotions or stress affect the early development of mental capacities? What structures of the brain handle emotions, learning and memory, language, and stress?

2. What are the benefits to infants' health, if any, of trained nurses making home visits to pregnant women and first-time mothers?

3. How and to what extent does the government provide nutritional assistance to children in our society? Are supplemental nutrition programs accountable and effective? Explain your answer.

4. What are the health consequences to children of teenage child-bearing? Of poverty? Of homelessness? Of alcohol, tobacco, or drug use by the mother? Of multiple births?

5. Freedberg (1983) asserts that next to farm and chemical workers, children face the greatest health risks from pollution and hazardous wastes. Do current policies prohibit construction of playgrounds or child-care settings on abandoned industrial sites or landfills? Are children exposed to dangerous pesticides, lead poisoning, or wood preservatives on playgrounds or at child-care sites? How can healthier environments be developed in family, community, and child-care settings? (See U.S. Department of Health and Human Services [1997]. *Training guides for the Head Start learning community: Sustaining a healthy environment.* Washington, DC: U.S. Government Printing Office.)

6. If children have lower tolerance levels for toxins than do adults, do current federal environmental standards protect children? What progress has the proposed Children's Environmental Protection Act made in Congress (see www.senate.gov/~boxer/sprfund.html)? How can parents and children's advocates get more information about the health effects of environmental pollutants on our nation's children? (See, for example, www.epa.gov/epadocs/child.htm and Appendix 1 for other websites.)

7. In a preschool program, why is it more important to provide concrete preparation experiences with food and to hold conversations about necessary ingredients and the preparation process than to show food pictures and to ask questions like "Are peas vegetables?"

8. At Tiny Tikes Child Care Center, a small group of 3-year-olds sat at the art table as their preschool teacher ladled from a big bowl a glob of chocolate pudding for each child. Then the teacher told the children that today they were going to fingerpaint with pudding! The 3-year-olds began cautiously to stick their fingers in

the pudding. One child giggled and squeezed the pudding through his fingers. Another child spread the pudding around and then slapped her hands on the table several times. Next, a child stuck a pudding-covered hand in her mouth and grinned. The other children began to lick pudding from their hands and to giggle at each other's chocolate-covered hands and faces. What attitudes and values about food are being conveyed by this activity? Discuss the choice of food as a medium for art.

9. What characteristics are associated with attention deficit disorders? Why might this disorder be misdiagnosed in early childhood? Does research link consumption of sweeteners, food additives, or lead to this disorder? What environmental adaptations might be helpful for a child with an attention deficit disorder? Is use of stimulant drugs such as Ritalin an appropriate or effective treatment for young children? Why or why not?

10. If a child in your program tests HIV positive or has AIDS, what steps should you consider taking to effectively meet this challenge and to maintain a safe educational environment (see Wadsworth and Knight, 1996)?

11. What early childhood resources are available to young children in homeless shelters in your area or state?

■ Advocacy and Leadership Strategies

1. What progress is your state making and how does it compare with other states on the health-related criteria for Goal 1—Ready to Learn—of the National Education Goals? (See "State Scorecards" at the National Education Goals Panel website: www.negp. gov and "Children in the States" at the Children's Defense Fund website: www.childrensdefense.org) Write to your state legislators about what you learned about child health issues in your state. (See Appendix 3 for letter-writing tips.)

2. In 1997, the enactment of Title XXI, the State Children's Health Insurance Program (CHIP) was a huge step forward for children's health. Investigate what choices your state has made in regard to children's health insurance and access to health care as a result of this program (see Children's Defense Fund, 1998a, 1998c; National Association of Child Advocates, 1998). Should access to health care be a child's right (see Appendix 11)? Why or why not?

3. Investigate the availability, affordability, developmental appropriateness, and coordination of children's mental health services in your community. (For further information on this issue, see the Children's Defense Fund website as listed in Appendix 1.)

4. Suppose that you are composing a parent newsletter for your preschool program. What parent/child activities might you suggest to strengthen positive attitudes toward good nutrition?

5. Invite a WIC representative to speak to your group about WIC eligibility requirements, screening forms, and the application process. Also discuss efforts to reach possible participants, and the nature of their nutrition consultation program.

6. After reading about the WIC program and listening to presentations about or visiting a local WIC program, make arrangements to visit one of your county legislators or supervisors. (See Appendix 5 for additional tips on visiting public officials.) Be prepared to discuss the purposes and accomplishments of WIC. Point out that WIC checks bring money into the county and that the WIC program provides employment for people in the county. Make plans to discuss the feasibility of more county support for the WIC program (e.g., greater coordination of social service programs, more assistance in contacting eligible WIC participants or development of management information systems).

7. Request an interview with a grocery store employee. Explain that you want to learn more about how the WIC program works and want to discuss the employee's impressions of the program. (Be sure that the grocery store employee has had sufficient experience with WIC customers.) Based on the readings in this chapter as well as information received from a WIC representative (if available), compose four to six interview questions that you wish to ask this person. In framing your questions, consider issues such as:

   a. Do grocery store employees or vendors understand the purposes of WIC, WIC eligibility requirements, and what foods are acceptable for WIC purchases?

   b. Do they encounter pressure to allow substitute purchases?

   c. Do they believe that the program is necessary and effective in supplementing the nutrition of the women and children enrolled in the program?

   Take notes during the interview in order to obtain a record of the interviewee's responses. After the interview, write a synopsis of the interview, including the interview questions asked, the interviewee's responses, and your interpretation and comparison of these responses in relation to chapter readings and information, if any, from a WIC representative.

8. At your field-study site, interview the program director about what steps, if any, are taken to prevent the spread of disease in relation to the following categories:

   a. Diaper changing

   b. Coughing and sneezing

c. Hand washing

d. Attendance policies for children with diarrhea

e. Ventilation and amount of outdoor play

f. Cleaning/disinfecting tables, dishes, and utensils

g. Handling, serving, or storing food

h. Serving leftovers

i. Use of latex or vinyl gloves

Also inquire as to when and how the local health department inspects the program, if at all. (For additional information, see U.S. Department of Health and Human Services [1996]. *Training guides for the Head Start learning community: Preventing and managing communicable diseases*. Washington, DC: U.S. Government Printing Office.)

References and Suggested Readings

American Academy of Pediatrics. (1999a). Children's health care coverage. [Online]. Available: www.aap.org/advocacy/washing/chichcc.htm

American Academy of Pediatrics. (1999b). Immunization protects children: 1999 immunization schedule. [Online]. Available: www.aap.org/family/parents/immunize. htm

Bernstein, N. (1995, January/February). Learning to love. *Mother Jones* [Online], 3 pages. Available: www.bsd.mojones.com/mother_jones/JF95/bernstein. html

Centers for Disease Control and Prevention (CDC). (1998a). 10 things you need to know about immunization. [Online]. Available: www.cdc.gov/nip/vacsafe/q10vac.htm

Centers for Disease Control and Prevention (CDC). (1998b). You, your community, and state immunization laws. [Online]. Available: www.cdc.gov/nip/vacsafe/fs/statelaw.htm

Center on Hunger, Poverty, and Nutrition Policy. (1994). *The link between nutrition and cognitive development in children*. Medford, MA: Tufts University. (ERIC Document Reproduction Service No. ED 374 903)

Children's Defense Fund. (1998a, March 19). CHIP and child health: Questions and answers. [Online]. Available: www.childrensdefense.org/health_qu. html

Children's Defense Fund. (1998b). *Poverty matters: The cost of child poverty in America*. Washington, DC: Author.

Children's Defense Fund. (1998c). Progress report: Implementing the State Children's Health Insurance Program (CHIP). [Online]. Available: www. childrensdefense.org/health_progress.html

Cook, J. (1996). Poor kids more undernourished. In *Connecticut Kidslink* [Online]. Available: www.statlab.stat.yale.edu/cityroom/kidslink2/issues. html#anchor650296

Cooper, R. T. (1997, June 5). Teen-pregnancy myths debunked. *The Seattle Times* [Online], 3 pages. Available: www.seattletimes.com/extra/browse/htm197/altteen_060597.html

Evans, S. K. (1997). *Nutrition education materials and audiovisuals for grades preschool through 6*. Beltsville, MD: U.S. Department of Agriculture, Food and

Nutrition Information Center. (ERIC Document Reproduction Service No. ED 409 204)

Food Research and Action Center (FRAC). (1998). Hunger in the U.S. [Online]. Available: www.frac.org/html/hunger_in_the_us/hunger_index.html

Freedberg, L. (1983). *America's poisoned playgrounds: Children and toxic chemicals.* Paper presented at the Conference on Alternative State and Local Policies, Washington, DC. Oakland, CA: Youth News. (ERIC Document Reproductive Service No. 231 519)

Fujimoto, G. (1997, July–August). Visiting new moms: Home visiting promotes babies' healthy development by supporting their mothers. *Children's Advocate* [Online], 3 pages. Available: www.4children.org/news/7-97hvis.htm

Harris, I. B. (1996). *Children in jeopardy: Can we break the cycle of poverty?* New Haven, CT: Yale University Press.

Howerton, M. (1998, March–April). Safe kids in Harlem: Communities mobilize to prevent childhood injuries. *Children's Advocate* [Online], 3 pages. Available: www. 4children.org/news/398harlm.htm

Jang, M. (1998, May–June). Washing away the germs: Simple programs of enforced handwashing produce dramatic gains in children's health. *Children's Advocate* [Online], 3 pages. Available: www.4children.org/news/598handw. htm

Kleinman, R. E., Murphy, J. M., Little, M., Pagano, M., Wehler, C. A., Regal, K., & Jellinek, M. S. (1998). Hunger in children in the United States: Potential behavioral and emotional correlates. *Pediatrics* [Online], 6 pages. Available: www.pediatrics.org/cgi/content/ full/101/1/e3

Livingston, K. (1997). Ritalin: Miracle drug or cop-out? *The Public Interest, 127,* 3–18.

Lustman, N. M. (1998). Attention deficit disorders: The basics. In *Connecticut Kidslink* [Online]. Available: statlab.stat.yale.edu/cityroom/kidslink2/issues. html#anchor650296

Mogharrenban, C., & Nahikian-Nelm, M. (1996). Autonomy at mealtime: Building healthy food preferences and eating behaviors in young children. *Early Childhood Education Journal, 24* (1), 29–32.

National Association of Child Advocates. (1998, February). The State Children's Health Insurance Program: Is your state making the best choices for children? [Online]. Available: www.childadvocacy.org/publicat.html

Ogden, C. L., Troiano, R. P., Briefel, R. R., Kuczmarski, R. J., Flegal, K. M., & Johnson, C. L. (1997). Prevalence of overweight among preschool children in the United States, 1971 to 1994. *Pediatrics* [Online], 7 pages. Available: www.pediatrics.org/cgi/content/full/99/4/e1

Portner, J. (1997, September 10). Volunteerism reduces teen pregnancy, study finds. *Teacher Magazine* [Online], 2 pages. Available: www.teachermag.org/ we/vol-17/02teen.h17

PR Newswire. (1996, June 13). Groundbreaking study on teenage childbearing quantifies devastating consequences to parents, children and society. [Online]. Available: www.kidsource.com/kidsource/content/news/teen_pregnancy

Thomson, M., & Caulfield, R. (1998). Teen pregnancy and parenthood: Infants and toddlers who need care. *Early Childhood Education Journal, 25* (3), 203–205.

Wadsworth, D. E., & Knight, D. (1996). Meeting the challenge of HIV and AIDS in the classroom. *Early Childhood Education Journal, 23,* 143–147.

Wolraich, M. L., Lindgren, S. D., Stumbo, P. J., Stegink, L. D., Appelbaum, M. I., & Kiritsy, M. C. (1994). Effects of diets high in sucrose or aspartame on the behavior and cognitive performance of children. *The New England Journal of Medicine, 330,* 301–307.

C h a p t e r 5

Abuse, Neglect, and Violence in Children's Lives

Fast Talk with Fast Foods

Observation Notes:

6:25 P.M.   A mother, about 21 years old, walks toward a restaurant table followed by 6-year-old Jason and 4-year-old John. Straggling at the rear is 2-year-old Johanna. The mother sets the tray and her purse on the table and takes off her jacket. She doesn't help the kids with their jackets. John tugs on the strap of her purse; she swats his hand and caustically remarks, "Why don't you break that like you break everything else?"

Jason and John sit down on one side of the booth, the mother and Johanna on the other. The mother shoves a Cheery Meal in front of each child, and they open the boxes. Jason wails, "I didn't want a burger!"

"I didn't *give* you a burger," his mother snaps.

"I wanted fries, too," Jason peevishly mumbles.

"I don't care. Don't ask for anything else for the rest of the day," yells the mother.

Johanna takes a bite of her hamburger and then spits it out, exclaiming, "No like pickles! No like pickles!"

The mother grabs the hamburger away and says, "So don't eat them."

They all sit in silence for a few seconds.

John pulls out his package of Legos from the Cheery Meal box and asks, "Can I open the Legos?"

The mother responds, "No! Will you be quiet and just eat? We're *not* staying." John sighs and eats a couple of fries.

6:30 P.M.   Jason demands, "Gimme one," and grabs at his brother's fries. John quickly pulls away his fries.

The mother intervenes: "John, give him one. You always hog everything. How many times have I told you to share stuff with your brother?"

John stands up on the bench. The mother growls, "Sit! We're gonna go, so *eat.*" Jason starts to kick his feet against the bench so hard that the booth shakes. His mother glares, raises her hand, glances around, and then withdraws it. She warns, "Jason, we're going now; you better be ready." She leaves the table to throw out the garbage.

When she returns, Jason whines, "Johanna messed her pants, Johanna messed her pants." Johanna starts to whimper and shrinks back into the corner of the booth.

The mother grabs Johanna by the arms, shakes her, and shrieks, "You're gonna get it! You dirty, dirty girl! Don't I have enough to do!" The mother drags sobbing Johanna off to the bathroom.

Questions

1. Are there clues to suggest that the dynamics displayed are typical patterns for this family? Or do they represent "just one of those days when nobody should have gotten out of bed"? Support your answer.

2. Consider the interaction in this episode. In what ways did the actions of the mother influence the actions of the children? In what ways did the actions of the children precipitate the actions of the mother?

■ Preview

In the past two decades, we have witnessed an upsurge in reports of suspected child abuse and neglect. This upsurge reflects, in part, dramatic changes in laws and in public concern about the problems of abuse and neglect. On the other hand, exposure to violence in our society has been on the rise, too. For example, the media often strive to capture viewers' attention by glamorizing and increasing violence in programs. According to Concerned Educators Allied for a Safe Environment, such exposure is detrimental to children and to public health. James Garbarino, however, wonders if the nation can make a public research-based case against child abuse, much as it has for smoking. In the second reading of this chapter, Garbarino reflects on some of the societal beliefs that we need to confront if we are to advance such a campaign. Derry Koralek then offers some anecdotal accounts of how to look for signs of abuse and neglect in early childhood settings.

The Effects of Violence on Children's Lives

Concerned Educators Allied
for a Safe Environment

■ ■ ■

Children, caught in the crossfire, are dying. Every day in the U.S. 10 children die from gunfire and 30 are wounded. The second most frequent cause of death, ages 15 to 19, is gunfire. Every day 135,000 children bring guns to school. Thirty percent of families with children keep a loaded gun in their home.

Children watching television see 25 violent acts per hour. Children learn from television that violence is the way to solve conflicts, that violence is power, entertainment and the way to respond to shame and humiliation. Children buy the toy weapons that TV sells. TV desensitizes children to the suffering of others.

Violence as punishment heightens aggressiveness. Corporal punishment is widely accepted in schools and homes. Most parents who were abused in their childhood, abuse their own children. Reports of child abuse and neglect have risen 259% in the last ten years.

Children witness the outbursts of violence that occur when the stresses of poverty, and rage at the injustices of discrimination, become more than the adults around them can bear. Unemployment is the primary correlate with spouse abuse and child abuse.

Children and Families Need to Be Surrounded with Services and Protection at the Community, National, and International Levels

Children who live with chronic violence show severely disturbed behaviors:

■ *extremes of aggression or withdrawal,*
■ *trouble remembering, difficulty concentrating,*
■ *learning problems,*
■ *deep distrustfulness,*
■ *pervasive sadness.*

It is hard for them to imagine a future for themselves or for the world.

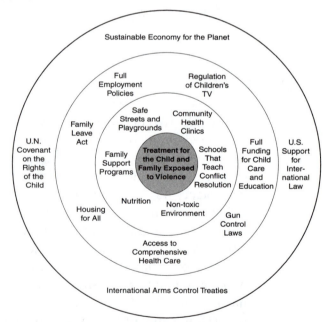

Sources: Beyond Rhetoric, report of the National Commission on Children, 1991; Children's Defense Fund; American Psychological Ass. Commission on Violence; National Association for the Education of Young Children, Panel on Violence; Garbarino, Debrow, Kostelny, Pardo, *Children in Danger.*

Concerned Educators Allied for a Safe Environment (CEASE). (undated). *The effects of violence on children's lives* (Information sheet #10). Cambridge, MA: CEASE. Reprinted by permission of the publisher.

CAN Reflections on 20 Years of Searching

James Garbarino

■ ■ ■

For the last 20 years, I have been studying childhood in the United States and around the world (with visits to more than 20 countries). This work has had several themes, many of them brought together in my most recent book, *Raising Children in a Socially Toxic Environment* (1995). But through it all, one question has remained at the center, "Can we prevent child abuse?" I began addressing this question 20 years ago as a freshly minted Ph.D. from Cornell University. Two decades later, I have returned to Cornell as Director of the Family Life Development Center and Professor of Human Development, and this question still provides a focal point for my work. I track my progress (and to some extent the progress of our field) through the evolution of this question, and I want to share some reflections of my personal struggle, in the hope that doing so can shed light on the progress of our field, represented as it is by our primary journal, *Child Abuse & Neglect [CAN], The International Journal.*

Can we prevent child abuse? As I look back over the evolution of my answer to this question, I am drawn to the issue of smoking as a useful analogy. When I first began flying in airplanes in the 1950s as a child, it used to drive me crazy that people would light up cigarettes right next to me. As one who is very sensitive to cigarette smoke, this made flying very difficult. At the time it seemed almost inconceivable that within four decades we would have prohibited smoking on airplanes entirely (at least on domestic flights). How did this happen? It required a systematic, coordinated assault on a set of values, on a set of beliefs, and on a set of assumptions about what rights people possessed.

It required the amassing of a database that documented the risk posed by smoking to health and well-being. It required a dogged, relentless campaign to communicate that database to the people, and it required consistent advocacy in the halls of government—local, state, and national. What is more, all of this had to take place in the face of a well-financed tobacco industry lobby *and* the power of nicotine addiction itself in the lives of the many millions of addicts.

The results are impressive. Smokers now constitute a minority whose social position is increasingly marginal. This is not to say that smoking has ceased and desisted. Indeed, marginal groups in the society—particularly youth—continue to smoke in disproportionate numbers (overall about 23%). Can we prevent smoking? The answer is "yes" if we don't equate prevention with a one-time eradication but rather with a staged reduction that eventually confines the behavior to a small group who are beyond social influence, and for whom only social control will suffice as an intervention. The confining of a behavior to marginal groups is one measure of the success of a social change movement because it makes possible coercive social interventions—such as smoke-free workplaces. I might add that this point is quite relevant to child abuse prevention, where one measure of success is the fact that "mainstream groups" such as two parent middle-class families have dramatically changed their child-rearing attitudes and behaviors in recent decades.

Looking back over the last two decades, I see reason to be hopeful about the prospects for child abuse prevention, principally because I see that in the midst of much social deterioration generally (Garbarino, 1995) there is a shifting of attitudes, beliefs, and behavior that points away from the foundation for child abuse, such as hitting children. This shifting is evident in the consciousness of children. Nearly a decade ago, when we got to talking about a newspaper article on "corporal punishment" at my house, and as I was reading some of the piece aloud,

James Garbarino. (1996). CAN reflections on 20 years of searching. *Child Abuse and Neglect, 20*(3), 157–160. Reprinted by permission from Elsevier Science.

89

my 6-year-old daughter said, "You mean people hit children? Teachers hit children? That's terrible." She said, "Don't they realize they'll learn to hit other kids and they'll grow up to hit their own kids?" Years earlier at age 6, my son had put crayon and pencil to paper to produce his first book, entitled simply *Hitting Children Is Bad*.

The response of my children had, I think, two meanings. First, as children, they were struggling themselves with the issue of how to deal with aggression, in their own behavior and in the behavior of others. They need all the help they can get in responding to their own aggressive impulses. They need role models and cultural support for learning nonviolent ways to respond when they are frustrated, angry, or simply want to exert their will. If the adults in their life use assault as a tactic under those conditions, how are they, as young children, supposed to "know better"—and do better. The prospect of adults hitting kids is frightening to them as they are trying to learn how to manage their lives.

But there is also a second meaning to their response. The fact that it was inconceivable to them that hitting is good is itself a measure of success, just as the fact that it's inconceivable that people would get along *without* hitting kids is evidence of the problem we face as a society. But we have to start with the recognition that we *have made* some progress on this issue. Many of us have in our personal lives. We have institutionally when we note that a majority of American schools prohibit physical assault against children, what they call "corporal punishment." I think we must acknowledge and promote public consciousness of that progress. The question is not simply whether we can eradicate physical assault against children in one fell swoop, but whether we can tip the balance in the American value system so that we will be where we are with smoking now in the coming years; maybe it's 10 years, maybe it's 20 years.

By making the case against hitting with scientific evidence, with personal testimony, with group demonstration of "a better way," we will build a credible cultural foundation upon which to proceed with policies to regulate, to confine, and to gradually eradicate assault against children. This is the key to answering the question, "Can we prevent child abuse?" I think the tactical and the strategic issues we face can be broken into several areas.

One is the issue of language, the power of language to push people's consciousness in the direction we want. I think one way to prevent child abuse is to push against the use of language that describes physical punishment as something other than it is. I think we will make progress as we reshape the dictionary of talking about violence. Let's simply talk about the use of "assault against children as punishment," not about "discipline," not "corporal punishment," and, not even "physical punishment" (because many physical punishments do not involve assault).

Picking up a squalling 2-year-old in the midst of a temper tantrum, sitting him down, and saying, "you will stay here because I will not let you act this way" is certainly physical control, and it is *physical* because it moves the body. Restraining a child who's fooling around is a kind of physical punishment, but it's not assault. I think an important part of our agenda is to get the public to focus on "assault as discipline." Many people still find this concept disorienting. But that, of course, is what we have to do—disorient people, jar them out of the comfort of terms like "a good licking." Let's make people come right out and say, "I favor assaulting children—for their own good, of course."

Confront the objective empirical realities of what we're talking about by piercing some of the euphemistic language. That can push things along. Here we might look to other campaigns for social change, like the smoking movement. There we know we must pierce the advertisements that portray smoking as glamorous and instead show what smoking really means—to the lungs, for example.

Beyond language, a second issue we must confront is this: "Is physical child abuse simply too much of a good thing?" Is physical child abuse qualitatively different from normal assault—the normal violence that most American parents use as part of their childrearing? Or, is it simply an extreme form of a common "normal" behavior? Do we have a continuum on which when you get to 85 on a scale of 100, it's child abuse? Or, are these two fundamentally different phenomena—normal assault and child abuse? What is the relevance of undermining normal physical assault to the goal of preventing child abuse?

Our approach to sexual child abuse is very different. There we define any sexual contact as inappropriate and probably damaging. The evidence tells us that the more "normal" assault that's present in a parent-child relationship, the *more* likely it is that there will eventually be abuse (Straus, 1994). And yet, it's desirable to assault children—as long as it doesn't become extreme. Of course, people differ in what they consider to be extreme: Whereas 52% of adults living in the northeastern U.S. think that hitting a child with a belt or a switch not hard enough to leave marks is abuse, only 18% of Southerners think so.

Another survey (conducted in the 1970s) reported that parents who *don't* hit their kids were made to feel like deviants, that they're not doing something good. Preventing child abuse is about the setting of minimal standards of care for children. It's not about discovering a set of preexisting criteria. It's about *setting* standards based on knowledge and beliefs. And the process of setting standards is a matter of science-based child advocacy. It's a matter of getting people to agree upon the minimal standard of care with respect of caregiving, with respect to the use of force (and with respect to sexuality and with respect to meeting basic physical and emotional needs).

Underlying the process of setting minimal standards of care is the question, "Does all violence lead to more violence?" Based on his review of the evidence, Jeffrey Goldstein adopts the following position: "Aggressive behavior used to achieve a personal goal, such as wealth or power, and that may be perceived by the actor as justified, or even as nonaggressive, is a primary cause of aggressive and criminal behavior of others." His model leaves a kind of a loophole—"to achieve a personal goal." It is not a simple one-for-one contagion model that *all* violence leads to violence. It leaves open socially defined violence as possibly noncontagious. Another view—commonly associated with Murray Straus—offers a more straightforward one-to-one correspondence model—*all* violence produces violence somewhere down the line. Indeed, this is the core of Straus' book *Beating the Devil Out of Them* (1994), the idea that all punishment by assault is pathogenic (like all smoking).

Goldstein has pulled back from this "radical" view to allow the possibility that violence can be confined to social purposes without spilling over into other contexts. But from a child's point of view, the whole world is "personal." Certainly a child's relationship with his or her parents is profoundly personal. In their future behavior and their view of the world, children tell us that hitting them increases the likelihood that they will hit others. Nonetheless, there's certainly a lively debate on this topic. I believe our progress in preventing child abuse will hinge on our ability to communicate this perspective to adults in our society, to improve the ability and motivation to understand what children can tell us about the experience of violence (Garbarino & Stott, 1989).

Related to this issue of what constitutes "personal" within the family is the important issue of what constitutes "private" in the family's relationship with the community. I think that in our campaign to prevent child abuse it is necessary to refute the popular contention that childrearing is a private matter. Alice Rossi (1968) provided the foundation for this perspective in her analysis of a bio-social perspective on parenting. Rossi makes a very persuasive argument that parenting evolved in our species in a situation of stable, close, intimate relationships with lots of monitoring by others, lots of shared responsibility for child care, and lots of supportive feedback about childrearing. Her point is that as a species we developed the capacity to parent in that kind of environment, which makes it "unnatural" to ask people to parent on their own—perhaps as single parents living in single houses or nuclear families living without a lot of community connection. And that may well be why things are so bizarre for us in our society.

We've erected a cultural superstructure around privacy and autonomy that is fundamentally not in the human best interest because it asks people to do something unnatural to them. If that's true, then we do indeed have a big agenda in changing this orientation, an orientation that says that children are the private matter of their parents. We have to see that every child is a social matter and that being a parent is a social act.

And if we are successful in accomplishing this agenda, will we prevent child abuse? I believe we will, that we will push abuse into an ever more marginal social position, in which we can surround it with efforts to assess and document emergent problems and then intervene early to protect the children and "control" the perpetrators. At that point, we won't have achieved utopia, but we will have fulfilled our professional and civic mandate. I, for one, would be delighted to be able to report completion of that task when the time comes to celebrate the 40th anniversary volume of this journal.

REFERENCES

Garbarino, J. (1995). *Raising children in a socially toxic environment.* San Francisco, CA: Jossey-Bass.

Garbarino, J., & Stott, F. (1989). *What children can tell us.* San Francisco, CA: Jossey-Bass.

Goldstein, J. (1986). *Aggression and crimes of violence.* New York: Oxford University Press.

Rossi, A. (1968). Transition to parenthood. *Journal of Marriage and the Family,* 26–39.

Straus, M. (1994). *Beating the devil out of them: Corporal punishment in American families.* Lexington, MA: Free Press.

Recognizing Child Abuse and Neglect

Derry Koralek

■ ■ ■

Making a Difference[1]

Sandra is the mother of a 4-year-old girl, Kelly. Three months ago Sandra visited a community clinic for help to stop drinking and to separate from Kelly's father, Frank, who is also an alcoholic. Frank has physically abused Sandra and Kelly in the past, but both of them, especially Kelly, still feel close to him. Recently, Kelly has been very withdrawn and depressed.

The counselor at the clinic suggested that Sandra find child care for Kelly as part of her treatment plan, both for her own peace of mind and for Kelly's safety. Because Kelly was at risk for abuse, the family was eligible for State-subsidized respite care. The counselor told Sandra about the local resource and referral (R&R) agency that could help her find child care and described the various types of care available. Kelly had never gone to child care before.

Sandra received several referrals from the R&R and enrolled Kelly in a half-day child care program, where she is making friends and getting help from her caregivers in expressing her feelings. Sandra and Kelly are temporarily living in a shelter for women. During the time Kelly is at child care, Sandra attends a treatment program, looks for work and a new place to live, and gathers the strength she needs to start a new life.

The clinic counselor keeps in contact with Kelly's child care program to share ideas on how to help the family and especially on how to handle Frank, who has become very angry about losing custody of Kelly.

Ruth was 19 when her first son, Anthony, was born premature and very frail. She found Anthony very difficult to care for and sometimes shook or hit him when he cried for long periods. At age 3, Anthony was hospitalized with pneumonia at the same time that a second normal and healthy son, Brian, was born. Six months later, Ruth's husband left her. Ruth found a restaurant job and enrolled Anthony and Brian in her neighbor Marie's family day care home.

At age 3, Anthony was barely talking but had become very active, violent, and hard to control. Ruth favored Brian because he was an "easier" baby, but raising them both on her own was causing greater and greater strain. Ruth was fired from her job and started using severe physical punishment when she was angry. She began asking Marie for help.

Marie told Ruth about some local counseling and support groups and took care of the boys occasionally in the evening or for part of the weekend, but she began to see that the punishment had become physical abuse. As required by law, Marie reported the abuse to the local child welfare agency and then told Ruth that she had done so. Ruth had become frightened enough of her own violent behavior that she was willing to accept intervention.

The children spent over a year in foster care while continuing to attend Marie's program. Child care was their greatest comfort and continuity during this difficult period. Marie was able to get some free training from the local community health center on how to set firm limits for the two boys while showing them the affection they needed.

The boys are now 7 and 4. Anthony, in a special class because of a learning disability, joins Brian at family day care after school each day. Marie still cares for the boys on occasional weekends. Anthony and Brian continue to be very challenging to care for, but Anthony has become much more confident about making friends. Learning to read is still very hard for

Adapted from Derry Koralek. (1992). Recognizing child abuse and neglect. In *Caregivers of young children: Preventing and responding to child maltreatment* [Online]. Washington, DC: U.S. Department of Health and Human Services, National Center on Child Abuse and Neglect. Available: www.calib.com/nccanch/pubs/caregiv/section2.htm

him, but Marie is teaching him to play the guitar, since Anthony has always had an exceptional ear for music.

Roberta and John are affluent, upwardly mobile working parents. Their 7-year-old son, Steven, attends second grade and an afterschool program. Three-year-old Lynn goes to a child care center. Both children are cared for by a housekeeper until late in the evening and frequently on weekends. Both Roberta and John are working toward advances in their careers; they are often away for evening meetings, work-related social events, and business trips.

When they have time to spend with the children, they are often distracted, low-energy, and tense. They expect their children to be very bright and successful and sometimes find them disappointing. John is especially upset and critical about Steven's below-average performance in school.

The teachers at Steven's afterschool program have begun to feel concerned about his withdrawn behavior and his lack of friends. He spends most of his time alone in fantasy play, which often involves grown-ups attacking or ridiculing the "baby." Lynn's preschool teachers are also concerned; she frequently whines and clings to adults and has had chronic colds and sore throats.

Roberta and John did not take the afterschool staff's concerns very seriously until they began to hear from Lynn's preschool program. Parent conferences at both programs helped them understand that they have been neglecting their children's emotional needs.

After nearly a year of discussion, both have made some adjustments and sacrifices. Steven and Lynn are slowly starting to join group activities with other children. John is beginning to confront his emotionally abusive relationship with Steven, which is very much like the pressure and ridicule he received from his own father.

When Andrea graduated from high school she wasn't sure what kind of job she wanted. A friend suggested that she try working as a child caregiver. She came from a large family, and had always liked babysitting for her brothers and sisters ("little kids are so cute"), so she decided to apply for a job at the Bo Peep Child Development Center. Although she had no experience working with young children and had no formal education in child development or in meeting the needs of young children, Bo Peep's director, Ms. Kelly, offered her a job as an aide working with the toddler group. Ms. Kelly was sure that Andrea's positive attitude and love of children would be an asset to the program.

Most of Andrea's training occurred on the job as she and the lead caregiver, Theresa, planned and carried out a program of activities for the 14 toddlers in their care. Theresa gave Andrea several articles on activities for toddlers and helped her learn about "what makes toddlers tick." Andrea thought it was all very interesting, but, as she was the oldest child in a family of seven, she already knew how to care for the children. She had seen four brothers and sisters grow up and knew how to keep them in line.

Unfortunately, Andrea soon learned that dealing with a group of toddlers can be very demanding and stressful. She was exhausted by the end of each day. One minute a child would ask to be held and cuddled, and the next she would cry because she wanted to do something for herself.

Theresa recognized that this was typical toddler behavior and created ways for the toddlers to express their independence. When a child yelled "no" it didn't bother her, and she calmly redirected the child to another activity. Andrea soon began feeling that Theresa was spoiling the children. Despite Theresa's attempts to help Andrea understand what toddlers were like and what they needed from adults, Andrea refused to listen. She would develop her own ways for handling the "problem" children.

One day two of the children refused to put on their coats to go outdoors. Andrea grabbed them both by their arms and squeezed hard until the children both began wailing. Theresa turned and saw a red-faced Andrea and two screaming children. Theresa saw that Andrea had lost control, and stepped in to console the crying children, giving them both hugs and reassuring them that everything would be all right. Then she asked Andrea to take a break to regain control of her behavior. Andrea agreed to go take a walk around the neighborhood until she had calmed down.

Later that day, Theresa and the program director met with Andrea and explained that her behavior was absolutely inappropriate for a caregiver. They suggested that Andrea might want to seek another kind of employment. Andrea willingly resigned her position, saying that she now understood that caring for young children required knowledge and skills that she did not have. In addition, she said that she didn't think that she had enough patience to do a good job working with a group of toddlers. Theresa and the program director thanked Andrea for her honesty and wished her good luck in her next job.

Caregiving professionals who have ongoing, daily contact with children are often able to detect and report suspected child maltreatment that otherwise might go unnoticed. To recognize and report child maltreatment effectively, it is necessary to have a common understanding of the various types of maltreatment and how they are defined.

The Child Abuse Prevention and Treatment Act, as amended by the Child Abuse Prevention, Adoption, and Family Services Act of 1988 (Public Law 100-294) defines child abuse and neglect as "the physical or mental injury, sexual abuse or exploitation, negligent treatment, or maltreatment of a child under the age of 18, or except in the case of sexual abuse, the age specified by the child protection law of the State by a person (including any employee of a residential facility or any staff person providing out-of-home care) who is responsible for the child's welfare under circumstances which indicate that the child's health or welfare is harmed or threatened thereby." The Act defines sexual abuse as "the use, persuasion, or coercion of any child to engage in any sexually explicit conduct (or any simulation of such conduct) for the purpose of producing any visual depiction of such conduct, or rape, molestation, prostitution, or incest with children." As a result of the Child Abuse Amendments of 1984 (Public Law 98-457), the Act also includes as child abuse the withholding of medically indicated treatment for an infant's life-threatening conditions.

Each State and community and many early childhood education programs also have definitions of child maltreatment. For example, Head Start and all branches of the military have specific definitions of child maltreatment. Caregiving professionals should find out what definitions are applicable in their community and program.

Evidence of each form of child abuse and neglect (physical abuse, neglect, sexual abuse, and emotional maltreatment) can be found in young children from birth through age 8. Sensitive early childhood education professionals can pick up clues of possible maltreatment by observing the child at the program or during routine conversations with parents. In addition, early childhood education professionals need to be alert to the behaviors of children and other staff within the program.

Physical signs of abuse or neglect are those that can actually be seen. Whether mild or severe, they involve the child's physical condition. Frequently, physical signs are bruises, bone injuries, or evidence of lack of care and attention manifested in conditions such as malnutrition.

Behavioral clues may exist alone or may accompany physical indicators. They might be subtle clues, such as a "sixth sense" that something is wrong, or sexual behaviors in young children indicating sexual knowledge not ordinarily possessed by young children, for example, sexual aggression toward younger children. Early childhood education professionals are trained to be skillful observers of children's behavior. They are aware of the range of behavior that is appropriate for children of a given age and are quick to notice when a child's behavior falls outside this range. Many programs maintain anecdotal records based on observations of individual children. Reviewing observation notes recorded over a period of time can provide useful information about changes in a child's behavior or pattern of development. These changes might indicate that the child is a victim of child abuse or neglect.

Early childhood education professionals have daily informal contacts with parents as they drop off and pick up their children from the child care center or family child care home, and more formal conversations during periodic parent conferences. During these conversations, parents might make statements about their children that indicate that they have abused or neglected their child or may be at risk for doing so. For example, a young mother comments, "Sam doesn't listen to anything I say. He is just like his father; I would be better off without him." A parent's negative comments or indifference to the child's progress in the program may cause the caregiving professional to observe the child more carefully to determine if the child shows any signs of having been maltreated.

Early childhood education professionals also use their observation skills to identify signs that child abuse and neglect might be taking place within their child care programs. For example, over a period of time a teaching assistant notices that several children avoid spending time alone with the teacher. She reports her concerns to the director. Or, a staff member sees a colleague slap a child who talked back to her or shake an infant who wouldn't stop crying. These behaviors should be considered to be child abuse and should be reported.

In the past, materials on recognizing child abuse and neglect included lists of physical and behavioral indicators for each of the types of abuse. These lists tended to be misleading, however, because recognition of child maltreatment is based on the detection of a cluster of indicators rather than observation of one or two clues.

Cultural Differences[2]

In the United States, people come from many different cultures: African American, Asian, European, Hispanic, and Native American, to name a few. During the past 20 years, the United States has experienced a great influx of immigrants from all over the world: Afghanistan, Cambodia, Cuba, El Salvador,

Ethiopia, India, Iran, Mexico, Nicaragua, the Philippines, Thailand, Vietnam, and so on. Because the children and families served by early childhood education programs reflect this cultural diversity, it is extremely important that caregivers of young children learn about and show sensitivity to the cultures and ethnic groups of the children in their care. This sensitivity will help caregivers distinguish between cultural child-rearing practices that are merely different and those that are defined by law as abusive or neglectful.

Caregivers may encounter some parents whose values or customs are different from their own. When this happens, caregiving professionals should take an honest and direct approach and ask the parents to explain their views and beliefs so that they can better understand the environment in which the child is being raised.

Child-rearing practices vary among families, cultures, and ethnic groups. In some families, children are expected to obey their parents without questioning the reasons for a parent's request. In many cultures, children are taught not to express negative feelings or opinions in front of their elders. While some cultures teach children to avoid making eye contact with adults, others chastise children who do not make eye contact: "Look at me when I'm talking to you." Most early childhood education programs in the United States encourage children to be independent because educators believe that this helps children to develop positive self-esteem. Yet many cultures encourage preschoolers to be dependent on their parents until they are school age, believing that young children need to feel that they will be taken care of. Clearly, there can be more than one right way to care for young children.

It is important to remember, however, that legal definitions of child abuse and neglect are not flexible. Even when an abusive practice is considered to be a cultural practice, it is still child abuse, and caregivers of young children are mandated to report it.

Recognizing Child Abuse and Neglect through Conversations and Interviews

Early childhood programs are generally family oriented, providing a great deal of formal and informal communication between program staff and families of the children in the program. Caregivers may gather important information about the family from routine conversations with parents and children. During daily dropoff and pickup times and at scheduled conferences, parents provide details of family life,

discuss discipline methods, or ask for help with problems. Young children enjoy talking about their families so they, too, may provide information about the family's interactions and home life.

Conversations with the parent can provide clues to how the parent feels about the child. The presence of child abuse and neglect may be indicated if the parent constantly:

Blames or belittles the child ("I told you not to drop that. Why weren't you paying attention?")

Sees the child as very different from his/her siblings ("His big sister Terry never caused me these problems. She always did exactly what she was told to do.")

Sees the child as "bad," "evil," or a "monster" ("She really seems to be out to get me. She's just like her father, and he was really an evil man.")

Finds nothing good or attractive in the child ("Oh well. Some kids are just a pain in the neck. You can see this one doesn't have anything going for her.")

Seems unconcerned about the child ("She was probably just having a bad day. I really don't have time to talk today.")

Fails to keep appointments or refuses to discuss problems the child is having in the program ("That's what I pay you for. If she's getting into trouble it's your job to make her behave.")

Misuses alcohol or other drugs.

When the caregiver knows a family well, he/she is in a better position to gauge whether a problem may be child abuse and neglect or something else, a chronic condition or a temporary situation, a typical early childhood problem that the program can readily handle, or a problem that requires outside intervention. Family circumstances may also provide clues regarding the possible presence of abuse or neglect. The risk of abuse or neglect increases when families are isolated from friends, neighbors, and other family members or if there is no apparent "life-line" to which a family can turn in times of crisis. Marital, economic, emotional, or social crises are some causes of family stress that can lead to child abuse or neglect.

When considering the possibility of child abuse and neglect, a caregiver of young children may want to talk with a child about a particular incident. Before having this conversation, the caregiver must be convinced that such a conversation will not put the child in further danger. Such a conversation is appropriate provided it is handled nonjudgmentally, carefully, and professionally.

Remember, an early childhood education professional does not need to prove child abuse or neglect beyond a reasonable doubt before reporting. All he/she needs is to have a reasonable ground for suspecting the presence of abuse or neglect. It is CPS' role to conduct a thorough investigation to determine whether child abuse and/or neglect exists.

Talking with the Child

When children's verbal skills are advanced enough for them to participate in conversations, they may be able to answer questions about their injuries or other signs of maltreatment. The caregiver should keep in mind that the child may be hurt, in pain, fearful, or apprehensive. Every effort must be made to keep the child as comfortable as possible during the discussion.

The primary purpose for the discussion is to gather enough information from the child to make an informed report to the CPS agency. Once the essential information has been gathered, the caregiver should conclude the conversation. *When the early childhood education professional is talking with the child, he/she is not conducting an interrogation and is not trying to prove that abuse or neglect has occurred.*

The person who talks with the child should be someone the child trusts and respects, such as a caregiver, family child care provider, or teacher. The conversation should be conducted in a quiet, private, nonthreatening place that is familiar to the child. In nice weather, a pleasant spot outdoors might be appropriate.

For example, a teacher might see the child alone in the book corner reading a book. She could sit with the child, strike up a conversation, and try, in the course of the conversation, to steer the discussion toward his/her injuries. She might say, "I noticed that new bruise on your arm this morning. It must have hurt when you got it. Would you like to talk about it?" The teacher should then wait to see if the child wants to talk about the bruise or change the subject to something else. If the child changes the subject, the teacher should go along with the change in conversation and not push the child to talk about the injury.

When children are willing to discuss their injuries, they should be reassured that they have done nothing wrong. Maltreated children often feel, or are told, that they are to blame for their own abuse or neglect and for bringing trouble to the family. Therefore, it is important to reassure children that they are not at fault. The caregiving professional talking with the child must be very careful not to show any verbal or nonverbal signs of shock or anger when the child is talking about what happened to cause the injury.

It is important for caregivers of young children to use terms and language the child can understand. If a child uses a term that is not familiar (such as a word for a body part), the caregiving professional may ask for clarification or ask the child to point to the body part he/she means. Caregivers of young children should not make fun of or correct the child's words; it is better to use the same words to put the child at ease and to avoid confusion. If the child is showing sexual knowledge that is inappropriate for that age group, the caregiver could ask in a quiet, low-key tone, "Where did you learn about. . . ?"

Children should not be pressed for answers or details that they may be unable or unwilling to give. For example, it would be inappropriate to ask, "Did you get that bruise when someone hit you?" If the child changes what he/she has already said, the caregiver should just listen and note the change. The caregiving professional should not ask "why" questions. *Caregivers of young children can actually do the child more harm by probing for answers or supplying the child with terms or information.* Several major child sexual abuse cases have been dismissed in court because it was felt that the initial interviewers biased the children.

If children want to show their injuries, the caregiver should allow them to do so. But if a child is unwilling to show an injury, the caregiver should not insist, and, of course, no child should be pressed to remove clothing.

Caregivers must be sensitive to the safety of the child following the disclosure; the child might be subject to further abuse if he/she goes home and mentions talking with someone at the program. If a caregiver of young children feels that the child is in danger, CPS should be contacted immediately. Support from CPS may provide protection for the child. A CPS caseworker may need to interview the child at the program. If so, the program should provide a private place for the interview, and a caregiver, teacher, or provider whom the child trusts should be present throughout the interview. If it is necessary for the CPS caseworker to remove the child from the program for a medical examination, caregivers should request a written release from the CPS caseworker.

Talking with the Parent(s)

There are several points at which caregivers of young children might want to communicate with a parent about suspected child abuse and neglect. These points range from a teacher observing some possible signs of child maltreatment and wanting to get to know the family better to letting parents know that someone at the program has filed a report of suspected child abuse and neglect.

The caregiver should confer with supervisors or colleagues to identify the most appropriate person to meet with the parents. In some cases, this will be the person who provides direct care for the child: the caregiver or teacher. In other cases, the program director, social worker, education coordinator, or mental health specialist will be preferred. Sometimes a team approach is best, with the person who works closest with the child accompanied by an administrator or support staff. If a family child care provider is part of a network, he/she may want to have a colleague or supervisor present.

It is never appropriate for a caregiving professional to try to "prove" a case of maltreatment by accusing parents or demanding explanations for a child's injuries or behavior. At the same time, if a teacher fears that the discussion of possible maltreatment might make the child even more vulnerable to abuse, it is essential to talk with CPS prior to scheduling or conducting the meeting with the parents.

Parents may be apprehensive or angry at the prospect of talking with the program staff about an injured or neglected child. The caregiver may know the parents well from daily interactions with them and because their child has been in the program for a long time. The caregiving professional should hold the meeting in a private place and try to make the parents as comfortable as possible. At the beginning of the conversation, the caregiver must clearly explain the reasons why the meeting was called. If program staff have taken any action or will in the near future (filing a report of suspected child maltreatment, for example), the legal authority for the action should be explained. Parents may not realize that early childhood education professionals are mandated to report suspicions of child abuse and neglect.

In talking with the parents, the early childhood education professional should respond in a professional, direct, and honest manner. If parents offer explanations, staff members may demonstrate empathy. Staff should never display anger, repugnance, or shock. Keeping in mind that situations that appear to be maltreatment might turn out to be something else, caregivers should avoid placing blame or making judgments or accusations

It is important to assure parents that the discussion is confidential; however, make it clear whether some of what is discussed must be revealed to a third party (for example, the CPS agency). Caregivers of young children should avoid prying into matters extraneous to the subject at hand and *never betray the child's confidence to the parents* (for example, it is inappropriate to say, "Your child said . . .").

Parents have a right to know that a report has been made. They need to hear that the program will continue to support them through this difficult time. The caregiving professionals should let parents know that program staff care about them and their child and will continue to provide the same high-quality care as in the past. It is important not to alienate the family. Family members will be more open to assistance if they know that staff members are willing to help.

When program staff do not tell the parents, they often feel betrayed or that someone has "gone behind their back." In these instances, the parents are not likely to trust the program staff and may remove their child from the program. Also, although CPS is mandated *not* to reveal the name of the referral source, the parents nearly always know where the report has come from, and attempts at concealment only anger them further.

When working with young children and their families, it is not easy to remain objective about the signs of abuse and neglect. Knowledge of the children and their families cannot help but influence how a caregiver interprets a child's physical injury or behavior. An educator may ignore signs and think that this child's mother or father, or his/her colleague, couldn't possibly be abusive or neglectful. The response of the caregiving professional will also be influenced by cultural values, personal values, and training. The early childhood educator must remember that abuse and neglect occur in all kinds of families. Parents who maltreat their children come from every race, income level, gender, and culture.

Despite this warning that personal biases and feelings will influence the ability to recognize child abuse and neglect, caregivers of young children should remember that sometimes it is extremely difficult to recognize abuse and neglect. It is crucial to remember that there are large gray areas that might be considered abuse or neglect by some people and not others. Families may frequently pass in and out of this gray area, and this movement influences the way the family is labeled and treated.

The caregiver's responsibilities regarding child abuse and neglect include recognition followed by reporting. The staff member is not responsible for investigating an occurrence of suspected abuse or neglect. Once the signs lead to a suspicion of child abuse or neglect, a report must be filed.

ENDNOTES

1. The first three examples in this section are reprinted from California Child Care Resource and Referral Network, *Making a Difference* (San Francisco: California Child Care Resource and Referral Network, 1986).

2. Information in this section was adapted from U.S. Department of Health and Human Services, *A Guide for Education Coordinators in Head Start* (Washington, DC: Head Start Bureau, 1986), 59–63.

■ Ask Yourself

Identifying Issues for Advocacy

1. Does society have the right to interfere in a family's private life? In domestic violence? Why or why not? How are these positions reflected or not reflected in "The Rights of the Child" (see Appendix 11)?

2. How might certain values in U.S. society (e.g., beliefs in self-reliance, individual control, or the rights of those in authority positions to use force, if necessary, to maintain authority) contribute to potential situations of child abuse?

3. What consideration should be given to family contexts and diverse cultural practices of child rearing when identifying suspected instances of child abuse or neglect?

4. What happens to someone in your state when he or she reports a suspected case of child abuse or child neglect? Can a reporter be held liable for an unfounded report? Should a reporter be able to remain anonymous? Why or why not?

5. Suppose the interaction reported in the vignette at the beginning of this chapter occurred at a school-sponsored family picnic. In small groups, discuss the following issues:

   a. Is there enough evidence here to file a report of suspected child abuse? Why or why not?

   b. Should the school get involved? Why or why not?

   In reaching a decision, use the indicators of child abuse included in Appendix 12 as well as your state's legal definition of child abuse and your state's reporting guidelines.

6. If a child in your early childhood program reported observing repeated spousal abuse at home, would you consider this an instance of suspected child neglect? Why or why not (see Dowling, 1998; National Clearinghouse on Child Abuse and Neglect, 1998d)?

7. Should states release the names of people with unsubstantiated reports of child abuse or neglect to child-care directors or employers? If you were a child-care director, would you interview someone from another part of the state with an unsubstantiated

report of child abuse for a position as an early childhood teacher or caregiver? Why or why not?

8. What staff behaviors in a preschool setting would you consider to be forms of physical, sexual, or emotional maltreatment? Would you include overemphasis on academic skills, overreliance on packaged materials, belittling particular children, or physical coercion (Paulson, 1983; Polakow, 1993)? Why or why not?

9. As an early childhood teacher, what precautionary measures should you take and how would you respond to allegations of sex abuse (Mikkelsen, 1997)? Should children in an early childhood program be hugged or cuddled by early childhood teachers and caregivers? Why or why not?

10. Should pregnant women who abuse alcohol or drugs be charged with child abuse or neglect? Or, as in Wisconsin, should pregnant mothers who consume alcohol or cocaine be detained and pushed to the front of the line for treatment but not judged or convicted for any crime? Support your answer.

11. If a woman has killed her baby, allegedly as a result of postpartum depression, should she be allowed to reunite with her two other young children? Why or why not? What, if any, limits are there to the Family Reunification Act?

12. In fall 1997, the national media drew public attention to the murder trial of *au pair* Louise Woodward, who was accused of causing a child's death by shaking. What are the indicators of Shaken Baby Syndrome (Palmer, 1997)? Why was this case controversial (see www.child. cornell.edu)? What advocacy efforts are being taken to prevent Shaken Baby Syndome?

13. Should early childhood programs provide working parents with video access at a website so they can observe their child's activities during the day? Might hackers and child predators be able to access the site?

14. Should covert videotape surveillance be used in settings where caregivers or parents are suspected of being abusive toward children ("Using Video," 1997)? Why or why not?

15. How effective are "good touch–bad touch" programs for young children (Jordan, 1993)?

16. According to an estimate from the Centers for Disease Control and Prevention, nearly 1.2 million latchkey children have access to loaded and unlocked firearms in their homes (Brady, 1996). Should adults be held responsible and liable for the safe storage (locked/unloaded) of guns? Should guns be "personalized" so they can only be fired by the owner (i.e., by the owner wearing a radio-frequency tag, placed in a ring or wrist band, that transmits a signal recognized by a chip in the gun)? Should gun owners have to sign for specially coded ammunition, which can be identified even after impact (Canada, 1995)? Why or why not?

■ Advocacy and Leadership Strategies

1. Request an interview with a child protective services caseworker. Explain to the individual that you wish to learn more about the prevention, identification, and treatment of child abuse and neglect. Based on information gathered from readings, class presentations, and your own personal experiences, compose at least six interview questions to ask this person. (Consider issues such as who is reporting, confidentiality or anonymity of reporting, types of abuse and neglect reported, the investigation process, investigation of the report in the home or at school, responses of alleged victim and perpetrator and of other family members, the percentage of unfounded cases, removal of the child from the home, child custody battles, delivery and time frame of services, and caseload.) Take notes during the interview in order to obtain a record of the interviewee's responses. After the interview, write a synopsis of the interview, including the interview questions asked, the interviewee's responses, and your interpretation based on chapter readings and other information gathered from class presentations. Cite references used. Share and discuss your report with your classmates.

2. Interview a school nurse, guidance counselor, or center director about the incidence of child abuse and neglect cases among the children. In framing your interview questions, consider readings, Appendix 12, class presentations, and your own experiences related to issues such as identification, reporting procedures, school/home relations, linkages with social and public health agencies, and pupil classroom adjustments. (Also remember to respect the interviewee's need to maintain confidentiality.) Take notes during the interview. After the interview, write a synopsis of the interview, as described in the previous strategy activity.

3. Investigate what is happening with the implementation of Megan's Law in your state (see Breig, 1996; Tong, 1998a; U.S. House of Representatives, Committee on the Judiciary, 1996).

4. Develop a packet for families aimed at preventing child abuse (see National Committee to Prevent Child Abuse, 1998c). Make copies of the packet available in a laundromat, a pediatrician's office, or a well-baby clinic.

5. Develop a peace project for an early childhood classroom (Levin, 1994; Schmidt, Brunt, & Solotoff, 1993).

6. Interview several parents about the reactions of young children to violence shown on the television news (see Chapter 3 of this book and Thomas-Lester, 1998).

7. Develop and distribute a brochure for parents about gun safety and where trigger locks are available in your community.

8. Organize a Stop the Violence campaign in your community (Miller, 1996). With a friend, other teacher, or administrator, identify

people or organizations who might share your commitment to violence reduction. Contact and invite them to a meeting to suggest collaborating on campaign activities. Plan for press releases and perhaps public displays of children's artwork, distribution of fliers and grocery bag stuffers, or an event sponsored by one or more of the businesses in your community. (See Appendices 2 and 5 for help in this area.) Some possible groups to consider are:

a. Local doctors or the State Medical Association
b. Health insurance organizations
c. Local television broadcasters or local newspaper writers
d. Police department
e. Women's shelters
f. Local theater groups
g. Department of human services
h. Mental health centers
i. Community education or extension services
j. League of Women Voters
k. Senior centers
l. Crime prevention councils or neighborhood watch groups
m. School districts
n. After-school programs
o. Lions, Rotary, Kiwanis, Junior League, and other service organizations
p. Early childhood professional organizations
q. Local businesses and business groups
r. Local religious groups
s. Community action groups

9. Develop a mini-grant proposal to fund a workshop, local information distribution, or community-based activities to raise public awareness of violence. For further details and an application form, write to CEASE, Mini-grants, 55 Frost St., Cambridge, MA 02140.

10. Organize a book club of four to five people (fellow students, worksite colleagues, or community members) and read and discuss one of the following books:

Gilligan, J. (1997). Violence: Reflections on a national epidemic. New York: Vintage Press.

Pelzer, D. J. (1995). A child called "it": One child's courage to survive. Deerfield, FL: Health Communications.

Richards, K. N. (1998). Tender mercies: Inside the world of a child abuse investigator. Washington, DC: Child Welfare League of America.

11. At your field-study site, interview the program director about what precautions are taken to minimize the risk of a child in the program being maltreated. Include questions related to the following categories:

a. Staff selection strategies used to screen out individuals who might represent a risk to children's safety and well-being

> **b.** Steps taken to identify and alleviate sources of staff stress in the work environment
>
> **c.** Types of staff training offered that might reduce the risk of child maltreatment
>
> **d.** Operational policies and practices adopted to minimize the risk of child maltreatment.

■ References and Suggested Readings

Action Alliance for Children. (1997, July–August). Fact sheet: Domestic violence and young children. *Children's Advocate* [Online], 2 pages. Available: www.4children.org/news/7-97fact.htm

American Academy of Pediatrics. (1995). Raising children to resist violence (brochure). [Online]. Available: www.aap.org/family/parents/resist.htm

Bergsgaard, M. (1997). Gender issues in the implementation and evaluation of a violence-prevention curriculum. *Canadian Journal of Education, 22* (1), 33–45.

Brady, S. (1996, November 29). Perspective on handguns: A way to cut the deadly toll. *Los Angeles Times*, p. 7B.

Breig, J. (1996). Labeling sex offenders won't protect children. *U.S. Catholic, 61* (11), 13–14.

Canada, G. (1995). The best way we know how. *Young Children, 51* (1), 26–29.

CEASE FIRE. (1997, October 6). Frank Shelly hid his 9mm Glock so well, it took his daughter 4 years to find it. *New Yorker*, p. 75.

Dowling, C. G. (1998, July/August). Violence lessons. [Online]. Available: www.motherjones.com/mother_jones/JA98/dowling.html

Edleson J. L. (1997). Children's witnessing of adult domestic violence. [Online]. Available: www.mincava.umn.edu/papers/witness.htm

Gilligan, J. (1997). *Violence: Reflections on a national epidemic.* New York: Vintage Press.

Jordan, N. H. (1993). Sexual abuse prevention programs in early childhood education: A caveat. *Young Children, 48* (6), 76–79.

Kamii, C., Clark, F. B., & Dominick, A. (1995). Are violence-prevention curricula the answer? *Dimensions of Early Childhood, 23* (3), 10–13.

Levin, D. E. (1994). Building a peaceable classroom: Helping young children feel safe in violent times. *Childhood Education, 70,* 267–270.

Mikkelsen, E. J. (1997). Responding to allegations of sexual abuse in child care and early childhood education programs. *Young Children, 50* (3), 47–51.

Miller, S. (1996). *Stop the violence.* Workshop presented at the Conference of the Association for Childhood Education International, Minneapolis, MN.

Minnesota Center Against Violence and Abuse. (1998). A gallery of art from child witnesses of violence. [Online]. Available: www.mincava.umn.edu/kart.asp

National Association for the Education of Young Children. (1997). NAEYC position statement on the prevention of child abuse in early childhood programs and the responsibilities of early childhood professionals to prevent child abuse. *Young Children, 52* (3), 42–46.

National Crime Prevention Council. (1994). *Working together to stop the violence: A blueprint for safer communities.* Washington, DC: Author. (ERIC Document Reproduction Service No. ED 402 246)

National Clearinghouse on Child Abuse and Neglect. (1998a). In fact . . . Answers to frequently asked questions on child abuse and neglect. [Online]. Available: www.calib.com/nccanch/pubs/infact.htm

National Clearinghouse on Child Abuse and Neglect. (1998b). Lessons learned: Conclusions. [Online]. Available: www.calib.com/nccanch/pubs/lessons/concls.htm

National Clearinghouse on Child Abuse and Neglect. (1998c). Lessons learned: Introduction. [Online]. Available: www.calib.com/nccanch/pubs/lessons/intro.htm

National Clearinghouse on Child Abuse and Neglect. (1998d). What is child maltreatment? [Online]. Available: www.calib.com/nccanch/pubs/whatis.htm

National Committee to Prevent Child Abuse. (1996a). An approach to preventing child abuse. [Online]. Available: www.childabuse.org/fs15.html

National Committee to Prevent Child Abuse. (1996b). Child sexual abuse. [Online]. Available: www.childabuse.org/fs19.html

National Committee to Prevent Child Abuse. (1996c). Prevention of child abuse and neglect fatalities. [Online]. Available: www.childabuse.org/fs9.html

National Committee to Prevent Child Abuse. (1996d). The relationship between domestic violence and child abuse. [Online]. Available: www.childabuse.org/fs20.html

National Committee to Prevent Child Abuse. (1996e). The relationship between parental alcohol and other drug problems and child maltreatment. [Online]. Available: www.childabuse.org/fs14.html

National Committee to Prevent Child Abuse. (1997). Selected child abuse information and resources directory. [Online]. Available: www.childabuse.org/resource.html

National Committee to Prevent Child Abuse. (1998a). Child abuse and neglect statistics. [Online]. Available: www.childabuse.org/facts97.html

National Committee to Prevent Child Abuse. (1998b). Prevention advocacy. [Online]. Available: www.childabuse.org/13ar97.html

National Committee to Prevent Child Abuse. (1998c). Prevention packet info. [Online]. Available: www.childabuse.org/capm1.html (also capm2, 3, and 4)

Palmer, S. (1997). Shaken baby syndrome. [Online]. Available: www.TheArc.org/faqs/Shaken.html

Paulson, J. S. (1983). Covert and overt forms of maltreatment in the preschools. *Child Abuse and Neglect: The International Journal, 7*, 45–54.

Pelzer, D. J. (1995). *A child called "it": One child's courage to survive.* Deerfield, FL: Health Communications.

Polakow, V. (1993). *Lives on the edge.* Chicago: University of Chicago Press.

Richards, K. N. (1998). *Tender mercies: Inside the world of a child abuse investigator.* Washington, DC: Child Welfare League of America.

Schmidt, F., Brunt, E., & Solotoff, T. (1993). *Peacemaking skills for little kids.* Miami: Peace Education Foundation. (ERIC Document Reproduction Service Number ED 363 847)

Straus, M. A., & Donnelly, D. A. (1994). *Beating the devil out of them: Corporal punishment in American families.* San Francisco: Jossey-Bass.

Thomas-Lester, A. (1998, March 31). Helping children cope with violence: Preschoolers face very specific fears. *The Washington Post,* p. 6D.

Tong, D. (1998a). Child protection laws: Are they really protecting our children? [Online]. Available: www.abuse-excuse.com/laws.htm

Tong, D. (1998b). False accusation charges: How to survive when you have been wrongly accused. [Online]. Available: www.abuse-excuse.com/tips.htm

U.S. House of Representatives, Committee on the Judiciary. (1996). *Megan's Law: Report together with additional views (to accompany H. R. 2137)* (Report to the House of Representatives, 104th Congress, 2nd session, No. Y 1.1/8: 104–555). Washington, DC: U.S. Government Printing Office.

Using video to stop child abuse. (1997, October 28). *USA Today,* pp. 1D, 4D.

■ *Chapter 6*

■ **Diversity and Equity**

Thanksgiving: Time for a Unit on Native Americans?[*]

Mrs. Jones teaches kindergarten in a middle-sized city in the Northeast. Through the grapevine, she learns that there are three children in her class who are said to be Native Americans:

> Ramona and her family have just moved to the city from a southwestern reservation, where she attended a government-sponsored Head Start program for Native American children. She is bilingual in her native language and English.

> Mary has heard that she has a Native American great-grandmother on her father's side of the family. The family does not know where this great-grandmother was born and does not know any Native American people who might help them trace their ancestry.

> Tom's parents have lived in the city for 15 years, but the family keeps in touch with relatives living in a Native American community 100 miles away. Tom's mother belongs to the city's Native American Cultural Center and occasionally attends dinners and social dances there, but Tom's father hasn't attended for some years; the dinners conflict with his bowling league. Tom doesn't speak a Native American language.

[*]Adapted from Z. Chevalier and S. Roark-Calnek. (1982, November). Meeting the challenge of cultural pluralism. Workshop presented at the National Conference of the National Association for the Education of Young Children, Washington, DC.

Mrs. Jones decides to teach a unit on traditional Native American culture "because that's part of our history, our past." This is the only unit using ethnic or cultural content that she will teach this year; she wants to "make the Native American children feel special." The unit will be taught at Thanksgiving time. She sets up a Plains-style tipi in her room and plans a series of learning activities on a buffalo-hunting theme.

On the day that she introduces the unit, Mrs. Jones announces to her class, "We have three real Native Americans in this room and they're going to help us learn about themselves." She encourages other children to direct questions to Tom, Mary, and Ramona.

As Mrs. Jones begins her lesson, Ramona goes to the bathroom and hangs around the sink, washing her hands. She pulls out paper towels one by one and carefully drops them in the wastebasket. When Mrs. Jones calls on her to answer a question, she looks away, answers "dunno," and sits down in the back of the story circle, behind another child.

Mary has moved up to sit next to Mrs. Jones, who is reading a story and showing its illustrations to the children. She reaches over and pats Mrs. Jones on the leg, smiling at her. When Mrs. Jones addresses questions to Mary, she answers readily at first but soon begins to fidget. Mrs. Jones asks her why the Native American boy in the story is wearing a feather in his hair, and Mary hesitates before stammering out an answer. She's interrupted by several other children: "Dummy! You made that up. When I saw that on TV . . . ." Mary bursts into tears.

Ramona, Mary, and Tom are given notes to take home to their parents and told, "I'm asking your mommies and daddies to come in and tell us about how Native Americans live. Maybe they can bring in something your grandmas and grandpas used a long time ago."

Tom slouches down when he hears this and mumbles, "I bet I'm going to lose that note!" He remains stonily silent during the course of the day. At the end of the day, he rips the note from his jacket and stuffs it down behind a cushion. Mrs. Jones is distressed.

Questions

1. Using the evidence in the vignette, why do you think Ramona, Mary, and Tom are reacting in these ways?

2. What is Mrs. Jones trying to accomplish? What should she know about these children? What suggestions would you make to help her learn about the children or how to accomplish her goals?

■ Preview

Different views on diversity and equity often stem from values attributed to a unified, "melting-pot" culture versus a pluralistic, "salad" culture. Those who espouse the first position believe that society's needs will best be served when everyone works toward reaching consensus on norms and values. Those who favor the latter view believe that acknowledging differences in ethnic and cultural traditions as well as diverse ways of communicating contribute to the freshness, richness, and openness of a society. Which of these positions best meets the needs of all children and their families? Should we assume that all people wish to retain their distinctive cultural identities? Do some wish to blend in more readily with the dominant culture? Or is it possible or even beneficial to have "the best of both worlds"?

In the first two selections of this chapter, Louise Derman-Sparks and Debbie Reese examine the detrimental effects of societal bias on young children and suggest ways that teachers can incorporate multicultural and antibias practices into their programs. Another diversity and equity issue is: In what language(s) should children with a dominant language other than English be educated? The debate centers on the effectiveness of bilingual education programs. In this chapter, Laurel Shaper Walters takes a closer look at the history of this issue in the United States and reviews related research literature. When teachers attempt to address the diverse needs of all children in their classrooms, they often must find ways to adapt their roles and to expand their relationships with other profession-als. The inclusion of children with disabilities is one example of the diversity and equity issues that teachers are confronting today. In the last selection, Joan Lieber, Paula J. Beckman, Marci J. Hanson, Susan Janko, Jules M. Marquart, Eva Horn, and Samuel L. Odom present research findings describing how some teachers are changing their roles and relationships in inclusive programs for young children.

Empowering Children to Create a Caring Culture in a World of Differences

Louise Derman-Sparks

■ ■ ■

Children's Development of Identity and Attitudes

Take a moment to listen to the voices of children. Members of the Anti-Bias Curriculum Task Force developed the anti-bias approach after a year spent collecting and analyzing children's thinking and trying out activities. They collected the following anecdotes:

- Steven is busy being a whale on the climbing structure in the 2-year-old yard. Susie tries to join him. "Girls can't do that!" he shouts.
- Robby, 3 years old, refuses to hold the hand of a dark-skinned classmate. At home, he insists, after bathing, that his black hair is now "white because it is clean."
- "You aren't really an Indian," 4-year-old Rebecca tells one of her child care teachers. "Where are your feathers?"
- "Malcolm can't play with us. He's a baby," Linda tells their teacher. Malcolm, another 4-year-old, uses a wheelchair.

Those voices reflect the impact of societal bias on children. Now, listen to voices of children in programs that practice anti-bias curriculum:

- Maria, 4 years old, sees a stereotypical "Indian warrior" figure in the toy store. "That toy hurts Indian people's feelings," she tells her grandmother.
- Rebecca's kindergarten teacher asks the children to draw a picture of what they would like to be when they grow up. Rebecca draws herself as a surgeon—in a pink ball gown and tiara.
- After hearing the story of Rosa Parks and the Montgomery bus boycott, 5-year-old Tiffany, whose skin is light brown, ponders whether she would have had to sit in the back of the bus. Finally, she firmly asserts, "I'm Black and, anyway, all this is stupid. I would just get off and tell them to keep their old bus."
- In the school playground, 5-year-old Casey and another white friend, Tommy, are playing. Casey calls two other boys to join them. "You can't play with them. They're Chinese eyes," Tommy says to him. Casey replies, "That's not right. All kinds of kids play together. I know. My teacher tells me civil rights stories."

Children do not come to preschool, child care centers or elementary school as "blank slates" on the topic of diversity. Facing and understanding what underlies their thoughts and feelings are key to empowering children to resist bias. The following is a brief summary of research about how children develop racial identity and attitudes:

- As early as 6 months, infants notice skin color differences. (Katz, 1993)
- By 2 years of age, children not only notice, they also ask questions about differences and similarities among people. They soon begin forming their own hypotheses to explain the diversity they are seeing and hearing. When my daughter was 3, she commented one day, "I am think-

ing about skin color. How do we get it?" I launched into an explanation about melanin, which was clearly above her level of understanding. Finally, I asked her, "How do you think we get skin color?" "Magic markers!" she replied. (Derman-Sparks, Tanaka Higa & Sparks, 1980)

At my family's 1991 Passover Seder (the Seder honors the ancient Jewish Exodus from slavery in Egypt), my niece announced, "I'm half Jewish." "Uh huh," I replied (one parent is Jewish). She continued, "The Jewish people went through the water and they didn't get wet. They got to the other side. The people who weren't Jewish got drowned."

"That is what the Passover story tells us, that the Egyptian soldiers drowned," I affirmed, but her expression remained quizzical. So, I decided to ask her, "What do you think happened to the people who were half Jewish?"

"They got to the other side, too," she replied, paused and then concluded, "but they got a little bit wet." Afterward, a cousin wondered, "How did you ever think of that question?" (the Passover story does not mention people being "half Jewish").

I don't know if my question was "right" in any absolute sense, but trying to follow my niece's line of thinking, I sensed that the issue was important to her. She seemed emotionally satisfied with her solution. Moreover, it was a cognitively clever one—she got to the other side safely AND she acknowledged her identity as she understood it.

- How we answer children's questions and respond to their ideas is crucial to their level of comfort when learning about diversity. Statements such as, "It's not polite to ask" "I'll tell you later" or "It doesn't matter," do not help children form positive ideas about themselves or pro-diversity dispositions toward others. (Derman-Sparks & ABC Task Force, 1989)
- Between 2 1/2 to 3 1/2 years of age, children also become aware of and begin to absorb socially prevailing negative stereotypes, feelings and ideas about people, including themselves. All children are exposed to these attitudes in one form or another, usually through a combination of sources (parents, extended family, neighbors, teachers, friends, TV, children's books, movies). (Derman-Sparks & ABC Task Force, 1989)
- Throughout the early childhood period, children continue to construct and elaborate on their ideas about their own and others' identities and their feelings about human differences. In the primary years, children's development goes beyond the

individual to include a group identity. Some researchers believe that after age 9, racial attitudes tend to stay constant unless the child experiences a life-changing event. (Aboud, 1988)

- The research literature also points to the great damage racism, sexism and classism have on *all* children's development. Young children are harmed by a psychologically toxic environment. How they are harmed depends on how they are affected by the various "isms"— whether they receive messages of superiority or inferiority. (Clark, 1955; Dennis, 1981)

For children of color, the wounds can be overt. Often, however, they are quite subtle. Chester Pierce calls these subtle forms of racism "micro-contaminants" (Pierce, 1980). Kenyon Chan notes that these micro-contaminants "are carried by children like grains of sand, added one by one, eventually weighing children down beyond their capacity to carry the sand and to grow emotionally and intellectually to their fullest" (Chan, 1993).

Racism attacks young children's growing sense of group, as well as individual, identity. Thus, the children are even less able to resist racism's harm. Chan cites an example: A Chinese American girl enrolled in a suburban kindergarten in Los Angeles. Her European American teacher claimed that her name was too difficult to pronounce and promptly renamed her "Mary," calling it an "American" name. This young child is forced to wonder what is wrong with her name and what is wrong with her parents for giving her such a "bad" name. And her doubts originated with the very person who is responsible for supporting and cultivating her development.

Moreover, as Lily Wong-Fillmore's research documents, young children who come from homes where a language other than English is spoken pay a terrible price if they experience a too-early loss of continued development in their home language. The price includes the gradual impoverishment of communication between the child and parents (and other family members) and the potentially serious weakening of the "family's continued role in the socialization of its children" (Wong-Fillmore, 1991).

White, English-speaking children also experience psychological damage. Although this issue has been less studied, the research we do have suggests some disturbing problems:

- First, racism teaches white children moral double standards for treating people of racial/ethnic groups other than their own. This leads to the possibility of general ethical erosion (Clark, 1955) and to a form of hypocrisy that results in primary school-age children saying words that sound like acceptance of diversity, while acting in ways that demonstrate the opposite (Miel, 1976).

- Second, children may be constructing identity on a false sense of superiority based on skin color. White children's self-esteem will be rather vulnerable if/when they come to realize that skin color does not determine a person's value.

- Third, racism results in white children developing fears about people different from themselves. They do not gain the life skills they need for effectively interacting with the increasing range of human diversity in society and the world.

Racial stereotyping is not the only danger. Children's absorption of gender stereotypes limits their development. As young as 3 and 4, children begin to self-limit their choices of learning experiences because of the gender norms they are already absorbing. One of the negative consequences of this process is a pattern of uneven cognitive development, or "practice deficits," related to the types of activities boys and girls choose (Serbin, 1980, p. 60). Girls tend to function below potential in math and boys in expression of their feelings.

Furthermore, research on children's development of ideas and feelings about disabilities indicates that by 2 and 3, they notice, are curious about and sometimes fear people with a disability and their equipment (Froschl, Colon, Rubin & Sprung, 1984; Sapon-Shevin, 1983). Children's fears appear to come from developmental misconceptions that they might "catch" the disability, as well as from adults' indirect and direct communication of discomfort. Moreover, the impact of stereotypes and biases about people with disabilities affects primary age children's treatment of any child who does not fit the physical "norms" of attractiveness, weight and height.

Research also suggests that young children who learn about people with disabilities through a variety of concrete activities are much more likely to see the whole person, rather than just focusing on the person's disability.

What Empowering Children to Create a Caring Culture Requires of Us

Clarity about Goals

The following goals are for *all* children. The specific issues and tasks necessary for working toward these goals will vary for children, depending on their backgrounds, ages and life experiences.

- *Nurture each child's construction of a knowledgeable, confident self-concept and group identity.* To achieve this goal, we must create education conditions in which all children are able to like who they are without needing to feel superior to anyone else. Children must also be able to develop biculturally where that is appropriate.
- *Promote each child's comfortable, empathic interaction with people from diverse backgrounds.* This goal requires educators to guide children's development of the cognitive awareness, emotional disposition and behavioral skills needed to respectfully and effectively learn about differences, comfortably negotiate and adapt to differences, and cognitively understand and emotionally accept the common humanity that all people share.
- *Foster each child's critical thinking about bias.* Children need to develop the cognitive skills to identify "unfair" and "untrue" images (stereotypes), comments (teasing, name-calling) and behaviors (discrimination) directed at one's own or others' identities. They also need the emotional empathy to know that bias hurts.
- *Cultivate each child's ability to stand up for her/himself and for others in the face of bias.* This "activism" goal requires educators to help every child learn and practice a variety of ways to act: a) when another child acts in a biased manner toward her/him, b) when a child acts in a biased manner toward another child, c) when an adult acts in a biased manner. Goal 4 builds on goal 3 as critical thinking and empathy are necessary components of acting for oneself or others in the face of bias.

These four goals interact with and build on each other. We cannot accomplish any one goal without the other three. *Their combined intent is to empower children to resist the negative impact of racism and other "isms" on their development and to grow into adults who will want and be able to work with others to eliminate all forms of oppression.* In other words, the underlying intent is not to end racism (and other "isms") in one generation by changing children's attitudes and behaviors, but rather to promote critical thinkers and activists who can work for social change and participate in creating a caring culture in a world of differences.

Preparing Ourselves

Effective anti-bias education requires every teacher to look inward and commit to a lifelong journey of understanding her/his own cultural beliefs, while changing the prejudices and behaviors that interfere with the nurturing of all children. Teachers need to know:

- how to see their own culture in relationship to society's history and current power realities
- how to effectively adapt their teaching style and curriculum content to their children's needs
- how to engage in cultural conflict resolution with people from cultural backgrounds other than their own
- how to be critical thinkers about bias in their practice
- how to be activists—engaging people in dialogue about bias, intervening, working with others to create change.

Achieving these goals takes commitment and time, and is a developmental process for adults as well as for children. One must be emotionally as well as cognitively involved and ready to face periods of disequilibrium and then reconstruction and transformation.

Implementation Principles and Strategies

To create a caring culture in which children can be empowered, teachers must be "reflective practitioners" who can think critically about their own teaching practice and adapt curriculum goals and general strategies to the needs of their children.

Critical Thinking

Be aware of "tourist multicultural curriculum" and find ways to eliminate tourism from your program. Tourist multicultural curriculum is the most commonly practiced approach in early childhood education and elementary school today. The majority of commercial curriculum materials currently available on the market and many published curriculum guides reflect a tourist version of multicultural education. Unfortunately, tourist multicultural curriculum is a simplistic, inadequate version of multicultural education.

In a classroom practicing a tourist approach, the daily "regular" curriculum reflects mainstream European American perspectives, rules of behavior, images, learning and teaching styles. Activities about "other" cultures often exhibit the following problems:

- *Disconnection:* Activities are added on to the curriculum as special times, rather than integrated into all aspects of the daily environment and curriculum.

- *Patronization:* "Other" cultures are treated as "quaint" or "exotic." This form of tourism does not teach children to appreciate what all humans share in common.
- *Trivialization:* Cultural activities that are disconnected from the daily life of the people trivialize the culture. A typical example is multicultural curriculum that focuses on holidays—days that are different from "normal" days. Children do not learn about how people live their lives, how they work, who does what in the family—all of which is the essence of a culture. Other forms of trivialization include: turning cultural practices that have deep, ritual meaning into "arts and crafts" or dance activities, or asking parents to cook special foods without any further lessons about the parents' cultures.
- *Misrepresentation:* Too few images of a group oversimplifies the variety within the group. Use of images and activities based on traditional, past practices of an ethnic group rather than images of contemporary life confuse children. Misusing activities and images that reflect the culture-of-origin of a group to teach about *the life of cultures in the U.S.* conveys misconceptions about people with whom children have little or no face-to-face experience.

In sum, tourist multicultural curriculum does not give children the tools they need to comfortably, empathetically and fairly interact with diversity. Instead, it teaches simplistic generalizations about other people that lead to stereotyping, rather than to understanding of differences. Moreover, tourist curriculum, because it focuses on the unusual and special times of a culture and neglects how people live their daily lives, does not foster children's understanding and empathy for our common humanity. Moving beyond tourist multicultural curriculum is key to our profession's more effective nurturing of diversity.

Incorporate multicultural and anti-bias activities into daily curriculum planning. Diversity and anti-bias topics are integral to the entire curriculum at any education level. One practical brainstorming technique for identifying the numerous topic possibilities is "webbing."

Step one is determining the center of the "web." This can be: 1) an issue raised by the children (e.g., a person who is visually impaired cannot work); 2) any number of traditional preschool "units" (e.g., my body, families, work); 3) High/Scope's (Weikart, 1975) "key experiences" (e.g., classification or seriation); 4) any of the traditional content areas of the primary curriculum (science, math, language arts, physical and health curriculum).

Step two involves brainstorming the many possible anti-bias, multicultural issues that stem from the subject at the web's center. *Step three* involves identifying specific content for a particular classroom based on contextual/developmental analysis. *Step four* involves listing possible activities that are developmentally and culturally appropriate for your particular class.

Cultural Appropriateness: Adult/Child Interactions

Effective teaching about diversity, as in all other areas, is a continuous interaction between adults and children. On the one hand, teachers are responsible for brainstorming, planning and initiating diversity topics, based on their analyses of children's needs and life experiences. On the other hand, careful attention to children's thinking and behavior, and to "teachable moments," leads educators to modify initial plans.

Find ways to engage children in critical thinking and the planning and carrying out of "activism" activities appropriate to their developmental levels, cultural backgrounds and interests. Critical thinking and activism activities should rise out of real life situations that are of interest to children. The purpose of such activities is to provide opportunities for children, 4 years old and up, to build their empathy, skills and confidence and to encourage their sense of responsibility for both themselves and for others. Consequently, activities should reflect *their* ideas and issues, not the

teacher's. The following two examples are appropriate activism activities.

In the first situation, the children's school did not have a "handicapped" parking space in their parking lot. After a parent was unable to attend open school night because of this lack, the teacher told the class of 4- and 5-year-olds what had happened and why. They then visited other places in their neighborhood that had "handicapped" parking and decided to make one in their school lot. After they did so, they then noticed that teachers were inappropriately parking in the "handicapped" spot (their classroom overlooked the parking lot), so they decided to make tickets. The children dictated their messages, which their teacher faithfully took down, and drew pictures to accompany their words. They then ticketed those cars that did not have "handicapped parking" plaques in their windows.

In the second example, a class of 1st- through 3rd-graders visited a homeless shelter and talked to the director to find out what people needed. They started a toy and blanket collection drive, which they promoted using posters and flyers. They visited several classrooms to talk about what they were doing. They also wrote to the Mayor and the City Council to say that homeless people needed more houses and jobs.

Parents and Family Involvement

Find ways to involve parents and other adult family members in all aspects of anti-bias education. Education and

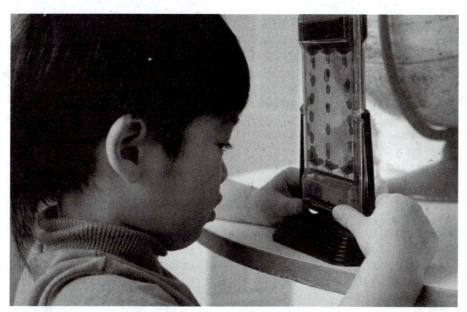

Careful attention to children's thinking and behavior can lead educators toward culturally appropriate interactions and plans.

collaboration with parents is *essential*. Educators have to be creative and ingenious to make this happen. Parents can help plan, implement and evaluate environmental adaptations and curricular activities. They can serve on advisory/planning committees with staff, provide information about their lifestyles and beliefs, participate in classroom activities and serve as community liaisons. Teachers can send home regular short newsletters to share ongoing plans and classroom activities, and elicit parent advice and resources. Parent meetings on child-rearing and education issues should also incorporate relevant diversity topics.

When a family member disagrees with an aspect of the curriculum, it is essential that the teachers listen carefully and sensitively to the issues underlying the disagreement. Objections may include: 1) family's belief that learning about differences will "make the children prejudiced" ("color-blind" view), 2) parent's belief that teaching about stereotyping and such values belongs in the home, not at school, 3) family members' strong prejudices against specific groups.

Staff need to find out all they can about the cultural and other issues that influence the family's concerns, and then work with family members to find ways to meet their needs while also maintaining the goals of anti-bias education. The techniques for working with parents on anti-bias issues are generally the same as those used for other child development and education topics. The difference, however, lies in the teachers' level of comfort about addressing such topics with other adults.

Teacher Education and Professional Development

Teacher training must incorporate liberating pedagogical techniques that:

- engage students on cognitive, emotional and behavioral levels
- use storytelling to enable students to both name and identify the ways that various identity contexts and bias have affected their lives
- use experiential activities that engage learners in discovering the dynamics of cultural differences and the various "isms"
- provide new information and analysis that give deeper meaning to what is learned through storytelling and experiential activities
- create a balance between supporting and challenging students in an environment of safety, not necessarily comfort.

The most useful way to work on our own development is to join with others (staff, or staff and parents) in support groups that meet regularly over a long period of time. By collaborating, sharing resources and providing encouragement, we can work on our self-awareness issues, build and improve our practices, strengthen our courage and determination and maintain the joy and excitement of education.

In sum, children of the 21st century will not be able to function if they are psychologically bound by outdated and narrow assumptions about their neighbors. To thrive, even to survive, in this more complicated world, children need to learn how to function in many different cultural contexts, to recognize and respect different histories and perspectives, and to know how to work together to create a more just world that can take care of all its people, its living creatures, its land.

Let's remember the African American novelist Alice Walker's call to "Keep in mind always the present you are constructing. It should be the future you want" (Walker, 1989, p. 238).

REFERENCES

Aboud, F. (1988). *Children and prejudice.* London: Basil Blackwell.

Chan, K. S. (1993). Sociocultural aspects of anger: Impact on minority children. In M. Furlong & D. Smith (Eds.), *Anger, hostility, and aggression in children and adolescents: Assessment, prevention, and intervention strategies in schools.* Brandon, VT: Clinical Psychology Publishing.

Clark, K. (1955). *Prejudice and your child.* Boston: Bacon.

Dennis, R. (1981). Socialization and racism: The White experience. In B. Bowser & R. Hunt (Eds.), *Impacts of racism on White Americans* (pp. 71–85). Beverly Hills, CA: Sage.

Derman-Sparks, L., Tanaka Higa, C., & Sparks, B. (1980). Children, race, and racism: How race awareness develops. *Bulletin, 11*(3 & 4), 3–9.

Derman-Sparks, L., & ABC Task Force (1989). *Anti-bias curriculum: Tools for empowering young children.* Washington, DC: National Association for the Education of Young Children.

Froschl, M., Colon, L., Rubin, E., & Sprung B. (1984). *Including all of us: An early childhood curriculum about disability.* New York Educational Equity Concepts.

Katz, P. (May, 1993). *Development of racial attitudes in children.* Presentation given to the University of Delaware.

Martin, B., Jr. (1987). *I am freedom's child.* Allen, TX: DLM Teaching Resources.

Miel, A. (1976). *The short-changed children of suburbia.* New York: Institute of Human Relations Press.

Pierce, C. (1980). Social trace contaminants: Subtle indicators of racism in TV. In Withey & Abelis (Eds.), *Tele-*

vision and social behavior. Hillsdale, NJ: Lawrence Erlbaum.

Sapon-Shevin, M. (1983). Teaching young children about differences. *Young Children, 38*(2), 24–32.

Serbin, L. (1980). Play activities and the development of visual-spatial skills. *Equal Play, 1*(4), 5.

Walker, A. (1989). *The temple of my familiar.* New York: Pocket Books.

Weikart, D. (1975). *Young children in action.* Ypsilanti, MI: High Scope Press.

Wong-Fillmore, L. (1991). Language and cultural issues in early education. In S. L. Kagan (Ed.), *The care and education of America's young children: Obstacles and opportunities. The 90th yearbook of the National Society for the Study of Education* (pp. 3–49). Chicago: University of Chicago Press.

■ *Louise Derman-Sparks is director, Anti-Bias Leadership Project, Pacific Oaks College, Pasadena, California.*

Teaching Young Children about Native Americans

Debbie Reese

■ ■ ■

Young children's conceptions of Native Americans often develop out of media portrayals and classroom role playing of the events of the First Thanksgiving. The conception of Native Americans gained from such early exposure is both inaccurate and potentially damaging to others. For example, a visitor to a child care center heard a four-year-old saying, "Indians aren't people. They're all dead." This child had already acquired an inaccurate view of Native Americans, even though her classmates were children of many cultures, including a Native American child.

Derman-Sparks (1989) asserts that by failing to challenge existing biases we allow children to adopt attitudes based on inaccuracies. Her book is a guide for developing curriculum materials that reflect cultural diversity. This digest seeks to build on this effort by focusing on teaching children in early childhood classrooms about Native Americans. Note that this digest, though it uses the term "Native American," recognizes and respects the common use of the term "American Indian" to describe the indigenous people of North America. While it is most accurate to use the tribal name when speaking of a specific tribe, there is no definitive preference for the use of "Native American" or "American Indian" among tribes or in the general literature.

Stereotypes Children See

Most young children are familiar with stereotypes of the Native American. Stereotypes are perpetuated by television, movies, and children's literature when they depict Native Americans negatively, as uncivilized, simple, superstitious, blood-thirsty savages, or positively, as romanticized heroes living in harmony with nature (Grant & Gillespie, 1992). The Disney Company presents both images in its films for children. For example, in the film *Peter Pan*, Princess Tiger Lily's father represents the negative stereotype as he holds Wendy's brothers hostage, while in the film *Pocahontas*, Pocahontas represents the positive stereotype who respects the earth and communicates with the trees and animals.

Many popular children's authors unwittingly perpetuate stereotypes. Richard Scarry's books frequently contain illustrations of animals dressed in buckskin and feathers, while Mercer Mayer's alphabet book includes an alligator dressed as an Indian. Both authors present a dehumanized image, in which anyone or anything can become Native American simply by putting on certain clothes. *Ten Little Rabbits*, although beautifully illustrated, dehumanizes Native Americans by turning them into objects for counting. *Brother Eagle, Sister Sky* (Harris, 1993) contains a speech delivered by Chief Seattle of the Squamish tribe in the northwestern United States. However, Susan Jeffers' illustrations are of the Plains Indians, and include fringed buckskin clothes and teepees, rather than Squamish clothing and homes.

An Accurate Picture of Native Americans in the 1990s

Native Americans make up less than one percent of the total U.S. population but represent half the languages and cultures in the nation. The term "Native American" includes over 500 different groups and reflects great diversity of geographic location, language, socioeconomic conditions, school experience, and retention of traditional spiritual and cultural practices. However, most of the commercially prepared teaching materials available present a gener-

Debbie Reese. (1996). *Teaching young children about Native Americans.* ERIC Digest. Champaign, IL: ERIC Clearinghouse on Elementary and Early Childhood Education. (ERIC Document Reproduction Service No. ED 394 744)

alized image of Native American people with little or no regard for differences that exist from tribe to tribe.

Teaching Suggestions

When teachers engage young children in project work, teachers should choose concrete topics in order to enable children to draw on their own understanding. In teaching about Native Americans, the most relevant, interactive experience would be to have Native American children in the classroom. Such experience makes feasible implementing anti-bias curriculum suggestions. Teachers may want to implement the project approach (Katz & Chard, 1989), as it will allow children to carry on an in-depth investigation of a culture they have direct experience with. In these situations, teachers may prepare themselves for working with Native American families by engaging in what Emberton (1994) calls "cultural homework": reading current information about the families' tribe, tribal history, and traditional recreational and spiritual activities; and learning the correct pronunciation of personal names.

Positive Strategies

A number of positive strategies can be used in classrooms, regardless of whether Native American children are members of the class.

1. *Provide knowledge about contemporary Native Americans* to balance historical information. Teaching about Native Americans exclusively from a historical perspective may perpetuate the idea that they exist only in the past.
2. *Prepare units about specific tribes,* rather than units about "Native Americans." For example, develop a unit about the people of Nambe Pueblo, the Turtle Mountain Chippewa, the Potawotami. Ideally, choose a tribe with a historical or contemporary role in the local community. Such a unit will provide children with culturally specific knowledge (pertaining to a single group) rather than overgeneralized stereotypes.
3. *Locate and use books that show contemporary children of all colors engaged in their usual, daily activities*—playing basketball, riding bicycles—as well as traditional activities. Make the books easily accessible to children throughout the school year. Three excellent titles on the Pueblo Indians of New Mexico are: *Pueblo Storyteller,* by Diane Hoyt-Goldsmith; *Pueblo Boy: Growing Up in Two Worlds,* by Marcia Keegan; and *Children of Clay,* by Rina Swentzell.
4. *Obtain posters that show Native American children in contemporary contexts,* especially when teaching younger elementary children. When selecting historical posters for use with older children, make certain that the posters are culturally authentic and that you know enough about the tribe depicted to share authentic information with your students.
5. *Use "persona" dolls* (dolls with different skin colors) in the dramatic play area of the classroom on a daily basis. Dress them in the same clothing (t-shirts, jeans) children in the United States typically wear and bring out special clothing (for example, manta, shawl, moccasins, turquoise jewelry for Pueblo girls) for dolls only on special days.
6. *Cook ethnic foods* but be careful not to imply that all members of a particular group eat a specific food.
7. *Be specific about which tribes use particular items,* when discussing cultural artifacts (such as clothing or housing) and traditional foods. The Plains tribes use feathered headdresses, for example, but not all other tribes use them.
8. *Critique a Thanksgiving poster depicting the traditional, stereotyped pilgrim and Indian figures,* especially when teaching older elementary school children. Take care to select a picture that most children are familiar with, such as those shown on grocery bags or holiday greeting cards. Critically analyze the poster, noting the many tribes the artist has combined into one general image that fails to provide accurate information about any single tribe (Stutzman, 1993).
9. *At Thanksgiving, shift the focus away from reenacting the "First Thanksgiving."* Instead, focus on items children can be thankful for in their own lives, and on their families' celebrations of Thanksgiving at home.

Besides using these strategies in their classrooms, teachers need to educate themselves. MacCann (1993) notes that stereotyping is not always obvious to people surrounded by mainstream culture. Numerous guidelines have been prepared to aid in the selection of materials that work against stereotypes (for example, see Slapin and Seale [1992]).

Practices to Avoid
Avoid using over-generalized books, curriculum guides, and lesson plans; and teaching kits with a "Native American" theme. Although the goal

of these materials is to teach about other cultures in positive ways, most of the materials group Native Americans too broadly. When seeking out materials, look for those which focus on a single tribe.

Avoid the "tourist curriculum" as described by Derman-Sparks. This kind of curriculum teaches predominantly through celebrations and seasonal holidays, and through traditional food and artifacts. It teaches in isolated units rather than in an integrated way and emphasizes exotic differences, focusing on specific events rather than on daily life.

Avoid presenting sacred activities in trivial ways. In early childhood classrooms, for example, a popular activity involves children in making headbands with feathers, even though feathers are highly religious articles for some tribes. By way of example, consider how a devout Catholic might feel about children making a chalice out of paper cups and glitter.

Avoid introducing the topic of Native Americans on Columbus Day or at Thanksgiving. Doing so perpetuates the idea that Native Americans do not exist in the present.

Conclusion

Much remains to be done to counter stereotypes of Native Americans learned by young children in our society. Teachers must provide accurate instruction not only about history but also about the contemporary lives of Native Americans.

REFERENCES

Derman-Sparks, Louise. (1989). *Anti-Bias Curriculum: Tools for Empowering Young Children.* Washington, DC: National Association for the Education of Young Children. ED 305 135.

Emberton, S. (1994). Do Your Cultural Homework. Editorial. *National Center for Family Literacy Newsletter* 6:(3, Fall): 5–6.

Grant, Agnes, and LaVina Gillespie. (1992). *Using Literature by American Indians and Alaska Natives in Secondary Schools.* ERIC Digest. Charleston, WV: ERIC Clearinghouse on Rural Education and Small Schools. ED 348 201.

Harris, V. (1993). From the Margin to the Center of Curricula: Multicultural Children's Literature. In B. Spodek, and O. N. Saracho (Eds.), *Language and Literacy in Early Childhood Education.* New York: Teachers College Press. ED 370 698.

Katz, L. G., and S. C. Chard. (1989). *Engaging Children's Minds: The Project Approach.* Norwood, NJ: Ablex.

MacCann, D. (1993). Native Americans in Books for the Young. In V. Harris, (Ed.), *Teaching Multicultural Literature in Grades K–8.* Norwood, MA: Christopher Gordon Publishers.

Slapin, Beverly, and Doris Seale. (1992). *Through Indian Eyes: The Native Experience in Books for Children.* Philadelphia: New Society Publishers. ED 344 211.

Stutzman, Esther. (1993). *American Indian Stereotypes: The Truth Behind the Hype.* An Indian Education Curriculum Unit. Coos Bay, OR: Coos County Indian Education Coordination Program. ED 364 396.

■ *Debbie Reese is a Pueblo Indian who studies and works in the field of early childhood education.*

The Bilingual Education Debate

Laurel Shaper Walters

■ ■ ■

This year marks the 30th anniversary of the federal Bilingual Education Act, the original legislation that created special programs for students who are learning to speak English. Yet instead of celebrations, bilingual education is facing attacks and reexamination from all sides.

In California, the state with the largest percentage of limited-English-proficient (LEP) students, voters will decide on June 2 whether bilingual classrooms should be eliminated and replaced with one-year, sheltered English-immersion classes (see "Models of Language Instruction"). Officially named Proposition 227, the California ballot question comes in the wake of complaints by immigrant parents and some bilingual educators that students are languishing in bilingual classes without learning enough English.

Throughout the country, the California initiative has sparked a renewed debate about the relative effectiveness of the many different approaches to educating the growing population of LEP students. And it is also provoking some soul-searching among bilingual advocates who are arguing for the reform of bilingual education rather than its elimination.

After three decades, research on bilingual education is extensive, with hundreds of studies available. Yet much of it has been called into question by conflicting interpretations or has even been dismissed as methodologically unsound. In a 1996 review of the literature, for example, Boston University's Christine Rossell found only 25 percent of 300 program evaluations to be methodologically acceptable. The others often failed to use control groups or did not include a statistical control for socioeconomic or other differences.

Most research findings so far have failed to demonstrate the superiority of transitional bilingual programs, the most common type, in which students are taught in their native language while learning English. A few recent studies, however, have turned up some provocative new evidence of benefits for students who get a strong foundation in more than one language. "Late-exit" transitional bilingual programs and two-way programs that are intended to develop literacy in both the native language and English appear to help LEP students perform better throughout high school.

The Great Divide

In 1974, the U.S. Supreme Court ruled in *Lau v. Nichols* that schools must take "affirmative steps" to help students who do not speak English. The Court did not specify the type of program required, however. Today, the different approaches to teaching minority-language students comprise a dizzying list. Methods break down into different models, including those that incorporate the native language such as transitional bilingual education, as well as English-language programs, which include structured immersion and English as a Second Language.

Of the nearly 3 million LEP students nationwide, 74 percent are Spanish speakers, according to the National Center for Education Statistics. Vietnamese is the next largest language group, at 3.9 percent. Arguments about how best to teach LEP students usually focus on how soon they should be taught in English-only classrooms. The arguments are often motivated by political agendas, with strong views on both sides.

Part of the political debate stems from disparate goals. Many supporters of bilingual education view English learners as an opportunity to create truly bilingual and biliterate graduates. Opponents argue that tax dollars should not be spent on maintaining a child's native language and culture. The goal, from

Laurel Shaper Walters. (1998, May/June). The bilingual education debate. *The Harvard Education Letter, 14* (3), 1–4. Reprinted by permission of the Harvard Graduate School of Education.

Models of Language Instruction

Bilingual Immersion Students are taught in a separate classroom with most instruction in English. Part of the day, however, is set aside to develop concepts, literacy, and critical-thinking skills in the native language. The goal is for students to improve their English so they can join regular classrooms in two to four years.

Early-Exit Transitional Bilingual The most common model in use. The student's native language is used as a bridge, beginning with entry into school until they learn enough English to function in a regular classroom, theoretically two to three years. Programs vary in how rapidly English is introduced and which subjects are taught in the native language. The goal is to develop English skills without delaying academic content.

English as a Second Language (ESL) Students get special instruction in English from a trained specialist, either in the regular classroom or in a pull-out program varying from 30 minutes to half the day. The goal is to assist students who are learning subjects primarily in English.

Late-Exit Transitional Bilingual Education (Maintenance or Developmental Bilingual Education) Students receive some instruction in their native language until 6th grade, with the increasing use of English. The goal is to foster literacy in the native language as a foundation for later literacy in English, as well as to instill a positive attitude toward the native culture.

Sheltered English Immersion (Structured Immersion) Academic content is taught in simple English using context and gesture to explain meaning. Some programs allow teachers to use students' home language for clarification or have native language aides available when needed. The goal is to mainstream students quickly.

Two-Way Bilingual Education Language-majority and language-minority students are taught together in the same bilingual class. Most programs are English/Spanish, but some are available in other languages. The goal is for all students to develop fluency in both languages.

---

this perspective, is to help students learn English as quickly as possible and move into mainstream classrooms.

At the same time, both sides want to be sure students keep up with their peers in academic coursework. Bilingual supporters say this is best accomplished by teaching in the native language and gradually introducing more English as students gain literacy in their first language. Critics say this transitional approach isolates students from their peers for too long and delays the acquisition of English.

But in schools whose students speak many different languages, models that include instruction in the native language—particularly the two-way model—are not always practical. Classrooms with students from a variety of backgrounds often rely on English as a Second Language programs, which offer intensive English instruction from a specially trained teacher for part of the day.

Shortcomings of Bilingual Education

Studies comparing different models have failed to demonstrate the superiority of transitional bilingual programs, despite widespread federal support and implementation of this approach. One of the most comprehensive studies in the field is a 1991 federally financed project that followed more than 2,000 elementary children over four years. It looked at three programs: structured English immersion (special instruction in English only), early-exit transitional bilingual education (students mainstreamed into English-only classrooms by the end of first or second grade), and late-exit transitional bilingual education (students not mainstreamed until the end of sixth grade).

This evaluation, known as the Ramirez study after its principal author, has been used as both support for transitional bilingual education and ammunition against it. Students in all three programs learned English and made progress. Therefore, the study concluded, providing substantial instruction in a student's primary language does not delay acquisition of English. Yet it did not demonstrate that this approach boosted achievement or was superior to the immersion program.

Studies have also shown that many students stay in bilingual classrooms longer than the three years usually prescribed by the transitional bilingual model, and that when they are mainstreamed into regular classrooms they often lag behind their English-speaking peers.

Even the staunchest bilingual proponents readily admit that the current system of transitional bilingual education is failing many students. "A lot of bilingual programs aren't as good as they ought to be," says Catherine Snow, a researcher and professor at Harvard University's Graduate School of Education. "It's not surprising that parents of kids in those programs end up being dissatisfied." Snow chaired a National Research Council committee that announced in March that "initial reading instruction for children who do not speak English is best carried out in the child's home language."

A Case for the Long View

Recent research, however, suggests that a long-term view may be necessary in evaluating the effectiveness of language programs. In several studies—including the Ramirez study and studies by Virginia P. Collier and Wayne P. Thomas of George Mason

University—children schooled in English-language programs made faster gains in English than comparable children in bilingual programs. But around the third or fourth year, the children who were taught at least partially in their native language began to catch up in English. While these students began to reduce the gap between their achievement and that of their native English-speaking peers, students who received English-only instruction failed to sustain their academic progress in late elementary and secondary school. Collier and Thomas looked at scores from nationally normed tests in all subjects, not just English, to judge the effectiveness of six different bilingual models.

Collier blames short-term studies for producing inconclusive research results on bilingual education programs. "In our current research," she says, "we have found data patterns similar to those often reported in other short-term studies focused on Grades K–3—little difference between programs." Significant differences show up only after students continue their schooling in mainstream courses, says Collier, whose ongoing research follows students through 11th grade. The preliminary findings show that only students who receive both English and native-language instruction through grade 5 or 6 are continuing to do well through high school (see chart).

In fact, the question of how long it takes students to become proficient in a new language is at the heart of the bilingual education controversy. Collier's research suggests that it takes students who receive English-only instruction longer (7 to 10 years) to reach average achievement, compared to students provided with strong native-language support (4 to 7 years).

But some critics say the Collier and Thomas study has not been subjected to peer review. "We only have their stated findings," says Rosalie Pedalino Porter, director of the READ Institute in Amherst, MA, an organization advocating English-language programs for LEP students. "I just cannot believe any child sitting in an American classroom can need 10 years to learn English." Collier and Thomas recently posted a 96-page research summary on the World Wide Web for review by other researchers and practitioners.

How Long Does It Take?

There appears to be no one answer to the question of how long it takes for a non-English speaker to become fluent enough to keep up in the classroom. What often gets lost in the discussion is the highly variable nature of language acquisition, says Snow. Students of normal intelligence can take vastly

Patterns of K–12 English Learners' Long-Term Achievement in Normal Curve Equivalents (NCEs) on Standardized Tests in English Reading Compared across Six Program Models (data are based on 42,000 student records collected from five districts between 1991 and 1996)

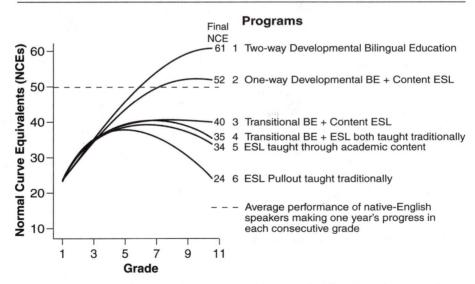

Source: From *School Effectiveness for Language Minority Students* by W. P. Thomas and V. P. Collier, 1997, Washington, DC: National Clearinghouse for Bilingual Education <www.ncbe. gwu.edu>. Reprinted by permission.

different amounts of time to master English. Socioeconomic background also plays a role.

Another important variable is age. "What you need to do for 13-year-olds and 5-year-olds is quite different," Snow says. Considerable research supports the theory that students who learn the "mechanics of literacy" in their native language can translate that knowledge into learning another language more easily. Therefore, says Snow, "the group that's really highly at risk are the students who arrive at school not knowing how to read. They're the ones that we really need to worry about."

The widespread myth that younger children learn languages more easily than older ones confuses the issue further. In fact, research shows that older students who are literate in their native language are faster second-language learners.

Mary Cazabon, director of bilingual programs in the Cambridge, MA, public schools, sees this in her district. "If students come in at the high school level literate and fully on grade level in their native language, they make a smooth transition into English and don't need 7 to 9 years," she says. "The younger children need to develop bilingually in order to maximize their learning potential," she believes.

In Cambridge, most Spanish-speaking students are taught in two-way bilingual programs with native English speakers. Research shows strong academic gains for both native-English and LEP students in two-way programs. Yet Cazabon recognizes that such a model is impractical for all languages and all ages. "You can't say that there is one exact model that is going to work for every child," she says.

Evaluation of Bilingual Classrooms

Some research, in fact, concludes that the specific models and languages of instruction may be less important than the quality of teaching that language-minority students receive. Researchers note the lack of interactive instruction in many programs for LEP students. When students have little opportunity to speak in class, they don't learn as quickly. There is also a concern about the lack of books available to students in bilingual programs.

"Many concerned educators realize that in order to improve the education of bilingual students, we need to go beyond the debate on language choice and support for particular models. . . . Issues of pedagogy need to be addressed," writes Boston University professor Maria Estela Brisk in her 1998 book, *Bilingual Education: From Compensatory to Quality Schooling.*

Even in schools using the same model, there can be drastic differences in instructional approaches. In the Ramirez report, for example, students who attended one of the late-exit schools performed significantly better than students at the other late-exit schools. The researchers noted that the higher scoring students attended a kindergarten that emphasized critical-thinking skills in the native language. Another study noted dramatic differences in instructional practices between the lower and upper grades of the models compared, resulting in more differences between grade levels than between models.

"The focus needs to switch from languages to schools," concludes Brisk. "Schools, not languages, educate students."

FOR FURTHER INFORMATION

D. August and K. Hakuta. *Improving Schooling for Language-Minority Children.* Washington, DC: National Academy Press, 1997.

M. E. Brisk. *Bilingual Education: From Compensatory to Quality Schooling.* Mahwah, NJ: Lawrence Erlbaum Associates, 1998.

V. P. Collier and W. P. Thomas. *Language Minority Student Achievement and Program Effectiveness: Research Summary of Ongoing Study.* George Mason University, 1998; http://www.ncbe.gwu.edu/ncbepubs/resource/effectiveness.

National Research Council. *Preventing Reading Difficulties in Young Children,* 1998; Available from National Academy Press, 202-334-3313; http://www. nap.edu.

R. P. Porter. *Forked Tongue: The Politics of Bilingual Education.* New Brunswick, NJ: Transaction Publishers, 1996.

J. Ramirez et al. *Final Report: Longitudinal Study of Structured English Immersion Strategy, Early-Exit and Late-Exit Transitional Bilingual Education Programs for Language Minority Children* (Vols. 1 and 2 prepared for the U.S. Department of Education). San Mateo, CA: Aguirre International, 1991.

C. H. Rossell and K. Baker. "The Educational Effectiveness of Bilingual Education." *Research in the Teaching of English, 30,* no. 1 (February 1996): 7–74.

■ *Laurel Shaper Walters is an education writer living in St. Louis, Missouri.*

The Impact of Changing Roles on Relationships between Professionals in Inclusive Programs for Young Children

Joan Lieber, Paula J. Beckman, Marci J. Hanson, Susan Janko, Jules M. Marquart, Eva Horn, and Samuel L. Odom

■ ■ ■

As inclusion of young children with disabilities into preschool programs has become more prevalent, there have been concomitant changes in the roles assumed by the professionals and paraprofessionals in these programs. In this [article] we examine the ways in which inclusive models influence the roles assumed by the program staff and the factors that affect the ability of staff members to assume these roles. Data, which included interviews, participant observation and document analysis, were collected as part of a multi-site national study of inclusive education programs and practices. From these data, themes emerged regarding the changing roles and relationships of staff members in inclusive early childhood programs. These themes are discussed as both facilitators of and barriers to successful inclusive programs.

The Impact of Changing Roles on Relationships between Professionals in Inclusive Programs for Young Children

Two converging trends in the United States have resulted in increased interest in the inclusion of preschool children who have disabilities in settings with children who do not have disabilities. First, students with disabilities are increasingly being included in educational programs for typically developing children at the elementary and secondary levels (Zigmond, 1995). Second, since 1991, all states have been required to provide educational programs for preschool-age children with disabilities (Rose & Smith, 1994). As a result, the inclusion of young children with disabilities has become more prevalent (Lamorey & Bricker, 1993). While a few programs, such as Head Start, have included children with disabilities for a number of years, others are just beginning to engage in these efforts.

As programs have attempted to become inclusive, it has become increasingly clear that the success of these efforts, for children with and without disabilities, depends on a complicated and interrelated array of factors. Some researchers (Bronfenbrenner, 1977; Guralnick, 1982; Odom, et al., in press; Peck, 1993) suggest that factors outside of the children themselves can influence their participation in inclusive settings. For example, although children may not be directly involved in interactions that take place between adults in inclusive settings, they may be affected by these relationships (Baker & Zigmond, 1995; Ferguson, 1995; Sindelar, 1995). Inclusive settings, almost by definition, require staff members to assume new roles and forge new relationships. This is true for at least two reasons. First, inclusion often requires staff members to work with many more people than they might have in the past. For

Joan Lieber, Paula J. Beckman, Marci J. Hanson, Susan Janko, Jules M. Marquart, Eva Horn, and Samuel L. Odom. (1997). The impact of changing roles on relationships between professionals in inclusive programs for young children. *Early Education and Development, 8* (1), 67–82. Reprinted by permission.

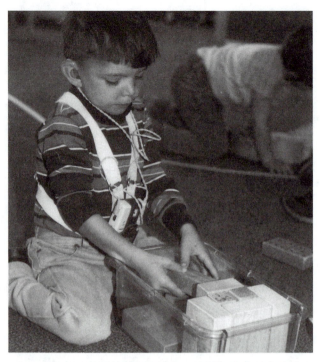

Inclusion of young children with disabilities has become increasingly prevalent.

example, regular education personnel must begin working more closely with special educators as well as related service personnel (Baker & Zigmond, 1995; Giangreco, Dennis, Cloninger, Edelman, & Schattman, 1993). This change can sometimes lead to important questions about how to define the roles of various staff members and the relationship of these staff members to one another (File & Kontos, 1992; Ferguson, Meyer, Jeanchild, Juniper, & Zingo, 1992). Second, the process of assuming new roles frequently requires staff members to collaborate in new ways and to acquire new skills (Baker & Zigmond, 1995; Friend & Cook, 1996; Marchant, 1995; Pugach, 1995). In some programs, teachers who are used to operating independently may become co-teachers. In others, special education personnel may serve as consultants to regular classroom teachers. As Sindelar (1995) has noted, there are many different ways to collaborate, and individual teachers may assume very different roles as part of this collaboration. Thus, Sindelar argues it is important to understand the impact of different models in inclusive settings.

The purpose of this [article] is to describe the ways in which inclusive models may influence the roles assumed by program staff members and to examine factors that affect the ability of these staff members to assume new roles. The results presented are based on a larger, qualitative study of inclusion in early childhood settings which is being conducted

as part of the Early Childhood Research Institute on Inclusion (ECRII).

Method

This study was designed to reflect multiple perspectives and multiple settings. This ecological approach (Bronfenbrenner, 1977) requires the use of multiple data collection methods and multiple sources of data. Therefore, the research design included purposive sampling of constituents across multiple levels of the child's and family's ecology. We also used a field study approach (Zelditch, 1962), described below.

Purposive Sampling

Investigators at universities participating as national research sites for ECRII each studied four inclusive preschool programs. This resulted in 16 programs nation-wide. Programs were purposefully selected to represent a range of inclusive models as well as diversity in geography, socio-economic status, population density, ethnicity, and language use. Participating programs included community-based child care, public school, and Head Start programs and reflected a variety of approaches to inclusion. In one approach, described here as an integrated activity model, there were two separate classrooms, one led by a regular educator and the other by a special educator. These teachers joined their classes for a portion of the day. In another model, the special education teacher model, responsibility for planning, implementing and monitoring classroom activities was assumed by a special education teacher. Little contact occurred with regular educators. There was contact, however, with classroom assistants and related services providers. In this model a few children without disabilities were included in a class consisting primarily of children with disabilities. A third approach, an itinerant teaching model, was comprised of classrooms led by regular educators who received support or direct services from special educators and the appropriate related services providers on a regular, ongoing basis. In programs using this approach, children with disabilities were represented in approximately the same proportion as in naturalistic settings. Finally, some programs used a fourth approach, a co-teaching model, in which children were co-taught by a regular and a special education teacher. In these programs, children with disabilities were represented in approximately the same proportion as in naturalistic settings.

Data collection methods were consistent with our desire to reflect an insider or emic view of inclusion (i.e., to understand the perspectives of those who construct or experience inclusive education practices first-hand). Members of the following three constituency groups from each of the 16 programs provided their perspectives: (a) parents and caregivers of 5 children with disabilities and 2 children without disabilities (caregivers of 112 children across the 16 programs); (b) direct service providers (regular and special education teachers, classroom assistants, and related service providers); and (c) administrators and policy makers (community program directors, school principals, regional coordinators, Head Start program directors). In larger districts and in schools, districts, and programs that were organizationally complex, and incorporated multiple categorical programs, or both (e.g., Head Start and public school-funded special education programs), administrators from each program component were interviewed.

Field Study Approach

Our field-study approach employed three data collection strategies: open-ended interviews, participant observation and document analysis. Interviews with professionals and paraprofessionals focused on staff members' roles and responsibilities in the program, relationships with families and with other staff members, issues faced when including children with disabilities in the classroom, program policies and procedures, funding issues, and personal perceptions of barriers and facilitators of inclusion. Each interview lasted between 60 and 90 minutes, with follow-up interviews as needed. All interviews were audiotaped and transcribed verbatim.

Participant observations occurred from 2 to 3 times per week for extended periods of between 6 and 16 weeks. Participant observers focused on adult-child and adult-adult relationships during instructional time, as well as formal and informal meetings among families and professionals. Each observation lasted from 1 to 5 hours and was recorded in the form of field notes that included information about date, place, time, and duration of the observation; the persons present; descriptions of the physical environment; events that occurred; and comments made or information offered by those observed. Staff members and administrators also provided documents describing their program policies and other written information relevant to the program, for example, handbooks about the program which were given to parents.

Cross-Site Data Analysis

We used a grounded-theory approach to data analysis. This approach is inductive in nature and is used to discover information and generate theories based on the content of the data (Glaser & Strauss, 1967; Charmaz, 1983). This approach was supplemented by cross-site analysis techniques allowing synthesis of data from each of the four national research sites participating in ECRII and permitting nationalization of our findings without sacrificing in-depth description and understanding (Firestone & Herriot, 1984).

Our final coded categories, and the interpretations and theories they represent, are presented in this paper with the primary data that were the basis of our understanding of roles and relationships between staff members in inclusive settings. From the beginning of the study, data collection and analysis proceeded simultaneously, but analysis strategies can be conceptualized as occurring in four phases (Charmaz, 1983). During the first phase, interview transcripts and field notes were analyzed line-by-line and coded according to [an] individual researcher's understandings about the meanings of the data. During the initial phase of coding, categories were frequently labeled using primary data (i.e., the words of those interviewed) (Wolcott, 1990). Key codes and interpretations were recorded in the form of analytic memos. Analytic memos were dated and maintained as a record for the dual purposes of auditability and the creation of conceptual maps.

During the second phase, researchers within each site met weekly to review and discuss initial coding, to generate data categories and subcategories, and to develop initial explanations and interpretations of the categories. During the third phase, six months after data collection began, a formal process of cross-site analysis was initiated by an experienced educational ethnographer. Researchers from each of the four national sites met to synthesize and define conceptual categories and to develop questions and strategies for additional data collection that would promote investigation of those categories and theory development. One of the large conceptual categories identified during this process was roles and relationships. During the final phase of data collection and analysis, we refined, elaborated, and exhausted our theoretical hunches through a process of theoretical sampling. Follow-up interview protocols were developed to further explain, confirm, or disconfirm our developing theories. In addition, individual participants were questioned to verify and clarify information that they had previously shared. For purposes of this paper, interviews, field notes, and documents that directly pertained to the changing roles and relationships among staff members were analyzed.

Results

Several important themes emerged from the data regarding the roles assumed by staff members in inclusive early childhood programs. Each theme reflected issues that affected the ability of staff members to adapt to changing roles and relationships. These themes are described below.

Investment in the Program

One of the emerging themes that related to roles and relationships was the extent to which staff members had a personal investment in the program. Even when inclusion initiatives originated at an administrative level, staff member participation in developing the program seemed to contribute to their sense of ownership and to their efforts to make inclusion work. This dynamic was observed in almost all of the programs. For instance, in one program that used a co-teaching approach, the program was initiated by the principal, but the responsibility for the program's design belonged to the teachers. As one teacher described the program's inception, the principal was

> . . . instrumental in getting this program going. She's the one who approached Betty and I both, individually, about co-teaching and doing an inclusion program. . . . She gave us the opportunity to design and do it any way we wanted to. So we did. It's better figuring out how we want to do it than having someone tell us how we're going to do it. So she gave us the freedom to do it however we wanted.

Similarly, in a program that used integrated activities, participation of staff members was voluntary, and teachers had a considerable amount of freedom in planning their joint activities. The principal described the evolution of this program by saying:

> They kind of expanded it at a pace that they were comfortable with. It wasn't a "This is what we're going to do" plan. As I look across the building, the inclusion experiences that have been really positive have been those outgrowths of people that want to work together, are committed to working together, and have gradually increased the amount of time that they work together.

In contrast, when teachers had little input into the development of the program, problems with roles and relationships were identified. For instance, in one co-teaching program, staff members were not well prepared for change. Children with disabilities began the school year one month earlier than the typical children. When the children with disabilities began their program, they moved into a classroom that had been occupied by the early education teacher for the previous four years. The early educa-

tion teacher came back to school to find her room completely rearranged. As she said, "You know it's like if you leave home on vacation and you come back and all of your stuff is somewhere else." The special education teacher agreed that it would have worked much better if she had not ". . . come into somebody's classroom already existing, [to] start a new classroom."

A Shared Philosophy

Sharing a program philosophy facilitated positive relationships among staff members in inclusive classrooms. One teacher said, "The most important [quality] is holding a shared philosophy. Both [teachers] have to believe and agree on what it is you are trying to accomplish."

In programs where staff members did not share a philosophy, ideological differences contributed to stressful relationships. In one co-teaching program an early education teacher noted that

> Our [program philosophy] is a little more free, it is not as structured. . . . [In the special education philosophy] you take them to an area but you're actually telling them each move to make whereas ours is more open.

Similarly, a special education teacher explained,

> Whereas [the early education teacher] would just kind of let them choose what [the children] wanted to do and kind of supervise what was going on . . . I'm more in there, and these kids need more hands-on.

She admits that

> there's been some real bumpy roads . . . the [early education] teacher and assistant were under the assumption that the children were not going to need much hands-on, so I think that's hurt a lot in the beginning.

A difference in philosophies appeared to have less effect on relationships in programs that relied on integrated activities. One special education teacher described the differences in her philosophy by saying, "[The early education teacher] is more child-directed. [I] lead more than [I] let the children lead." In spite of these differences in style, the teachers' relationship with each other was not affected, at least in part because their groups were together for only a limited portion of the day.

Perceived Ownership of the Children

Programs also varied in the extent to which responsibility for the children was assumed jointly by regular and special education professionals. For example, as one teacher in a co-teaching program described, "When it comes time to write report cards, we work together on that. . . . When it comes time to writing IEPs, we work together on that." In programs using the integrated activities model, responsibility for the children was retained by the children's assigned teacher. In a program using itinerant teaching model, the difficulty of perceived ownership was described in this way:

> I think you have a large group of special education teachers who have their own classrooms . . . nobody ever comes and looks at what they do. . . . Then you are telling these people, we want you to change your job description in a very significant way. Not only do we want to take away your classroom, we want you to have . . . the interpersonal skills to communicate and translate what you know inside a regular classroom. You don't have your own group of kids. You may have five or six different classrooms that you have to work with. . . .

Thus, joint ownership proved difficult to achieve in a number of programs using an itinerant approach. In some of those programs, typically developing children were the responsibility of the early childhood teacher while the children with disabilities were sometimes perceived to be the responsibility of the special education staff. In one program the early education teacher made a distinction between a child who had a disability and his fellow students in terms of responsibility for progress toward his educational goals saying, "The itinerant teacher follows Daniel around. . . . It's her job to work on his IEP . . . that is what she is here to do. . . . [He] came in with an IEP so we don't work on that." As the director of another program pointed out, "ownership is really big. . . . It is intrinsic to the itinerant model." The problem of ownership was explained by one of the itinerant teachers saying:

> It's a problem that all of us itinerants in general have. . . . The biggest barrier is this idea that a lot of teachers have, "they're your special needs kids, you're only here one day a week for [X] minutes or whatever's on the IEP, you don't understand what we go through on a daily basis." I want them to know that I do understand and I'm here to help you. Sometimes . . . they listen but they're not ready to accept or they don't feel . . . like special needs children belong in their program. They feel like they're a hindrance to their program, "I can't do circle, we couldn't even get that pumpkin made because your child was talking or was out of his seat. . . ."

For some teachers, this sense of ownership seemed to meet the needs of individual staff members and prevented them from initiating inclusion more extensively. As one teacher using integrated activities said, "Well, we each have our own room and you have your own this and that and I just haven't been ready to give that all up. I still see that as a box that I'm in. . . ."

Staff Communication

Communication among program staff members was also a major determinant of how successful their relationships were and how successfully the program functioned. In one co-teaching program, staff members clearly did not communicate effectively with one another. The special education teacher said,

> I don't know if I'm expecting too much from other staff . . . and they [early education staff] won't tell me what's going on. I mean I'll hear other things, they kind of talk to [the special education assistant] a little bit but they won't talk to me.

In another instance, a special educator assigned specifically to work with a particular child explained, "And I had been going in every week and offering and [asking] 'when can I come and talk to you?' That was the biggest problem, the lack of communication."

Communication was a particularly salient issue in models where special education teachers or related service personnel provided consultation to the classroom staff. However, those difficulties were overcome somewhat when professionals worked directly in the classroom rather than taking the children out of the room to work with them. One occupational therapist saw improved communication as an advantage to working in the classroom:

> Just the communication back and forth while you're working. I mean we can bounce ideas off of each other, point out things. It's more real than writing in the notebook or calling her on the phone and trying to describe. I think the ideal situation is really when you all work together in the classroom at the same time.

Dedicated Planning Times. One strategy that some programs used to facilitate communication was to formalize planning and provide opportunities for staff members to meet and work collaboratively. Frequently, however, this time was quite limited. At one program that used integrated activities, the principal asked teachers to set aside one hour a month for planning between the early education and special education classes. Still other programs tried to arrange regular meeting times but were not always successful. In a program using the special education teacher model, an occupational therapist said, "[The teacher] and I try and set up regular meeting times. They don't always happen . . . unless we actually write in on our calendars and schedule it, it's hard to fit it in." A similar problem was identified by another occupational therapist who explained, "We haven't got the time. We haven't figured out the time to get together."

Informal Communication. Opportunities for informal contact between staff also facilitated communication. Such contact often occurred during lunch or when staff members met in the hallways. One teacher whose program used the special education teacher model explained, "[We] get along beautifully. We usually all eat lunch together and sometimes we just talk about stuff." Informal contact was important according to the program's speech therapist who said,

> It's more of just like meeting here and there. Like we'll probably sit down once a month and really talk about all the kids. But it's more of just like okay catch her on the playground [and talk about] this child.

Role Release

To a large extent, the ability of staff to release their previous roles seemed to contribute to good working relationships. According to one special educator in a co-teaching model:

> I am not just a special educator in our model. I work with all the children. We are following the traditional pre-K curriculum. So when we are doing circle time, we have a theme. I'm before the children. Gwen and I take turns. And I'm working with everybody, just as she is.

The early education teacher concurred saying, "We're almost like one person. It's gotten so bad that, at times, we even finish each other's sentences."

In several programs, the lead teacher and assistant had built visibly collaborative working relationships. In one classroom using the special education teacher model, the teacher and assistant had a very interactive working style, with interchangeable roles and cooperative teaching. They planned together almost daily and took turns in leading activities. In a classroom using integrated activities, the special education teacher described her interaction with the assistant as good teamwork. The assistant concurred saying, ". . . We basically just alternate, whoever feels like doing something that day, you know, alternate what we do."

In another program, however, role release was not accomplished easily. According to one commu-

nity-based itinerant teacher, one of the biggest challenges faced by itinerant teachers was

> releasing our role as a classroom teacher to going into someone else's center and classroom. . . . It's learning how to consult and not want to take over but provide what they need from their point of view and not what we think.

Role Clarity and Role Satisfaction

While the ability to release roles was helpful in some circumstances, in others staff members perceived a lack of clarity in their roles. Ill-defined and poorly understood roles sometimes affected teachers' satisfaction with their role and served to undermine working relationships. A lack of clear role definition was especially difficult in the initial stages of inclusion, or whenever there was a change in roles.

In one co-teaching program the lack of role clarity led to an uncertainty for the special education teacher about how much she should suggest to the early education teacher when she was working with children with disabilities. When a child who was blind was unoccupied and given little assistance in an activity led by the early education staff, the special education teacher commented:

> It is hard to see this happen, and then you try to intervene [by making a suggestion] but it's like how much do you do? It's like what is our role, are we mother or boss?

In another instance, there was considerable role confusion about a teacher who was placed in a class to provide a highly-structured program for a child with autism. The child's parent described the issue by saying:

> [Her] role in the classroom kind of evolved. I think when she first got there, [the other teachers] tried to treat her as an aide. Then the next two months they treated her like a rookie teacher. And now I think . . . the relationship is more at the peer–peer level.

In a program that used a co-teaching model, the roles and responsibilities were not equivalent. On returning to school to find her classroom changed and a substantially different curriculum used, the early education teacher questioned her role as a teacher, a role she had had since 1972. She felt that her role had become an "assistant to the assistant." She went on, "You know you come in and your room is, you know it's nothing that you had any input into and . . . you really don't know what you're doing. I mean you don't even know what's expected."

However as roles and relationships were sorted out there was often satisfaction with the way they evolved. For example, the relationship between the teachers and the speech therapist in one co-teaching program seemed satisfactory to all the participants. According to the special education teacher, "We organized this model with support staff and we wanted the support staff to come to us. We did not want the speech pathologist to pull children out who were identified [as having a disability]." This role was supported by the speech pathologist who said that working with the children in the classroom "is easier for the kids I think. It's the transition from going from the classroom to my room that upsets some of the children. Or they just seem to enjoy being still in the same area."

Stability in Adult Relationships

In addition to role clarity, familiarity with the other adults often had a positive impact on the relationships among the adults. In some programs, the stability of the community increased professionals' familiarity with each other. According to one director of special education:

> Our staff has been very stable. It's also an area that's fairly small. People get to know each other so there's a high degree of cooperation. . . . All these different people get to know each other because they stay here. So when something like an inclusion effort comes along, we have an advantage, I think. Being that people are pretty happy about themselves and about where they live, and know their colleagues. There's a built-in and positive atmosphere and a high level of cooperation among people.

In contrast when there was a lack of stability in the professional staff, a level of familiarity and an opportunity to build a relationship could not occur. One early education teacher who worked with the special education staff in an itinerant teaching model described her relationships in this way:

> I don't know how they work it as a team, I really don't. I don't know [the special education coordinator] very well. I knew the one from last year but I didn't know her well either. They are all over the place, and they have so many special needs children right now, they've left my kids behind in my class.

Further, in a new program a lack of familiarity can impede the development of staff relationships. A number of professionals in one program that initiated a co-teaching model indicated that they wished they had spent time at the beginning of the year, before the children arrived, establishing a positive relationship. An occupational therapist said:

> . . . to build a relationship and I think that's the crucial thing that makes it work, is that you have a positive relationship with the child[care] teacher and director and they know that you'll be there if they need you.

Initiative

Because inclusive programs required staff members to assume new roles, someone typically needed to take the initiative to foster program activities. The importance of this initiative could be seen in several programs. For instance, one teacher in an integrated activity model noted that "When [the early education teacher] and I want to do something we just do it and [the principal] doesn't mind."

In another example, this initiative was reflected by who "opened the door." As one staff member in the program tells it,

> [The special educator] has worked very, very hard to keep the doors open between the two classes. . . . When [they started the program, the special educator] was always the one who would open the door. And now I've seen on more than one occasion, [the other teacher] opening the door. . . .

In contrast, when one participant felt that another was not taking enough initiative, it adversely influenced the relationship. In one co-teaching program, these difficulties exemplified ongoing problems between the teachers and their aides:

> I don't like having to tell an adult who should be able to see that something is out of place, "Could you please go take care of that?" I don't feel like I have to give orders. I'm not a drill sergeant. But with most of the assistants, it's like you have to tell them everything to do.

In some instances, staff had to take special initiative to establish good working relationships. This initiative was often evident in successful programs using an itinerant teaching approach. According to one occupational therapist:

> We just have to adapt per student, per teacher . . . I think it's still hard for people, but it's getting easier. You have to adapt your personality to the teacher you're working with, just like you would do it if it was a patient.

Administrative Support

A final factor that contributed to relationships among the adults was the availability of administrative support. Such support also facilitated implementation of the model and sometimes contributed to a willingness to continue an inclusive program.

In one program the principal provided support for any teachers who chose to implement integrated activities. She said, "I would support any initiative that people take. . . . Anything that [the teachers] ask in terms of support to make that work, I try and provide."

Support from administrative staff came in a variety of forms. One way that administrators demonstrated support was by listening to the concerns of staff members. In one program the teacher director described her role in this way: "I like to encourage the teachers . . . to work as a team together, to support . . . each other. I tell them any problem, anything you have, come and talk to me, I will try to help you. . . ."

Support was also provided by administrators who let the staff know they had confidence in their abilities:

It's what you're going to do that we're going to support. And with you knowing the curriculum . . . we'll be there and we will be throwing in things that will help you. . . . But know that you're still in charge just like you always were.

Another administrator said:

One thing that I think is good in any place where people are being together . . . and they're trying to get along is to back off a little, you know don't be in their face observing them every day . . . let them have some time to kind of gel together and decide their pecking order . . . they need time to come up with their own communication styles. . . .

In still another program a crucial variable was the administrator's willingness to allocate resources for training and planning as the program was being developed. Training was accomplished by hiring a coordinator with a child development background and requiring all staff members to participate in staff development training together, form a joint philosophy and policies, and continue learning in the program after its inception. The director provided this support because

You can't always get teachers who really believe or are comfortable leaving their classroom . . . and being a consultant and engineering the integration . . . I don't know that it's changed philosophy as much as given people more confidence that they can do it. It's given them the know-how to do it.

Thus, administrative support in the form of allowing teachers planning time and training resources appears to facilitate more successful inclusion experiences.

Discussion

The push for the inclusion of young children with disabilities in educational settings with typically developing youngsters has come from multiple directions. Some inclusive programs have had the luxury of extensive resources and planning time to merge or develop programs; other programs have made alterations seemingly overnight. The transfiguration in the roles and relationships of professionals and paraprofessionals coming from both early education and special education backgrounds, has created many opportunities and challenges.

The themes identified in this study, while not exhaustive nor mutually exclusive, highlight important barriers and facilitators to collaborative relationships among staff members in inclusive preschool settings. The results from this investigation have both confirmed and extended previous literature in a number of ways. Our findings confirm the work of previous authors who have argued that relationships between adults frequently influence outcomes in inclusive programs (Baker & Zigmond, 1995; Ferguson, 1995; Giangreco et al., 1995; Peck et al., 1993). With the exception of Peck and his colleagues, however, most of this work has not focused on preschool-age children. Peck and his colleagues (1993) found that many of the difficulties in nonsurviving inclusive preschool programs were with relationships among adult participants. For example, differing philosophies and lack of substantive involvement of staff in planning for inclusion. Our findings also extend this work by further delineating specific aspects of roles and relationships which may influence the success of inclusive programs for young children. Although it is reasonable to predict that a particular program model would influence relationships among the adults in systematic ways, we found instead a good deal of variation within program models. For most of our themes, specifically communication, role release, role clarity and satisfaction, familiarity, initiative and administrative support, there was no one model which contributed to more successful relationships among the adults. It should be noted, however, that there were two themes for which the program's model seemed to have more an effect. One of the themes, shared philosophy, had less impact on adult relationships in programs using models where teachers spent less time together (e.g., integrated activities). Second, the theme of perceived ownership had less effect on relationships in coteaching programs and no effect in models where special education and early education teachers retained control of their own classes (i.e., integrated activities). In contrast, in itinerant teaching models, ownership of children was an issue that affected adult relationships. Further research is needed to systematically address the impact of program models on relationships among staff members.

The methodological approach undertaken in this study has allowed the researchers to examine the roles and relationships among professionals and paraprofessionals from an insider's perspective. In-depth interviews of personnel were conducted to solicit the perspectives of the key players and these same individuals were observed extensively as they worked in their classrooms. The data that emerged from these multiple sources produced a rich account of the challenges and successes in preschool classes, and allowed the cross-checking of individual perspectives. Likewise, the cross-site analysis of information from programs across the country has strengthened support for these findings.

Implications for facilitating successful inclusion experiences can be identified from an examination of these emerging themes. First, a sense of shared philosophy or joint ownership of children appears to produce more positive experiences. Though models may differ substantially, key features are associated with these positive outcomes. In general, the importance of an investment in the program on the part of participants was clear. This investment was often created by active involvement in designing and developing the program. Also a sense of well-being appeared to exist in programs with a philosophy jointly agreed upon by the major participants. This philosophy seemed to emerge from informal communications and relationships among staff members or from more formalized, targeted joint planning and support. This is consistent with other literature suggesting the importance of a shared philosophy or framework (Baker & Zigmond, 1995; Giangreco et al., 1993). Less investment was noted when the initiative for inclusion was one-sided or dominated by a single teacher or organization, or when a change was "sprung" on an existing program or individual. Similarly, as in other studies (Baker & Zigmond, 1995; Ferguson et al., 1995; Pugach, 1995; Thousand & Villa, 1992), opportunities for both formal and informal joint planning and communication enhanced the satisfaction of staff members and appeared to help clarify their roles. Finally, the pivotal influence that a key person—either an administrator or a teacher within the existing program—could exert was evident. One person with a vision and the energy and know-how to effect change could make the difference in a program's success or failure in smoothly implementing inclusive practices.

There are a number of implications of these findings for training needs and preparation of staff members who work in inclusive early childhood programs. Previously personnel preparation has been child-centered. However, as programs that serve young children have become more inclusive, adult roles are changing radically. The ways in which adults work with, communicate to, and collaborate with other adults is assuming primary importance. Efforts to prepare personnel are critical so that participants develop the skills necessary to collaborate effectively in a variety of new roles.

Needs may differ for adults who co-teach and adults who serve as consultants. For adults in co-teaching situations, there is a need to negotiate who delivers instruction and the equality of their roles. In contrast, adults who make the transition from classroom teacher to consultant spend more time working with other adults than with children. They need to develop skills in motivating their colleagues to learn new approaches such as implementing IEP goals for children with disabilities.

Related service personnel face changing roles as well. Formerly therapy was provided using a "pull out" model. Now therapists coordinate more closely with classroom staff and may even provide group activities for children who are not identified as requiring special education services.

The results of this study and a review of the related literature highlight the importance of roles and relationships among professional staff including administrators, assistants and related service staff as well as between early education teachers and special education teachers who must work together effectively for the successful inclusion of preschool children with disabilities in educational settings with typical peers. Interventions and support must begin with the acknowledgment of the importance of this factor and the provision of strategies for facilitating more fruitful interactions. We are reminded of the proverb: "Both together do best of all."

REFERENCES

Baker, J. M. & Zigmond, N. (1995). The meaning and practice of inclusion for students with learning disabilities: Themes and implications from the five cases. *The Journal of Special Education, 29*(2), 163–180.

Bricker, D. (1995). The challenge of inclusion. *Journal of Early Intervention, 19*(3), 179–194.

Bronfenbrenner, U. (1977). Toward an experimental ecology of human development. *American Psychologist, 32,* 513–531.

Charmaz, C. (1983). The grounded theory method: An explication and interpretation. In R. M. Emerson (Ed.), *Contemporary field research* (pp. 109–126). Boston: Little, Brown.

Ferguson, D. (1995, December). The real challenge of inclusion: Confessions of a 'rabid inclusionist.' *Phi Delta Kappan,* 281–287.

Ferguson, D., Meyer, G., Jeanchild, L., Juniper, L. & Zingo, J. (1992). Figuring out what to do with the grown-ups:

How teachers make inclusion "work" for students with disabilities. *Journal for Persons with Severe Handicaps, 17*(4), 218–226.

File, N. & Kontos, S. (1992). Indirect service delivery through consultation: Review and implications for early intervention. *Journal of Early Intervention, 16*(3), 221–233.

Firestone, W. A. & Herriot, R. E. (1984). Multisite qualitative policy research: Some design and implementation issues. In D. M. Fetterman (Ed.), *Ethnography in educational evaluation.* Beverly Hills, CA: Sage Publications.

Friend, M. & Cook, L. (1996). *Interactions: Collaboration skills for professionals.* White Plains, New York: Longman Publishers.

Giangreco, M. F., Dennis, R., Cloninger, C., Edelman, S. & Schattman, R. (1993). "I've counted Jon": Transformational experiences of teachers educating students with disabilities. *Exceptional Children, 59*(4), 359–372.

Guralnick, M. (1982). Mainstreaming young handicapped children: A public policy and ecological systems analysis. In Spodek (Ed.), *Handbook of research in early childhood education* (pp. 456–500).

Glaser, B. & Strauss, A. (1967). *The discovery of grounded theory: Strategies for qualitative research.* Chicago: Aldine.

Lamorey, S. & Bricker, D. D. (1993). Integrated programs: Effects on young children and their parents. In C. A. Peck, S. L. Odom, & D. D. Bricker (Eds.), *Integrating young children with disabilities into community programs: Ecological perspectives on research and implementation* (pp. 249–270). Baltimore: Brookes.

Marchant, C. (1995). Teachers' views of integrated preschools. *Journal of Early Intervention, 19*(1), 61–73.

Odom, S. L., Peck, C. A., Hanson, M., Beckman, P. J., Kaiser, A. P., Lieber, J., Brown, W. H., Horn, E. M., & Schwartz, I. S. (in press). Inclusion at the preschool level: An ecological systems analysis. *Social Policy Report—Society for Research in Child Development.*

Peck, C. (1993). Ecological perspectives on implementation of integrated early childhood programs. In C. Peck, S. Odom, & D. Bricker (Eds.), *Integrating young children with disabilities into community programs: Ecological*

perspectives on research and implementation (pp. 3–16) Baltimore: Paul Brookes.

Peck, C., Furman, G. & Helmstetter, E. (1993). Integrated early childhood programs: Research on the implementation of change in organizational contexts. In C. Peck, S. Odom, & D. Bricker (Eds.), *Integrating young children with disabilities into community programs: Ecological perspectives on research and implementation* (pp. 187–206). Baltimore: Brookes.

Pugach, M. (1995). On the failure of imagination in inclusive schooling. *Journal of Special Education, 29*(2), 212–223.

Rose, D. & Smith, B. J. (1994). Providing public education services to preschoolers with disabilities in community-based programs: Who's responsible for what? *Young Children, 49*(6), 64–68.

Sindelar, P. T. (1995). Full inclusion of students with learning disabilities and its implications for teacher education. *Journal of Special Education, 29*(2), 234–244.

Thousand, J. S. & Villa, R. A. (1992). Collaborative teams: A powerful tool in school restructuring. In R. A. Villa, J. S. Thousand, W. Stainback & S. Stainback. *Restructuring for caring and effective education* (pp. 73–108). Baltimore: Brookes.

Thousand, J. & Villa, R. A. (1995, December). Inclusion: Alive and well in the green mountain state. *Phi Delta Kappan,* 288–291.

Wolcott, H. (1990). *Writing up qualitative research.* Beverly Hills, CA: Sage Publications.

Zelditch, M. (1962). Some methodological problems of field studies. *American Journal of Sociology, 67,* 566–576.

Zigmond, N. (1995). An exploration of the meaning and practice of special education in the context of full inclusion of students with learning disabilities. *The Journal of Special Education, 29*(2), 109–115.

The study is supported by a grant (H024K40004) from the U.S. Department of Education. We wish to acknowledge the contribution of Shouming Li, Deirdre Barnwell, Karen Herring, Diane Grieg, Pamela Wolfberg, Sonya Gutierrez, Craig Zercher, Maria Morgan, Kristen Anderson, and Carolyn Cottam.

■ Ask Yourself

Identifying Issues for Advocacy

1. Is bilingualism detrimental to school achievement and the development of social competence? Why or why not? Should children from immigrant families be taught in their dominant or native language for no more than two years upon immigrating to the United States? Why or why not (see Anderson, 1996; Bronner, 1998; Crawford, 1998; National Association for the Education of Young Children, 1996)?

2. Is preserving customs of immigrants detrimental to their child's educational attainment? Why or why not? Should schools strive for cultural continuity between home and school? Why or why not (see Barta & Winn, 1996; National Association for the Education of Young Children, 1996)?

3. Are programs for bilingual/multicultural education effective? Why or why not?

4. Write a story or a brief autobiography about significant encounters with diversity in your life (see Reddy, 1996).

5. If "telling" is not the best way to develop multicultural understanding, then what would be developmentally appropriate learning experiences for young children (see Chapter 8 of this book and The Teaching Tolerance Project, 1991)?

6. Do holidays still have a place in early childhood programs? Some educators argue that the festivals, food, and fashion approach to multicultural education is better avoided, particularly if done in isolation. They claim this approach perpetuates stereotypes and fails to address cultural bias. Others claim that sharing holiday celebrations can further intercultural understandings and relationships. What do you think and why? How would you, as a teacher, address the raft of holidays that occur between November and February?

7. Honeysuckle Day Care and Nursery School is located in an upper middle-class, all-White community. Most children come from two-parent, working families. Noting the community in which this program is located, the director explains that there has never been a need for bilingual education. She is uncertain how the staff would "handle such a situation if it were to arise." She guesses that probably the center would not accept the child because he or she most likely would be considered a child with special needs, and the center does not accept children with special needs. Analyze the assumptions and value positions held in this situation in terms of views expressed by the National Association for the Education of Young Children (1996) and the authors of your readings.

8. Some people espouse the position that cultural traditions should be taught only by members of that society. They argue that outsiders are cultural "foreigners," unable to grasp the subtleties of another person's culture. Moreover, one's thoughts and feelings are sifted through one's own cultural lenses. Thus, attempts to teach children about their culture when it is different from one's own are seen as paternalistic and patronizing. What implications does this view have for the early childhood teacher? Does this preclude finding out about other cultures and societies? Why or why not (see Ladson-Billings, 1994)?

9. What are the rights of parents of a young child with disabilities? What are the rights of children with and without disabilities? What are the rights of teachers (see Appendix 11)?

10. Do children with physical disabilities create unnecessary fears in their preschool peers without disabilities? Why or why not?

11. What are the effects on the child with disabilities when he or she is socially isolated by peers? Are children with disabilities often social isolates in regular classrooms?

12. What knowledge and skills do teachers need to have to be able to work with children with disabilities (see Cartledge & Johnston, 1996)?

13. What measures should be taken to ensure appropriate educational placements for children at risk or with disabilities (see Fuchs & Fuchs, 1998; Sapon-Shevin, 1996)?

14. How valid is developmental delay as a category for disabilities services? How about attention deficit hyperactivity disorder? Are identification strategies adequate? Are services effective? Why or why not (see The Arc of the United States, 1997; Committee on Children with Disabilities, 1994; Committee on Children with Disabilities and Committee on Drugs, 1996; Division for Early Childhood, 1996; Jensen et al., 1997)?

15. Sue, a legally blind child, is enrolled in Sandbox Nursery School. As part of the special education aid provided for Sue, a special education teacher from the Board of Cooperative Education Services (BOCES) comes three times a week to work with Sue. This teacher works with her during a time of the session when Sue will not miss out on specially planned activities. The special education teacher also incorporates activities that involve the entire class. The directors contacted an organization called Lighthouse to help them get Sue's parents to accept her disability. Sue has come a long way. When she was first enrolled, she could not participate during snack-time because she could not feed herself and refused to hold a cup. The changed attitudes of her parents also have fostered quicker progress at home. Examine and discuss this situation in light of suggestions made by authors of your readings.

16. Renting space from a church for many years, a child-care director suddenly discovers that the church now has begun to rent space in the same building to a preschool special education program. In the upper-income community, she notices that new attitudes about her program are beginning to surface. The church is becoming known as a center for children with special needs, and parents, concerned that their children will be perceived as having special needs, now hesitate to enroll them in her child-care program. If you were the director, how would you respond?

17. Should all publicly funded playgrounds be made accessible for children with disabilities? Why or why not?

■ Advocacy and Leadership Strategies

1. Visit museums, festivals, ethnic restaurants, and other places that expose you to cultural patterns and lifestyles different from your own.

2. Organize a book club of four to five people (fellow students, worksite colleagues, or community members) and read and discuss one of the following books:

   Creaser, B., & Dau, E. (1995). The anti-bias approach in early childhood. Watson, Australia: Australian Early Childhood Association. (ERIC Document Reproduction Service No. ED 399 049)

   Derman-Sparks, L., & Phillips, C. B. (1997). Teaching/learning anti-racism: A developmental approach. New York: Teachers College Press.

   Poinsett, N., & Burns, V. (1995). Rainbow children: A racial justice and diversity program for ages 5–8. Boston: Unitarian Universalist Association.

   Reddy, M. T. (Ed.). (1996). Everyday acts against racism: Raising children in a multiracial world. Seattle, WA: Seal Press.

   Slapin, B., & Seale, D. (1992). Through Indian eyes: The native experience in books for children. Philadelphia, PA: New Society Publishers.

   Tatum, B. D. (1997). "Why are all the Black kids sitting together in the cafeteria?" New York: Basic Books.

3. Carefully read the following letters and then consider what ways of coping with ethnicity each of these letters exemplifies. Write a response to each letter. In your response, concentrate on the child's perspective and what the 4- or 5-year-old child is learning. Should the school ignore these requests? Why or why not?

   > Dear Teacher,
   >
   > I would appreciate it if you did not call attention to Shenoa's Cherokee background during Thanksgiving. My new husband has adopted Shenoa. He wants her to be a real Yankee like himself, and so do I.
   >
   > Thank you,
   >
   > Mrs. Sally Porter

   > Dear Teacher,
   >
   > I didn't get much of a chance to talk to you at Open House last Thursday night because there were so many people standing around. However, I want you to know that even though Rhonda's skin is as fair as yours and mine, she is African American. And I want her to be proud of her African heritage. So please, when you begin to talk about Black History on Martin Luther King's birthday, be sure to ask Rhonda to tell the class about the many struggles of our people for equal rights. For a 5-year-old,

she is extremely well informed. She has been attending the Title IV program and knows a lot about her ancestry.

Thank you,

Mrs. Janice Bethany

Dear Teacher,

I won't be coming to International Night at the school, and I would rather not send in my recipe for churros. When my husband, Jose, and I emigrated from Puerto Rico and came here, we decided on two things:

1. We would practice our old ways only at home with our friends and family.
2. With strangers and on our jobs, we would try to blend in with other people.

We want our children to do the same things that we do. They know who they are, but they know that it's a competitive world out there, and that they will have to be like everyone else in order to get ahead.

Thank you,

Mrs. Rorita Rodriguez

4. At your community or school library, search for children's books that convey authentic messages about people of color and for books that convey stereotypical or racist messages. Using this information, work with the librarian, parents, or teachers to make improvements in the quality of books available to children (see Appendix 14 and Slapin & Seale, 1992).

5. Show the videocassette "Anti-Bias Curriculum" (Louise Derman-Sparks, 1989, Pacific Oaks Bookstore, 5 Westmoreland Place, Pasadena, CA 91103) to staff or parents of an early childhood program and lead a discussion.

6. At your field-study site, interview one of the teachers using "Diversity in the Classroom: A Checklist" (see Appendix 13) and invite the teacher to discuss the questions and his or her responses (see Boyd, 1997).

7. Develop a classroom project or curriculum unit that addresses antibias concerns.

8. If you are a teacher in grades K–3, apply to Teaching Tolerance for a grant to implement a tolerance project in your school and community. For details, see www.splcenter.org/teachingtolerance/tt-5.html

9. Visit a bilingual classroom and record the teaching strategies used. Interview the teacher about choice of curriculum strategies, development of English fluency, and making the transition to greater use of English. Compare and contrast what you observe and hear with the viewpoints expressed in the readings of this chapter. (If possible, volunteer your assistance in the classroom.)

10. Submit an op-ed article to your local newspaper on bilingual education or request that the newspaper reports on bilingual education programs in your area (see Appendix 4).

11. With three to five other classmates, organize a debate on bilingual education or full inclusion (see Appendix 8 for debate guidelines).

12. In order to better understand diverse perceptions and responses to children with special needs, interview a nursery-school teacher, a day-care teacher, and a kindergarten teacher. Request an interview with each teacher and state your purpose (i.e., to gather information about identification of and curricular adaptations for learners with developmental delays or disabilities). Based on information gathered from this chapter, compose four to six interview questions that you wish to ask each person. (Avoid questions that can be answered with a yes-no only response.) Take notes during the interview in order to obtain a record of the interviewee's responses. After the interviews, write a synopsis of the interviews, including the questions asked, each interviewee's responses, and your interpretation of responses in relation to readings in this chapter. Then compare interview findings with guidelines for developmentally appropriate curriculum practices (Bredekamp & Copple, 1997). Share your information in class in a panel discussion.

13. On October 8, 1986, PL 99-457 was signed into law. These amendments to PL 94-142 provide federal assistance to states for intervention services and preschool programs for children with disabilities (birth to 5 years) and for intervention services aimed at high-risk infants and toddlers. All states decided to apply for these funds. Contact an early childhood special education representative in your state (e.g., in the State Education Department or in the State Mental Health Department). Find out how your state implements the provisions of this amendment. What "lead agency" is designated to oversee and monitor implementation of these provisions? What types of agencies or institutions are the major providers of services (e.g., public versus private)? How are young children with disabilities or at risk identified? What proportion of the children served in the state have language delays or other speech difficulties? What proportion of the children served in the state have each of various disabling or at-risk conditions? What provisions exist to train staff for these programs?

14. At your field-study site, investigate what provisions are made for children with disabilities. Also research how staff are prepared for inclusion of children with disabilities. Interview a sample of teachers and parents about their ideas about inclusion (see Poulson & Cole, 1996).

15. Developmental screening can be an important step in identifying children with disabilities. When administration of a screening instrument indicates that a child may have a serious learning or developmental problem, a referral should be made for more thorough assessment. Developmental screening, however, can satisfy the requirements of the Individuals with Disabilities Education Act (IDEA) for identification of children with disabilities and therefore is open to serious misuse (Shepard, 1997). Another concern about assessment instruments expressed by the Goal 1 Technical Planning Group of the National Education Goals Panel is if such assessment tools are responsive to cultural variation (Kagan, Moore, & Bredekamp, 1995). In the past, attempts to make assessment culturally sensitive focused on translating the assessment tool in the child's language or reviewing the cultural appropriateness of the information solicited by the questions. Today, however, we also recognize that cultural patterns and values predispose children to approach learning in different ways and that assessment instruments must accommodate cultural variations in learning styles and must allow for alternative expressions of valued outcomes. Identify a standardized screening or evaluation instrument that is intended for use with young children (e.g., Battalle Developmental Inventory Screening Test, Brigance Preschool Screen, Denver Developmental Screening, or DIAL-R). Review the appropriateness of the instrument for use with culturally diverse children. Ask yourself questions such as:

a. With what cultural group or groups and ages was this instrument normed?

b. Do you think the instrument has any cultural biases? If so, what are they?

c. Does the screening or evaluation instrument focus on activities that are familiar to children from diverse cultural backgrounds and that appeal to their interests?

d. Can the instrument accommodate cultural variations in learning styles?

e. What child-rearing practices would this instrument seem to assume? Or what assumptions seem to be made about typical child development patterns? Do these assumptions fit with the child-rearing practices and patterns of child development in culturally diverse communities in your geographic area?

f. In these communities, how might you involve parents and other family members in reviewing this instrument and in gathering information for screening and evaluation?

Summarize what you learned about cultural sensitivity and the appropriateness of this assessment instrument. Report to the class.

References and Suggested Readings

Anderson, M. P. (1996). Frequently asked questions about NAEYC's linguistic and cultural diversity position paper. *Young Children, 51* (2), 13–16.

Apter, D. S. (1994). From dream to reality: A participant's view of the implementation of Part H of P.L. 99-457. *Journal of Early Intervention, 18* (2), 131–140.

The Arc of the United States. (1997). Early intervention and early childhood services. [Online]. Available: www.TheArc.org/posits/earlyinter.html

Barta, J., & Winn, T. (1996). Developmentally appropriate practice: Involving parents in creating anti-bias classrooms. *Journal of Early Education and Family Review, 4* (2), 7–10.

Bizar, M., Koerner, M., & Zemelman, S. (1996). A design for multicultural education: Leveling the playing field. [Online]. Available: www.ncrel.org/mands/docs/5-14.htm

Boyd, A . L. (1997). An anti-bias approach to early childhood education. [Online]. Available: www.naspweb.org/family/ho/ANTIBIAS.htm

Bredekamp, S., & Copple, C. (Eds.). (1997). *Developmentally appropriate practice in early childhood programs* (rev. ed.). Washington, DC: National Association for the Education of Young Children.

Brett, A. (1997). Assistive and adoptive technology—Supporting competence and independence in young children with disabilities. *Dimensions of Early Childhood, 25* (3), 14–15, 18–20.

Bronner, E. (1998, June 10). In bilingual schooling setback, educators see another swing of the pendulum. *New York Times* [Online], 3 pages. Available: www.ourworld.compuserve.com/homepages/JWCRAWFORD/NYT12.htm

Carter, M. (1996, Fall). Uses of persona dolls. *Educational Doll Plans: The People of Every Stripe Newsletter* [Online], 2 pages. Available: www.teleport.com/~people/margiec.htm

Cartledge, G., & Johnston, C. T. (1996). Inclusive classrooms for students with emotional and behavioral disorders: Critical variables. *Theory into Practice, 35* (1), 51–57.

Committee on Children with Disabilities. (1994). Screening infants and young children for developmental disabilities (RE9414: A policy statement of the American Academy of Pediatrics). *Pediatrics, 93* (5), 863–865. Available: www.aap.org/policy/00207.html

Committee on Children with Disabilities and Committee on Drugs. (1996). Medication for children with attentional disorders (RE9627: A position statement of the American Academy of Pediatrics). *Pediatrics, 98* (2), 301-304. Available: www.aap.org/policy/01494.html.

Crawford, J. W. (1998). What's new on the language policy web site. [Online]. Available: www.ourworld.compuserve.com/homepages/JWCRAWFORD/new.htm

Creaser, B., & Dau, E. (1995). *The anti-bias approach in early childhood.* Watson, AUS: Australian Early Childhood Association. (ERIC Document Reproduction Service No. ED 399 049)

Davis, S. (1997). The human genome project: Examining The Arc's concerns regarding the project's ethical, legal, and social implications. [Online]. Available: www.ornl.gov/hgmis/resources.arc.htm

Derman-Sparks, L., Gutiérrez, M., & Phillips, C. B. (n.d.) *Teaching young children to resist bias: What parents can do* (brochure). Washington, DC: National Association for the Education of Young Children.

Derman-Sparks, L., & Phillips, C. B. (1997). *Teaching/learning anti-racism: A developmental approach.* New York: Teachers College Press.

Division for Early Childhood (DEC). (1996). *Developmental delay as an eligibility category* (a position paper). Denver, CO: Division for Early Childhood of the

Council for Exceptional Children. (ERIC Document Reproduction Service No. ED 412 707)

Fennimore, B. S. (1994). Addressing prejudiced statements: A four-step method that works! *Childhood Education, 70,* 202–204.

Fleer, M. (1996). Theories of "play": Are they ethnocentric or inclusive? *Australian Journal of Early Childhood, 21* (4), 12–17.

Fuchs, D., & Fuchs, L. S. (1998). Competing visions for educating students with disabilities: Inclusion versus full inclusion. *Childhood Education, 74,* 309–316.

Hildebrand, V., Phenice, L., Gray, M., & Hines, R. (1996). *Knowing and serving diverse families.* Englewood Cliffs, NJ: Prentice-Hall.

Jensen, P. S., Mrazek, D., Knapp, P. K., Steinberg, L., Pfeffer, C., Schowalter, J., & Shapiro, T. (1997). Evolution and revolution in child psychiatry: ADHD as a disorder of adaptation. *Journal of the American Academy of Child & Adolescent Psychiatry, 36* (12), 1672–1681.

Kagan, S. L., Moore, E., & Bredekamp, S. (Eds.). (1995). *Reconsidering children's early development and learning: Toward common views and vocabulary* (Report No. 95-03). Washington, DC: Goal 1 Technical Planning Group, National Education Goals Panel.

Koplow, L. (1996). *Unsmiling faces: How preschools can heal.* New York: Teachers College Press.

Ladson-Billings, G. (1994, May). What we can learn from multicultural education research. *Educational Leadership, 51* (8), 22–26.

National Association for the Education of Young Children (NAEYC). (1996). NAEYC position statement: Responding to linguistic and cultural diversity—Recommendations for effective early childhood education. *Young Children, 51* (2), 4–12.

Poinsett, N., & Burns, V. (1995). *Rainbow children: A racial justice and diversity program for ages 5–8.* Boston: Unitarian Universalist Association.

Poulsen, M. K., & Cole, C. K. (1996). *Project Relationship: Creating and sustaining a nurturing community* (manual and video). Los Angeles, CA: Los Angeles Unified School District, Infant Preschool Programs. (ERIC Document Reproduction Service No. ED 408 742)

Reddy, M. T. (Ed.). (1996). *Everyday acts against racism: Raising children in a multiracial world.* Seattle, WA: Seal Press.

Roth, M. (1996). You have to start somewhere. In M. T. Reddy (Ed.), *Everyday acts against racism* (pp. 3–11). Seattle, WA: Seal Press.

Sapon-Shevin, M. (1996). Full inclusion as disclosing tablet: Revealing the flaws in our present system. *Theory into Practice, 35* (1), 35–41.

Shepard, L. A. (1997). Children not ready to learn? The invalidity of school readiness testing. *Psychology in the Schools, 34,* 85–97.

Skibinski, L. (1996, Fall). A *Pocahontas* persona doll story. *Educational Doll Plans: The People of Every Stripe Newsletter* [Online], 3 pages. Available: www.teleport.com/~people/pocahont.htm

Slapin, B., & Seale, D. (1992). *Through Indian eyes: The native experience in books for children.* Philadelphia, PA: New Society Publishers.

Swick, K. J., Boutee, G., & Van Scoy, I. (1996). Families and schools building multicultural values together. *Childhood Education, 72* (2), 75–79.

Tatum, B. D. (1997). *"Why are all the Black kids sitting together in the cafeteria?"* New York: Basic Books.

The Teaching Tolerance Project. (1991). *Starting small: Teaching tolerance in preschool and early grades.* Montgomery, AL: Southern Poverty Law Center.

Weiss, L. (1997, May–June). Care for special needs. *Children's Advocate* [Online], 2 pages. Available: www.4children.org/new/5-97need.htm

When voters handcuff educators (editorial). (1998, June 10). *Milwaukee Journal Sentinel* [Online], 1 page. Available: www.ourworld.compuserve.com/homepages/JWCRAWFORD/MJS1.htm

Chapter 7

The Family: Parenting Education and Family Involvement in Education

A License to Help?

Mrs. Yancey, a kindergarten teacher, watches the departing father of 5-year-old Pete with tears in her eyes. "Where did I go wrong? I was only trying to help. I even offered to help Pete get some exercise by taking him ice skating after school. I know that Mr. Freeman works long hours and has his hands full as a single parent. I sure had a tough time getting him in here, and now he's left in a huff! I only casually mentioned that I thought Pete's grandmother shouldn't send four peanut butter and jellies, two creme-filled cupcakes, a banana, and a can of pop for lunch when the child is 25 pounds overweight. I just suggested that Pete's compulsive eating habits would be relieved if Mr. Freeman spent more time with his son."

Questions

1. Suppose you were Mr. Freeman. How would you describe the conference with Mrs. Yancey?

2. Was Mrs. Yancey justified in her comments to Mr. Freeman? Why or why not?

3. What should a teacher do when he or she believes a child is nutritionally at risk?

4. What is the next step Mrs. Yancey should take after this regrettable first conference with Mr. Freeman?

Preview

For the past 30 years, families have been changing from the traditional model where the man is the breadwinner and the woman stays home. Today, many children, at some point, will experience living in a single-parent family. If early childhood programs play a role in supporting the family, how can they best help strengthen today's family? At the very least, teachers need to be sensitive to family circumstances, routines, and values. Also, parent involvement in school programs can strengthen the connections between home and school and can enhance the meaningfulness of the curriculum for the child. As part of parent involvement, parents should be informed about their child's developmental progress, but parents should also be encouraged to communicate to the teacher their knowledge of the child and their expectations as well as their concerns for the child. Teachers should be sensitive to the need for communication to occur in both directions.

In the first selection in this chapter, Marge Scherer leads David Elkind to examine the ways in which families have changed, why these changes have occurred, and the effect these changes have on our children. In the next two articles, the Family Involvement Partnership for Learning and Brent A. McBride and Thomas R. Rane highlight the importance of family involvement in education, with particular emphasis on the role of father/male involvement in the lives of young children. Glenna Zeak and Penny Hauser-Cram then offer specific examples and insights about parent involvement and communication. Finally, Sharon L. Kagan, addressing the changes in and stresses on the modern family, discusses the importance of both parenting education and family support programs and delineates the issues surrounding such programs.

On Our Changing Family Values

A Conversation with David Elkind

Marge Scherer

■ ■ ■

Most of us are familiar with the term "nuclear family." And we are also aware that the demographics have changed, that there are many more nontraditional families today. You take the idea further and introduce the idea of the postmodern family. Would you explain that concept?

The modern nuclear family—two parents, two and one-half children, with one parent at home with the children—is fast disappearing. We now have the postmodern family, what I call the permeable family—two parents working; single-parent families; adoptive families; remarried families; and so on. The permeable family is more fluid, more flexible, and more obviously vulnerable to pressures from outside itself. It mirrors the openness, complexity, and diversity of our contemporary lifestyles.

In Ties That Stress *you explain some of the historical forces that have shaped families of the past and families today. Would you give us a capsule history?*

Around the '50s, most of us lived in nuclear families. We operated under the assumptions that women should stay home, men should be the providers, and the children were to be protected. Then many events changed us, like World War II, the atomic bomb, the Holocaust, then later the Women's Rights movement, the Civil Rights movement, Watergate. These events and their consequences challenged our basic ideas about how the world works. For example, we began to doubt the notion that after World War II, there would never be another major war; that every day and in every way, we're getting better and better.

And how has this new, more pessimistic thinking about the world changed family values?

As a consequence of these events, we began to see the sentiments of the modern nuclear family as overly idealized and blind to the dark side of human behavior. For example, couples used to believe in romantic love—that there was just one person in the whole world for you and once you found that person you would live happily ever after, without having to work at the relationship. Our divorce rate contradicts the notion.

Second, there was the notion of maternal love, the belief that women possessed a maternal instinct to be with their children all the time, and make a nest, and that if they didn't, something was wrong with them. When the maternal love notion became very prominent, husbands began to think that they should be included within that maternal love and should be looked after in the manner of children. It put a heavy burden on women. Today we talk more about shared parenting than maternal instinct.

A third sentiment of the nuclear family was domesticity and the idea that the home was the center of one's life. That really grew out of the movement into cities and industrialization. The factory was a cold hard place, and the factory worker was a cog in a machine. In contrast, the home was a warm, welcoming place in a heartless world. And in that home, the mother was the center. She had had—up until the turn of the century—creative outlets such as quilting, canning, cooking, and baking. The industrialization of home products robbed women of creative outlets. Women were told not to grind their own coffee because they could buy it vacuum-packed, not to bake their own bread because they could buy Wonder Bread, not to make their own clothes because factory-made clothes were much cheaper. Women were turned into consumers, which eventually contributed in a very important way to the women's movement.

Those were the three major sentiments of the nuclear family, and they've been supplanted with new sentiments, those of consensual love, shared parenting, and urbanity.

We talk a lot about family values. The real family value that grew out of the nuclear family sentiments was that of togetherness. It's the notion that the family is the most important relationship in one's life. Parents don't divorce because family is more important than personal needs or happiness. In the same way, business comes after, not before the family. Obviously all families didn't live by these rules, but togetherness was the ideal.

And these notions are gradually being eroded and replaced with new sentiments that are not idealistic?

I want to make it very clear. I'm not arguing that the nuclear family was good and the postmodern, permeable family, bad, or vice versa. There is a lot of misunderstanding about post-modernism. Some identify it with trendy fads in literature and the arts. But it is a more general movement that argues that the modern beliefs—for example, the belief in progress—have to be modified in light of world events. Postmodernism really challenges some of the ideas of modernity, but it also tries to incorporate what is good from the past, just as postmodern architecture takes what it sees as good from the past but also discards what doesn't work.

What happened to the family was, thanks to the sexual revolution and new contraceptive methods, premarital sex became socially acceptable. And that had the effect of making virginity lose its value. That's a significant point because it means that relationships are very different today. The implicit contract based on an exchange of virginity for commitment no longer exists. The basis of the contract has become consensual. Marriage is an agreement between two equals, with the idea that we'll stay in the relationship as long as it serves our purposes and needs. It's more egalitarian, and it gives adults many more options.

Talk more about the family values of today that supplant the old values, like autonomy replacing togetherness.

Instead of togetherness, we have a new focus on autonomy. The individual becomes more important than the family, not because of egocentrism or narcissism, but rather because of a rapidly changing society and economy. We hear about layoffs everyday. Occupations that never even existed before are invented, and whole other occupations disappear. It's a difficult time for people occupationally.

When I lived in Rochester, generations had worked for Eastman Kodak. Your parents worked there, you were working there, your kids were going to work there. The company—they called it Mother Kodak—had recreation centers, health centers. And you bought stock and you had security. All of that has changed.

Parents today have to protect themselves first, much as in an airplane they must put the breathing mask on themselves before they put it on their child. To make sure that their children are provided for, they devote tremendous time to working and refurbishing their skills. So, too often, parents are focused on their own activities, forcing kids to be autonomous as well—to be much more independent, to be home alone, to get their own meals, to organize their own time.

The notion of autonomy is that each person should be free to follow his or her own trajectory. The family meal has gone by the board. It used to be a gathering place for the nuclear family. Today soccer practice or a business meeting takes precedence over dinner because personal needs are more important than the family.

You don't urge people to have the family meal anymore, or do you?

If possible, it's wonderful but increasingly difficult in today's world. Rituals are, nonetheless, very important for children, and even if you don't have a family meal, at least you should have certain rituals on birthdays or holidays. They may not be every day or every week, but it's important to have a time when the family can come together.

We talk a lot about quality time, but it's not really the quality of the time that is important. What is critical is that the children feel that they are important enough in their parents' lives that the parents are going to sacrifice something for them. Real quality time is when parents say, "Look, I know I have this meeting but you are more important, and I am going to come to your recital." Children need to know they are important in their parents' lives.

Children used to be thought of as innocent. But our TV shows today often depict kids as smarter than their parents. You've even said that **Home Alone** *is the perfect metaphor for our concept of childhood. Did the concept of competent children come out of popular culture or child psychology?*

It didn't come from any new discoveries in child development. We have no data indicating that children are more competent today than we knew them to be in another time in history. The perception of child competence comes directly from social changes and from our need as parents and adults to have competent children. As society has changed, we can no longer protect children in the way we once did. So now we believe we have to prepare them by exposing them to everything and anything.

Television is the prime culprit, but not the only one. We can no longer control the information flow to children. When we were dealing with print media, children had to have a certain level of intellectual ability and skill to decipher words. With television, even young children can get information visually. After the tragedy in South Carolina when a mother drowned her children, a woman called me and said, "What do I say to my 5-year-old? She saw the news on TV and she is asking, 'Mommy, are you going to kill me?'" It's a whole different world today. As a result, parents and society have to see children as competent. It's a way for us to stay sane to say, "Well, you know, they are seeing all this stuff, but they can handle it. It will prepare them for the real world."

You don't think that children today are more savvy than they used to be?

We overestimate their competence. As I travel and lecture across the country, teachers tell me routinely that they see much more aggressive behavior and much more hostility on the playgrounds. We see many more learning problems. We see much more depression in children. These are all the stress symptoms of kids who are expected to be more competent in handling all sorts of experiences than they really are.

You call this the new morbidity, all the stress-related illnesses that affect children and families.

Right. The pediatrician Robert Haggerty and his colleagues called it that. Up until mid-century, most young people died from polio, tuberculosis—from disease. Fortunately, medical science conquered these illnesses, but today we lose as many young people through stress-related causes as we once lost through disease. We lose 10,000 youngsters a year in substance abuse-related automobile accidents. We lose 5,000 kids a year in suicide. We have two million

alcoholic teenagers. All of these are stress-related problems arising from the fact that in our society the needs of children and youth are simply weighted less heavily than the needs of adults. A few decades ago, women consumed millions of pounds of tranquilizers because their needs were not being met. Today children and adolescents are reacting to stress in equally self-destructive ways.

If we really want to attack this problem, we can't just talk about drug and sex education. They are important, but we have to talk about how we can better meet the needs of children and youth. Their needs for love and care and adult supervision and guidance. Their need for more space for activities. More age-appropriate curricula. More sense that they are important in their parents' lives and in the life of society.

I was watching a documentary program last night. The reporters were asking a group of kids about stealing and lying. These kids had no strong moral sense about doing these things. They didn't worry about whether the person would be hurt or damaged by taking something from them. It's not true for all of our children, but I think that to the extent we don't really care about kids, kids are not going to care about other people.

Are they a lost generation?

No, not entirely. The question is, Can a society survive when the number of kids who are lost gets larger than the number of kids who are not?

Returning to the idea of the competent child, do schools buy into that notion, too? Are there practices at school that might be creating too much stress?

One of the most serious examples of schools buying into the notion of childhood competence is the whole early childhood issue. Up until the '60s, fewer than half of children had been in early childhood programs prior to kindergarten. Today 85 percent of children enter kindergarten with some preschool experience. As a result, administrators tend to believe that a child entering 1st grade should know letters and numbers. If children don't have those literacy and numeracy skills, they are held back or put in transition classes. Nationally, we are retaining 10 to 20 percent of kids; in some communities, 50 percent. The average age in many of the suburban 1st grades now is 7.

You are saying that children this age shouldn't be retained because they might just need a few more years to develop?

Right. What people don't recognize is that the 4–7 age period is one of very rapid intellectual growth, much like the period of rapid physical growth in early adolescence. Children grow at different rates, quite independently of their intellectual potential. If a 6-year-old isn't able to read, it may have nothing to do with his or her motivation or ability and everything to do with intellectual immaturity. And we punish children simply for having different growth rates.

Pushing the curriculum down to lower grade levels is another example. The decimal fractions that used to be taught at 6th grade in a week or two are now being taught at 4th grade. It takes 4th graders a month and they still don't understand it. There are a great many things that children can learn in 4th grade. They don't have to learn decimal fractions. We should have them learning things that are challenging at their level but not so daunting that they feel frustrated.

I hear the same thing at the high school level. One instructor used to teach organic chemistry at 12th grade. Parents pushed the school to teach it at 10th grade. Many 10th graders were in tears over that course. Yet we hold to the idea that somehow anything can be taught at any time and kids can learn it.

At the same time schools are being criticized for not challenging students or for not having high standards.

There isn't sufficient individualization in the schools. High standards are best met by individualization. Most of the printed curriculum material makes little provision for wide differences in learning styles. It's not that we shouldn't have expectations and standards, but we need to recognize that children don't all learn in the same way at the same rate.

One of the most important findings of the Tennessee study (STAR) is that class size makes a difference. It's the amount of one-on-one time between teacher and child that has the most impact.

Of course, it's easier for us to have a one-size-fits-all curriculum. And it's economically easier to have larger classes. But those concerns speak to the adult issues, not to child issues. If you reduced class size to 18, did just that one thing across the country, you'd see a remarkable improvement in education across the board.

If you are a teacher and you see children in your classroom who aren't receiving much attention from their parents, what do you do?

One of the things I tell our student teachers is that children want to be loved, as we all do, by the people whom they love. If that love is not reciprocated, we can't replace it. Certainly loving and caring teachers are important, but they cannot fulfill the parental role. Teachers cry out for these children, but they have to recognize there are limits to their role as providers of the kind of affection and love that kids need.

How can schools help families feel more connected to a larger community?

Many schools already are reaching out to families by providing the quality child care that is so difficult for parents to find and afford.

Another important thing schools can do is to provide parenting classes. There is a wonderful program (Parents as Teachers) in 14 midwestern states where the school systems send trainers on home visits to help young mothers engage in developmentally appropriate activities with their infants.

A lot of other things can be done—schools are bringing grandparents in, using tutors, bringing social services and health services into the school.

We have to recognize, however, that we are a very, very diverse society, not a homogeneous one. You can go to Brownsville, Texas, where 98 percent of the kids speak Spanish. You can go to some towns in California, where the kids speak eight different languages. In Groton, Connecticut, most fathers are in the Navy, and get transferred out of town every three years. The result is that no child both starts and finishes the elementary school. In communities around Pittsburgh, kids still walk to school and go home for lunch. You could lift those neighborhoods out of the '20s or '30s.

We don't sufficiently appreciate the extraordinary diversity of our society. It's one of our great strengths. There is no one way to interact with the community. Schools have to work with the community in ways that are meaningful in their particular miniature world.

One last question. Some of us have grown up in nuclear families and are experiencing all the stresses of postmodern families today. What's next for families?

I am hopeful that we will move beyond the permeable family to a *vital* family that meets the needs of both parents and children. The problem with the postmodern permeable family was that it went to extremes. Erik Erikson once said something to the effect that to be heard in our society, you have to take an extreme position and shout it loudly. Once your position is heard and taken seriously, then you can move back to a middle ground. I hope that we are moving back toward a more balanced family. I see some signs of it, especially in our concern with community.

Statistics show that young people are marrying later and are having fewer children. They are trying in their own lives not to make the mistakes their parents made. They don't want to go through divorce. When they do get into a relationship, they want to make it work. This bodes well for the family. At schools, there is a new excitement about change. Hopefully, we will individualize more and begin to place the needs of teachers and children on a par with political and economic considerations. That's the most significant way schools can help families.

■ *David Elkind is professor of child study at Tufts University, 105 College Ave., Medford, Massachusetts 02155. He is the author of many books, including* Ties That Stress: The New Family Imbalance *(Cambridge: Harvard University Press, 1994).*

■ *Marge Scherer is managing editor of* Educational Leadership.

Partners in Learning

How Schools Can Support Family Involvement in Education

Family Involvement Partnership for Learning

■ ■ ■

> ### The Family Involvement National Education Goal
>
> We believe that strengthening the connection between families and schools is so important that we have made it one of America's National Education Goals. The Goal declares that by the year 2000, "Every school will promote partnerships that will increase parental involvement and participation in promoting the social, emotional, and academic growth of children."
>
> *Richard W. Riley*
> *U.S. Secretary of Education*

Learn to Communicate Better

At times, parents feel that educators talk down to them or speak in educational jargon they do not understand. School signs often seem unwelcoming. Schools should make every effort to reach out and communicate with parents in a clear way and listen to what they have to say. To ensure that all parents have access to information, written material should be concise and easily readable. Schools should be parent-friendly. Some school newsletters for parents include a glossary of terms to help parents understand school improvement efforts. Other schools use regularly scheduled telephone calls to stay in contact with families.

Encourage Parental Participation in School Improvement Efforts

When schools develop improvement plans, families ought to be included at every stage of the process to get their input and to give them a sense of shared responsibility. Many schools, supported by the new Goals 2000: Educate America Act, are now developing such plans. They are working to raise academic standards, improve teaching, make schools safer, introduce computers and other learning technologies into the classroom, and to make many other vitally needed changes. The full involvement of parents and other members of the community is instrumental to the success of these efforts.

Involve Parents in Decision-Making

Schools can give parents a more effective voice by opening up the school governance process so that more parents can participate. Many schools hold evening and weekend meetings and conferences to accommodate families' work schedules.

Give Teachers the Tools to Reach Out to Families

Staff development can help teachers to understand the benefits of family involvement and show them how to remove barriers to involvement. It can also

Family Involvement Partnership for Learning. (1997). *Team up for kids! How schools can support family involvement in education.* Washington, DC: U.S. Department of Education.

explain techniques for improving two-way communication between home and schools, and suggest ways to help meet families' overall educational needs.

Make Parents Feel Welcome

Often the first time a parent comes to school is when a child is in trouble. Schools can help reduce tensions by making initial contacts with parents friendly and respectful. Schools can also reduce distrust by arranging contacts in neutral settings off school grounds. Home visits by family liaison personnel can be particularly helpful. Some programs have used home-school coordinators to run weekly clubs for parents, helping to build parenting skills and trust between families and schools. Schools might also encourage parents, teachers, and students to meet at the beginning of the school year to agree on goals and develop a common understanding.

Overcome Language Barriers

Reaching families whose first language is not English requires schools to make special accommodations. Translating materials into a parent's first language helps, but written communication alone is not enough. Ideally, a resource person, perhaps another parent, should be available to communicate with parent in their first language. Interactive telephone voice-mail systems that have bilingual recordings for families are also useful. In addition, English-as-a-second-language classes for parents and grandparents may be helpful.

Use Technology to Link Parents to the Classroom

Educators can creatively use new technology—from voice-mail to homework hotlines to educational CD-ROM programs—to get parents more involved in the learning process. For example, voice mail systems have been installed in several hundred schools across the country. Parents and students can call for taped messages that describe classroom activities and daily homework assignments. Audiotapes and videotapes can also be used to enhance communication with parents. These are especially helpful in reaching family members who do not read. Even with all the new technology, teachers and other school staff can still use the old telephone to connect with parents. Schools can help by providing teachers with classroom phones.

Encourage Communities to Join School-Family Partnerships

This can be especially effective in reducing school safety problems that are connected to problems in surrounding neighborhoods. Parents, community residents, and law enforcement officials can help by joining together in voluntary organizations, friendship networks, and neighborhood watches to solve common problems. Schools and community and religious organizations can help by offering after-school cultural and recreational activities. Community-supported student services have also succeeded when families, schools, and community representatives have made the effort to get involved.

Father/Male Involvement in Early Childhood Programs

Brent A. McBride and Thomas R. Rane

■ ■ ■

Parents, educators, researchers, and policymakers all assert the value of positive home-school partnerships. This focus on parental involvement in school settings comes at a time when early childhood programs increasingly consist of children from single-parent households, recombined or blended families, foster-parent homes, extended families with relatives, or a variety of other family situations (Epstein, 1988). A major challenge for family support professionals working in early childhood settings is to restructure program policies and practices aimed at increasing parent involvement to reflect the new realities of family structure, lifestyle, and ethnic characteristics. This effort is crucial as an increasing number of states and local public school systems move toward offering pre-kindergarten programs for children from economically disadvantaged and "high-risk" backgrounds (Karweit, 1993).

Father/Male Involvement in Early Childhood Settings

An important yet often overlooked strategy in the effort to increase parent involvement in early childhood programs is involving fathers or other significant male role figures. The notion that all fathers of children from low-income and high-risk backgrounds absent themselves from child rearing is a myth that permeates program development efforts in this area. For example, in a recent study of a pre-kindergarten at-risk program, McBride and Lin (in press) found that a majority of the mothers surveyed reported their children had regular and consistent interaction with a father or other male role figure despite the high proportion of single-parent families being served

by the program. In a nationwide survey of Head Start programs serving low-income families, Levine (1993) found that a man is present (whether the father, mother's boyfriend, or other male relative) in approximately 60 percent of Head Start families. Furthermore, in a similar nationwide survey of Head Start programs, Gary et al. (1987) found that the majority of parents and staff members felt that emphasis should be placed on getting Head Start fathers involved in the program.

The myths and stereotypes surrounding men in low-income and high-risk households have had a significant negative impact on policies relating to programs that benefit disadvantaged families (Levine, 1993). Generally these policies identify "parents" as targets for their outreach initiatives, yet program implementation typically discourages the participation of men in parent involvement activities. The lack of initiatives designed to encourage male involvement in pre-kindergarten programs for children who are at risk for later school failure does not build upon the strengths that many of these men can bring to the parenting situation—strengths that can be utilized in the development of effective home-school partnerships. When men become actively involved, they can have positive impacts on many aspects of children's development (see Lamb, in press, for a comprehensive review).

Getting Fathers/Males Involved

Given the support for increased involvement of parents in their children's schooling and the positive contributions men can make to their children's development, it is important to reach out specifically

Brent A. McBride and Thomas R. Rane. (1996, October). *Father/male involvement in early childhood programs.* ERIC Digest. Champaign, IL: ERIC Clearinghouse on Elementary and Early Childhood Education. (ERIC Document Reproduction Service No. ED 400 123)

to fathers or other significant males in parent involvement efforts for pre-kindergarten and early childhood programs. In doing so, however, it is important to recognize at the outset that several barriers must be overcome in order to successfully get men more involved. Levine (1993) has outlined four factors that constrain Head Start and state-funded pre-kindergarten programs from encouraging father involvement:

1. fathers' fears of exposing inadequacies;
2. ambivalence of program staff members about father involvement;
3. gatekeeping by mothers; and
4. inappropriate program design and delivery.

Each one of these barriers must be overcome as programs attempt to encourage and facilitate increased involvement of fathers in their children's school experiences.

McBride and his colleagues (McBride, Obuchowski, & Rane, 1996) have identified several key issues that need to be explored as early childhood programs struggle to build stronger home-school partnerships through the development and implementation of parent involvement initiatives targeted at men.

1. *Be specific about goals.* Early childhood educators need to be specific in their reasons for developing parent involvement initiatives targeted at men. Prior to developing such initiatives, educators must ask themselves why they think such efforts are important and how they can enhance the services being provided to children and families. There are clear benefits to encouraging male involvement in early childhood programs for enrolled children, their families, and the programs in general. Focusing on male involvement because it is currently a "hot" social issue increases the likelihood that such efforts will wane when the next big issue emerges.

2. *Acknowledge resistance to initiatives.* Not everyone will be committed to the concept of parent involvement initiatives targeted at fathers or other significant males. The lack of male involvement and "responsible" fathering behaviors is often cited as a major reason for children's later school failure, and many people will question why resources should be targeted at these men when they are viewed as the primary cause of the problems facing children. This resistance may come from mothers, teachers, school administrators, and community leaders. Since support from

these groups is critical to the success of parent involvement initiatives designed for men, educators will need to build a strong rationale for developing such initiatives, a rationale that can be clearly articulated to these groups in order to gain their support for such efforts.

3. *Identify the significant male role figures.* Educators will need to be specific about whom to target in their efforts to encourage male involvement. Research data have indicated that children growing up in low-income and single-parent homes often have regular and consistent interactions with a father figure, although not necessarily their biological father. Focusing efforts on biological fathers will exclude a large proportion of men who play significant roles in the lives of these children. The key for educators will be to identify who the men are in the lives of these children who can then become targets for these efforts.

4. *Provide training and support services for staff.* Most early childhood educators have received little, if any, formalized education and training in the area of parent involvement. This is especially true in the area of male involvement in early childhood programs. If such efforts are to be successful, teachers will need staff development and in-service training experiences that will allow them to develop a knowledge base from which to develop and implement initiatives that are designed to encourage male involvement in their programs.

5. *Train female facilitators to accept male involvement.* Although having male staff members provide leadership to initiatives designed to encourage male involvement in early childhood programs would be desirable, such expectations are not always realistic because the majority of professionals in this field are female. Women can be successful in these efforts, but they must acknowledge and build upon the unique strengths that men bring to the parenting realm and be sensitive to differences in the ways in which men and women approach parenting and interacting with young children.

6. *Don't neglect mothers.* Research has indicated that mothers tend to be the "gatekeepers" to their children for fathers or other significant male role figures. As educators develop initiatives to encourage male involvement, they must not do so at the expense of efforts targeted at mothers. Mothers need to be involved in the development of these efforts from the beginning. They need

to be made aware of why resources are being put into developing these activities and how they and their children will benefit. Eliciting the support and involvement of mothers in developing such initiatives can help insure the initiatives' success.

7. *Go slowly.* As with any other initiative, early childhood educators must proceed slowly in their efforts to encourage male involvement in their programs. The key to success for these efforts is in building a male-friendly environment that facilitates a culture of male involvement in the program. However, building such a culture is a long-term process, and educators shouldn't expect too much, too soon. They should start slowly and build upon their successes.

8. *Don't reinvent the wheel.* Many early childhood programs serving children who are at risk for later school failure already include comprehensive parent involvement components, although they tend to be targeted primarily at mothers. When developing initiatives for male involvement, educators should first evaluate the parent involvement components already in place and explore how they may be adapted to reach out to men in order to meet their unique needs.

Conclusion

Successful resolution of these issues will provide early childhood programs with a solid foundation from which to develop and implement parent involvement initiatives designed for men. Through such initiatives, men can become valuable resources as educators struggle to build stronger home-school partnerships aimed at strengthening family units that will help young children achieve success as they progress through the educational system.

FOR MORE INFORMATION

Epstein, J. L. (1988). How Do We Improve Programs for Parent Involvement? *Educational Horizons* 66(2): 58–59. EJ 364 521

Epstein, J. L. (1992). School and Family Partnerships. In M. C. Alkin (Ed.), *Encyclopedia of Educational Research* (6th ed.) (pp. 1130–1151). New York: Macmillan.

Gary, L., L. Beatty, and G. Weaver. (1987). *Involvement of Black Fathers in Head Start.* (Final report submitted to the Department of Health and Human Services, ACYF, Grant No. 90-CD-0509). Washington, DC: Institute for Urban Affairs and Research, Howard University. ED 309 213

Karweit, N. (1993). Effective Preschool and Kindergarten Programs for Students At-Risk. In B. Spodek (Ed.), *Handbook of Research on the Education of Young Children* (pp. 385–411). New York: Macmillan. ED 361 107.

Lamb, M. E. (in press). *The Role of the Father in Child Development* (3rd ed). Hillsdale, NJ: Lawrence Erlbaum.

Levine, J. A. (1993). Involving Fathers in Head Start: A Framework for Public Policy and Program Development. *Families in Society,* 74(1): 4–19.

McBride, B. A., and H. Lin. (in press). Parental Involvement in Prekindergarten At-Risk Programs: Multiple Perspectives. *Journal of Education for Students Placed At-Risk.*

McBride, B. A., M. Obuchowski, and T. Rane. (1996). Father/Male Involvement in Prekindergarten At-Risk Programs: Research Guiding Practice. Workshop presented at the Family Resource Coalition Biennial Conference, Chicago, IL, May.

Portrait of a Head Start Parent

A Teacher's Story, A Teacher's Reflections

Glenna Zeak

■ ■ ■

Introduction

Mrs. M. was the mother of three children between the ages of 1 and 3. She spent most of her days at home, tending her children and looking forward to the afternoon soaps. Mrs. M. was also the wife of an abusive alcoholic. She often prayed that her husband would come home and pass out on the couch, but most of the time she would get a beating instead.

One afternoon, a Head Start representative came to visit. Mrs. M. was embarrassed not only by her bruised and battered appearance, but also by the condition of her house. Dust and clutter weren't the major problems, her house was literally falling apart. Mrs. M. thought about the hole in her bathroom floor from which the basement below was clearly visible. Mrs. M. pictured in her mind's eye several places in the walls that her husband had punched through and hoped that the visitor from Head Start wouldn't ask to come in. Thankfully, she didn't. They talked at the door instead. The woman introduced herself as Ruth Anne and mentioned that she knew there were young children in the home who might be eligible for Head Start. Krista, Mrs. M.'s eldest child, would be 3 in November, so she was old enough to begin classes. If Krista was enrolled, she would be picked up by bus three days a week and spend three hours each day in a preschool classroom. Mrs. M. was delighted. This program promised to make her life a bit easier. After all, caring for two children would be easier than managing three. Mrs. M. accepted Ruth Anne's invitation and consented to have her child begin the program.

As the months went by, Krista seemed really to enjoy going to school. One afternoon, the phone rang, and the woman on the other end of the line identified herself as Romaine, the parent involvement coordinator from Head Start. Romaine invited Mrs. M. to come to the center the following Tuesday to meet with a group of parents who were planning a Christmas party for the children. Mrs. M. declined, saying that she was far too busy that day. Then, after hanging up the telephone, the young mother returned to the sofa. A month later, Romaine called again. She mentioned that the parent group still needed help with the Christmas party and even offered to provide child care for the babies if Mrs. M. would agree to participate. The meeting was to be held the following Tuesday in a local church basement. Reluctantly, Mrs. M. attended. She observed briefly, and when it seemed as if little was being accomplished, Mrs. M. offered some suggestions that sparked a productive conversation. Everyone appeared to relax with one another, and a successful party was planned. Mrs. M. felt pretty proud of herself. Not only had she spoken up, but the other parents had listened, and her opinion had been valued. She was glad she had come. Before the meeting ended, Romaine requested that this group of parents meet on a monthly basis to plan other activities for the children and to provide mutual support for the participants. Romaine also suggested that the group elect a committee chairperson, and Mrs. M. was elected. Mrs. M. was elated, yet worried about what her husband would say. Would he let her participate? Despite her concerns, Mrs. M. accepted the responsibility and resolved to do well. After the meeting, the new committee chairperson was elected to

Glenna Zeak. (1996). Portrait of a Head Start parent. *Early Childhood Education Journal, 23* (4), 247–248. Reprinted by permission of Plenum Publishing Corporation.

the role of something called policy council representative. This was the decision-making board of the program, consisting of parents, the Head Start director, and community representatives. The thought was a bit overwhelming, but Romaine assured Mrs. M. that she could simply observe the first few times. Romaine also expressed confidence that the young mother could handle the responsibility and excel in her new role.

As she considered all of this, Mrs. M. decided simply to tell her husband about her plans. After all, he wasn't home during the day. That evening, when she nervously brought up the subject and broke her big news, her husband was too drunk to take much notice.

On the day of the policy council meeting, Mrs. M. observed as planned, but not for long. Someone noticed that she had been busy writing notes all through the meeting, and with that, Mrs. M. was selected as secretary for the group.

Although Mrs. M. had always been a very quiet, introverted person and her self-esteem had reached an all time low of late, her personality began to change with her involvement in Head Start. Throughout the year, Mrs. M. continued to serve as policy council representative and to work on several additional committees. The following year, with her second child enrolled at Head Start, Mrs. M. became even more involved. That year, the policy council elected Mrs. M. state representative and policy council chairperson. This meant that she would attend the state-level meetings and be responsible for sharing and obtaining information for Blair County Head Start. As Mrs. M. met those new challenges, her confidence in herself continued to grow.

Another year passed by, and Mrs. M.'s youngest child was enrolled in Head Start. Mrs. M. was elected policy council chairperson, continued as the state representative, and became a national representative for Head Start. This meant a trip to a national conference in Colorado, an experience that proved to be an awakening for her. While she was away from all of the stress of home for a week, with the children cared for by Grandma, Mrs. M. realized that she did not have to live in an abusive environment. She saw that she was worthwhile and valued. At that conference, she promised herself to make major changes for her children's sake as well as for her own.

On her return home, Mrs. M. secretly planned to file for divorce but wanted to wait for the "right time." That time came all too soon, when one of her husband's episodes of violence lasted for hours. All the while, she held on, determined that this would be the last time she would ever endure this treatment. She turned to Head Start for help, and Romaine arrived and guided Mrs. M. and her children through every step, from hospital to lawyer to shelter. Her life as the wife of an abusive alcoholic had ended, but her life as a Head Start teacher had just begun.

In the fall, she enrolled at Pennsylvania State University, where she received her undergraduate degree in early childhood education. She returned to Head Start as a teacher, hoping to repay a debt of gratitude by giving families the care and support her family had experienced from the moment that Ruth Anne, the Head Start representative, had first knocked at the door. As a result of her firsthand experiences in Head Start, Mrs. M. knew that the parent involvement practices of Head Start had much to offer families. She had learned an important lesson: Every successful parent involvement effort is built on sincerity, friendship, and a nonjudgmental attitude. Even when the parents of children in her class did not choose to be involved in Head Start in ways that she had hoped, Mrs. M. did not assume lack of interest or laziness. Instead, she thought about how different her own life might have been if Head Start staff hadn't taken the time to draw her out and seek a variety of ways to include her. What a waste of human potential it would have been if the Head Start professionals hadn't searched for Mrs. M.'s subtle strengths, gradually nurtured her self-confidence, and helped to educate all three of her children! In her interactions with parents, Mrs. M. sought to keep in touch with the feelings she had experienced when first approached by Head Start personnel: embarrassment about her living conditions, fear of failure, a low self-concept, and anguish about her family's situation.

Over the years, Mrs. M. grew to understand Head Start from both sides, first as a parent and later as a teacher. In the spring, she began working toward her master's degree in early childhood education so that she could continue to learn and develop as a professional. Every detail of Mrs. M.'s life described in this Head Start teacher's story is true. I know, because I am the former Mrs. M.

Acknowledgment. The author would like to express her appreciation to Mary Renck Jalongo for helping her to write this story.

Backing Away Helpfully

Some Roles Teachers Shouldn't Fill

Based on an Interview with
Penny Hauser-Cram

■ ■ ■

I suspect that if you asked for a definition of a good teacher most families would describe a cross between a chameleon and Wonderwoman—someone who is part developmental scholar, pediatrician, artist, and therapist, with a little bit of toy designer, janitor, and athlete mixed in. But based on my years as a teacher and a director, I have come to believe that there are at least some roles that teachers can't and shouldn't fill. Two roles that I have seen cause tension and hard feelings come immediately to mind: the role of family therapist and the role of parenting expert.

Parents need and want other adults in each of these roles. Since teachers and parents share an intimate, ongoing relationship centered on children they both care about, it is tempting for all sides to move from educational and developmental issues to personal, and even therapeutic, ones. A big challenge for teachers is to help parents find the help they need, without adopting those helping roles themselves.

Sharing Children's Development

Parents and teachers really do share children. Together they are involved in seeing one [child], and sometimes several children, through some of the largest developmental events of the early years: the transition from the home to school or a center, the process of making friends, the joys and struggles of learning to talk or even to begin reading. Because of daily involvement with a child, a teacher is often the first outsider to know the in's and out's of a family's workings: whether they ignore or attend to a child's illness, when they have had periods of disorganization, how they handle the stresses of being late, bathroom accidents, or a missing favorite book or toy. A teacher also learns a great deal of very revealing information

about individual children: how late or early a baby sits up, walks, says a first word; how shy or aggressive a three year old is; how challenging or cooperative a four year old may be. Unlike friends or neighbors, who may have similar insights, teachers are in a position to evaluate—they can compare a family or a child to many others they know.

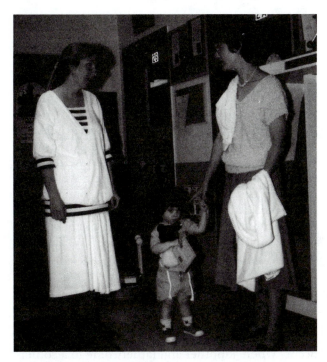

Together parents and teachers are involved in seeing children through some of the major developmental events of the early years.

Backing away helpfully: Some roles teachers shouldn't fill. (1986, Spring). *Beginnings,* pp. 18–20. Reprinted with permission from Child Care Information Exchange, P.O. Box 2890, Redmond, WA 98073, 1-800-221-2864.

153

A Charged Situation

Since parents are often deeply invested in how their children are developing, their discussions with teachers are often charged with emotion. Some parents resent or distrust teachers, particularly in cases where teachers and family members see the child or the purposes of early education differently. For example, imagine what happens when a father sees a boy as active and a teacher sees that child as aggressive or when a mother wants her three year old to practice number facts and a teacher insists blocks and beads provide the right kinds of early mathematical experiences.

Other parents react to a teacher's knowledge by thinking: "Here is someone who already knows and cares about us. At last, here is someone I can really talk to." Then, when a teacher asks a question in a conference related to a child's life at home, the parent may see it as an invitation to go far beyond issues of the child's behavior or schooling. Suddenly, the teacher is catapulted into the role of a therapist or expert.

Spotting Difficult Situations

Sometimes teachers can anticipate that parents may desire additional advice, especially when a child's behavior has undergone a dramatic change. Discussing that change with parents is an important part of a teacher's responsibility, but such discussions can sometimes lead to areas beyond the scope and expertise of the teacher.

Imagine that during a conference a teacher says: "I have been wondering about Michael. The last two weeks he hasn't been playing with friends. He seems listless and tired. Has he been sleeping well?" The parent comes back with: "You're right. I'm glad you mentioned it. Things have been tough . . . there have been a lot of fights at night. We're thinking of separating, and I'm worried about Michael. What shall I do?" Without meaning to, the teacher touched a nerve. The parent responded with a flood of intimate information and a request for help. Within a few moments, the teacher has become a parent's counselor.

A different type of difficult situation sometimes occurs when a mother and father come to a conference with different points of view. Before the teacher can say much, it is clear that they see their child quite differently. One insists: "Shelly is a cry-baby." The other interrupts: "She is not. She is just more sensitive than other children." Both turn to the teacher for confirmation. Suddenly, the teacher is playing the part of an arbitrator in a family dispute.

It is early Wednesday morning. Lucia, rubbing her eyes, comes into the classroom dragging behind her father. A teacher greets her and then comments to Lucia's father that she looks a bit tired. Sighing, he replies: "She's so difficult at home. We can't get her to eat her dinner or go to sleep at a reasonable hour. And she's always starting fights with her brother. We're exhausted. What can we do?" All at once, the teacher has gone from making an observation to being the dispenser of advice.

Each of these is a delicate situation—parents are genuinely seeking help. But they are also asking their children's teachers to go beyond what teachers can reasonably do. The requests are tempting—they complement teachers' knowledge, and often they seem like only a small extension of teachers' concern for children's development.

Backing Away Helpfully

Far from being trapped, teachers can take steps to help parents understand the difference between the roles of teachers, therapists, and experts—steps that clarify without abandoning or ignoring the distress or confusion that parents may feel.

1. *Acknowledge what has been said.* When parents open up their private lives, they make themselves vulnerable. If a teacher tries to change the topic or gloss over the issues raised, the parent may be hurt or angry. Teachers must recognize what's been revealed: "That helps me to understand why Michael has been tired. It sounds difficult for all of you."

2. *Categorize the kind of problem.* Once a parent has talked about a problem, a teacher must decide: Is this a classroom problem, a mild developmental issue, or an acute issue in children's or parents' lives deserving professional help? Deciding is not always easy, but here are some examples which may help:

   - *Classroom problems:* Learning to concentrate on a task; being able to take turns or share with other children; conflicts between parents and teachers over how early to start toilet training; a child's reluctance to come to school in the morning.

   - *Mild family issues:* A child being unwilling to play at other children's homes; a child being afraid of monsters and refusing to go to sleep at night; parent-child conflicts over eating habits, thumb sucking, getting dressed in the morning.

- *Acute problems:* Marked delay in the child's development; extreme aggression, fears, or apathy in children; marital conflict; family abuse; severe mental or physical illness or death in the family.

It is important to categorize because teachers have the skills and information to work on classroom issues. Venturing into family issues or acute problems saddles teachers with responsibilities and demands too great to handle.

3. *Make a plan for classroom issues.* It is vital that parents know teachers are willing and able to work on problems of learning, behavior, and development in the classroom. Go right to work: find out what is bothering the parent, describe your view of the issue, work out joint strategies, and arrange a time to talk over progress in the near future.

4. *For other kinds of problems, inform parents of other resources.* If a parent brings up something other than a classroom issue, she should not be left alone with her problem neglected. Teachers can help responsibly by alerting parents to other, more appropriate resources:

- *Resources for mild developmental issues:* I have seen two kinds of center-based parent resources work very well. At Eliot-Pearson, we have a parents' group led by a social worker (trained in child development), not a teacher. The group meets at the school, with no teachers or director attending. Since the group mixes parents of children of different ages and from different classrooms, the discussion doesn't turn to teachers or curriculum. Also, because of that mix, parents of younger children can learn from the mothers and fathers of older children. Parents of older children can look back and appreciate all the distance they have come.

    At the Brookline Early Education Project, there were specific *call-in hours* each week—just as some pediatricians have. Trained social workers and child development specialists took calls from parents concerned about issues such as sleep difficulties, sibling relationships, or changes in behavior.

- *Resources for acute issues:* Always have a list of community resources on hand: When parents announce their needs, they are feeling them acutely. That is not the time to say: "Hmmm, I once had a friend who used a good family counselor. Let me see if I can find out who that was." Instead, it is the time to offer a well thought-out list of resources. The list should include a variety of services in a range of areas: developmental screening clinics, therapists who work with children, family therapists, marriage counselors. The list should contain services in a number of different locations and at varying levels of expense. Every resource listed must have been carefully checked.

5. *Agree to collaborate.* By limiting their roles, teachers aren't signing off. They can agree to work with families and outside resources to solve issues. They can work closely with parents to help children develop better eating habits or self-control. They can share information about what works in the classroom or offer observations when parents come to pick up children. They can offer to talk to a professional who will be testing the child, make it possible for that person to observe in the classroom, and meet with parents to go over any final reports.

Conclusion

The way in which teachers are pulled into acting as therapists or experts is part of a much larger situation. Families often have nowhere else to turn. Many, maybe even most, parents live apart from their own families of origin. Few pediatricians or nurses are trained to discuss and solve developmental issues. For over a century, parents have been *trained* to turn to outside experts—like Gesell or Spock—for answers. For many people, it is a large, bewildering, and expensive step to start hunting for professional help. Not surprisingly, it is teachers who inherit the flock of questions, concerns, and worries parents have.

The other side of the coin is that teachers are trained to notice and respond to the needs of other human beings. For many of them, saying "No" to a request for help feels wrong, like shutting off some very basic perception. But I am not suggesting that teachers turn a cold shoulder on family's needs. Instead, teachers should think about where they can be most helpful and where being helpful lies in pointing the way to more appropriate resources.

The Changing Face of Parenting Education

Sharon L. Kagan

■ ■ ■

Today's families face monumental stresses associated with daily living. A stagnant economy routinely demands family employment in two or three jobs, leaving little time for effective parenting. Job insecurity often fuels family discontinuity and fragmentation. Unemployment, once the condition of the unskilled, has affected pink and white collar workers, causing more and more parents regularly to face complexities that make nurturing children difficult. Finally, the rise in the number of single parents, many of them teenage or never married, places heavy burdens on families and on society.

As these dramatic demographic changes have occurred, so have equally profound advances in our knowledge about the relationship between demographic conditions, family life, and child outcomes. We know, for example, that economically deprived single mothers are more likely to abuse their children physically (Gelles, 1989), that premature low-birthweight babies born into poverty have a poorer prognosis of functioning within normal ranges (Bradley et al., 1994), and that family income and poverty are powerful correlates of the cognitive development and behavior of young children (Duncan et al., 1994). Conversely, we know that when economic conditions of families are improved, or when services such as parent education and support are offered, outcomes for children, siblings, and families improve (Roberts & Wasik, 1990; Seitz & Apfel, 1994).

Such advances in scientific knowledge—while perhaps not fully understood by parents—have filtered into public consciousness. American parents recognize that parenting is important and that they can benefit from help in meeting their parenting duties. A recent survey by the Public Agenda (1994),

for example, noted that one-third of parents feel that teachers today are doing a worse job than teachers of the previous generation. But 55% also said that they themselves are doing a worse job of parenting than their parents did. When asked if a child was more likely to succeed if he or she came from a stable and supportive family but attended a poor school, or if he or she came from a troubled family but attended a good school, 61% of the parents said the child with the more stable family had the better chance of success.

In short, Americans understand the importance of parental competence; that is why they flock to bookstores to buy parenting magazines and why they cruise electronic bulletin boards that offer advice and conversation.

Parenting Education: Timely and Useful

Not insensitive to parents' needs, social service providers are recontouring their efforts to provide parent education and family support programs. Parent education programs are growing in number and becoming increasingly diverse on virtually every dimension imaginable: sponsorship, funding mechanisms, audience, intensity, staffing patterns, and evaluation strategy.

What binds these diverse programs together? Contrary to the approach used in the days when parent education had a didactic, if not somewhat elitist, orientation, today's approach is more universally adapted. While programs differ in how they carry out activities, they tend to embrace a common set of principles: (1) a focus on prevention and optimization rather than treatment; (2) a recognition of the

Sharon L. Kagan. (1995, May). *The changing face of parenting education.* ERIC Digest. Champaign, IL: ERIC Clearinghouse on Elementary and Early Childhood Education. (ERIC Document Reproduction Service No. ED 382 406). Adapted from Sharon L. Kagan. (1995). On Building Parental Competence: The Nature of Contracts and Commitments. In *The Challenge of Parenting in the '90s.* Washington, DC: The Aspen Institute.

need to work with the entire family and community; (3) a commitment to regarding the family as an active participant in the planning and execution of the program rather than as a "passive client" waiting to receive services; (4) a commitment to nourishing cultural diversity; (5) a focus on strength-based needs analyses, programming, and evaluation; and (6) flexible staffing (Dunst & Trivette, 1994). In practice, adherence to these principles suggests that today's parent education and support programs endow families with primary responsibility for their children's development and well-being; envision healthy, functioning families as the basis of a healthy society; and understand families as a part of a system that includes neighborhood and community.

Current Issues in Parenting Education

Changes in nomenclature represent one of several current issues in parent education. Terminology used—besides parent education—includes parent empowerment, family education, family life education, parent support, and family support. Some other issues include:

- *The equity issue.* Parent education is alive and well in the marketplace, with affluent consumers exercising choice and purchasing information. Low-income parents have far more limited access to formal parenting programs and less discretionary income with which to purchase information. If parent education is left to market forces alone, the wealthy will become more information rich, while the poor will become comparatively and actually more information poor.
- *The voluntary/involuntary issue.* Presently, most programs are voluntary, with parents determining the nature and length of their engagement. Increasingly, as programs receive public funding and are designed to ameliorate a particular problem (substance abuse or child abuse, for example), their voluntary nature comes into question. Changing from a voluntary to a required program may alter the intent and nature of family support and violate its basic principles.
- *The cultural competence issue.* Beneath the face of parent education and support lie widely different ideas about what constitutes effective parenting, varying often with cultural predispositions and orientations (Caldwell et al., 1994). Discerning multiple understandings of what constitutes competence across and among cultures and delineating effective ways to build parental competence while nourishing diversity remain a challenge.
- *The quality issue.* Because parent education and family support efforts have grown fairly rapidly, and because they have emerged from different professional traditions, attempts to address program quality are only beginning to emerge. Uncertainty regarding specific variables associated with quality outcomes prevails. Overall, there is little specification regarding the competencies, training, or credentials needed for working in the programs. Tools to evaluate program quality and methods of program accreditation are only now being developed.
- *The results issue.* While it is appropriate to demand results from parenting education and family support efforts, the programs must be recognized for what they are and are not. They do not replace efforts in community development or major employment initiatives. They do enhance parents' overall competence and self-efficacy, knowledge of child development, and capacities to parent more effectively. It is for these outcomes that parent education should be held accountable. To date, only sporadic evaluation of parent education and family support has taken place. Much of the data collected have been on pilot programs and have been conducted by the program developers without random assignment of participants (Powell, 1994). More emphasis needs to be placed on durable, scientific, objective evaluations that measure those results that the interventions are designed to accomplish.
- *The linkage/coordination issue.* The need to engage in cooperative planning, coordination of service delivery, and infrastructure development across programs, communities, and states is becoming acute. In some locales, voluntary networks of parent education and family support programs are developing, fostering linkages that promote coordination and access.

Potential Government Strategies

If parent education and family support are an important national priority, policymakers can support such programs by fostering public-private collaborations and supporting publicly funded efforts for low-income parents. The conditions of families are affected also by every piece of social legislation, and family support can be infused into a broad range of social supports. As the nation considers many new contracts, let us remember that the most significant contract of all is the familial contract we undertake with our children.

FOR MORE INFORMATION

Bradley, R. H., L. Whiteside, D. Mundfrom, P. Casey, K. Kelleher, and S. Pope. (1994). Early Indications of Resilience and Their Relations to Experiences in the Home Environments of Low Birthweight Premature Children Living in Poverty. *Child Development* 65 (2, April): 346–360. EJ 483 917.

Caldwell, C., A. Green, and A. Billingsley. (1994). Family Support in Black Churches: A New Look at Old Functions. In S. L. Kagan and B. Weissbourd (Eds.), *Putting Families First: America's Family Support Movement and the Challenge of Change* (pp. 137–160). San Francisco: Jossey-Bass. PS 023 276.

Duncan, G., J. Brooks-Gunn, and P. Klebanov. (1994). Economic Deprivation and Early Childhood Development. *Child Development* 65(2, April): 296–318. EJ 483 914.

Dunst, C., and C. M. Trivette. (1994). Aims and Principles of Family Support Programs. In C. Dunst, C. M. Trivette, and A. G. Deal (Eds.), *Supporting and Strengthening Families: Vol. 1 Methods, Strategies, and Practices* (pp. 30–48). Cambridge, MA: Brookline Books.

Gelles, R. (1989). Child Abuse and Violence in Single Parent Families: Parent Absences and Economic Deprivation. *American Journal of Orthopsychiatry* 59: 492–501.

Powell, D. R. (1994). Evaluating Family Support Programs: Are We Making Progress? In S. L. Kagan and B. Weissbourd (Eds.), *Putting Families First: America's Family Support Movement and the Challenge of Change* (pp. 442–470). San Francisco: Jossey-Bass. PS 023 276.

Public Agenda. (1994). *First Things First: What Americans Expect from the Public Schools.* New York: Author.

Roberts, R. N., and B. H. Wasik. (1990). Home Visiting Programs for Families with Children Birth to Three: Results of a National Survey. *Journal of Early Intervention* 14 (3, Summer): 274–284. EJ 420 056.

Seitz, V., and N. Apfel. (1994). Parent-Focused Intervention: Diffusion Effects on Siblings. *Child Development* 65(2): 677–683. EJ 483 938.

■ Ask Yourself

Identifying Issues for Advocacy

1. Will parent involvement in school programs and in policy decisions minimize the influence of the professional educator? Why or why not?

2. Should parents' expectations for their child in an early education program (as revealed by talking with them) influence a teacher's curriculum decisions? Explain.

3. What adjustments, if any, should a teacher make when working with single parents? Justify your response.

4. David Elkind (1994) hopes to see the emergence of the *vital family*. Do you see this happening among your friends and relatives? Was it ever absent?

5. David Elkind (1994) states that the increase in learning problems and aggressive behavior in children is symptomatic of stress in their lives. Do you agree? Why or why not? What can you do as an early childhood educator to reduce the stress in young children's lives?

6. In this chapter, McBride and Rane refer to the "unique strengths" and "the different approach to parenthood" that fathers bring to parenting. Do you agree? To what specifically do you think the authors were referring? Do patterns of fathering behavior differ

across cultures (Furstenberg, 1994; Mindel, Habenstein, & Wright, 1998; Staples, 1994)? Explain.

7. One concern of school psychologists, who see increased disruptions and discipline problems in the classroom, is that parents are not spending enough time with their children. Do you share their concern? Why or why not (Hochschild, 1998; Levine & White, 1994)?

8. What new initiatives at the national level relate to parenting? (Refer to the Family and Medical Leave Act and the U.S. Department of Education.)

9. How would you, as a classroom teacher, respond to a parent who dropped her son off at preschool and said, "Tommy was a bad boy this morning, so I told him he's not allowed to have any of Beth's birthday treat at snack time today"?

Advocacy and Leadership Strategies

1. To better understand how parents interpret involvement in their child's education, interview a preschool and an elementary school parent. Request an interview and state your purpose (i.e., to learn about how the parent wishes to be involved in his or her child's education). Compose four to six questions to ask each parent about how he or she is, or hopes to be, involved in school activities and decision making and what obstacles he or she may see to involvement. (See Coleman & Churchill, 1997, and research other readings to guide your question preparation.) Include a bibliography of these readings with your final report. Write open-ended questions, avoid suggesting specific responses, and avoid questions that can be answered with a yes-no only response. Take notes during the interviews; write a summary, including the interview questions and follow-up probe questions, the responses of each interviewee, and your interpretation and analysis of responses in terms of how this information might be helpful to a teacher. Compare and contrast responses of the preschool and the elementary school parent. Incorporate ideas from readings in your interpretations. To extend this activity, visit the website for the National Coalition for Parent Involvement in Education (www.ncpie.org) and investigate the new initiatives to involve parents in their child's education.

2. La Leche League International is an organization that promotes breast-feeding and gives support to new mothers. Contact a member of La Leche League in your area and ask to attend a monthly meeting. Before attending, research the history and current scope of La Leche League and the research on the benefits of breast-feeding. Talk with the members about the needs of new mothers,

the role that La Leche League has played in their lives, the value of home visiting programs for new mothers, and other support available in the community for new parents. If there is a need expressed for more support for new parents in your area, develop an action plan to further investigate this issue. Report all of your findings to the class. To extend this activity, refer to the WIC article in Chapter 4 and read about WIC's National Breast-Feeding Promotion Campaign. What strategies are being implemented by your state to promote this campaign? Interview a peer counselor for breast-feeding mothers and inquire about the success of the program in your area and the training needed for peer counseling. Include these findings in your report.

3. Research the Family and Medical Leave Act (FMLA) of 1993 and corporate-sponsored and/or on-site corporate child care (www.familiesandwork.org). Then interview personnel representatives from two corporations in your area, one with more than 50 employees and one with less than 50 employees. Prepare interview questions based on your research. Include in your questions the following: Does the smaller company provide unpaid leave? Why or why not? How frequently do employees at the larger company file for leave under FMLA? Do male employees take family leave? What concerns, if any, do corporate leaders have about FMLA? How do employees support themselves while on 12 weeks of unpaid leave? Also inquire if either company provides child-care support to employees. Is there a need for on-site child care and/or corporate-subsidized care? If there is on-site child care at a corporation in your area, ask to visit the facility and to talk to parents about the benefits of such a program. How might corporate employees propose child-care support to management? Prepare such a presentation that is based on research, is convincing, and is feasible. (See Appendix 2 for suggestions on preparing the presentation.) Present your proposal to the class along with the findings from your investigation.

4. Prepare an extensive annotated list of available resources in your area (city and county) for families with young children (e.g., Even Start, Head Start, or HIPPY). While gathering the information, attend a local government board meeting and inquire about community policies, programs, municipal events, and services affecting young children and families. What recreational or educational programs does the community sponsor for families with young children? Other sources of information about available programs for young children may be the library, museum, zoo, parks office, YMCA, YWCA, cooperative extension office, Junior League, and Chamber of Commerce. Present the comprehensive list in a colorful, eye-catching brochure format and distribute to parents of young children in your community. (*Hint:* Funding for printing such a publication may be obtained from the Board of Real-

tors, Chamber of Commerce, or a local philanthropic organization.)

5. Based on your field-study observations, how do teachers and parents interact with each other? What seem to be their assumptions about their roles in this situation? What does the teacher and center or school do to promote involvement (e.g., activities planned, press releases, home visits, PTA, or parent resource personnel)? What is the response from parents and the community? Include your observations in your field-study report.

6. Read and discuss two books by Stephanie Coontz: *The Way We Never Were: American Families and the Nostalgia Trap* (1992) and *The Way We Really Are: Coming to Terms with America's Changing Family* (1997). Compare and contrast these books with *Ties That Stress: The New Family Imbalance* by David Elkind (1994).

7. Investigate the Temporary Assistance for Needy Families (TANF) program in your state and its impact on children and child care. Are the needs of children and families in your state being met? Does your state guarantee child-care assistance to needy families? What are the reimbursement rates to child-care providers? Is there a local or state advocacy organization dedicated to meeting the needs of children and families living in poverty? If so, invite a representative of this organization to discuss the initiative and advocacy agenda with the class. What can you, as an early childhood advocate, do to support their agenda? (See Appendix 2.)

8. Many early childhood settings have intergenerational programs where senior citizens spend time with the children. How might elders and young children in your community benefit from such interactions? Is there an intergenerational program in your field-study site? Interview an intergenerational volunteer, a classroom teacher involved in such a program, and a coordinator of placements from an organization such as the Foster Grandparent Program. From your interviews and from your investigation of the research on intergenerational programs, prepare a report for the class that defines how to maximize the effectiveness of such a program in your classroom.

9. What are the current national, state, and local initiatives to promote responsible fatherhood? If there is an organization in your area, invite a representative to speak to the class. If there is not a local program, is there a need for one? Research the impact such programs are making across the country. Also, watch several popular sitcoms, cartoons, and children's movies to see how fatherhood is portrayed in the media. In what ways are your findings consistent with research on the topic?

10. Do teenagers at your local junior/senior high school learn about parenting in their curriculum? What provisions does the local

high school make for teenage parents? Also, investigate the availability of parenting programs in your area, other than those offered as part of the school curriculum. Who sponsors the area programs? Is there a fee? Are there limitations on who can attend the classes? Next, research the effectiveness of parenting programs. What are examples of exemplary parenting programs? Finally, observe a parenting class and interview an instructor. After investigating this issue, decide if there is a need for more and/or better parenting programs in your area. If so, develop an action plan to meet this need. (See Appendices 2, 3, and 4.)

11. Goal 8 of the National Education Goals, as set out in the Goals 2000: Educate America Act, is: "Every school will promote partnerships that will increase parental involvement and participation in promoting the social, emotional, and academic growth of children." Contact the U.S. Department of Education (1-800-USA-LEARN) and request progress reports and resource materials relating to this goal. Since 1989, what progress has been made in reaching this goal in your community? Write a report on the status of local and state initiatives to meet this goal and make three specific suggestions of innovative ways to stimulate parent and community involvement in education in your school district. Present this report at a school board meeting.

■ References and Suggested Readings

Allan, L. (1997, May). Do you resent and stonewall parents? Matthew's line. *Young Children, 52* (4), 72–73.

Berger, E. (1995). *Parents as partners in education: The school and home working together* (4th ed.). New York: Prentice-Hall.

Briggs, N., Jalongo, M. R., & Brown, L. (1997). Working with families of young children: Our history and our goals. In J. P. Isenberg & M. R. Jalongo (Eds.), *Major trends and issues in early childhood education* (pp. 56–69). New York: Teachers College Press.

Coleman, M., & Churchill, S. (1997, Spring). Challenges to family involvement. *Childhood Education, 73* (3), 144–148.

Coontz, S. (1992). *The way we never were: American families and the nostalgia trap.* New York: Basic Books.

Coontz, S. (1997). *The way we really are: Coming to terms with America's changing family.* New York: Basic Books.

Elkind, D. (1994). *Ties that stress: The new family imbalance.* Cambridge, MA: Harvard University Press.

Epstein, J. L. (1995). School/family/community partnerships: Caring for the children we share. *Phi Delta Kappan, 76* (9), 701–712.

Furstenberg, F. (1994). Good dads—Bad dads: Two faces of fatherhood. In A. Skolnick & J. Skolnick (Eds.), *Families in transition* (8th ed.) (pp. 348–367). New York: HarperCollins.

Hansen, K., & Garey, A. I. (Eds.). (1998). *Families in the U.S.: Kinship and domestic politics.* Philadelphia: Temple University Press.

Hochschild, A. R. (1998). Ideals of care: Traditional, postmodern, cold-modern, and warm-modern. In K. Hansen & A. I. Garey (Eds.), *Families in the U.S.: Kinship and domestic politics* (pp. 527–538). Philadelphia: Temple University Press.

Levine, R., & White, M. (1994). The social transformation of childhood. In A. Skolnick & J. Skolnick (Eds.), *Families in transition* (8th ed.) (pp. 273–293). New York: HarperCollins.

Mindel, C., Habenstein, R., & Wright, R. (Eds.). (1998). *Ethnic families in America: Patterns and variations* (4th ed.). Upper Saddle River, NJ: Prentice-Hall.

Pipher, M. (1996). *The shelter of each other: Rebuilding our families*. New York: Ballentine.

Rasinski, T., & Fawcett, G. (1996, June/July). The many faces of parental involvement. *Reading Today*, p. 21.

Sanders, M. (1996, November). Building family partnerships that last. *Educational Leadership*, pp. 61–66.

Skolnick, A., & Skolnick, J. (Eds.). (1994). *Families in transition* (8th ed.). New York: HarperCollins.

Staples, R. (Ed.). (1994). *The black family: Essays and studies* (5th ed.). Belmont, CA: Wadsworth.

Thorkildsen, R., & Stein, M. (1998, December). *Is parent involvement related to student achievement? Exploring the evidence*. Research Bulletin, No. 22. Bloomington, IN: Phi Delta Kappa, Center for Evaluation, Development, and Research.

U.S. Department of Education. (1994). *Strong families, strong schools*. Washington, DC: Author.

U.S. Department of Education. (1996). *Reaching all families: Creating family-friendly schools*. Washington, DC: Author.

U.S. Department of Education, National Center for Education Statistics. (1997). *Fathers' involvement in their children's schools* (NCES 98-091). Washington, DC: Author.

Weissbourd, R. (1996). *The vulnerable child: What really hurts America's children and what we can do about it*. Reading, MA: Addison-Wesley.

Westheimer, M. (1997). Ready or not: One home-based response to the school readiness dilemma. *Early Child Development and Care, 127-128*, 245–257.

Workman, S., & Gage, J. (1997, May). Family-school partnerships: A family strengths approach. *Young Children, 52* (4), 10–14.

■ Chapter 8

■ Developmentally
■ Appropriate and
■ Educationally
■ Worthwhile Practice

The Delight of Learning to Read?

Grandma Kramer, Cindy's mother-in-law, breezes in the front door with a package under her arm and exclaims, "How's my darling grandson? Come here, sweetie. Look at the nice present Grandma brought you!" With a gleeful twinkle in her eye, Grandma Kramer shakes the box. Jimmy toddles toward her as she starts to open it. Grandma Kramer gushes, "Oh, Cindy, I found the most marvelous kit for teaching a 2-year-old to read. It's just what our genius, Jimmy, needs." Grandma Kramer produces an assortment of word cards, phrase cards, and picture books (cost = $29.95).

"Cindy, the kit is as easy as pie to use. It'll take you only a few minutes a day to teach Jimmy to read. Oh, what a thrill it will be to hear little Jimmy read his first words!" exudes Grandma Kramer. Grandma continues, "Besides, you know we can't depend on today's schools to teach children—especially young boys—to read. If we use this kit with Jimmy now, we can be sure our little darling will never have a reading problem in school. Don't you think that would be worth the few minutes a day this kit takes, Cindy?"

Questions

1. If a child spends time learning to read in the preschool years, might other critical areas of development be slighted? Explain.

2. Why is there a trend in today's society to expose children to school-related activities, especially literacy activities, at earlier ages? Can this instruction be harmful for children? Explain.

3. Suppose Jimmy does learn to recognize some sight words through exposure to this kit. Is this really reading? Is there value in teaching Jimmy to recognize some sight words (e.g., names of body parts) at this young age? Explain.

4. If Jimmy learns to read before he starts kindergarten, will he be bored in kindergarten? Why or why not?

■ Preview

The prevailing point of view about teaching young children has shifted from nurturant waiting for certain indicators of readiness to appear to active efforts to provide appropriate early experiences that promote learning at the child's present level of development. Today, the early childhood teacher needs not only to identify appropriate early experiences to broaden children's understanding, but must build on children's existing knowledge and experiences and must implement individual education plans (IEPs) for children with disabilities. In the last 30 years, the explosion of child development research as well as the expansion and diversity of early childhood programs led the National Association for the Education of Young Children to develop and publish a position statement and set of guidelines for developmentally appropriate practice for children, from birth to age 8. Questions and debate about what is developmentally appropriate practice, however, will continue as times and our knowledge about children change (Bredekamp & Copple, 1997).

In the first selection in this chapter, Ruth A. Wilson describes the distinctive characteristics of young children's learning. She then explains how these characteristics can be taken into account when planning learning experiences, particularly environmental education activities, and why developmentally inappropriate practices are detrimental to young children. Next, Rosalind Charlesworth makes the case for NAEYC's developmentally appropriate practice guidelines being applicable to the education of all children in our diverse society. Finally, David Ruenzel reflects on his personal experiences and observations of kindergartens and on alternatives to increased academic pressures found in some kindergartens today.

Developmentally Appropriate Interpretation with Preschool Children

Ruth A. Wilson

■ ■ ■

The preschool child's way of learning differs from that of older children and adults.

During the first few years of life, young children learn about the world around them primarily through their senses and by being physically involved with it. While children can and do develop cognitive understandings about the natural world during their preschool years, they arrive at such understandings not by what adults tell them or explain to them, but by way of active learning opportunities involving direct experiences with nature and natural systems, under the guidance of caring adults (Cohen, 1992).

For young children, perception conducts thought —that is, their thinking actually depends on concrete perceptual information. Thus, what young children see, feel, hear, smell, and taste serves as the medium, or channel, for developing concepts and understandings. Perception for adults, on the other hand, obeys thought. Adults perceive the world as reflections of the cognitive models they've developed to represent the world. Thus, the adult's approach to understanding the natural world tends to be in relation to models, rather than on investigating nature as a complex entity (Sebba, 1991).

The Uniqueness of the Child's Way of Knowing

Some research suggests that young children's perception of the world is based on a "primal seeing" or "primal knowing," which allows them to experience the world around them in a primitive, but fundamental way. Some would suggest that this puts children in touch with "the embodiment of things, their very quintessence" (Sebba, 1991, p. 415). It is this type of knowing which tends to foster the imagination and a sense of wonder in young children (Cobb, 1977).

The perceptual closeness that young children seem to experience with nature relates to the fact that they are physically closer and less mediated in their response to the natural world (Hart, 1993). Their greater immersion in sensory perception, however, doesn't necessarily mean that young children have a more caring relationship to it (Hart, 1993). Their behavior, in fact, often indicates that they do not. Such behaviors as pulling wings off butterflies or squashing ants on the sidewalk are not unusual for young children.

Thus, children seem to be at once both closer to and further from nature (Hart, 1993). There are, in fact, indications that young children are conceptually distant from nature. Piaget (1963), for example, identified a tendency of children to ascribe intention and consciousness to inanimate things (stones, twigs, etc.). Recent research, too, indicates that young learners (four to six year olds) "frequently possess blurred or inaccurate understanding of processes and events in the world around them" (Palmer, 1995, p. 44).

Planning Developmentally Appropriate Experiences

The difference between the child's and the adult's understanding of the natural world— and their differing approaches to arriving at such understanding—should be taken into careful consideration when

Ruth A. Wilson. (1996). Developmentally appropriate interpretation with preschool children. *Legacy*, 7 (1), 31–33. Reprinted by permission of the National Association for Interpretation.

planning interpretive experiences. When planning for young children, their approach to learning about the world should be understood and respected. Because of the way young children learn, environmental educational programs for them should provide direct access to the natural environment. Designers of such programs should build in rich opportunities for sensory absorption and physical manipulation. This means that children should be "doers" in the process, not just "listeners" and "watchers." This also means that children should be given opportunities to experience the natural world through all their senses—opportunities to feel a wide variety of natural textures, smell the earth and the variety of things that grow on the earth, listen to whispers in the wind and roars in the water, taste the sweetness of honey and the tartness of rhubarb, and view the intricacies of a bird's nest or a spider's web.

Environmental educational programs for preschoolers should also provide many opportunities for young children to explore freely and joyfully. This can be done through such activities as digging in the dirt, splashing in the water, and walking barefoot in the grass. The emphasis should not be on analyzing and naming, but on stimulating the children's senses and bringing joy and excitement to their actions, their thoughts, and their feelings.

An important consideration in providing interpretive experiences for preschool children is that of developmental appropriateness. Principles of devel-

opmentally appropriate practices have been outlined by the National Association for the Education of Young Children and focus on providing experiences and learning opportunities for young children that match their level of development (Bredekamp, 1987). Key concepts related to developmentally appropriate practices include active versus passive learning opportunities, direct versus abstract experiences, and child-initiated explorations.

While best practices in environmental education suggest a combination of aesthetic perception and disciplined thinking at all levels of development (Sebba, 1991; Wilson, 1993), the primary focus during the early childhood years should be on aesthetic perception. This focus should gradually change as the child matures in his or her thinking; yet both approaches to learning should be included in interpretive programs at all levels of maturity [see the next page].

An experience that focuses on aesthetic (or sensory) perception is one "in which the child is actively involved, with his body, his senses, and his awareness" (Sebba, 1991, p. 395). Such experiences represent a developmental "match" to the preschool child in that young children tend to be "conscious of their senses and . . . are involved in listening to them" (Sebba, 1991, p. 405). According to Cobb (1969), "the child, like the poet, is his own instrument. His whole body, eroticized and highly sensitized by the necessities of nurture and touch, is the tool of his

Emphasis should be on stimulating children's senses and bringing joy and excitement to their actions, thoughts, and feelings.

Suggested Ratio of Aesthetic Perception to Disciplined Thinking

Early Childhood		Middle Childhood		Adulthood	
Aesthetic Perception	Disciplined Thinking	Aesthetic Perception	Disciplined Thinking	Aesthetic Perception	Disciplined Thinking

mind, and serves with a passionate enjoyment in a creative engagement with the forces of nature" (p. 128).

Aesthetic perception is not totally divorced from cognitive activity. The mental activity involved might be referred to as "undirected cognition," whereas disciplined thinking involves a more "directed cognition." "Undirected cognition" has been described as an "exciting and important kind of cognition" consisting of "free association, dreams, or reveries . . . including the free flow of thoughts that occur continually as the child walks home or stares at the window" (Mussen, Conger, & Kagan, 1979, p. 242).

Concerns about Inappropriate Practices

Opportunities for experiences which foster aesthetic perception are especially important during the early childhood years. This is due to the child's "unique and unrepeatable ability . . . to grasp surroundings" (Sebba, 1991, p. 398). "The interaction between the child and the natural environment is . . . an authentic childhood experience that carries with it the original stamp of childhood and that will disappear with its passing" (Sebba, 1991, p. 410).

As the child's unique way of knowing and experiencing the natural world tends to fade over time, an inappropriate educational approach can result in serious childhood deprivation—i.e., depriving the child of a sense of joy and wonder in getting to know the natural world. Cobb (1977) suggests that denying young children experiences that foster a sense of wonder may result in early psychic injury with long term negative implications on the status of one's mental health. A similar concern has been expressed by David Elkind (1987), who refers to the introduction of formal instruction during the early childhood years as "miseducation" and suggests that this practice puts young children "at risk for short-term stress and long-term personality damage" (p. 125).

While children are likely to suffer from inappropriate approaches to learning about the natural en-

vironment, so will the human/Earth relationship. "The way young children learn about the natural environment determines, in part, the nature of their life-long relationship with it" (Cobb, 1977, p. 107). Thus, if children learn that the natural environment is something to be labeled, dissected, analyzed, and used, their behavior toward the environment may be governed more by power, ownership, and indifference than by respect and caring.

Guidelines and Suggestions

Fostering a life-long love and respect for the natural world begins with a child-centered approach to learning about nature. The child-centered approach matches the way in which young children learn and reflect "best practices" in early childhood education (Bredekamp, 1987). Presented [on the next page] is a brief reference guide outlining some of the major characteristics of preschoolers, the nature of appropriate learning activities for young children, and examples of developmentally appropriate environmental education activities for preschool children. Additional guidelines and suggested activities are presented in *Fostering a Sense of Wonder During the Early Childhood Years* (Wilson, 1993), an early childhood environmental education curriculum guide designed to infuse nature-oriented activities throughout all aspects of an early childhood program.

Summary

Respecting the child's way of knowing offers benefits to the child—including his or her cognitive, aesthetic, emotional, and social development. Respecting the child's way of knowing also has the potential for making a difference in improving the human/Earth relationship. The child's way of knowing focuses on appreciation, wonder, and love. It fosters a personal, caring relationship with the natural environment. Valuing the child's way of know-

Reference Guide for Appropriate Environmental Education Activities for Preschool Children

Characteristics of Young Children	Nature of Appropriate Learning Activities for Preschool Children	Examples of Appropriate Learning Activities for Preschool Children
Active	Action oriented	Digging in sand or soil
Playful	Grounded in play	Jumping in a pile of leaves or hiding in tall grass
Curious	Explorative	Looking in holes and under logs
Creative/Inventive	Imaginative	Building dens and making nature collages
Concrete Learners	Real vs. abstract	Digging potatoes or planting beans vs. coloring pictures of vegetables or playing with "pretend" foods
Observant	Rich in variety	Watching wildlife around a pond or bird feeder
Sensorimotor	Rich in sensory stimulation and opportunities for hands-on involvement	Extracting the fruit from a pumpkin shell
Social Learners	Reflect sound ecological practices	Recycling and reusing

ing and carrying some of the characteristics of childhood into adult life may help us, as a society, live more joyously and harmoniously with the world around us.

REFERENCES

Bredekamp, S. (1987). *Developmentally appropriate practice in early childhood programs serving children from birth through age 8.* Washington, DC: National Association for the Education of Young Children.

Cobb, E. (1969). The ecology of imagination in childhood. In P. Shepard and D. McKinley, *The subversive science.* Boston: Houghton Mifflin (pp. 122–132).

Cobb, E. (1977). *The ecology of imagination in childhood.* New York: Columbia University Press.

Cohen, S. (1992). Research on children and ecology. *Childhood Education,* 68(5), 260.

Elkind, D. (1987). Miseducation. *Parents,* October, pp. 124–128, 130.

Hart, R. (1993). Affection for nature and the promotion of earth stewardship in childhood. Presentation for the American Horticultural Society's National Children's Gardening Symposium.

Mussen, P. H., Conger, J. J., & Kagan, J. (1979). *Child development and personality.* New York: Harper & Row.

Palmer, J. A. (1995). Environmental thinking in the early years: Understanding and misunderstanding of concepts related to waste management. *Environmental Education Research* 1 (1), 35–45.

Piaget, J. (1963) (orig. French, 1947). *The psychology of intelligence.* Totowa, NJ: Littlefield Adams.

Sebba, R. (1991). The landscapes of childhood: The reflection of childhood's environment in adult memories and in children's attitudes. *Environment and Behavior,* 23(4), 395–422.

Wilson, R. A. (1993). *Fostering a sense of wonder during the early childhood years.* Columbus, OH: Greyden Press.

■ *Dr. Wilson is associate professor in the Department of Special Education, Bowling Green State University, Bowling Green, Ohio 43403-0255.*

Developmentally Appropriate Practice Is for Everyone

Rosalind Charlesworth

■ ■ ■

In 1987, the National Association for the Education of Young Children (NAEYC) published guidelines for developmentally appropriate practice for young children ages birth through age eight (Bredekamp, 1987). The initial impetus for this publication was the implementation of the NAEYC accreditation process, which required accredited programs to exhibit "developmentally appropriate activities, materials, and expectations" (Bredekamp & Copple, 1997, p. v). Centers seeking accreditation, however, could not refer to any published guidelines that outlined developmentally appropriate practice. In addition, the guidelines were a response "to a growing trend toward more formal, academic instruction of young children" (Bredekamp & Copple, 1997, p. v). Prekindergarten teachers were being increasingly pressured to use a curriculum that seemed more suitable for elementary school. The 1987 guidelines (Bredekamp, 1987) described best practice, as recognized by early childhood professionals with many years of teaching young children. The book represented "the early childhood profession's consensus definition of developmentally appropriate practice in early childhood programs" (p. iv).

The 1987 document, which connected developmentally appropriate practice (DAP) to the areas of age and individual appropriateness, defined the basic elements of quality instructional practice with young children as no previous publication had. Since its publication, it has become the most influential document guiding the field of early childhood education. While thousands of early childhood professionals embraced the document, others criticized it for using developmental theory (especially Jean Piaget's) as the conceptual base. Many called for a reconceptualized DAP, built on the basis of cultural, historical and political theory (e.g., Bloch, 1992;

Fowell & Lawton, 1992; Jipson, 1991; Kessler, 1991a, 1991b; Lubeck, 1994, 1996; Walsh, 1991). Critics particularly questioned whether DAP could apply to the education of children from diverse cultures. NAEYC attempted to respond to the diversity question in the revised edition of the guidelines. A more in-depth description of the DAP view of cultural appropriateness gave equal attention to age, individual *and* cultural appropriateness (Bredekamp & Copple, 1997). This article will present evidence that DAP is for everyone, whatever their socioeconomic status, culture, race, gender, age or special needs.

What Is Development?
What Are DAP and DIP?

Development refers to changes in individuals across the lifespan. We know, for example, that young children sit before they crawl, crawl before they walk, understand spoken language before they speak, etc. The DAP approach is meant to provide guidelines for what is appropriate educational practice, relative to young children's current, as well as future, development.

Both the 1987 and 1997 versions of the NAEYC guidelines include examples of Developmentally Appropriate Practice (DAP) and Developmentally Inappropriate Practice (DIP). DAP refers to a child-centered approach to instruction that views the child as the primary source of the curriculum and recognizes young children's unique characteristics. Teachers can support children's growth by offering appropriate materials and activities that match their observations of children's emerging cognitive, physical/motor and affective/social development. With knowledge of cultural aspects and of both typical and atypical development, teachers can construct

Rosalind Charlesworth. (1998). Developmentally appropriate practice is for everyone. *Childhood Education, 74,* 274–282. Reprinted by permission of Rosalind Charlesworth and the Association for Childhood Education International. Copyright © 1998 by the Association.

a curriculum that meets the needs of all children, using the NAEYC suggestions to guide their planning (e.g., Bredekamp & Rosegrant, 1992; Dugger-Wadsworth, 1997; Escobedo, 1993; Hale, 1992; Stremmel, 1997). DAP provides children with choices that allow for individual differences and ensure success for all. The guidelines (Bredekamp & Copple, 1997) include a general position statement, an overview of the teacher as a decision-maker, and more specific examples and guidelines for DAP with infants and toddlers, 3- through 5-year-olds, and 6- through 8-year-olds.

The guidelines provide examples of DAP and DIP in contrasting extremes for each age group. For example, the following example is from the section for 6- through 8-year-olds, under the heading "Creating a Caring Community of Learners" (Bredekamp & Copple, 1997, p. 161):

- *Appropriate practices.* Teachers ensure that primary-grade rooms function as caring communities of learners in which all children and adults feel accepted and respected. Children learn personal responsibility, how to develop constructive relationships with other people, and respect for individual and cultural differences, as well as important skills and knowledge to enable them to function in society.
- *Inappropriate practices.* No efforts are made to build a sense of the group as a community. To maintain classroom order, teachers continually separate children from friends and discourage conversation. Some children who lack social skills are isolated or rejected by peers and receive no assistance from teachers in developing positive relationships within the classroom.

These contrasts define the extremes of DIP and DAP. Some research supports the view that teaching practice ranges from one extreme to the other (Charlesworth, Hart, Burts, Mosley & Fleege, 1993b; Stipek, Daniels, Galluzo & Milburn, 1992).

At one extreme, the DIP teacher uses lectures, drill-and-practice, and workbooks and worksheet activities. DIP separates content areas (i.e., mathematics, science, social studies, reading/language arts, etc.) with little, if any, integration, and few hands-on, concrete experiences. DIP teachers keep order by punishing students for unacceptable behavior and offering extrinsic rewards for obedience. Children are not guided toward an understanding of appropriate behavior, nor to building self-control and motivation. Little, if any, attention is paid to individual differences, and assessment focuses on weekly quizzes, end-of-unit tests and standardized test scores.

In contrast, DAP (as defined in the guidelines) emphasizes the whole child (physical, social, emotional and cognitive), while taking into account gender, culture, disabilities, socioeconomic status, family factors and any other important elements in order to meet the individual child's needs, developmental level and learning style. Teachers make informed decisions based on their knowledge of child development, individual children and cultural and social context (Bredekamp & Copple, 1997). The curriculum integrates the content areas and provides for active exploration and concrete, hands-on activities. Children are motivated to learn by their natural curiosity and their desire to make sense of the world. Hart, Burts and Charlesworth (1997) offer a more detailed description of this type of curriculum.

Why DAP Is for Everyone

Research demonstrates that both preschool and kindergarten-age children enrolled in less developmentally appropriate classrooms exhibit about twice the levels of stress behaviors when compared with those in more developmentally appropriate programs (Burts, Hart, Charlesworth, Fleege, Mosley & Thomasson, 1992; Burts, Hart, Charlesworth & Kirk, 1990; Hart, Burts, Durland, Charlesworth, DeWolf & Fleege, 1998; Love, Ryer & Faddis, 1992).

Children in preschool and kindergarten classes that practice inappropriate academic activities have been found to do less well in academic achievement (Bryant, Burchinal, Lau & Sparling, 1994; Frede & Barnett, 1992; Mantzicopoulos & Neuharth-Pritchett, 1995; Marcon, 1993), rate lower on behavioral evaluations (Mantzicopoulos & Neuharth-Pritchett, 1995; Marcon, 1994) and tend to be perceived as less motivated (Hirsh-Pasek, 1991; Stipek, Feiler, Daniels & Milburn, 1995), when compared with children attending more child-initiated/DAP programs. In addition, these studies suggest that children who attend more child-centered DAP programs perform better in all of these areas. Achievement findings favor DAP curriculum approaches, even when compared with programs that use mixed curriculum models (Marcon, 1992, 1994).

The results of studies that followed students from kindergarten into the elementary grades are consistent with preprimary findings, suggesting that less developmentally appropriate preschool and kindergarten classroom experiences are linked in the future to: (1) poorer academic achievement; (2) lower conduct and work-study habit grades; (3) more distractibility; and (4) less prosocial, conforming behavior during the early grade-school years. These results contrast with those for children who attended

DAP programs. Attendance in DAP programs appears to be related to overall positive benefits in terms of later level of achievement and behavioral outcomes for elementary school students from varying backgrounds (Burts et al., 1993; Charlesworth, Hart, Burts & DeWolf, 1993a; Hart, Charlesworth, Burts & DeWolf, 1993; Larsen & Robinson, 1989; Marcon, 1994).

DAP and Equity

The findings from the LSU studies (Charlesworth et al., 1993a) indicate that developmentally appropriate curriculum promotes equity in developmental outcomes, at least when considering African American and European American children from socioeconomically diverse backgrounds. This research program targeted preschool and kindergarten children who attended both DAP and DIP programs.

DAP programs in preschool and kindergarten appeared to lower children's stress levels. Males, low SES (socioeconomic status) [children], and African Americans were most adversely affected by DIP programs. All children in DAP classrooms (regardless of SES, racial background or gender) exhibited less stressful behavior (Burts et al., 1992; Hart et al., 1998).

All children from different SES backgrounds who attended DAP kindergartens also benefited academically. Children in DAP classrooms outperformed their DIP classroom counterparts on the California Achievement Test (CAT). The lower SES DAP students did as well as the lower SES DIP students on the CAT, while the higher SES DIP students did better than the lower SES DIP students. These results are congruent with previous studies indicating that standardized test scores favor high SES students (Alexander & Entwisle, 1988; Patterson, Kupersmidt & Vaden, 1990; Shakiba-Nejad & Yellin, 1981), but they also suggest that DIP instruction may be to blame.

Other researchers also have found that DAP classroom settings may be beneficial for low income African American children. Marcon (1992, 1994) found both short- and long-term benefits for low SES African American children who attended child-initiated (DAP) preschool and kindergarten programs. Bryant et al. (1994) obtained similar short-term results for African American students enrolled in Head Start. Other studies also support the equitable nature of DAP (Hirsh-Pasek, Hyson & Rescorla, 1990; Mantzicopoulos, Neuharth-Pritchett & Morelock, 1994; Schweinhart, Barnes & Weikart, 1993).

Fuson (1996) developed a mathematics program for Latino 1st- and 2nd-grade students in Chicago that is based on the students' concrete, everyday experiences. This program is very much in the DAP mode. The 1st-graders' test scores were equal to or better than those of other students taught in a variety of styles. The students from the experimental program did exceptionally better than children taught with basal texts.

Equity in Activity Type Participation

DAP classrooms provide children from diverse backgrounds with greater access to developmentally appropriate activities. One set of studies (Charlesworth et al., 1993a) found that low SES and African American children have less access than European American children to the few developmentally appropriate experiences available in DIP classrooms. By contrast, the researchers found that all students had equal access to such activities in DAP classrooms. It appears that some teachers direct minority children into more teacher-led group activities that require a high degree of conformance. Many teachers and parents believe that these children need this structure and conformity in order to succeed in the mainstream culture (e.g., Delpit, 1988, 1995; Goldenberg, 1994; Knapp & Shields, 1990; Lubeck, 1994, Pine & Hilliard, 1990; Stipek, 1993). Some evidence indicates that parents with low incomes and relatively poor education are more likely to endorse rigidly structured, basic skills-oriented programs for young children (Rescorla et al., 1990; Stipek et al., 1992).

Greater exposure to conformance-oriented activities may be particularly damaging for African American children, even though many members of their culture appear to prefer such programs (Delpit, 1988). Compared to their European American counterparts, research indicates that African American children tend to thrive more on people-oriented activities that offer freedom, variation and novelty (Charlesworth, 1996). Consequently, African American children need a more physically active, socially oriented environment to support their high energy level (Hale, 1981, 1992). Results of the analysis by Abshire (1991) indicated that African Americans, as compared to their European American counterparts, were more frequently involved in whole group, waiting and group-managed transitional activities in DIP kindergartens and had less access to group story, music and centers. African Americans in DAP kindergartens had equal access to the concrete hands-on experiences that better fit their learning style.

Recent brain development research indicates that brain growth is maximized through meaningful activities that include interaction with concrete materials and other people. Language also plays a key role—the more words that infants and toddlers hear, the more capable they will be with language in later years. Ordinary conversation, as well as songs and rhymes (in contrast to drill-and-practice on the alphabet and counting), stimulate brain development. These kinds of activities are very much in line with DAP principles (Newberger, 1997).

Educating Our Diverse Population

The 1997 revision of the DAP guidelines emphasizes the importance of focusing on the strengths and the needs of culturally and linguistically diverse children. It is also important, however, to review the developmental commonalities "that cut across socioeconomic, cultural and language groups such as maturation, sequential developmental stages, and a learning mode based on active, concrete-based experiences" (Escobedo, 1993, p. 215). Such linguistically and culturally diverse preschoolers need ". . . access to high quality and developmentally appropriate preschool experiences" (Kagan & Garcia, 1991, p. 427). Furthermore, educators and curriculum developers "must address not only considerations of child development but also those matters that are culture- and language-specific" (Escobedo, 1993, p. 214).

In their text on methods of teaching young children in multicultural classrooms, Robles de Melendez and Ostertag (1997) cite DAP as the core of the early childhood education profession. They believe certain developmental tasks, such as those identified by Erik Erikson and by Jean Piaget, are common across cultures. Knowledge of these tasks enables teachers to develop programs based on a particular age group's general characteristics. "Developing a program based on the children is also a basic principle of multicultural education" (p. 117). Robles de Melendez and Ostertag also tie multicultural education to the individually appropriate principle of DAP. "Developmentally responsive education and multicultural education both have the role of building common human experiences unique to individuals and to specific cultures" (p. 121). They view DAP and multicultural education as equal partners in supporting diversity.

Hispanic/Latino/Chicano children and families are receiving increased attention because they represent an ever-greater segment of the population in the United States. Eugene E. Garcia (1997), in a review of research on the education of Hispanics in early childhood, supports the NAEYC position statement on linguistic and cultural diversity (NAEYC, 1996). He believes the primary culture must be respected and preserved while children are gradually assimilated into the school culture. Yazmin Elizabeth Kuball (1995) describes how she changed from skill-based teaching to developmentally appropriate language education in her bilingual kindergarten. Kuball accepted another teacher's advice and initially used dittoed skill sheets and sheets with letters to trace. She began with "A" and drilled through the letters, one each week. She found, however, that while her students had learned the alphabet, it was out of context. Her students were unable to compose a letter to a friend, because, they said, they didn't know how to write.

The next year, Kuball removed the desks, kept two round tables, and set up areas for dramatic play, art, reading, woodworking and science, as well as a space for a garden. She then instituted a whole language literacy program, surrounding the children with print and starting them out with writing as composition. The photos and writing samples she shares in her article document the success of her DAP program with children whose primary language is Spanish.

James St. Clair also teaches a bilingual kindergarten class, evenly divided between English-speaking and Spanish-speaking students. His students attend Spanish immersion half the day and English immersion the other half. St. Clair teaches the English immersion half of the day, but he also is fluent in Spanish. He describes (St. Clair, 1993) how his classroom is stocked with a multitude of manipulative materials, including a water table and a sand table, for use with mathematics. St. Clair found he could easily and accurately assess the students' progress by observing them as they worked with these materials to solve problems.

Paula Carter (1997) describes what she learned regarding teaching English to Grace, an Asian American 1st-grader. Grace was reluctant to speak English at school. After consulting with Grace's mother, who spoke only Cantonese at home, Carter suggested that Grace and her mother spend some time each day speaking English together. Carter then started using concrete language experiences, rather than phonics workbooks. She and Grace talked, read and wrote about things that were familiar to Grace. This concrete approach proved to be very successful.

James P. Comer (Goldberg, 1997) believes that schools with predominantly impoverished populations, especially African American children, can become communities through the application of certain principles of psychiatry and the behavioral sciences. The Comer Project for Change in Education is based on improved mental health and school, family and community partnerships and involvement. Comer believes that educators must foremost consider child development, which should guide decisions regarding curriculum, instruction and assessment. The Comer model has been very successful and has been adopted in many schools across the United States.

Lee Little Soldier, a leading advocate for the culturally appropriate early education of Native American children, noticed that Native American children in Head Start classrooms are very communicative (Little Soldier, 1992). These classrooms are characterized by openness and informality, opportunities for freedom and autonomy, and strong bonds of trust between students and adults, which have developed from work on cooperative projects. Native American students tend to remain silent and withdrawn in public school classrooms, where lecture/recitation dominates (Little Soldier, 1992). Their culture values group cooperation and interaction, rather than the individualized, competitive approach common to DIP classrooms. Little Soldier believes that DAP approaches, such as noncorporal punishment discipline, flexible time schedules and opportunities for creative experiences, are a better fit to the Native American culture.

Susan Evans Akaran teaches Native American Alaskan kindergartners. She was puzzled when she had difficulty motivating her students to write stories, since she knew that Native American Alaskans have a rich cultural tradition of oral storytelling. Akaran recounts how she turned to the DAP guidelines (Bredekamp & Rosegrant, 1992) for help (Akaran & Fields, 1997). She noted that the Native American Alaskans shared more of an oral, not written, tradition; consequently, she needed a way to bridge the gap. She achieved this task by asking the parents to tell stories to their children. Each of the children then dictated those stories to their teacher and illustrated the dictation. Then, the stories were bound into books, one for each child, that the students read to each other in school and to their parents at home. This experience demonstrated for the children the relationship between oral and written storytelling. The children acquired an enthusiasm for bookmaking and maintained the oral/written language connection, as evidenced in their continued interest in writing.

Donna Dugger-Wadsworth (1997) describes the relationship of DAP and programs recommended for children with disabilities by the Division of Early Childhood/Council on Exceptional Children. Such programs teach specific skills to children with disabilities during naturally occurring classroom activi-

ties. Teachers should watch for the moment when a child has found an activity of interest and insert direct instruction at an opportune moment that fits the ongoing activity. More specifically, teachers need to learn how to modify materials and activities so that special needs children can be included in regular classroom activities. Congruent with DAP, Early Childhood Special Education (ECSE) has a history of family involvement that has been strengthened through legislative mandates. As with any group, special needs children should receive respect and be valued as individuals.

Summary and Conclusions

This article presents support for the value of the principles of developmentally appropriate practice (DAP) for all children in our diverse society. Emerging supportive research indicates that more appropriate practices support the psychological, social and academic well-being of young children from diverse ethnic and socioeconomic groups. DAP appears to place children from diverse backgrounds on a level playing field. Furthermore, many professionals who are, themselves, members of minority groups and/or who have taught young minority children support practices that would fall in the developmentally appropriate category. As Sue Bredekamp (1997) points out, early childhood teachers are decision-makers who inform their practice using their knowledge of child development, social and cultural contexts, and their own empirical observations.

It is extremely important that the guidelines be used with care. Hsue & Aldridge (1995) caution that if any part of DAP appears to conflict with a child's culture, resolution should be sought through constructive dialogue with the family. Furthermore, early childhood professionals should be educated regarding their students' cultures, a point that the revised guidelines (Bredekamp & Copple, 1997) make clear. The guidelines are not intended as doctrine, but rather as a way to plan for providing supportive environments for young children. Child development theories, as opposed to historical or other theories, are used as DAP's foundation because, as William Ayers (1993) suggests, "Theories of child development, including developmental psychology, can help by reminding us that childhood is a unique, distinct time and place in the growth of a person" (p. 34). He warns that adopting theory as a doctrine can be dangerous; it should only be a guide. This same caution is relevant to the guidelines themselves.

REFERENCES

Abshire, S. (1991). *A study of developmentally appropriate and developmentally inappropriate kindergarten classrooms: Activity types and experiences.* Unpublished master's thesis, Louisiana State University, Baton Rouge.

Alexander, L. L., & Entwisle, D. R. (1998). Achievement in the first two years of school: Patterns and processing. *Monographs of the Society for Research in Child Development, 2,* 95–108.

Akaran, S. E., & Fields, M. V. (1997). Family and cultural context: A writing breakthrough? *Young Children, 52*(4), 37–40.

Ayers, W. (1993). *To teach: The journey of a teacher.* New York: Teachers College Press.

Bloch, M. N. (1992). Critical perspectives on the historical relationship between child development and early childhood education research. In S. Kessler & B. B. Swadner (Eds.), *Reconceptualizing the early childhood curriculum: Beginning the dialogue* (pp. 3–20). New York: Teachers College Press.

Bredekamp, S. (Ed.). (1987). *Developmentally appropriate practice in early childhood programs serving children from birth through age eight.* Washington, DC: National Association for the Education of Young Children.

Bredekamp, S. (1997). Developmentally appropriate practice: The early childhood teacher as a decisionmaker. In S. Bredekamp & C. Copple (Eds.), *Developmentally appropriate practice in early childhood programs* (rev. ed.) (pp. 33–52). Washington, DC: National Association for the Education of Young Children.

Bredekamp, S., & Copple, C. (1997). (Eds.). *Developmentally appropriate practice in early childhood programs* (rev. ed.). Washington, DC: National Association for the Education of Young Children.

Bredekamp, S., & Rosegrant, T. (Eds). (1992). *Reaching potentials: Appropriate curriculum and assessment for young children* (Vol. I). Washington, DC: National Association for the Education of Young Children.

Bryant, D. M., Burchinal, M., Lau, L. B., & Sparling, J. J. (1994). Family and classroom correlates of Head Start children's developmental outcomes. *Early Childhood Research Quarterly, 9,* 289–309.

Burts, D. C., Hart, C. H., Charlesworth, R., DeWolf, D. M., Ray, J., Manuel, K., & Fleege, P. O. (1993). Developmental appropriateness of kindergarten programs and academic outcomes in first grade. *Journal of Research in Childhood Education, 8,* 23–31.

Burts, D. C., Hart, C. H., Charlesworth, R., Fleege, P. O., Mosley, J., & Thomasson, R. H. (1992). Observed activities and stress behaviors of children in developmentally appropriate and inappropriate kindergarten classrooms. *Early Childhood Research Quarterly, 7,* 297–318.

Burts, D. C., Hart, C. H., Charlesworth, R., & Kirk, L. (1990). A comparison of frequencies of stress behaviors observed in kindergarten children in classrooms with developmentally appropriate versus developmentally inappropriate instructional practices. *Early Childhood Research Quarterly, 5,* 407–423.

Carter, P. (1997, February). Mother's words.* *Teaching Pre-K–8,* 51.

Charlesworth, R. (1996). *Understanding child development.* Albany, NY: Delmar.

Charlesworth, R., Hart, C. H., Burts, D. C., & DeWolf, M. (1993a). The LSU studies: Building a research base for developmentally appropriate practice. In S. Reifel (Ed.), *Advances in early education and day care: Perspectives on developmentally appropriate curriculum* (Vol. 5, pp. 3–28). Greenwich, CT: JAI.

Charlesworth, R., Hart, C. H., Burts, D. C., Mosley, J., & Fleege, P. O. (1993b). Measuring the developmental appropriateness of kindergarten teachers' beliefs and practices. *Early Childhood Research Quarterly, 8,* 255–276.

Delpit, L. D. (1988). The silenced dialogue: Power and pedagogy in educating other people's children. *Harvard Educational Review, 58,* 78–95.

Delpit, L. D. (1995). *Other people's children: Cultural conflict in the classroom.* New York: New Press.

Dugger-Wadsworth, D. (1997). The integrated curriculum and students with disabilities. In C. H. Hart, D. C. Burts, & R. Charlesworth (Eds.), *Integrated curriculum and developmentally appropriate practice: Birth to age eight* (pp. 335–362). Albany, NY: SUNY Press.

Escobedo, T. H. (1993). Curricular issues in early education for culturally and linguistically diverse populations. In S. Reifel (Ed.), *Advances in early education and day care: Perspectives on developmentally appropriate curriculum* (Vol. 5, pp. 213–246). Greenwich, CT: JAI.

Fowell, N., & Lawton, J. (1992). An alternative view of appropriate practice in early childhood education. *Early Childhood Research Quarterly, 7,* 53–73.

Frede, E., & Barnett, W. S. (1992). Developmentally appropriate public school preschool: A study of implementation of the High/Scope curriculum and its effects on disadvantaged children's skills at first grade. *Early Childhood Research Quarterly, 7,* 483–499.

Fuson, K. C. (1996, April). *Latino children's construction of arithmetic understanding in urban classrooms that support thinking.* Paper presented at the annual meeting of the American Educational Research Association, New York.

Garcia, E. E. (1997). Research in review. The education of Hispanics in early childhood: Of roots and wings. *Young Children, 52*(3), 5–14.

Goldberg, M. F. (1997). Maintaining a focus development: An interview with Dr. James P. Comer. *Phi Delta Kappan, 78,* 557–559.

Goldenberg, C. (1994, April). Rethinking the means and goals of early literacy education for Spanish-speaking kindergartners. In D. Stipek (Chair), *Reconceptualizing the debate on appropriate early childhood education.* Symposium presented at the annual meeting of the American Educational Research Association, New Orleans, LA.

Hale, J. (1981). Black children: Their roots, culture, and learning styles. *Young Children, 36*(2), 37–50.

Hale, J. (1992). An African-American early childhood education program: Visions for children. In S. Kessler & B. B. Swadner (Eds.), *Reconceptualizing the early childhood curriculum: Beginning the dialogue* (pp. 205–226). New York: Teachers College Press.

Hart, C. H., Burts, D. C., & Charlesworth, R. (1997). Integrated developmentally appropriate curriculum: From theory and research to practice. In C. H. Hart, D. C. Burts, & R. Charlesworth (Eds.), *Integrated curriculum and developmentally appropriate practice: Birth to age eight* (pp. 1–28). Albany, NY: SUNY Press.

Hart, C. H., Burts, D. C., Durland, M. A., Charlesworth, R., DeWolf, M., & Fleege, P. O. (1998). Stress behaviors and activity type participation of preschoolers in more and less developmentally appropriate classrooms. *Journal of Research in Childhood Education, 12*(2), 176–196.

Hart, C. H., Charlesworth, R., Burts, D. C., & DeWolf, M. (1993, March). *The relationship of attendance in developmentally appropriate or inappropriate kindergarten classrooms to first and second grade behavior.* Paper presented at the biennial meeting of the Society for Research in Child Development, New Orleans, LA.

Hirsh-Pasek, K. (1991). Pressure or challenge in preschool? How academic environments affect children. In L. Rescorla, M. C. Hyson, & K. Hirsh-Pasek (Eds.), *New directions in child development. Academic instruction in early childhood: Challenge or pressure?* (No. 53, pp. 39–46). San Francisco: Jossey-Bass.

Hirsh-Pasek, K., Hyson, M. C., & Rescorla, L. (1990). Academic environments in preschool: Do they pressure or challenge young children? *Early Education and Development, 1*, 401–423.

Hsue, Y., & Aldridge, J. (1995). Developmentally appropriate and traditional Taiwanese culture. *Journal of Instructional Psychology, 22*, 320–323.

Jipson, J. (1991). Developmentally appropriate practice: Culture, curriculum, connections. *Early Education and Development, 2*(2), 120–136.

Kagan, S. L., & Garcia, E. E. (1991). Educating culturally and linguistically diverse preschoolers: Moving the agenda. *Early Childhood Research Quarterly, 6*, 427–443.

Kessler, S. A. (1991a). Early childhood education as development: A critique of the metaphor. *Early Education and Development, 2*, 137–152.

Kessler, S. A. (1991b). Alternative perspectives on early childhood education. *Early Childhood Research Quarterly, 6*, 183–197.

Knapp, M. S., & Shields, P. M. (1990). Reconceiving academic instruction for the children of poverty. *Phi Delta Kappan, 71*, 753–758.

Kuball, Y. E. (1995). Goodbye dittoes: A journey from skill-based teaching to developmentally appropriate language education in a bilingual kindergarten. *Young Children, 50*(2), 6–14.

Larsen, J. M., & Robinson, C. (1989). Later effects of preschool on low-risk children. *Early Childhood Research Quarterly, 4*, 133–144.

Little Soldier, L. (1992). Working with Native American children. *Young Children, 47*(6),15–21.

Love, J., Ryer, P., & Faddis, B. (1992). *Caring environments: Program quality in California's publicly funded child development programs.* Portsmouth, NH: RMC Research Corporation.

Lubeck, S. (1994). The politics of developmentally appropriate practice: Exploring issues of culture, class and curriculum. In B. L. Mallory & R. S. New (Eds.), *Diversity and developmentally appropriate practices* (pp. 17–43). New York: Teachers College Press.

Lubeck, S. (1996). Deconstructing "child development knowledge" and "teacher preparation." *Early Childhood Research Quarterly, 11*, 147–168.

Mantzicopoulos, P. Y., & Neuharth-Pritchett, S. (1995, April). *Classroom environments, parental involvement, and children's school achievement and adjustment: Two-year results from a Head Start early school transition demonstration program.* Paper presented at the annual meeting of the American Educational Research Association, San Francisco, CA.

Mantzicopoulos, P. Y., Neuharth-Pritchett, S., & Morelock, J. B. (1994, April). *Academic competence, social skills, and behavior among disadvantaged children in developmentally appropriate and inappropriate classrooms.* Paper presented at the annual meeting of the American Educational Research Association, New Orleans, LA.

Marcon, R. A. (1992). Differential effects of three preschool models on inner-city 4-year-olds. *Early Childhood Research Quarterly, 7*, 517–530.

Marcon, R. A. (1993). Socioemotional vs. academic emphasis: Impact on kindergartners' development and achievement. *Early Childhood Development and Care, 96*, 81–91.

Marcon, R. A. (1994). Doing the right thing for children: Linking research and policy reform in the District of Columbia public schools. *Young Children, 50*(8), 8.

National Association for the Education of Young Children. (1996). NAEYC position statement: Responding to linguistic and cultural diversity—Recommendations for effective early childhood education. *Young Children, 51*(2), 4–12.

Newberger, J. J. (1997). New brain development research—A wonderful window of opportunity to build public support for early childhood education! *Young Children, 52*(4), 4–9.

Patterson, C. J., Kupersmidt, J. B., & Vaden, N. A. (1990). Income level, gender, ethnicity, and household composition as predictors of children's school-based competence. *Child Development, 61*, 485–494.

Pine, G. J., & Hilliard, A. G. (1990). Rx for racism: Imperative for America's schools. *Phi Delta Kappan, 72*, 593–600.

Rescorla, L., Hyson, M., Hirsh-Pasek, K., & Cone, J. (1990). Academic expectations of mothers of preschool children: A psychometric study of the educational attitude scale. *Early Education and Development, 1,* 165–184.

Robles de Melendez, W., & Ostertag, V. (1997). *Teaching young children in multicultural classrooms.* Albany, NY: Delmar.

St. Clair, J. (1993). Assessing mathematical understanding in a bilingual kindergarten. In N. L. Webb & A. F. Coxford (Eds.), *Assessments in the mathematics classroom* (pp. 65–73). Reston, VA: National Council of Teachers of Mathematics.

Schweinhart, L. J., Barnes, H. V., & Weikart, D. P. (1993). *Significant benefits: The High/Scope Perry Preschool study through age 27.* Monographs of the High/Scope Educational Research Foundation, No. 10. Ypsilanti, MI: High/Scope Press.

Shakiba-Nejad, H., & Yellin, D. (1981). *Socioeconomic status, academic, and teacher response.* (Report No. 022 355). Stillwater, OK: Oklahoma State University. (ERIC Document Reproduction Service No. ED 231 754)

Stipek, D. J. (1993). Is child-centered early childhood education really better? In S. Reifel (Ed.), *Advances in early education and day care: Perspectives on developmentally appropriate practice* (Vol. 5, pp. 29–52). Greenwich, CT: JAI.

Stipek, D., Daniels, D., Galluzo, D., & Milburn, S. (1992). Characterizing early childhood education programs for poor and middle-class children. *Early Childhood Research Quarterly, 7,* 1–19.

Stipek, D., Feiler, R., Daniels, D., & Milburn, S. (1995). Effects of different instructional approaches on young children's achievement and motivation. *Child Development, 66,* 209–223.

Stremmel, A. (1997). Diversity and perspective. In C. H. Hart, D. C. Burts, & R. Charlesworth (Eds.), *Integrated curriculum and developmentally appropriate practice: Birth to age eight* (pp. 363–388). Albany, NY: SUNY Press.

Walsh, D. J. (1991). Extending the discourse on developmental appropriateness: A developmental perspective. *Early Education and Development, 2,* 109–119.

■ ***Rosalind Charlesworth** is professor, Child and Family Studies, Weber State University, Ogden, Utah.*

Paradise Lost

David Ruenzel

■ ■ ■

For most adults, their kindergarten experience is a vague dream from which emerge singular details of great clarity. People will tell you they can't remember anything, and the next moment they're inspired poets, telling you of glass milk bottles jingling, notes in the milkman's crate, or of the cool thinness of the vinyl mats they floated on during nap time, or of the huge afternoon sun carving out pockets of the room.

But my own remembrances of kindergarten are far less lyrical, for I was the single member of the kindergarten class of 1960 determined unfit for the rigors of 1st grade. I was what they call "retained," forced to do another year of kindergarten. This was a terrible blow to my parents, and therefore a terrible blow to me, and even now, so many years later, I am still indignant at having been assessed such an early failure. How, after all, could one fail kindergarten? How could adults have the arrogance to so judge a mere child? How could the "children's garden"—where a century ago children were still analogized as "seeds" and the teachers as the "guardians of God's gift"—be such fallow ground?

Of course, school officials didn't use the word "failure" when discussing my case. They used the word "immature"—I remember my parents whispering this word back and forth over the dinner table—as if I only needed some more ripening in the kindergarten's greenhouse climate. But as a 5-year-old, I felt, on some ghastly intuitive level, that "immaturity" was a euphemism for failure, for some kind of gross inadequacy that would follow me through the years.

Just what my inadequacy was I did not know; I was, of course, lacking in that kind of self-awareness. But I think the news of my retention surprised me as much as it hurt because I was unaware of having a particularly difficult year or of causing difficulty. I thought of myself as one of the children—no more and no less. Like them, I built castles with the large wooden blocks, helped dispense snacks, and happily gathered on the floor around our gray-haired teacher, who sang to us while she played the piano. Only once do I remember trouble. I somehow disappeared into a grove of trees during recess and was later discovered missing from class. A search was mounted, and I was eventually found bouncing on a low branch and escorted from the woods by scolding adults. It was a bit like being hauled away from the scene of a crime.

In later years, I learned from my parents that my presumed inadequacy was social in nature; school officials had, in fact, deemed me "socially immature." It wasn't that I was a troublemaker but the very opposite: I was too quiet, too pliable, too solitary. In short, I was considered an introvert, a bit of a loner, and it seemed as if I might never be interested in "winning over friends and influencing people." In America, gregariousness is considered a kind of gift to be honed in any number of school clubs and associations, and in the land of the ambitious extrovert, I would always be somewhat suspect.

After my first year of kindergarten, school was never again a magical or even pleasurable place for me, and at least some of my dissatisfaction I attribute to that early false start. Being held back imparted to me not just a sense of shame; it also taught me that schooling, even at its earliest stages, is about conformity as much as learning and that if I wanted to get along with my teachers and progress through the system I would have to sacrifice a good chunk of my individuality. To this very day, I carry a deep-seated bias against schools that measure children against narrow definitions of social and academic success.

Still, I rarely thought about the nature of kindergarten—what it was, what it is now, and what it could be—beyond my personal experience until my daughter came home from kindergarten early in the school year with a list of letters she was expected to learn to sound out. My daughter, one of the youngest in the class, found a few of the letters difficult. She became anxious about what she felt was her ineptitude. And when the teacher told my wife and

David Ruenzel. (1996, May/June). Paradise lost. Reprinted with permission from *Teacher Magazine*, Vol. 7, No. 8, Date 5/96, pp. 26–29, 31–34.

me that this was important preparation for 1st grade, that we should work with her while we were, say, doing the dishes, I felt rising up in me my old sense of indignation. What could it matter if my daughter knew the sounds for "g" or "c" when she would certainly learn these things soon enough? (Actually, she mastered the letters within a month without any special assistance from us.) Why this imposition of basic skills upon a child so smitten with playing witch?

My daughter's case, I was soon to find out, was far from unique. As I began to ask other parents around the country about their children's kindergarten experiences, they told me that their 5-year-olds were already reading and writing, or at least being pushed to read and write. Sometimes, this meant work sheets and drills—the things we associate with the basics. Other times, it entailed things like invented spelling, which at one time meant the children were free to play with letters and words. Now, though, teachers talk about invented spelling as a skill, or as a task by which children acquire a skill. It is part of pre-writing, which, like pre-reading, is something done in what schools like to call "literacy-rich environments." But the very use of the prefix suggests that play is almost besides the point. "Pre-" places the emphasis on getting up to speed, on readiness for "real" writing and reading, much as "pre-algebra" suggests but a path to the "real" work of algebra.

A few parents I talked with suspected that an academic focus in kindergarten was unnecessary if not inappropriate, but they went along with what appeared to be an inexorable trend. After all, no one else seemed to be complaining. Still, acquiescing to the trend could have unhappy consequences. Not all children can sit still and remain quiet for long periods of time, something a formalized curriculum requires them to do. Inevitably, some of the parents I talked with had begun to worry about their perfectly healthy and robust youngsters. Normal immature behaviors of small, restless children—occasional temper tantrums, sulks, excitability—were seen as signs of anxiety, hyperactivity, even depression. And the children who lagged behind in reading were sometimes stigmatized as "slow learners," making them a target for early remediation.

Talking to anxious parents of small children, you sometimes get the sense that "Head Start" is not just the name of the favored government early education program but a sort of national advertising slogan. You can get your child a head start not only in reading and writing but also in French, soccer, and computers. It is never too early for anything. You can push your children into the real world, even if they sometimes go kicking and screaming.

The more I heard, the more I became convinced that kindergarten is in real danger of becoming a miniature 1st grade, that it is losing whatever innocence it may have had. And there is no doubt that kindergarten was intended to be innocent—using that word in its broadest sense. The idea was to provide children with rich experiences while sheltering them during their most vulnerable years from the harsh realities of the adult world.

Friedrich Froebel, the German schoolteacher and philosopher who practically invented kindergarten in 1837, was a romantic and mystic who believed that "the schoolmaster's function is to point out and make intelligible the inner spiritual nature of things." For Froebel, the "spiritual nature of things" was bound up with nature, to which the child was instinctively drawn. This is why Froebel called it "kindergarten": He wanted it to be full of the plants and flowers in which he was convinced children took great delight.

For Froebel and the early kindergarten teachers in Europe and America, almost anything was possible if children were nurtured in nature and presented with lofty ideals. "I see mankind about to start on a new course and enter another age," Froebel proclaimed ecstatically in 1828. Ten years later, writing about the objects he had devised for children's play (he termed them "gifts") in his new kindergarten, he wrote, "Each object is an America, a new world to explore."

"It's the whole kindergarten thing, Mom. I'm alone in there, swimming with the sharks."

Source: Drawing by Ziegler; © 1997, The New Yorker Magazine, Inc.

I may have been convinced that kindergarten had plunged from its early ideals, that it had become a much more functional place, but I could not find any "hard" studies on the issue. My evidence was only anecdotal. So I decided to ask Vivian Gussin Paley, perhaps the nation's most famous kindergarten teacher, if my impressions were hopelessly subjective.

"Your suspicions are correct," said the 67-year-old Paley, who this year retired after an illustrious career at the University of Chicago's Laboratory School during which she produced a number of notable books on teaching young children. "Look at the walls of almost any kindergarten in the country, and you'll find clues as to how 1st grade material has been brought down into the kindergarten. Word families on the board, for instance—can, man, ran. What is this if not the formal teaching of reading and writing? Wherever I go, and with little self-consciousness and absolutely no sense of guilt, teachers are doing this kind of thing. It's hardly even a subject for discussion."

Paley told me that when she first began teaching kindergarten at a public school four decades ago, children were expected to print their first names and learn "little A, big A" during the first week of 1st grade. In fact, 1st grade teachers were annoyed if their charges arrived already knowing these things: They were too young, the 1st grade teachers said. They would hold their pencils incorrectly; they would bring with them bad habits.

The kindergarten teachers were only too happy to leave well enough alone. Paley described them as "tigers defending the territory" against any perceived intrusion of elementary school ways. They were throwbacks to the early practitioners of the kindergarten movement who, according to Nina Vandewalker, a prominent educator writing in 1907, were "exponents of a new gospel." These idealists, Vandewalker wrote in *The Kindergarten in American Education*, saw "man as a creative being, and education as a process of self-explanation. They substituted activity for repression, and insisted upon the child's right to himself and to happiness during the educational process."

Paley, whose own writings about kindergarten above all celebrate storytelling and fantasy play, said that until the last few years the word "deficit" was never used in conjunction with kindergarten children. "The whole point of this first school year," Paley noted, "was to build on children's social and imaginative strengths, to give them a sense of confidence about what they could accomplish."

I told Paley about a conversation I'd had with a kindergarten teacher who'd asked: If the children are ready for the basic skills of reading, writing, and math, why not give it to them? "First of all," Paley responded, "many of the children are not ready. Most of this stuff plays to the top third in terms of their development of skills. There is also, particularly in boys, the unnecessary development of anxiety, a sense of not being able to handle school work. And we all know that if you start out uptight, it will be hard over the long haul to get on track."

Paley said basic skills in kindergarten often meant that teachers were trying to get children to spell "dog" by stuttering "d-d-d-d. . . ." "Think of what we could be discussing with children instead of this grunting," she said. "I wonder if these children think their teachers can't spell."

As discouraging as all of this sounded, Paley did offer an optimistic note: The subject she is most frequently asked to speak on is storytelling and play. The problem is that kindergarten teachers somehow think they can't focus on these things. "I tell them, 'Of course you can,'" Paley said, her exasperation coming across loud and clear over the phone. "No one is telling anyone that play can't be at the center of the curriculum. And you can't blame the parents. I have rarely met parents from any strata of society who do not want to be educated. They need to be told, 'First things first.' My feeling is that we in the educational establishment cannot explain properly what play is all about, what emerges out of dialogue and discourse. If we could explain ourselves properly, parents would say, 'Well, is it really true that the Bronte sisters did nothing but play, tell each other stories, and roam the moors, and yet became great English novelists?'"

At the beginning of each school year in the Hazelwood School District in suburban St. Louis, parents of kindergartners receive a seven-page booklet of minimum basic skills their children are expected to learn. They include 100 items, such as "identify eight basic colors," "use proper posture and paper position" when writing, "read and write numerals one to 10," and "state two public buildings within their community."

I paged through the booklet during an afternoon visit to the two kindergarten classes at the district's Barrington Elementary School, located in a vast subdivision of recently constructed houses. "We're the foundation to make sure the children know their basics," said Cheryl Meyer, the teacher in one of the classes and the district's 1993–94 Teacher of the Year. "We're mindful that the children are going to be going to 1st grade and that we need to do things that will mesh so that it will be a smooth transition."

I asked Meyer if students ever had to repeat kindergarten on account of their inability to master these basics. Only rarely, she said, thanks, in part, to careful screening and diagnostic testing. "We have a list of all the children which we go over: above average, average, need enrichment, remediation. If necessary, we'll refer them to the counselor."

As we talked, I was still looking through the lists of basic skills. I must have looked insufficiently impressed—actually I was incredulous—because Meyer noted, "We go well above and beyond that. You saw what we were doing today with sentences and punctuation."

Indeed, I had seen it, not only in Meyer's classroom but also when I was in school—in 2nd, 3rd, and 4th grades, and maybe even in high school. It seemed, in fact, as if I had been seeing such exercises forever.

The children were sitting at tables copying down a sentence that Meyer had written on the blackboard: "You can go down the street." As the kindergartners transcribed the sentence, the teacher fired off a series of questions: When we make our letters, do we start at the top or bottom? Left or right? What case do you need when you start a sentence?

At one juncture, when Meyer sensed flagging enthusiasm, she told the class she wanted to see more hands, and, sure enough, there were suddenly twice as many hands in the air. "Oh, I see lots of hands up, very good," she commented. Now the question-answer session became snappy, crisp.

"What kind of sentence is this?" she asked.

"Telling."

"What do you need between words?"

"A space."

"What would you need if this sentence had been asking a question?"

"A question mark."

Watching classes like these always reminds me of a remark by the late author and school critic John Holt: "A teacher in class is like a man in the woods at night with a powerful flashlight in his hand." Holt's point was that teachers, and classroom visitors, typically make the mistake of focusing only on those students called on to answer the questions. The problem with this is that you can only tell how a class is truly functioning by studying those lurking in the shadows—all of those students not under obvious scrutiny.

In this kindergarten class, those not volunteering responses—those out of the spotlight—were what most adults would call "well-behaved." Like little adults, they appeared remarkably serious, though their seriousness seemed somewhat tinged by apprehension. They stared straight ahead or downward,

clasping pencils, hoping, it seemed to me, for continued invisibility.

It must be said that most of the students' copied sentences were perfect or close to it: The tidy words were parked right between the lines. And when the teacher had the students convert the "telling" sentence into an "asking" sentence (Can you go down the street?), and then into an exclamatory sentence (You can go down the street!), they responded as if they had been working such exercises all their young lives.

There were a few exceptions, though. For instance, the girl sitting next to me kept writing her quivering letters backward, and they kept skewing above or below the lines. When Meyer stopped by to check her work, she offered a gentle suggestion or two, which didn't help much: Once Meyer left, the girl continued to write her letters backward. In an apparent attempt to reward the girl's effort, the teacher, when she returned again, drew a smiling face on the paper. But the girl did not return the smile, and, when she was alone once again, she resumed work on an elaborate, looping doodle centered like a coat of arms at the top of her paper. For the teacher, the doodle would most likely be superfluous, a distraction from the task at hand. But for the child, the so-called "telling" and "asking" sentences were apparently superfluous and the doodle an endeavor worth pursuing.

Meyer told me that the class had produced books during the course of the term, and she then turned to the children and asked, "What kind of books did we make?"

"My Missouri book," the children answered in unison.

"What is the name of our city?"

"St. Louis."

"What is the state tree?"

"The dogwood tree."

"What are the colors of the dogwood tree?"

"Pink and white."

It went on like this for a while. Then it was time for learning centers, during which children could play at an activity of their choice—Legos, trucks, housekeeping, etc. Even at their play, the children demonstrated remarkable self-control—it was extremely quiet for a kindergarten classroom—and I asked Meyer how she had established such a pronounced sense of order. "Well, it's not easy," she said. "You should have seen them at the beginning of the year. It takes a lot of time and an insistence that they obey classroom rules." She pointed to the three rules posted above the door: "1) Keep hands, feet, and objects to yourself. 2) No talking when anyone else is talking. 3) Follow my directions."

I also visited the kindergarten class next door, where Kyra Beckman, a young teacher who told me that she hoped eventually to become a principal, was reviewing with the students words she had printed on index cards: "five," "can," "six," "green," "she," "in," etc. Beckman was not particularly pleased with the children's performance and told them so. "You did better that time, but you still need to do better," she said. "However, a couple of you did well, and I have special stickers for you."

Later, a discussion ensued about what to do during a tornado, and the children practiced covering their heads with their hands. (It reminded me of the duck-and-cover drills of a different generation.) "Do you have any questions about tornadoes?" Beckman asked.

"I have a question, but not about tornadoes," a boy said.

"Then wait," the teacher said.

A few minutes later, the same boy began to launch into an anecdote about someone he knew who had seen a tornado, but the teacher cut him off. "That's a story, not a question," she said, "so you'll have to wait."

It seemed to me that this kindergarten class, like the previous one, was largely about waiting. Indeed, it was almost as if the critical yet unspecified lesson concerned the need to wait, to postpone pleasure. While the class was learning about tornadoes, they were waiting to play word bingo, and while they were playing word bingo—the words they covered were all from an assigned reading chart—they were waiting to go to the learning centers. And when this time finally came, it was dampened by an opening announcement: "I'm sorry to say that the kitchen will have to be closed today; there was too much fooling around there yesterday."

At the day's end, I asked Beckman how much of an authority figure a kindergarten teacher should be. "You've got to be on them at all times, or you lose control," she said. "Yet you've got to be there for them at all times, too. You're almost a motherly figure for them, and you have to listen to them tell stories about their lives. All day long, they want to tell you stories. But you have to draw a line. You have to say, this is the time we do our work, and this is the time we do our stories."

I told Beckman that there seemed to be an awful lot of material to cover in the Barrington kindergarten classes. "There is," she said. "It gets to the point where you're counting minutes—trying to fit in three more minutes of this or that."

There is no doubt that Meyer and Beckman are perfectly dutiful and professional teachers. In conducting classes that are models of efficiency, they are doing an excellent job of meeting the standards of their school and community. Barrington Elementary parents expect an intensive focus on the basics in an orderly environment, even at the earliest levels, and that is what these two teachers are providing. But community standards are not beyond reproach, and following them to the letter can extract a toll.

In an informal poll, I asked two dozen adults if they had liked kindergarten. All but a couple who claimed they could not remember it said yes—even those who described the rest of their schooling as a rather drab, dismal affair. Most talked about kindergarten as they might talk about a relaxing vacation in a sun-filled spot. Kindergarten was a "pleasant experience," "a happy time," "a place free of bells, announcements, and slamming lockers."

A 70-year-old man from Minnesota told me, "It was a transition year, getting used to school without having any of the pressure you usually have in school. I remember playing with my little friends and a lot of singing. I'd call kindergarten a very gentle introduction to school."

Adults as much as 35 years younger had much the same experience: Kindergarten was indeed school, yet it was very different from the rest of school. They remembered music and new friendships playing a central role. What they did not remember was academic learning; few remembered even being taken through the paces of the alphabet.

But this absence of formal academics does not mean that these kindergartens were places of unrestricted free play. To the contrary, the adults stated that there was in their kindergartens a time for everything: a time for rest, a time for song, a time to clean up. Their teachers believed in the breeding of good habits and consequently did their best to ensure that order prevailed over chaos, civility over indecorum.

Yet for all of their structure, these kindergartens were free of the tyranny of usefulness—the insistence, often unconscious, that even small children should be approached in terms of their future productivity, their ability to get a job done. Indeed, when people talk about what they liked best about kindergarten, they mention feeling at ease.

Why is it, then, that so many kindergartens have come to resemble 1st grade?

Some observers suggest that there is a tendency in what has always been a hierarchical system for the lower grades to imitate, over time, the practices of the higher. For instance, when the middle school movement began in earnest a couple of decades ago, the idea was to develop programs that were specifically tailored to the social, emotional, and academic needs of 12- and 13-year-olds. Eventually, though, the new middle schools, designed to be close-knit communities, came to resemble high schools in which students moved from class to class, having little contact with their teachers.

Likewise, kindergarten teachers adapt the approaches of primary school teachers. This occurs, at least in part, because of "self-esteem issues in early education," St. Louis kindergarten teacher Steve Zvolack told me. As Zvolack sees it, "A lot of teachers are worried about not being professional enough, and being professional, as a lot of people see it, means doing the kind of 'real' academic work elementary school teachers are doing."

But of all the factors that have worked toward changing the nature of kindergarten, perhaps nothing has had more of an impact than the inexorable movement to full-day classes. Twenty years ago, full-day kindergartens were scattered exceptions; now, full-day kindergarten is commonplace, with approximately 15 states providing funding (and many more planning to do so). Ten years from now, almost everyone agrees, virtually all kindergartens will be full day.

The trend is driven, to some degree, by the requirements of parents with full-time jobs; if their children cannot spend the entire day in kindergarten, parents must find an alternate source of child care. Furthermore, parents whose children have long been in day care and preschool often perceive a half day centered around play as a step backward. They want beginning reading and writing—not more play.

Suzie Nall, a professor of early childhood education at the University of Southern Illinois at Edwardsville and co-director of the national All-Day Kindergarten Network, told me that teachers moving into full day reported liking much about it: They know the families and children much better, and they no longer feel so rushed. But Nall also sounded a note of caution. "My concern is that we don't want full-day kindergarten becoming 1st grade," she said. "Teachers have a tendency to say, 'Well, I have a six-hour day now, and so I can fit in more.' We want to enhance the kindergarten program in a horizontal way, not in a vertical way."

By "horizontal," Nall means an expansion of an experientially based program, not the importation of an academic curriculum. Yet while she believes increasing numbers of parents understand the inappropriateness of pushing their 5-year-olds onto an academic track, she said the temptation to do so is strong nevertheless. "Some parents will go to the kindergarten teacher and say, 'I've been paying tuition for five years at the day-care center, at Montessori, and now it's your job to teach them to read. And the

papers—why aren't the papers coming home?' But if teachers have an active hands-on philosophy, then there are not a lot of papers going home."

At Mason Ridge Elementary School, in the affluent Parkway District of suburban St. Louis, I met, in a classroom replete with a fireplace, the school's two kindergarten teachers, Karen Gentry and Susan Wietzel, both 18-year veterans who had only recently begun to teach full day. Like Nall, they expressed concern about how teachers might be tempted to turn full-day kindergarten into a junior 1st grade. But they had another concern as well, namely that some of the children in full day—particularly those with professional parents who saw them only on evenings and weekends—were suffering from what sounded like battle fatigue.

"A lot of these children come to us having already had a lot of formal teaching in preschool, and so they're very bright," Gentry said. "But they have lots of behavioral problems. It's almost as if they've been in day care for so long that school has already gotten old for them, and they don't feel that it counts. The children who attend the latch-key program, for instance, you can almost point them out. They've learned not to listen, not to follow directions."

Wietzel, who taught full-day kindergarten for the first time in 1994 but is back to two half-day classes this year, added, "It's like they've had an adult in their faces for so long saying, 'Do this, do that.'"

"You tell them," Gentry interjected, "'We're going to paint now,' and they'll say, 'Well, I don't want to paint!'"

Wietzel said, "I have children who are home with their mothers for half a day, and, for them, their attitude about kindergarten is, 'This is so wonderful, so exciting!' vs. 'Here's this teacher going on and on.'"

These teachers were describing children who were already jaded; at 5 years old, these children were in the sort of rut associated with adults trapped in dead-end jobs. A deep cynicism about school was the likely result. I asked the teachers if their observations ever led them to think that kindergarten should be a place of its own, completely free from the stresses associated with traditional schooling.

"Kindergarten needs to be a special entity of its own, and yet it needs to count toward the future, too," Wietzel said. "So we do have a curriculum that prepares the children for 1st grade. Yet kindergarten is special, too, and needs leeway. If children don't like kindergarten, they'll have a long road ahead of them. So kindergarten is about stretching children's minds, but not about pushing them into the fast lane."

Both teachers said they emphasized effort, not results, and that they quickly backed off if they sensed frustration. "One of my students asked me, 'Is it OK to just try in high school like you do in kindergarten?'" Wietzel said. "Well, at some point, maybe not. But the nice thing about kindergarten is that just trying hard really is OK."

In passing, Wietzel had mentioned that raising children of her own had altered her kindergarten teaching, making her more flexible and open to improvisation. She had discovered that the relationship between parenting and teaching was far from casual. To do both well was less a matter of juggling roles than of being fully human. While this may seem like an obvious insight, it is frequently neglected. Author John Holt, reflecting on his own years of teaching, noted that many adults "hide themselves from children, pretending to be some idealized notion of 'Teacher.'" Realizing that this promoted aloofness if not downright phoniness, Holt asked teachers not to be afraid of revealing their real selves, as capricious as those selves may be. After all, Holt concluded, "Children looking into our eyes want to know if we're really there."

For the pioneers of the early kindergarten movement, being "there" meant that there had to be a radical redefinition of the stiflingly artificial relationship between teacher and student. It had to become more open, more natural. In the late 19th century, this meant that kindergarten teachers—all of whom were women—were to be more like "good" mothers than taskmasters. And as "good" mothers, they would bring the domestic sphere into the schoolhouse. Plants and pictures would enliven barren classrooms. Domestic pursuits—cooking, paper cutting, gardening—would take center stage. This, in effect, did happen. By the early 20th century, kindergarten was even influencing the activities of the primary grades, as elementary school teachers began to incorporate more of the manual, performing, and fine arts. By 1919, in Philadelphia alone, there were at least 20 kindergartens with outdoor gardens.

Nothing, though, was more important than for the teacher to get off her pedestal, so to speak, and take her place among the children. Shortly after the turn of the century, Nina Vandewalker wrote, "One must become a child with other children to succeed with them." Friedrich Froebel was even more straightforward. In an essay addressed to parents and teachers alike, he wrote, "Come let us live with our children."

The College School in St. Louis was the one place where I had a sense of Froebel's injunction as something fully lived. Here the two kindergarten teachers, Carol Filiatrault and Kathy Seibel, really did "live" with their children. In two adjoining rooms that felt more like working art studios than classrooms—a stained glass "window" made of a painted shower curtain was one of dozens of projects—the teachers worked alongside the students.

At the Barrington Elementary School, there were distinct times for work, play, and storytelling. At the College School, the elements blended together, the rhythms of one jostling the rhythms of the other. Children talked of vacations and family members while building their "dinosaur lands"; they fought dinosaur wars, which they interrupted for a snack; they roamed about collecting autographs, having just learned that signatures have value. At one point, the children asked to hear a song, and Filiatrault placed a record on a turntable. The children danced, moving in a circle as they held hands.

Later, one of the teachers described the children's activities as "social-dramatic play," a phrase with all the charm of a textbook heading. Yes, their play was socio-dramatic; it enhanced motor development, imagination, and a hundred other things. But play, which connects the child to the wider world, needs no adjective to justify it.

But I'm nit-picking about terms. Paley's behest to kindergarten teachers is simply, "Know your subject, play," and these two teachers at the College School obviously knew it. Their very relationships with the children were like the best kind of play: free, generous, and unrehearsed. They were unafraid to embrace a needy child or to call a child "sweetheart." They did not hesitate to share in the children's laughter. When these children looked at their teachers, they knew they were "really there."

Filiatrault told me that she had come to the College School from another private school where she had been teaching, as she put it, "1st grade in kindergarten." "Here," she said, "we don't concern ourselves with academic mastery. A lot of the things we do with the children are aesthetic because that's how children relate to the world."

The aesthetic emphasis was apparent in the displays of student work, which were, at all grade levels (including preschool), unlike anything I had seen at any other school. Everywhere—on table tops, walls, shelves—were sculptures, paintings, costumes, all created with extraordinary detail.

The detail of the displays, I learned, was due, in part, to the influence of an early childhood program run by the town of Reggio Emilia in Italy. The program was developed there in the early 1960s by an association of educators, parents, and community leaders. The title of a recent book about the Reggio Emilia approach, *The 100 Languages of Children*, is highly suggestive, the idea being that wire, paint, chalk, and so on are all "languages" in which children communicate.

Four years ago, Jan Phillips, director of the College School, visited a Reggio Emilia school in Italy and was stunned by the display of student work. "There were these breathtaking illustrations," Phillips said. "In fact, you couldn't help wondering if children really did this—it was too good. Yet there was a video demonstrating that children had, in fact, created it."

Phillips said she learned from her visit that children can do work of remarkable detail once they learn techniques for what she termed "coming back to the work." "My visit to Italy reaffirmed my belief that in teaching, the reflection upon an experience is as important as the experience itself," Phillips explained. "We constantly have the children think about what they'd like to add to their work or what they'd like to change about it."

Along a wall of the College School kindergarten is a mirror. Every month, the children study themselves in the mirror and then create a self-portrait. In a sense, every new self-portrait is a reflection on all the past portraits they have created. The first portrait is usually a stick figure with a circle for a head and arms emerging from, say, the cheeks. But over time, the portraits gather deepening form and structure, and the portraits become those of real children. It's a matter, the kindergarten teachers say, of letting children look in the mirror so they can see themselves through their own eyes.

■ Ask Yourself

Identifying Issues for Advocacy

1. How might an early childhood program undermine children's confidence in their own thinking (Jalongo, 1996; Katz, 1987)? How might assessment methods undermine young children's confidence in their own thinking (Committee on School Health and Committee on Early Childhood, Adoption, and Dependent Care, 1995)? How might assessment methods undermine teachers' confidence in their own observations and interpretations (Wein, 1997)? What would be alternatives to such programs or assessment methods (Fleer, 1996; French & Pena, 1997; Meisels, 1997; Segal, 1997)?

2. According to NAEYC (Bredekamp & Copple, 1997), what kinds of information should a professional consider when deciding what practices are developmentally appropriate? Should any other perspectives be considered? Why? Some educators, for example, believe that professionals should consider whether such practices contribute to development of the children's ownership of the learning process or help children become kind and caring participants in an inclusive and diverse world. Do you agree? Why or why not? Do you think the NAEYC's guidelines for developmentally appropriate practice are useful? Or are they too decontextualized and too open to diverse interpretations? Explain. (How might such guidelines be misused? What additional disclaimers, if any, should be made to guard against such misuses?)

3. The first of the six National Education Goals, endorsed in 1990 by the president of the United States and the governors from all 50 states, states that by the year 2000, all children in the United States will start school ready to learn. This call for action from our nation's political leaders sparked considerable debate in the

early childhood community about the appropriateness of this goal and the meaning of *ready to learn*. For example, at a 1998 research conference, psychology professor Craig Ramey declared, "Goal one is a silly statement. It's a political statement. Whoever wrote it didn't know anything about child development" (cited in Jacobson, 1998c, p. 12). Others have expressed concern about how this goal will be interpreted for linguistically and culturally diverse children, for children with disabilities, and for children living in poverty (Cooney, 1995; Farran & Shonkoff, 1994; Haynes, 1994; Prince & Lawrence, 1993). Does this goal imply, for instance, that all children should come to school knowing English? At the same time, some policy makers have attempted to move forward with the National Education Goals agenda and to focus attention at the federal and state levels on the healthy development of young children (Action Team on School Readiness, 1992; Boyer, 1993; Copple, 1997; Kagan, 1992; National Education Goals Panel, 1991; Resource Group on School Readiness, 1991). Do you think this is a worthwhile educational goal for our nation? Why or why not? What do you think *ready to learn* means? How should we assess children's readiness to learn?

4. Research on links between young children's brain development and early music experiences led Governor Zell Miller of Georgia to propose that his state distribute to every new mother a free classical music CD or cassette tape. Sony agreed to donate the CDs and tapes. In Florida, legislators proposed that state-funded child-care centers include daily doses of Beethoven in their curriculum. Neuroscientists, however, caution that some of the recommendations being made for educational practice have little, if any, scientific basis. What does brain research say about the effects of early musical listening or training (e.g., piano lessons) on children's nonmusical intellectual skills? Are babies who listen to classical music healthier or happier than babies who do not? (Does it matter whether infants hear Mozart or Metallica?) Is research evidence sufficient to recommend that music education programs for young children be improved and expanded? (See, for example, Bargreen, 1997; Campbell, 1998; Fuetsch, 1997; Jacobson, 1998a; Snyder, 1997; Viadero, 1998.) Other educators alluding to brain development research recommend the following early care and education practices to enhance intellectual skills:

- Drinking eight glasses of water every day
- Chewing peppermint gum
- Rubbing the skin between your toes
- Turning off the television
- Stringing beads and using clay and manipulatives that exercise small muscles
- By the age of 2, beginning to learn to work out conflicts peacefully with other children
- For children who can learn from flashcards, using round cards

- Eliminating use of worksheets until the child can draw a diamond

What, if any, evidence from brain development research supports these claims? Does other valid research support these recommendations? Is it far-fetched to base recommendations for educational and child-rearing practices on such evidence? Why or why not?

5. What does the word *curriculum* mean for toddler programs? Is the project approach developmentally appropriate for toddlers (Balaban & Cuffaro, 1992; Edwards & LeeKeenan, 1992; Lee-Keenan & Edwards, 1992)?

6. Gersten and White (1986) contend that equating child-initiated activities with active learning and teacher-directed activities with passive learning misrepresents various preschool curriculum models and preschoolers' actual experiences. They believe that early childhood education needs to move away from emotional phrases such as *high quality* and *whole child* and carefully examine what is happening in preschool settings. For example, is a quality learning experience one where a child moves to a sandbox, builds a sand castle, and then hears a teacher say that she or he did a nice job of castle building? Do you agree or disagree with these arguments? Explain. (Also see Schweinhart, 1997.)

7. Every day at Cross Roads Day-Care Center, the children gather at 9:15 for the calendar routine. For example, on the 24th of March, they counted the numbers on the calendar up to 24. Then they counted using the words *first, second, third,* and so on. Next, the preschoolers were asked what day it was, the weather outside, the name of the month, the name of the season, and the year. After this routine, the children moved into a circle for circle time and sang songs that they requested. Evaluate this routine in terms of the young child's early concept development (see Schwartz, 1994).

8. If children learn to read in kindergarten, will they be more likely to experience success in elementary school? What is an appropriate context for the literacy development of young children (International Reading Association and the National Association for the Education of Young Children, 1998; Snow, Burns, & Griffin, 1998; Whitehurst & Lonigan, 1998)?

9. Is the use of a computer by preschool children a significant educational experience in an early childhood program? Why or why not? (See Bredekamp & Copple [1997] as well as Elkind [1996] and Healy [1998].) Organize a debate on this issue with other classmates. (See Appendix 8 for debate guidelines.)

10. Why are worksheets inappropriate instructional materials for young children (see Ford, 1991; Kamii, 1985)?

11. *Looping* involves a teacher moving with his or her students to the next grade level at the end of a school year. What social and academic benefits can looping offer students (Burke, 1997)?

12. Some parents, believing that their children need extra time to mature socially or wanting to give them a competitive edge (either academic or athletic), seek to delay entry into kindergarten for a year. Some teachers recommend that students who are struggling in kindergarten or in a primary grade be held back a year or attend a transitional class. According to research evidence, what are the short-term and long-term effects or benefits of these practices (Byrd, Weitzman, & Auinger, 1997; Robertson, 1997; Shepard, 1997; Wang & Johnstone, 1997; Zill, Collins, West, & Hausken, 1995; Zill, Loomis, & West, 1997)? How do you account for the benefits of other instructional practices (e.g., Clay, 1993; Snow, Burns, & Griffin, 1998; Whitehurst & Lonigan, 1998) for students identified as being at risk or having difficulty?

Advocacy and Leadership Strategies

1. Imagine that Cindy, the young mother in the vignette at the beginning of this chapter, comes to you with concerns about the kit and wants advice about responding to Grandma Kramer. In a small group with your classmates, prepare strategies and arguments to convince Grandma Kramer that this kit is an inappropriate activity. Consider what young children can do and what young children should do. (Incorporate ideas from your readings and from Bredekamp & Copple, 1997.)

2. Visit a kindergarten or nursery-school classroom. Observe how much time is devoted to play or child-initiated activities. When are reading or literacy activities introduced? What types of literacy activities, if any, are occurring in the program? What types of science or math activities do you observe? What provisions are made for music learning? What types of teacher-led activities occur in the program? If computers are present, how are they used? (See Framework for an On-Site Study of an Early Childhood Program in Chapter 1.)

3. Lead a discussion group with a community group about developmentally appropriate practices or submit a column on developmentally appropriate practices to a local newspaper. (See Appendix 4: Working with the Media.)

4. Examine the NCTM math standards for grades K–4. Then read critics' viewpoints about the standards (e.g., Coombs, 1997; Hirsch, 1996; Quirk, 1997). Compare and contrast their arguments with what early educators identify as developmentally appropriate and educationally worthwhile practices (Bredekamp & Copple, 1997; Heckman & Weissglass, 1994; Jacobson, 1998b; Katz, 1987; Schwartz, 1994; Seefeldt, 1995; Viadero, 1996). Share your review with the class.

5. For a community organization or group that includes parents,

prepare a presentation on the following: What does brain development research say about raising smarter children?

6. Parents frequently ask what they can do at home to help their child get ready for kindergarten. The second objective of Goal 1 of Goals 2000 is: "Every parent in the United States will be a child's first teacher and devote time each day to helping such parent's preschool child learn, and parents will have access to the training and support parents need" (Shore, 1998, p. 1). As a class, design, organize, and present a program for parents and children that demonstrates developmentally appropriate activities that parents and preschool children can do together. These activities need to be low cost, age appropriate, interesting to preschool children, tied to firsthand experiences, and based on child development research (Seefeldt, 1995). Also have handouts with suggestions for more activities (e.g., Paulu, 1993; ReadyWeb, 1998). Target your audience, advertise your program, and make requests for funding from local organizations. After presenting your program, write a follow-up report, identifying successful strategies and suggestions for improvements.

7. What practices do teachers use to help young children make transitions from one care and/or educational setting to another? How do parents and teachers help the child make the transition from home to his or her first child-care or school setting? At the child-care center, how do both the infant and toddler caregivers help the children as they make the transition to the toddler room? From the toddler to the preschool room? What about the child entering kindergarten? What do the preschool and kindergarten teachers do to ease this transition? What strategies are used to help the child move easily from kindergarten to first grade? Each member of the class might interview an early childhood professional working at one of these levels and inquire about his or her transitioning strategies. Also look at research on transitioning practices (e.g., California Department of Education, 1997; Pianta, 1998). Make a comprehensive list describing best practices and ideas for easing children through transitions at each age level, and distribute it to early childhood professionals or submit it to an early childhood publication.

References and Suggested Readings

Action Team on School Readiness. (1992). *Every child ready for school*. Washington, DC: National Governors' Association Publications. (ERIC Document Reproduction Service No. ED 351 125)

Balaban, N., & Cuffaro, H. K. (1992). From our readers: Toddler projects? *Young Children, 48* (1), 3, 54.

Bargreen, M. (1997, August 31). Kids succeed more easily with a boost from music. *Seattle Times* [Online], 4 pages. Available: www.archives.seattletimes.com/web/index.html

Boyer, E. L. (1993). Ready to learn: A mandate for the nation. *Young Children, 48* (3), 54–57.

Bredekamp, S., & Copple, C. (Eds.). (1997). *Developmentally appropriate practice in early childhood programs* (rev. ed.). Washington, DC: National Association for the Education of Young Children.

Burke, D. L. (1997). *Looping: Adding time, strengthening relationships.* Champaign, IL: ERIC Clearinghouse on Elementary and Early Childhood Education. (ERIC Document Reproduction Service No. ED 414 098)

Byrd, R. S., Weitzman, M., & Auinger, P. (1997). Increased behavior problems associated with delayed school entry and delayed school progress. *Pediatrics, 100,* 654–661.

California Department of Education. (1997). *Continuity for young children: Positive transitions to elementary school.* Sacramento, CA: Author. (ERIC Document Reproduction Service No. ED 405 978)

Campbell, P. S. (1998). *Songs in their heads: Music and its meaning in children's lives.* New York: Oxford University Press.

Charlesworth, R. (1998). Response to Sally Lubeck's "Is developmentally appropriate practice for everyone?" *Childhood Education, 74,* 293–298.

Clay, M. (1993). *Reading recovery: A guidebook for teachers in training.* Portsmouth, NH: Heinemann.

Committee on School Health and Committee on Early Childhood, Adoption, and Dependent Care. (1995). The inappropriate use of school "readiness" tests. *Pediatrics, 95,* 437–438.

Coombs, M. (1997, June 17). New new math misses mark. *The Washington Times* [Online], 2 pages. Available: www.intres.com/math/coombs.htm

Cooney, M. H. (1995). Issues in education: Readiness for school or for school culture? *Childhood Education, 71,* 164–166.

Copple, C. (Ed.). (1997). *Getting a good start in school.* Washington, DC: National Education Goals Panel. (ERIC Document Reproduction Service No. ED 412 025)

Edwards, C., & LeeKeenan, D. (1992). From our readers: The authors respond. *Young Children, 48* (1), 54.

Elkind, D. (1996). Young children and technology: A cautionary note. *Young Children, 51* (6), 22–23.

Farran, D. C., & Shonkoff, J. P. (1994). Developmental disabilities and the concept of school readiness. *Early Education and Development, 5,* 141–151.

Fleer, M. (1996). Theories of "play": Are they ethnocentric or inclusive? *Australian Journal of Early Childhood, 21* (4), 12–17.

Ford, M. P. (1991). Worksheets anonymous: On the road to recovery. *Language Arts, 68,* 563–566.

French, J., & Pena, S. (1997). *Principals' ability to implement "best practices" in early childhood.* Paper presented at the annual meeting of the National Rural Education Association, Tucson, AZ. (ERIC Document Reproduction Service No. ED 413 149)

Fuetsch, M. (1997, September 6). Class feeds kids' budding musical appetites. *The Seattle Times* [Online], 2 pages. Available: www.archives.seattletimes.com/web/index.html

Gersten, R., & White, W. A. T. (1986, November). Castles in the sand: Response to Schweinhart and Weikart. *Educational Leadership,* 19–20.

Haynes, N. M. (1994). *School readiness and the non-mainstream urban child: An ecological approach.* New Haven, CT: Yale University. (ERIC Document Reproduction Service No. ED 379 383)

Healy, J. M. (1998). *Failure to connect: How computers affect our children's minds—For better and worse.* New York: Simon & Schuster.

Heckman, P. E., Confer, C. B., & Hakim, D. C. (1994). Planting seeds: Understanding through investigation. *Educational Leadership, 51* (5), 36–39.

Heckman, P. E., & Weissglass, J. (1994). Contextualized mathematics instruction: Moving beyond recent proposals. *For the Learning of Mathematics, 14* (1), 29–33.

Hirsch, E. D. (1996). *The schools we need & why we don't have them.* New York: Doubleday.

International Reading Association (IRA) and the National Association for the Education of Young Children (NAEYC). (1998). Learning to read and write: Developmentally appropriate practices for young children. *Young Children, 53* (4), 30–46.

Jacobson, L. (1998a, April 8). Education policymakers embrace brain findings. *Education Week, 17* (30), pp. 1, 20.

Jacobson, L. (1998b, March 11). Experts promote math, science for preschoolers. *Education Week, 17* (26), pp. 1, 12–13.

Jacobson, L. (1998c, March 4). Experts tackle transition to kindergarten. *Education Week, 17* (25), p. 12.

Jalongo, M. R. (1996). Why cute is still a four-letter word. *Early Childhood Education Journal, 24,* 67–70.

Kagan, S. L. (1992). Readiness past, present, and future: Shaping the agenda. *Young Children, 48* (1), 48–53.

Kamii, C. (1985, September). Leading primary education toward excellence: Beyond worksheets and drill. *Young Children, 40,* 3–9.

Katz, L. G. (1987, October). Lilian Katz: Let's not underestimate young children's intellects. *Instructor,* 16–19.

Kontos, S., & Wilcox-Herzog, A. (1997). Teachers' interactions with children: Why are they so important? *Young Children, 52* (2), 4–12.

LeeKeenan, D., & Edwards, C. P. (1992). Using the Project Approach with toddlers. *Young Children, 47* (4), 31–35.

Lubeck, S. (1998). Is DAP for everyone? A response. *Childhood Education, 74,* 299–301.

Martin, S. (1996). *Developmentally appropriate evaluation: Convincing students and teachers of the importance of observation as appropriate evaluation of children.* Paper presented at the annual meeting of the Association for Childhood Education International, Minneapolis, MN.

Meisels, S. J. (1997). Using work sampling in authentic assessments. *Educational Leadership, 54* (4), 60–65.

National Association of School Psychologists (NASP). (1998). NASP position statement: Student grade retention and social promotion. [Online]. Available: www.naspweb.org/center/contents/content.htm

National Education Goals Panel (NEGP). (1991). 1991 options for reporting on readiness for school. In *Measuring progress toward the National Education Goals: A guide to selecting indicators* (pp. 2–6). Washington, DC: Author. (ERIC Document Reproduction Service No. ED 334 278)

Paulu, N. (1993). Helping your child get ready for school. [Online]. Available: www.ed.gov/pubs/parents/GetReadyForSchool/index.html

Pianta, R. C. (1998, April). *Kindergarten transition practices.* Paper presented at the meeting of the American Education Research Association, San Diego, CA.

Prince, C. D., & Lawrence, L. A. (1993). School readiness and language minority students: Implications of the first National Education Goal. *NCBE FOCUS: Occasional Paper in Bilingual Education, 7.* Available: www.ncbe.gwu.edu/ncbepubs/focus/focus7.html

Quirk, W. G. (1997). The truth about the NCTM standards. [Online]. Available: www.wgquirk.com/TruthK12.html

ReadyWeb. (1998). Virtual library. [Online]. Available: www.ericps.ed.uiuc.edu/readyweb/library.html

Resource Group on School Readiness. (1991). Readiness for school: An interim report. In National Education Goals Panel (Ed.), *Measuring progress toward the*

National Education Goals: Potential indicators and measurement strategies (pp. 1–15). Washington, DC: National Education Goals Panel.

Robertson, A. S. (1997). *When retention is recommended, what should parents do?* Champaign, IL: ERIC Clearinghouse on Elementary and Early Childhood Education. (ERIC Document Reproduction Service No. ED 408 102)

Schwartz, S. L. (1994). Calendar reading: A tradition that begs remodeling. *Teaching Children Mathematics, 1* (2), 104–109.

Schweinhart, L. J. (1997). *Child-initiated learning activities for young children in poverty.* Champaign, IL: ERIC Clearinghouse on Elementary and Early Childhood Education. (ERIC Document Reproduction Service No. ED 413 105)

Seefeldt, C. (1995). Ready to learn! But what? *Contemporary Education, 66,* 134–138.

Segal, G. (1997, March). *A sociocultural model of learning and teaching in early childhood science education.* Paper presented at the annual meeting of the National Association for Research in Science Teaching, Oakbrook, IL. (ERIC Document Reproduction Service No. ED 406 150)

Shepard, L. (1997). Children not ready to learn? The invalidity of school readiness testing. *Psychology in the Schools, 34,* 85–97.

Shepard, L., Kagan, S. L., & Wurtz, E. (1998). *Principles and recommendations for early childhood assessments* (A report of the Goal 1 Early Childhood Assessments Resource Group). Washington, DC: National Education Goals Panel.

Shore, R. (1998). *Ready schools: A report of the Goal 1 Ready Schools Resource Group.* Washington, DC: National Education Goals Panel.

Silin, J. G. (1985, March). Authority as knowledge: A problem of professionalization. *Young Children, 40,* 41–46.

Snow, C. E., Burns, M. S., & Griffin, P. (Eds.). (1998). *Preventing reading difficulties in young children.* Washington, DC: National Research Council, National Academy Press.

Snyder, S. (1997). Developing musical intelligence: Why and how. *Early Childhood Education Journal, 24,* 165–171.

Sprung, B., Froschl, M., & Colon, L. (1996). *Playtime is science: An equity-based parent/child science program; An equity-based parent involvement program for early science education* (rev. ed). New York: Educational Equity Concepts.

Viadero, D. (1996, October 22). It all adds up. [Online]. Available: www.red. www.nsf.gov/ABOUT/articles/itaddsup.html

Viadero, D. (1998, April 8). Music on the mind. *Education Week, 17* (30), pp. 25–27.

Wang, Y. L., & Johnstone, W. (1997). *Evaluation of pre-first grade.* Paper presented at the annual meeting of the American Educational Research Association, Chicago. (ERIC Document Reproduction Service No. ED 409 348)

Wein, C. A. (1997). The impact of requirements for documentation on teacher practice in child care settings. *The Canadian Journal of Research in Early Childhood Education, 6* (1), 31–43.

Whitehurst, G. J., & Lonigan, C. L. (1998). Child development and emergent literacy. *Child Development, 69,* 848–872.

Zachlod, M. G. (1996). Room to grow. *Educational Leadership, 54* (1), 50–53.

Zill, N., Collins, M., West, J., & Hausken, E. G. (1995). Approaching kindergarten: A look at preschoolers in the United States. *Young Children, 51* (1), 35–38.

Zill, N., Loomis, L. S., & West, J. (1997). *The elementary school performance and adjustment of children who enter kindergarten late or repeat kindergarten: Findings from national surveys* (National Household Educational Survey; Statistical Analysis Report). Rockville, MD: Westat, Inc.

■ *Chapter 9*

■ Quality in Child Care
■ and Early Education

Pie Slicing?

"Thank you so much for taking time out of your busy schedule to see me, Assemblyman Toplure. I'll get right to the point. I'm here to discuss the need for an increase in state subsidy rates for child care. It is essential that you lift the freeze on these subsidy rates so that child-care providers are paid the current market rate for each eligible child in their program. The reimbursement rates in our state are so low that many child-care providers are unable to serve low-income children, and other providers are forced to limit the number of low-income children they can accept. We cannot expect poor families to stay in the workforce if they do not have access to stable, affordable child-care services. By increasing the reimbursement rates to child-care providers, without increasing the copayment for low-income parents, we can help assure that more of the poor children in our state are in quality, licensed child care while their parents are at work. If the subsidy rate is not increased, we will find more and more children in substandard care, which can threaten their health and safety and hinder their development."

"Well now, Mrs. Knight, I do understand that welfare reform has caused a surge in the demand for child care. And I think I can safely speak for the rest of my colleagues, Democrat and Republican. The problem with welfare payments and job training programs is that we only have so much funding available for child care. If we increase reimbursement rates to providers, then we cannot provide subsidies to all families currently eligible for child-care assistance in our state. If we put a freeze on reimbursement rates to providers, which is what we voted to do, then we can provide at least some child-care assistance to all families with incomes below 165 percent of the poverty level. And, if I remember correctly, the state subsidy is 75 percent of the market rate, but don't forget that families can

use this subsidy to pay neighbors, relatives, or friends to babysit. . . .
Oh, oh! The buzzer is sounding for a roll call vote. Sorry, I must go
now. But I do thank you for stopping in. It's always nice to meet one
of my constituents."

Questions

1. Suppose you had engaged in this exchange with a legislator in
   your state. What would be your next step?

2. What is the subsidy rate and market rate for child care in your
   state? Are the child-care needs of low-income families being
   met? Is there a waiting list for child-care subsidies in your state?
   Is your state using Temporary Assistance for Needy Families
   (TANF) funds to expand and support child-care services?

3. How can child care be made a priority for public spending?

■ Preview

The demand for child care, especially infant and after-school care,
continues to expand in the United States. With recent developments
in brain research, defining and providing quality child care is of
increasing concern. The first reading in this chapter, written by the
National Center for Early Development and Learning, outlines the
factors that define quality in child care. Next, Linda Jacobson looks
at the current status of child care in the United States. Valerie
Polakow then addresses the issues of affordability and accessibility of
quality care for all families and offers a description of a nationally
subsidized, high-quality child-care system. Finally, Joy Shioshita
explains the Worthy Wage Campaign and how inadequate wages for
child-care teachers undermine the quality of care that children
receive. These readings invite you to conduct a more in-depth study
of the many factors impacting the issue of quality care for all
children and help you to define your role as an advocate for young
children.

Quality in Child Care Centers

National Center for
Early Development and Learning

■ ■ ■

Millions of young children in the United States are cared for by someone other than their parents. Much of this care is provided by extended family members, friends, or neighbors. An increasingly large number of children, however, are cared for in child care centers. The need for affordable child care will increase under the new welfare provisions of Temporary Assistance for Needy Families (TANF), as access to child care becomes a critical ingredient of welfare recipients' employability.

What Are the Issues?

Quality child care is important for the well-being of young children. Higher quality ought to result in better outcomes for children. But what is quality and how can it be measured? How good is the quality of child care programs in the United States today? Most importantly, what do we know about the relationship between quality of child care and outcomes for children?

Quality in Child Care Centers

Quality can mean different things to different people. Some focus on structural features such as group size, child-staff ratios, physical space, teacher qualifications, staff training, wages, and safety. Others focus on how caregivers interact with children and the actual experiences children have. Useful measures have been developed so that the many dimensions of quality can now be assessed with accuracy and confidence.

Despite the availability of good measures, little nationally representative data are available. Thus researchers and policy makers must rely on knowledge from studies conducted in particular areas of the country or with particular types of centers. An analysis of these studies indicates that typical quality is considerably below what is considered good practice. The *Cost, Quality, and Child Outcomes Study* (CQO Team, 1995) reported that, of the more than 400 centers studied in four states, only 8% of infant classrooms and 24% of preschool classrooms were of good or excellent quality. In 10% of preschool programs and 40% of infant programs the quality was rated as poor. As displayed in the graph on page 196, less than adequate quality has been reported in a number of studies, and a synthesis of this research (Love, Schochet, & Meckstroth, 1996) suggests that the findings are so consistent as to raise broad concern about the quality of care in early childhood settings nationwide.

Three additional facts confirm that quality of care is less than what most parents would want for their children:

- The education credentials of staff who work in child care centers are often inadequate relative to the skills required. The CQO Study found that only 36% of teachers had a bachelor's degree or higher. The *NICHD Early Child Care Research Network* (1996) found that only a third of infant child care providers had any specialized training in child development and only 18% had a bachelor's degree or higher.
- Staff turnover is high, ranging from 25% to 50% per year. This means that children are constantly adapting to new caregivers and administrators are perpetually orienting and training new staff (Whitebook, Howes, & Phillips, 1990; CQO Team, 1995).
- Staff compensation, including wages and benefits, is exceptionally low. Child care staff are

National Center for Early Development and Learning. (1997, Summer). Quality in child care centers. *Early Childhood Research and Policy Briefs, 1* (1), 1–4. Reprinted here with permission from the National Center for Early Development and Learning.

among the lowest paid of all classes of workers in the U.S. Staff compensation is significantly related to the quality of care provided (Whitebook et al., 1990; CQO Team, 1995).

The Effects of Quality on Children

Over the past 15 years a number of studies have examined the effects of varying levels of quality on children's behavior and development. Each reached the same conclusion: *a significant correlation exists between program quality and outcomes for children* (Frede, 1995). Outcomes related to quality include cooperative play, sociability, language and cognitive development, creativity, ability to solve social conflicts, and self control. For example, findings from a recent NICHD study of early child care indicate that the quality of provider-child interaction is related to better cognitive and language scores for children and to more positive mother-child interactions across the first three years of life (NICHD Network, 1997).

What characteristics of child care are especially important? Features such as the number of children per adult and caregiver/teacher qualifications are important for setting the stage for better quality (Whitebook et al., 1990; NICHD Network, 1996). Alone, these features do not create quality. They provide the context, however, in which quality is more likely to occur. As research has become more sophisticated, it has also become more clear that features such as responsiveness of the caregiver, individualization of care, language used in the classroom, and the appropriateness of learning activities, are the key dimensions of quality that affect outcomes for children.

Some have argued that poor quality is of concern only for children living in poverty. Research suggests, however, that quality is important for all children, regardless of family income level (CQO Team, 1995; Love et al., 1996; NICHD Network, 1997).

Program Quality for Young Children across Multiple Studies

These 6 studies each rated the quality of a sample of programs for young children using either the *Early Childhood Environment Rating Scale* or the *Infant-Toddler Environment Rating Scale*. Each scale contains a set of items rated on a 1–7 scale, with ratings reflecting inadequate (1), minimal (3), good (5), or excellent (7) quality. The values on the chart represent the mean item rating for the centers observed. A rating of 5 is considered the minimum rating for reasonable quality. The figure shows that all studies reported average quality ratings below 5, and that infant programs were always rated lower in quality than preschool programs.

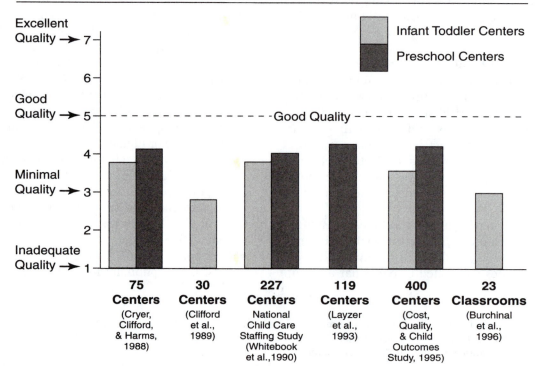

Program Quality for Young Children across Multiple Studies

What Do We Need to Learn?

Much research has documented quality in child care programs and the relationship between quality and outcomes. However, additional work is needed to inform both policy and practice. We recommend the following:

- *A periodic, nationally representative, study of child care practices and quality* would provide an important basis for understanding the current state of affairs and for evaluating the effects of changes in state and federal policies. States could implement their own systems for tracking quality, but a national study would provide better data and allow for comparisons. This study should involve on-site observations rather than relying solely on questionnaires.

- Most research has looked at the relationship between quality and outcomes. We need more *specific studies that identify unacceptable levels of quality below which children's development may be compromised,* as well as thresholds of quality that must be exceeded before programs can expect to have a meaningful impact.

- Although much is known about quality, *more research is needed to identify particular practices* that are especially important in promoting development. Such work should be experimental (in which different conditions are compared) rather than simply correlational (studies in which factors appear to be related to each other). We need to know the extent to which these practices are used, identify barriers to their use, and develop models and procedures for supporting improvement in caregiving.

- *Studies are needed in which children's development and behavior are tracked longitudinally.* We need to know how factors such as the home environment, family income, parenting style, family values, and parental choices about child care interact with program quality to affect outcomes for children.

What Policy Changes Are Needed?

Although more research is needed, *there is now little doubt that the quality of child care needs improving.* For this to occur, we urge legislators, agencies, and organizations to consider the following:

- *Strengthen standards and regulations for child care programs.* The CQO study found a relationship between state standards, the quality observed in centers, and outcomes for children. A recent study found that centers achieving accreditation by the National Association for the Education of Young Children were of higher quality than those that tried but did not achieve accreditation (Whitebook, Sakai, & Howes, 1997). Well-accepted professional standards exist for child-staff ratios, group size, and other structural variables, and states should require programs to adhere to these standards. States also need to set standards for quality caregiving, monitor the extent to which quality caregiving exists, and provide incentives as well as consequences for meeting these standards.

- *Require initial and ongoing training for staff working in child care programs.* Staff training and support are essential to quality caregiving. The profession must find ways to provide this training that are not expensive and allow caregivers to continue their work.

- *Find ways to recruit and retain more highly educated and skilled staff.* This translates to supporting higher wages, benefits, and improved working conditions.

- *Inform parents about the importance of quality child care and its effects on children.* Child care consumers need to be aware of the quality that is available in specific programs so that they can make informed choices. This calls for the development of guides for parents and other means of conveying this information on a regular basis, a role that could be assumed by resource and referral agencies.

- *Identify ways to support the costs of higher quality child care.* Improving the quality of child care in most instances will require more money. States, advocacy groups, providers, and consumers need to come together to develop a package of incentives and supports that makes high quality attractive to providers and consumers alike while creating conditions under which quality is affordable.

REFERENCES

Burchinal, M. R., Roberts, J. E., Nabors, L. A., & Bryant, D. M. (1996). Quality of center child care and infant cognitive and language development. *Child Development, 67,* 606–620.

Clifford, R. M., Russell, S., Fleming, J., Peisner, E., Harms, T., & Cryer, D. (1989). *Infant/toddler environment rating scale reliability and validity study: Final report.* Chapel Hill, NC: University of North Carolina at Chapel Hill, Frank Porter Graham Child Development Center.

Cost, Quality, and Child Outcomes Study Team. (1995). *Cost, quality, and child outcomes in child care centers: Public report.* Denver: Economics Department, University of Colorado-Denver.

Cryer, D., Clifford, R. M., & Harms, T. (1988). *Day care compliance and evaluation project: Final report.* Chapel Hill, NC: University of North Carolina at Chapel Hill, Frank Porter Graham Child Development Center.

Frede, E. (1995). The role of program quality in producing early childhood program benefits. *Future of Children, 5*(3), 115–132.

Layzer, J. I., Goodson, B. D., & Moss, M. (1993). *Life in preschool: Observational study of early childhood programs, final report, Volume 1.* Cambridge, MA: ABT Associates, Development Assistance Corporation, and RMC Research Corporation.

Love, J. M., Schochet, P. Z., & Meckstroth, A. (1996). *Are they in any real danger? What research does—and doesn't—tell us about child care quality and children's well-being.* Child Care Research and Policy Papers: Lessons from Child Care Research Funded by the Rockefeller Foundation. Princeton, NJ: Mathematica Policy Research, Inc.

NICHD Early Child Care Research Network. (1996). Characteristics of infant child care: Factors contributing to positive caregiving. *Early Childhood Research Quarterly, 11,* 269–306.

NICHD Early Child Care Research Network. (1997). *Mother-child interaction and cognitive outcomes associated with early child care: Results of the NICHD study.* Poster symposium presented at the Biennial Meeting of the Society for Research in Child Development, Washington, DC.

Whitebook, M., Howes, C., & Phillips, D. (1990). *Who cares? Child care teachers and the quality of care in America: Final report, National Child Care Staffing Study.* Oakland, CA: Child Care Employee Project.

Whitebook, M., Sakai, L., & Howes, C. (1997). *NAEYC accreditation as a strategy for improving child care quality.* Washington, DC: National Center for the Early Childhood Work Force.

Early Childhood Research and Policy Briefs is produced by the National Center for Early Development & Learning, Frank Porter Graham Child Development Center, University of North Carolina at Chapel Hill, under the Educational Research and Development Centers Program, Pit/Award # R307A60004, as administered by the Office of Educational Research and Improvement, US Department of Education. However, the contents do not necessarily represent the position of the National Institute on Early Childhood Development and Education, the Office of Educational Research and Improvement, or the US Department of Education, and you should not assume endorsement by the federal government. John M. Love, of Mathematica Policy Research, Inc., is primary author of this brief. Production of *Early Childhood Research and Policy Briefs* is a joint effort of faculty and consultants of the National Center for Early Development & Learning.

Yale Study Faults Child Care in All 50 States

Linda Jacobson

■ ■ ■

Child-care centers in all 50 states are operating under regulations that don't require high-quality care for infants and toddlers, according to a report on the status of state licensing guidelines.

Only 17 states have standards that the researchers described as "minimally acceptable." Four states—Idaho, Mississippi, South Carolina, and Wyoming—were found to have very poor or no regulations at all, and the rest were rated as poor.

The researchers, from Yale University and the Commonwealth Fund, a private foundation in New York City, based their evaluation on three categories: caregiver qualifications and training; grouping, meaning staff-to-child ratio and group size; and program, including the facilities, equipment, and approach toward children.

The report, published in the October edition of the *Journal of Orthopsychiatry*, serves to heighten the attention focused on early childhood education—especially during the first three years of life.

Research and Ratings

"Our new knowledge of rapid brain development in the early years underscores the importance of having enriching environments for our infants and toddlers," said Edward Zigler, a psychology professor at Yale and one of the founders of the federal Head Start preschool program for low-income children.

The report's release also came in the same week that President Clinton held a White House conference on child care, where he announced a proposed $300 million initiative to provide scholarships to 50,000 providers and give them financial incentives to stay in the child-care field. ("President Clinton Unveils Proposals to Upgrade Child Care," Oct. 29, 1997.)

The report confirms what previous studies have suggested: Child-care for children in their earliest years is often the worst.

The standards in only one state—Minnesota—were minimally acceptable or better in all three categories, according to the researchers' tabulations.

The researchers also noted that even when states earned good or acceptable ratings for child-care programs, they had poor or very poor ratings in the other two areas.

Comparing current state regulations with those on the books in 1982, the researchers also found that some states were relaxing training requirements for caregivers.

A No-Win Situation

When state officials do attempt to tighten guidelines, they often run up against tremendous opposition.

"It's a no-win situation. You can't please everyone," said Linda McCart, the director of Ohio's Family and Children First Initiative, a statewide effort to improve programs for young children and educate parents about infant development. "There are a whole group of folks that believe that as long as the teacher loves children, it doesn't matter what her qualifications are."

A crucial issue is who would pay for the kinds of improvements the experts espouse.

States fight an ongoing battle to balance "what's good for kids with what's good for business," said Sally Vogler, a policy director in Colorado Gov. Roy Romer's office who heads the state's First Impressions program, an early-childhood initiative.

Ultimately, Ms. Vogler said, the public will have to pay for early education the way it pays for public

Linda Jacobson. (1997, November 5). Yale study faults child care in all 50 states. Reprinted with permission from *Education Week*, Vol. 17, No. 10, Date 11/97, p. 7.

education. "But I think we're a decade away from that discussion," she said.

Despite the report's findings, numerous child-care centers throughout the country go above and beyond their states' minimum requirements, and many improve their programs to earn accreditation from the Washington-based National Association for the Education of Young Children.

A few states, including Florida, North Carolina, and soon Georgia, also offer their own stamps of approval, if centers meet additional standards.

"Our goal is making sure every child, no matter where they live, has access to quality," said Barbara Willer, the spokeswoman for the NAEYC.

The Yale study did not attempt to investigate how thoroughly states enforce the regulations they have. The researchers also did not consider caregiver pay and staff turnover, which also have been found to hurt quality.

Who Cares for the Children?

Denmark's Unique Public Child-Care Model

Valerie Polakow

■ ■ ■

The public authorities have an overall responsibility to create sound social frameworks and the best possible conditions for families with children. Furthermore, the public sector shall protect children and young persons against injustice and lack of care and, through guidelines and supportive measures, make it possible for parents to assume [their] responsibility as parents.[1]

Who cares for the children is a politically charged question in the United States in 1997—a question that confronts all working parents and particularly single mothers working in low-wage employment. The chronic lack of affordable, licensed, high-quality child care has a long tradition in this society, rooted in ideologies about motherhood, the family, and the role of government. However, it is instructive to consider an alternative tradition—one in which government and parents share responsibility for child care and public funding for the care of young children receives widespread support among citizens of all socioeconomic classes. In Denmark it is laid down by law that day-care facilities must be available to all children, and the government has assumed the cost of subsidizing a high-quality, comprehensive child-care system for infants and children from 6 months to 7 years of age, as well as an extensive after-school child-care system for school-age children.

During 1995–96 I lived in Denmark and spent many fascinating months researching Danish family and child-care policies, conducting interviews and observations from the top down and from the bottom up in order to develop an "in vivo" understanding of the strong public policies that support families and children. In this article I present a portrait of Denmark's unique national model of public child care.

Child Care and Universal Entitlements

In order for readers to understand the current success and popularity of the Danish child-care system, it is necessary to place the widespread support for child care within the context of the social democratic infrastructure of the Danish welfare state. Denmark has a long tradition of public family support policies and egalitarian values resulting in social policies that aim at uniting rather than dividing the population. Universalism is promoted as a goal for all entitlement programs. Public support and social services are seen as rights because the welfare of all citizens is seen as a collective social responsibility. Together with the other Nordic countries, Denmark has developed an impressive multi-tiered system of universal support policies for families, thereby removing chronic family and child poverty.[2] A comprehensive national child-care policy is seen as a vital component of this system, which is intended to sustain family life and parenting, irrespective of family form.

There is a statutory paid maternity leave (four weeks before birth and 14 weeks after) followed by a paid parental leave for one or both parents for an additional 10 weeks. When the infant is 6 months old, another 26-week parental leave, which is paid at a flat rate (about 80% of the level for maternity and initial parental leave), may be taken by one or both parents. This leave may be extended to 52 weeks with an employer's agreement. In addition, the system includes universal child and family allowances, a single-parent allowance, and a monthly social assistance stipend, as well as housing subsidies, generous unemployment benefits, and universal health care.

While working mothers in the United States, particularly low-income single mothers, wrestle daily

Valerie Polakow. (1997). Who cares for the children? Denmark's unique public child-care model. *Phi Delta Kappan, 78* (8), 604–610. Reprinted by permission of the author.

with a child-care crisis involving unavailable infant care, high costs, lack of access, and lack of regulation,[3] in Denmark high-quality child care is a guaranteed entitlement for every child, regardless of economic status. The Danish day-care system has for decades been internationally recognized for its extensive, high-quality services,[4] and there is increasing demand for those services. A comprehensive, subsidized public day-care system serves infants from the age of 6 months, and each local *kommune* (municipality) guarantees a child-care slot for all 1-year-olds, with single parents frequently receiving priority placement. Because day care is available, accessible, and widely supported by all segments of the population, mothers—both single and married—are able to work and become economically self-sufficient.

The Organization of the Public Day-Care System

The subsidized public day-care system, under the jurisdiction of the Ministry of Social Affairs, offers both professional center-based care for children from infancy through age 6 and paraprofessional home-based family day care for infants and toddlers up to age 3. With the maternity and parental leave policies, infants generally do not enter day care before the age of 6 months. Since formal schooling begins only at age 7, most Danish children are in day care for approximately six years.

Paraprofessional Family Day Care. The *Dagpleje* (family day care) is a neighborhood-based system administered by the local *kommune*. The caregivers, known as *dagplejemødre* (day-care mothers), receive three weeks of child development training during their first year and are supervised by a certified early childhood *pædagog* (teacher). Family day-care homes are inspected prior to licensing, and complete background and police checks are completed for all adult household members. If the day-care mother is selected as a potential applicant, other family members living at home are also screened by an early childhood supervisor. According to Eva Halse, director of the Copenhagen Østerbro Family Day Care Services, only about 25% of eligible applicants actually make it through the rigorous selection process. After the initial one-year period, early childhood supervisors visit "experienced" family day-care homes on a monthly basis and are on call to discuss any problems and offer ongoing professional support.

While official regulations permit a 1:5 caregiver-to-infant/toddler ratio,[5] I never found this arrangement in any of the sites I visited in metropolitan Copenhagen. The family day-care mothers there are regularly assigned three children, unless two are infants, in which case the ratio is 1:2. The day-care homes are grouped in neighborhood clusters of six or seven, and once a week each cluster of day-care mothers and their respective children spend the day together at a *legestue* (a three-room mini-day-care center fully equipped by the *kommune*), which is used on a rotating basis by five different neighborhood cluster groups. In this way the day-care mothers are not isolated in their homes and develop relationships with other caregivers and with the other children in their cluster. If a day-care mother falls ill or goes on vacation, she has back-up substitutes, each of whom is permitted to take on an extra child in her care. Once a month the cluster is also visited by its early childhood supervisor, who observes and meets with the caregivers during nap time. As unionized municipal employees, all family day-care mothers receive five weeks of paid vacation a year, full pensions, and a monthly salary of approximately 11,418 Dkr (U.S. equivalent: $2,003).

Day-Care Centers. There are several types of day-care centers serving infants and preschool children and providing after-school care. All the centers are run by certified *pædagoger* (teachers), assisted by paraprofessionals.[6] Both the teachers and the assistants are unionized municipal employees, with salaries for teachers in metropolitan Copenhagen ranging from 15,600 Dkr to 18,500 Dkr per month (U.S. equivalent: $2,736 to $3,245) and for assistants from 12,000 Dkr to 14,000 Dkr per month (U.S. equivalent: $2,105 to $2,456). All staff members receive pensions, get five weeks of paid vacation per year, and work between 30 and 37 hours a week.

- The *vuggestuer* are infant/toddler centers serving children between the ages of 6 months and 3 years. There are usually 30 to 40 children at a center, divided into smaller family groupings of eight to 10 children. The average ratio is one adult per 2.7 children,[7] and the staff members usually work in teams made up of one certified early childhood *pædagog* and one or two paraprofessional assistants.
- The *børnehaver* are preschool centers serving children from 3 to 6 years of age. They enroll from 20 to 80 children, usually divided into smaller family groups of 10 to 20 children, with an average ratio of one adult to 5.5 children.[8] The staff organization is similar to that of the infant/

toddler centers, with teams of one certified early childhood *pædagog* and one assistant.

- The *aldersintegrerede institutioner* (age-integrated centers) have become more widespread since the first experimental ones were established during the 1970s. These centers enroll children from 6 months to 14 years of age and account for about 20% of enrolled day-care children.[9] Philosophically, these centers promote play and social interactions across early and middle childhood, fostering responsibility on the part of older children (who attend the centers after school) and continuity and stability of adult/child and child/child relations, since the children may remain in these centers until early adolescence. Size and staffing ratios depend on the age of the children and follow the patterns of the *vuggestuer* and *børnehaver*.

In addition to the three types of centers described above, there are also after-school centers for elementary children between the ages of 6 and 9 and new experimental "forest schools" for children from 4 to 6 years of age, who spend the entire year experiencing intensive outdoor/environmental education. These "forest schools" have become increasingly popular among parents, particularly those living in the cities.

It is significant to note that the public day-care system is supported by government funds but is decentralized and run by each local *kommune*, which decides fees and ratios within the broad mandates of the Danish government, to which it is accountable for providing high-quality care for all children irrespective of their families' economic status. There is also a small private day-care sector run by private associations, but the private centers too receive approximately 80% of their funds from their local *kommune* and must follow the same operating guidelines.

While day-care costs exhibit slight variations from *kommune* to *kommune*, the tuition costs overall are fairly standardized (with $5 to $15 differences in monthly costs, depending on the area). In Copenhagen, for example, full-time care for an infant at either a family day-care home or an infant/toddler center in 1995–96 cost a maximum of 1,525 Dkr per month (U.S. equivalent: $267), and maximum full-time preschool costs were 1,325 Dkr (U.S. equivalent: $232). Fees are set on a sliding scale, with tuition waived for the lowest-income parents and then rising from approximately $11.60 per month to full tuition rates for those with annual incomes of more than $33,560.

The family day-care system is widely used in areas where there is high demand for infant care and in rural areas of the country, where centers are not as readily available. In some areas family day-care costs are a little lower than the center-based care (approximately $15 to $20 per month lower), with slightly longer hours. By combining a well-supervised paraprofessional system with a national public day-care center system, the Danes are attempting to meet working parents' increasing demand for day-care slots. While there is not yet full coverage, Danish family policy objectives aim toward that goal. It is significant to note that, in 1995, 60% of infants and over 80% of 3- to 6-year-olds were in public day care.[10]

While the structure, organization, and public financing of the day-care system are impressive, so too is the quality of infant and preschool care. During the fall of 1995, I visited five family day-care homes, attended the weekly cluster group meetings of family day-care mothers, and observed at seven different day-care centers. While the bulk of my observations took place in metropolitan Copenhagen, I also visited several sites in rural areas and interviewed staff members at all the day-care sites. In the following sections I present some brief snapshots of day care in action.

Stepping Inside:
Family Day Care in Action

Jytte[11] is a single mother in her late twenties with two children. Her 5-year-old attends a nearby preschool, and she takes care of her own 15-month-old daughter and two other toddlers, explaining that she chose to become a family day-care mother so that she could spend more time with her children.

I visited Jytte's home in the Nordhavn area—a lovely old neighborhood of flats and small shops near the harbor. Jytte's flat was on the second floor, comfortably furnished, with two bedrooms and a large living-room area. Jytte was returning from a morning outing with her daughter, Lise; Per, 18 months; and Bo, 12 months. All three toddlers were sitting in the large baby carriage supplied by her local *kommune*. Jytte lifted the two older ones out first and then picked up Bo, who had fallen asleep. After locking up the baby carriage outside, we entered the building, and the two toddlers clambered up the steps as Jytte unlocked the door, still holding Bo. As they entered the flat, Bo woke, and she took off his coat and mittens (it was a cold October morning) while the two toddlers peeled off their jackets and mittens and ran to take their slippers from the bedroom.

Jytte was calm and efficient, talking to the two toddlers softly while undressing Bo and eventually changing his diaper in the bedroom on a changing table. All three children then moved to the living-room area, where large blocks were set out, and Jytte went to prepare a snack in the kitchen. Milk and crackers and bananas were placed on the table, and when the children caught sight of the snack they went to fetch their bibs—including Bo, who crawled over to reach his. Jytte smiled as I remarked on how they each knew their own bibs (and earlier their slippers), telling me, "They are so clever—they always remind me if I forget to do anything." She lifted Bo into his high chair while Lise and Per climbed up onto theirs. Jytte began to sing a song while clapping her hands, and the toddlers followed suit, shouting out different sounds. Bo tried to pour his own milk, following the example of the two older toddlers, but he missed and the milk fell on the plastic cloth under the table. Jytte promptly produced a sponge and wiped it up, then held Bo's arm and encouraged him to pour again.

She cuddled all three children on the couch after the snack and then put Bo down for a nap in one of the three cribs in the bedroom, while the two older ones were playing on the couch. The atmosphere was warm and nurturing, and Jytte remained calm and unruffled as the children became cranky later in the morning. After their morning play period, when Jytte also read them several stories, she prepared lunch—milk and finger foods with fruit. Then she changed all three babies. Both Per and Lise went to fetch their own diapers from a large box, to which she smilingly replied "*tak*" (thank you); after they were changed and down in their cribs with pacifiers, Jytte relaxed in the living room, telling me, "This is my one hour of quiet! I treasure it."

Jytte has been a family day-care mother for more than four years, beginning when her older son was a baby. She appreciates the fact that she is able to count her own child as one of her day-care clients and speaks warmly of her supervisor as "always ready to help if there are any problems." As a family day-care mother, Jytte receives an allowance for food, diapers, and equipment, and one-third of her salary is tax free to compensate for the use of her home. All family day-care mothers are supplied with a large baby carriage, which seats up to four children. All the day-care mothers use these carriages as their main mode of transportation, and indeed it is a common sight on Copenhagen streets around 10 a.m. to see day-care mothers wheeling their young charges onto buses, off trains, through the downtown area, in parks, through wind and rain and fog. Even as

the icy winds of November blew in, there was no decrease of activity, as exercise and fresh air are considered an essential part of Danish child care at all ages. All the caregivers I interviewed, including Jytte, expressed satisfaction with their occupation. In addition, the other day-care mothers told me how important their weekly cluster meeting was: "We can share our problems and talk with each other as adults. If you are always alone talking to small children every day without a break, it can make you feel crazy."

Stepping Inside:
Day-Care Centers in Action

I visited seven day-care centers: three infant/toddler centers, three preschools, and one age-integrated institution. The diverse early childhood centers I observed in Copenhagen, Frederiksberg, and Herlev were all high-quality programs, providing flexible, play-based, developmental early education, with a strong focus on child-centered, child-initiated learning. Expressive group-oriented activities were fostered, and symbolic representation (as in the Reggio Emilia approach) was seen as a key to intellectual learning. Music and movement were central features of the morning, and the rest of the day was loosely and flexibly structured according to the children's play desires. Field trips took place several times a week—the preschoolers were taken via trains and buses to visit monuments, art galleries, outdoor theaters, libraries, parks, the harbor, and the forests. The programs were characterized by an open and flexible structure with an absence of teacher-directed learning. Autonomy and independence were fostered (4-year-olds were permitted to play alone in small groups with no adults present, both inside and outside), and cooperative play and socially inclusive group activities were emphasized.

There was a strong bias against any form of exclusion. When asked about the use of "time outs" with "difficult" children, Danish teachers uniformly reacted with horror at such an unthinkable practice, and one director told me, "No, never. We would never isolate a child—maybe that is one thing we in Denmark would get sued over!" Another head teacher remarked, "Often it is us. We have to look at how we are. Often we must change the way we are with the child or the way we say something, or sometimes we must look together with the parents at what is making the child angry or sad. But we should never isolate or punish the child who is having trouble." These perceptions about discipline and child management techniques were expressed by both directors and teachers at all the sites. In fact, the consistent responses across seven different centers serving diverse groups of children revealed key Danish educational tenets, influenced by N. F. S. Grundtvig (the Danish John Dewey): equality, social solidarity, cooperation, and gentle teaching. There were also strong injunctions against any formal "teaching" of reading or math readiness. All forms of early childhood intervention for vulnerable "at-risk" children were conducted within the child's center, where the services of a social worker and a psychologist were regularly available.

The following observations capture the flavor of a typical day at an age-integrated center.

I walked in to observe a lunch time with the youngest group of children. The cook, also a salaried municipal employee, was serving the food. Eleven babies and toddlers (ranging in age from 10 to 23 months) and three teachers were seated around a long table. The teachers tied on the children's feeding bibs and passed out forks (actual silverware) and china plates—even the youngest there picked up his fork, as the lox and ham and liverwurst spread on *smorrebrød* (open-faced sandwiches) were passed around. Bjarne (about 18 months old) poured his own milk with a great flourish, and others followed suit. The teachers moved quietly around, wiping up splashes of milk with wet washcloths.

Next came the second course: mini-quiche pieces with strong Danish cheese and slices of tomato. A 1-year-old ladled a piece onto her plate and then tried to stab it with her fork; on the third try she successfully speared the piece and put it in her mouth. She lunged for the pitcher and poured herself more milk, laughing as some splashed on her bib. The small pitchers were now empty, and a *"mere maelk"* (more milk) chant began. The toddlers banged with their forks, laughing uproariously, and the smiling teachers refilled the pitchers. Then the toddlers reached for them again, taking turns, amid many wild splashes. As the eating, pouring, and serving continued, no child fussed to come down from his or her high chair, and all valiantly ate with their forks, using chubby little fingers to collect what didn't quite make it to their mouths.

After about 25 minutes, Bjarne, the eldest, made a move to get down. A teacher gently told him to wait, and she brought out warm washcloths and passed them around. The toddlers wiped their faces with some help from the adults, who intervened only after the children had first tried to do it themselves. The teachers said *"tak for mad"* (thank you for the meal), which the toddlers repeated.

After lunch three toddlers went alone into the arts-and-crafts room, with a teacher watching from the open doorway. One toddler climbed onto a low table and, laughing, pulled a furry mobile down. A teacher looked in and told him *"nej"* (no) but left him on the table. He jumped down, picked up a puzzle piece, and threw it across the room. An older child (about 5 or 6 years of age) came in, told him *"nej"* sternly, and picked up the piece. As the older girl fit the piece into the puzzle, a teacher came in and took the toddler for a diaper change before putting him down for his outside nap in a *kommune*-supplied baby carriage. (I later learned that all babies and toddlers sleep outside unless the temperature drops below 0 degrees centigrade!)

The relaxed atmosphere at lunch was a common occurrence that I observed at different centers. The staff members were attentive but intentionally allowed the toddlers to experiment and rarely intervened. I was surprised to see the toddlers eat so competently and sit for such an extended period of time, but it was clear that autonomy and independence were being fostered—amid an acceptance of milky messes and many a miss—and that these young children were being socialized effectively for their future Danish dinners, which I subsequently discovered, often extended to midnight and beyond, with elaborate multiple courses of delectable and elegant cuisine!

The following description is drawn from a preschool I visited outside Copenhagen.

Four 3-year-olds were playing in the large activity room, which was essentially a free space until lunch, when tables were set up. The four were running together, colliding, and dissolving into gales of laughter. One began jumping on the couch, and the other three followed suit. Therese (the leader) jumped from the couch and pulled several large wooden blocks (which doubled as high chairs) to make "steps," and the children began a pattern of follow the leader on the couch and then balancing on the "steps." Suddenly Morten shouted to the other three to wait as he transformed the blocks into a "train," leaving one step to climb. He now assumed the lead, and the other three followed a new pattern of jumping on the couch, climbing onto the "step," and then riding the train. They all cooperated in the game, making train noises, and several others joined in so that there were now seven riding the train, with one serving as ticket collector for make-believe tickets. Several teachers walked by, smiling but not interfering, and the game continued for about half an hour.

I was fascinated by the cooperative nature of their play. No conflicts ensued, and several children inventively extended the initial game so that there were multidimensional forms of representation involving many symbols and artifacts. The key was that the children had complete autonomy; they had taken over the space and made it their own. Both children and adults looked on, respecting the world of the train riders. As one of the teachers commented, explaining her philosophy of early childhood education: "Never, never interrupt their play. We have an absolute emphasis on always respecting their play!"

In the arts-and-crafts room an extensive assortment of materials was arranged around the perimeter of the room, with Lego blocks in profusion, as well as books, pattern blocks, drawing/cutting/painting supplies, dozens of little plastic farm animals, farm people, and other miniatures. Three children, ranging in age from 3 to 6, were playing with the farm animals and different miniature flowers, sorting them into sets. One 4-year-old, Kresten, began building a symmetrical horizontal and vertical structure using the Lego blocks. I watched him; he was completely engrossed for about 20 minutes. Next to Kresten, Julie began to build a "garden." Inge entered the building area, picked up a Lego block, and threw it at Julie's garden, and Julie began to cry. A teacher walked over and immediately comforted Julie, but before the teacher could talk to Inge, Inge threw another block. Several of the adjacent children shouted "*nej, nej*" at Inge, and two repaired Julie's garden, saying "*så*" (a common exclamation equivalent to "there you go").

Inge stopped and watched as the teacher moved over and began to play with farm animals, telling a story in Danish about a duck who quacked loudly and who met other animals in Julie's garden, all of which made different sounds. The children were entranced, and all sat listening, including Inge. Meanwhile, the little builder, Kresten, who was both listening and building, now tried to fit the farm animals under an overturned box, next to his elaborate structure. But the large animals wouldn't fit. A little girl moved out of the story circle, came over and looked, and tried to lift the box. Together they figured out that Kresten needed to lift up the box and tilt it in order to fit the larger animals inside. As the story ended, the teacher took Inge on her lap. Two new children joined Kresten and his helper, who had now created a working farm with different tasks for the animals; all four children developed roles for themselves and continued their farm play for another 20 minutes. At lunch time they built a fence and left it standing as they moved to the lunchroom.

In this center, as in others I visited, the children had an autonomy of action that led to inventive transformational play. The respect accorded to children's expressive activities was in clear contrast to the approach that I have observed over the years in many child-care centers in the U.S., which are overly regimented and highly structured (despite guidelines embracing developmentally appropriate practice). In these Danish centers, gentle, respectful teaching à la Martin Haberman and Stacie Goffin[12] appeared to be the norm. Most impressive was the social/cooperative nature of group play, which clearly dominated daily experience. The above incidents of children intervening both to reprimand and to assist one another were not atypical. In fact, I observed such incidents at all seven sites.

What Can We Learn from the Danes?

While there were local differences between the various centers I visited—four had two or more male early childhood teachers on site, and two were ethnically diverse, with large numbers of immigrant children (particularly Turkish, Pakistani, and Bosnian)—all seven centers were nurturing, flexibly structured, and developmentally supportive, with a strong emphasis on social cooperation, expressive activity, child-initiated learning, and the "sacred" nature of play. These Danish day-care centers were part of a high-quality day-care system run by trained early childhood professionals with good paraprofessional assistance, and they were supported and appreciated by working parents. The family day-care homes, offering alternative infant care to parents, were well-organized, well-regulated, and carefully supervised by early childhood professionals. Clearly, the design of this paraprofessional system could be seen as one model for increasing access to and quality of infant- and toddler-care services in the U.S.

The Danish public day-care system is popular, and the status and respect accorded to early childhood teachers reflect the central place of day care in Danish family life. Day care is both accessible and affordable, and the operating costs and teacher salaries are subsidized by the local government; hence it is possible to run a high-quality system in which staff turnover is low. The widespread social support and the public economic base for a strong universal childcare system are phenomena from which we in the U.S. could learn a great deal; particularly impressive is the way in which a universal day-care system promotes equality of early educational opportunities for young children, because access to services does not depend on economic or family status. The families who are potentially most vulnerable—low-income single mothers and children, families experiencing domestic violence, immigrant families, refugee families, and "socially disabled" families—are given priority placement, because public day care is seen as both an equalizer and a potent force for the successful integration of the young into Danish society.

Contrast the Danish day-care system, which serves all children irrespective of their parents' economic status, with the current realities for poor families in the U.S. Head Start reached only 36% of income-eligible children in 1995 and remains underfunded.[13] There is also a national crisis of affordable child care for all American children whose parents are low-wage earners. The recent report released by the General Accounting Office, reviewing federally funded early childhood centers in different states across the nation, found severe health and safety violations in each of the states investigated and concluded that lack of regulation and monitoring was a critical cause.[14] Nancy Ebb also raised urgent concerns about the quality and availability of federally subsidized child care for families collecting AFDC (Aid for Families with Dependent Children) and for the working poor.[15] Meanwhile, with the dismantling of the federal welfare system, increasing numbers of poor single mothers will be forced into the workplace without adequate or affordable child care. The level of care is particularly inadequate for infants and toddlers, and findings from the *Cost, Quality, and Child Outcomes* study indicate that care for this age group may be even worse than previously documented.[16] In this study, child care at most centers in the U.S. was rated poor to mediocre. Only 8% of the infant/toddler rooms received a rating of "good" quality, and 40% received a rating of less than "minimal" quality.

Furthermore, in the absence of a nationally subsidized child-care system, private child-care costs are prohibitive—not only for poor parents but for middle-income families as well. Frequently costs run $800 a month for high-quality center-based infant care. In Michigan, for example, high-quality full-time infant care in Washtenaw County has risen to $10,000 a year—40% more than undergraduate tuition costs at the University of Michigan.

While participation in the labor force by mothers of young children in the U.S. is high—59.7% of women with children under 6[17]—there is a dearth of family-support policies to assist them. We have no paid maternity or parental leave, and the usual unpaid parental leave means that many mothers reenter the labor force when their infants are 12 weeks old or younger. We are the only country in the industrialized democratic world that fails its mothers and infants so abysmally in terms of family support and parental leave policies.

Denmark not only has generous maternal and parental leave policies, but its public day-care system has made a very different family life possible for working parents.

Denmark not only has generous maternity and parental leave policies, but its public day-care system has made a very different family life possible for working parents, particularly working and single mothers. Of all European Community (EC) countries, Denmark has the highest rate of working mothers with young children, approximately 79%.[18] The striking integration of day care into the fabric of society—there is literally a small center on almost every block in the city of Copenhagen—has created multilevel support from government and citizens and has become a part of the sacred universal system of benefits supported by high public taxes. While anti-tax discourse pervades public consciousness in the U.S. and has assumed the status of natural law, we might do well to pause and think about what we have lost by failing to create a publicly subsidized day-care system and a generous set of family support policies. "Who cares for the children?" is the perennial question. Clearly, in Denmark there is a sound partnership between parents and government, and their young children are the visible beneficiaries.

1. *Social Policy in Denmark: Child and Family Policies* (Copenhagen: Danish Ministry of Social Affairs, 1995), p. 4.

2. Sheila B. Kamerman and Alfred J. Kahn, eds., *Child Care, Parental Leave, and the Under 3's: Policy Innovation in Europe* (New

York: Auburn House, 1991); idem, *Starting Right: How America Neglects Its Youngest Children and What We Can Do About It* (New York: Oxford University Press, 1995); and Valerie Polakow, *Lives on the Edge: Single Mothers and Their Children in the Other America* (Chicago: University of Chicago Press, 1993).

3. Nancy Ebb, *Child Care Tradeoffs: States Make Painful Choices* (Washington, D.C.: Children's Defense Fund, 1994); U.S. General Accounting Office, *Review of Health and Safety Standards at Child Care Facilities* (Washington, D.C.: Department of Health and Human Services, 1993); and Suzanne Helburn, ed., *Cost, Quality, and Child Outcomes in Child Care Centers* (ERIC ED 386 297, 1995).

4. Marsden Wagner and Mary Wagner, *The Danish National Child-Care System* (Boulder, Colo.: Westview Press, 1976); David A. Corsini, "Family Day Care in Denmark: A Model for the United States?," *Young Children*, July 1991, pp. 10–15; and *Employment Equality and Caring for Children: Annual Report* (Brussels: European Commission Network on Child Care, 1993).

5. Jacob Vedel-Petersen, *Day Care for Children Under School Age in Denmark* (Copenhagen: Danish National Institute of Social Research, 1992), p. 18.

6. Teacher certification for *pædagoger* is a unique and separate 3-1/2-year training program for early childhood teachers, special needs teachers, and recreation specialists offered at 32 colleges of social education in Denmark.

7. Vedel-Petersen, p. 17.

8. Ibid.

9. Jytte Juul Jensen, "Age-Integrated Centres in Denmark," in *Employment Equality and Caring for Children: Annual Report* (European Commission Network on Child Care, 1992), pp. 35–38.

10. *Social Policy in Denmark*.

11. All names have been changed to protect confidentiality.

12. Martin Haberman, "Gentle Teaching in a Violent Society," *Educational Horizons*, vol. 72, 1994, pp. 131–35; and Stacie G. Goffin, "How Well Do We Respect the Children in Our Care?," *Childhood Education*, vol. 66, 1989, pp. 68–74.

13. *The State of America's Children 1996* (Washington, D.C.: Children's Defense Fund, 1996).

14. U.S. General Accounting Office, op. cit.

15. Ebb, op. cit.

16. Helburn, op. cit.

17. *The State of America's Children*, p. 93.

18. Bodil Stenvig, John Andersen, and Lisbeth Laursen, "Statistics for Work and the Family in Denmark and the EC," in Søren Carlsen and Jørgen E. Larsen, eds., *The Equality Dilemma: Reconciling Working Life and Family Life, Viewed in an Equality Perspective* (Copenhagen: Danish Equal Status Council, 1994).

■ *Valerie Polakow is a professsor in the College of Education, Eastern Michigan University, Ypsilanti.*

National Campaign Calls for Worthy Wages for Child Care

Joy Shioshita

■ ■ ■

Poverty-level pay. Fifty-hour work weeks. High exposure to illnesses. No health insurance. Every May 1, Worthy Wage Day calls public attention to these typical child care working conditions and to the result—high job-turnover rates undermining the quality of care that children receive. Research has repeatedly shown that children need consistent care from experienced, well-trained teachers.

Early childhood educators perform essential, highly skilled work supporting the development of the nation's children. Despite their above-average education levels, child care workers typically earn less than parking-lot attendants, and about one-third will leave their jobs this year, says the Center for the Child Care Workforce.

Good Child Care Jobs = Good Care for Children

"One of my biggest struggles is deciding whether to stay in the [early childhood] field. I absolutely love the work, but it's a struggle to make a living doing it," says Julia Gonzales, a lead teacher at Altadena Christian Children's Center near Pasadena.

Gonzales holds a bachelor's degree, has nine years' child care experience, and serves as a California state mentor teacher. Two of her friends, a postal clerk and a meter reader with only high school degrees, earn about $40,000 per year—twice her salary. Gonzales struggles to cover her rent, car insurance, and student-loan payments. "Most teachers have to depend on either a spouse or parents to make ends meet," she says.

During a typical week, Gonzales works during lunch and takes home 10 extra hours' worth of work:

writing weekly newsletters, gathering supplies, calling parents, and preparing for class.

"My whole feeling about early childhood is that it's the most important time of life, those formative years when children need the best care to lay a foundation for them," says Chandra Elstein, a teacher at the Tenderloin Childcare Center in San Francisco.

That's why it's such a problem that "the most educated and qualified people leave the [early childhood] field because of horrible pay," she says. Elstein is a living example. With a master's degree in early childhood education and over 10 years' experience in child care, she's now planning to enter another profession.

San Francisco parent activist Maria Luz Torre is well aware of the "very fast turnover of providers because of low wages." Parents, she explains, "want the really good ones to stay. They take care of our kids so we can work."

Continuous care from excellent child care teachers can make a huge difference in a child's life. Parent Deirdre Keane remembers how child care helped stabilize her youngsters during a rough divorce. Her daughter, Tierney, then age three, was "like a hurricane, hitting the walls, tearing things down" when she entered Tenderloin Childcare Center. Elstein patiently worked with Tierney on other ways to express her feelings. Tierney is now doing well in kindergarten, Keane reports.

Study Examines Child Care Staffing

The Center for the Child Care Workforce recently completed *Worthy Work, Unlivable Wages*: *The National Child Care Staffing Study, 1988–1997*. The report shows that:

Joy Shioshita. (1998, May/June). National campaign calls for worthy wages for child care. *Children's Advocate* [Online], 3 pages. Available: www.4children.org. The Children's Advocate is published by Action Alliance for Children, 1201 Martin Luther King, Jr. Way, Oakland, CA 98612. Phone: (510) 444-7136. Reprinted by permission of the publisher.

- *Child care teachers earn very low wages.* Teaching assistants and the lowest-paid teachers earn about $6 per hour. The highest-paid teachers, a much smaller group, earn an average of $10.85 per hour.

- *Staff turnover rates are very high.* During the past year, 20 percent of centers lost half or more of their teaching staff. 27 percent of teachers and 40 percent of teaching assistants left their jobs last year.

- *Most centers offer their staff limited or no health insurance.* Caring for young children heavily exposes workers to illnesses. Despite this fact, only 23 percent of centers offered fully paid health coverage to teachers, and only 21 percent offered such benefits to assistant teachers.

- *Centers paying higher wages kept more of their workers.* The study recommends a "well-targeted new investment of public funding to ease the child care burden on parents and caregivers alike," including:
  — More public money targeted to quality and pay
  — Extra pay for staff who receive further training
  — Higher reimbursement rates for child care programs
  — Stronger quality standards for programs receiving public funds

Bill Proposes Salary Supplements

California Assembly member Dion Aroner has introduced AB 2025, which would help raise wages of well-trained child care workers by:

- Paying yearly salary supplements to center-based or licensed family child care staff who stay at their jobs a year or longer; those with a bachelor's degree and/or bilingual skills would receive additional money

- Increasing government payments to programs that agree to raise their staff's salaries and to programs accredited by the National Association for the Education of Young Children or the National Family Child Care Association

Worthy Wage Pioneers

Some counties in New York and North Carolina already give salary boosts to child care staff. In North Carolina, state funds cover salary supplements in at least 25 counties, says Susan Russell, executive director of Day Care Services Association. DCSA administers one county's Child Care WAGE$ Project,

which rewards well-educated, lower-paid staff who stay at county-regulated programs. All eligible assistants, teachers, family child care providers, and directors receive between $200 and $2,000 a year, depending on their education level. The average turnover rate of eligible staff has dropped below 11 percent, compared to 36 percent before WAGE$ began, Russell says.

Nassau County, N.Y. provides yearly salary enhancements, $6,500 for teachers and $3,500 for assistant teachers in nonprofit child care centers contracting with the county. County taxes fund the program; the department of social services and the controller's office administer it. Gloria Wallick, executive director of the Child Care Council of Nassau, helped design the program and says that she'd like to see more incentives for training.

"Fight, Darlin'!"

A few years ago, Rhode Island family child care providers often went without health insurance. Many, earning poverty-level wages, couldn't afford private coverage and postponed medical treatment.

Now, after a five-year struggle, more than 100 family child care workers contracting with Rhode Island's welfare-related child care program receive fully paid, state-provided health coverage.

The family child care workers won this victory by mobilizing, with help from Direct Action for Rights & Equality (DARE), based in Providence, R.I. Executive Director Shannah Kurland describes the group as a grass roots, multiracial, "poor people's organization." Its specialty: "very confrontational" community organizing strategies.

After a DARE member first pointed to the problem of inadequate health coverage, horror stories accumulated. Kurland describes an uninsured woman who had provided family child care for nearly 20 years. When she finally received medical treatment, her doctor discovered a tumor "the size of a grapefruit."

DARE recruited more family child care workers as activists. Together with paid staff, they contacted child care providers and found many concerned about inadequate health coverage. The group then used numerous tactics to demand health insurance: storming the new governor's campaign headquarters, testifying before legislators, negotiating with state officials, and flooding state politicians with about 500 postcards, among other strategies.

Negotiations followed. At one point, says Kurland, the welfare department offered the workers Medicaid coverage requiring $150 monthly co-payments. DARE members held out for fully paid coverage, and they ultimately won.

Grace Brown, a family child care provider and DARE activist, has advice for other workers: "Fight, darlin'! Find the things that you really need and go after them." She's now involved with DARE's campaign promoting a "basic economic dignity" package for family child care workers contracting with the state. DARE's plan includes a $10 hourly wage, sick days, vacation, a pension, and pay for the actual number of hours worked.

To contact the Worthy Wage Campaign, call (800) UR-WORTHY.

■ Ask Yourself

Identifying Issues for Advocacy

1. What key factors define quality in an early childhood program? Does the degree and type of parent involvement relate to the quality of an early childhood program? If so, how? What effect, if any, does the work environment (organizational climate) for adults have on the quality of an early childhood program (Carter, 1998; Jorde-Bloom, 1997)? What would an ideal organizational climate for early childhood educators include? What factors influence the quality and quantity of teacher/child interactions (Kontos & Wilcox-Herzog, 1997)? What types of teacher/child interactions have you observed in your field study?

2. How does the *Code of Ethical Conduct and Statement of Professional Commitment* (Feeney & Kipnis, 1992) enhance the quality of early childhood settings? (This position statement is available online at www.naeyc.org/)

3. What steps should a parent take to choose a quality child-care setting (see Appendix 9)?

4. Goal 1 of the National Education Goals 2000 states: "All children will enter school ready to learn." What impact does the quality of a child-care or early education setting have on the achievement of this goal (Burchinal, Roberts, Nabors, Bryant, 1996; Kamii, 1994; Kontos & Wilcox-Herzog, 1997; National Institute of Child Health and Human Development Early Child Care Research Network, 1996; Peisner & Burchinal, 1997)?

5. In 1991, the National Institute of Child Health and Human Development (NICHD) began conducting a longitudinal study of the effects of child care on children's development. One research focus has been the effect child care has on mother/infant attachment. The laboratory measure used to assess attachment is known as the *Ainsworth Strange Situation* procedure. What is this procedure and is it a valid measure of attachment? (For a discussion of this procedure, see Belsky, 1986; Chess, 1987, Phillips, McCartney, Scarr, & Howes, 1987; and Rutter, 1981. *Note:* Belsky, Phillips, and McCartney are investigators participating in the current NICHD Early Child Care Study, so these readings provide back-

ground for the current project.) What are the research findings to date on attachment and on the effects of both quality and quantity of care? (Access the Early Child Care Study research results at www.nih.gov/nichd/html/childcar.html)

6. Should the cost of child care be funded by the federal and/or state government(s) in the same manner as are kindergarten and elementary education? Does your state provide funding to public school districts for a prekindergarten program (ages 3 to 4) (see Hendrie, 1998)?

7. Public libraries and bookstores have voiced concerns about parents regularly dropping off and leaving their children for hours as a substitute for child care. Should these facilities adopt rules prohibiting parents from leaving children unattended? Should they post signs warning parents that they can be prosecuted for child neglect if they leave their child unattended? Or do such actions create a punitive impression and indirectly discourage children from taking an interest in books?

8. How can we make the public aware of the need to establish strong licensing standards for child-care facilities (see Appendices 2, 3, 4, and 5)?

9. According to a Children's Defense Fund report, *Child Care Challenges* (Adams & Schulman, 1998), the average annual tuition for 4-year-olds in urban child-care centers exceeds $3,000 per child and is more than $5,000 per child in 17 states. What is the annual tuition at child-care centers in your area? What expenses are incurred in operating a child-care center? What are your thoughts about the cost and affordability of child-care programs?

■ Advocacy and Leadership Strategies

1. Does your state have a Resource and Referral Agency to direct parents to early care and education programs in their area? (This information is available from Child Care Aware at the National Child Care Information Center at www.nccic.org or at the National Association of Child Care Resources and Referral Agencies at www.naccrra.net) If so, have a representative from the program speak to the class about his or her role and about availability of care in your area. Inquire about before- and after-school programs (Seligson, 1997), evening/weekend care for shift workers, and sick-child care. If your state does not have a resource and referral agency or program, is there a need for one? If so, what can you do to help meet this need?

2. Develop a fact sheet on the affordability and accessibility of child-care and prekindergarten programs in your area (a Resource and Referral Agency may be a source for this data) to present to a

local legislator. Before meeting with the legislator, research any pending legislation that would have an impact on the affordabilty and/or accessibility of such programs. Be prepared with your recommendations regarding the pending legislation or suggestions for new legislation (see Mitchell, Stoney, & Dichter, 1997, and Appendices 5 and 7).

3. Read the National Association for the Education of Young Children's (NAEYC) official position paper on licensing and public regulation of early childhood programs (available online at www.naeyc.org). Invite a licensing agent from social services to your class to discuss state child-care regulations and how they are implemented or monitored. You may access your state's child-care licensing regulations online at the National Resource Center for Health and Safety in Child Care (www.nrc.uchsc.edu). Ask the licensing agent to estimate the impact of licensing on the quality of child care being provided in your state. Also investigate the procedure for accreditation of an early childhood program and its effectiveness as a strategy for improving the quality of child care (Bredekamp & Willer, 1996; Whitebook, Sakai, & Howes, 1997). Invite an early childhood program director or a validator who has participated in NAEYC's National Academy of Early Childhood Programs accreditation process to share his or her experiences with the class.

4. Using the Early Childhood Environment Rating Scale (ECERS) (Harms & Clifford, 1998), complete an evaluation of the overall classroom quality at your field-study site. If possible, first complete a group practice observation of an early childhood classroom. Later, compare and discuss item ratings. Read *Cost, Quality, and Child Outcomes in Child Care Centers Study: Key Findings and Recommendations* (1995) and Cryer and Phillipsen (1997) and discuss the results of your field study evaluation as compared to this larger study. You may also evaluate your field-study site using the Diversity in the Classroom Checklist in Appendix 13.

5. Is there a campus child-care center for children of students and faculty at your college or university? If so, inquire what you, either individually or as a class, can do to assist the child-care faculty and staff on a volunteer basis. If your college or university does not have a child-care center, find out if a needs assessment has been conducted and what the response has been. If this information has not been gathered, conduct a needs assessment. If it is determined that there is a need for such a facility, investigate the possibility for initiating a campus child-care center (Neugebauer, 1998) and develop an action plan for doing so. (See Appendix 2 for advocacy tips.)

6. At this time, the United States has no system of universal, publicly supported child care, although other advanced industrial societies do. After reading about Denmark's child-care model in this chapter, investigate the child-care policy of one other country

(Cochran, 1993; Jalongo & Hoot, 1997; Topolnicki, 1994). Also, research current national legislation in the U.S. (Kagan & Cohen, 1997). Is there movement in the United States toward a universal child-care system? What is the national agenda concerning child care? As part of this research, study the current legislation on Child Care and Development Block Grants, Dependent Care Tax Credits, Early Head Start and Head Start Programs, Early Learning Fund, and the Family and Medical Leave Act. How do U.S. policies compare to your study of child-care policies in other countries? Report your findings to the class and discuss the possibility of establishing one of these international child-care models in the United States. (See Appendix 10 for facts about child care in the United States.)

7. Numerous organizations are concerned about the quality of child care. In order to become familiar with the current advocacy efforts of several of these organizations and public-interest groups, each class member research one of these organizations (several examples are included in the following list, which is not exhaustive) and report to the class on the organization's philosophy, definition of quality care, membership, agenda, and website. (See Appendix 1 for web addresses of several organizations.) What role does each of these organizations play in improving the quality of care and education for young children? Some of the organizations are as follows:

> Action Alliance for Children; American Business Collaboration for Quality Dependent Care; Association for Childhood Education International; Child Care Action Campaign; Child Care Aware; Child Care Resource Center; Child Safety Forum; Child Welfare League of America; Children's Defense Fund; Families and Work Institute; National Association of Child Care Professionals; National Association for the Education of Young Children; National Association for Family Child Care; National Center for the Early Childhood Work Force; National Child Care Association; National Child Care Information Center; National Head Start Association; National Parent Teacher Association; National Resource Center for Health and Safety in Child Care; The Quality 2000 Initiative; School Age Child Care Project; U.S. Department of Education; U.S. Department of Health and Human Services—Child Care Bureau; USA Child Care; and Zero to Three—National Center for Infants, Toddlers and Families.

8. Factors found to have an impact on the quality of an early childhood program are the teacher's educational level, understanding of child development, and years of experience. What qualifications are required in your state for directors, teachers, and assistant teachers in licensed child-care centers and preschools? How do these requirements compare to those of other states? Interview the director of your field site about staff qualifications, pro-

fessional development, wages, and benefits. In a group of three or four, explore professional development initiatives and efforts to increase compensation for early childhood educators by contacting one or more of the following organizations: Center for Career Development in Early Care and Education (Wheelock College) <www.ericps.crc.uiuc.edu/ccdece/ccdece.html>, Center for the Childcare Workforce <www.ccw.org>, Council for Early Childhood Professional Recognition (call 800-424-4310), or National Institute for Early Childhood Professional Development (an initiative of NAEYC) <www.naeyc.org/naeyc>. Also read Azer, Capraro, and Eliot (1996); Bye (1995); *Child Care Bulletin*, July/August 1997 (Issue 16); NAEYC (1996a); and Shioshita (in this chapter). With this background knowledge and understanding of advocacy initiatives, decide how you, as a group and/or individually, can become involved in raising the level of professionalism and compensation for early childhood educators. Present both your research and your action plan(s) to the class. (Appendices 2, 3, 4, 5, 6, and 7 will be helpful in preparing your advocacy strategies.)

9. The following editorial cartoon appeared in a professional journal for education. Incorporating information from the readings in this text, write a model letter to the editor, responding to the editorial cartoon. You may want to refer to the implications of Goal 1 of the National Education Goals 2000: "All children will enter school ready to learn." As you compose your letter, consider the guidelines presented in Appendix 3: Writing Advocacy Letters.

Pett Peeves   **by Joel Pett**

Source: Copyright © 1994 Joel Pett. All rights reserved. Reprinted by permission.

10. At this time, the United States is one of two member nations not to ratify the United Nations' Convention of the Rights of the Child (see Appendix 11 and www.unicef.org/crc/). Organize a debate on support for and objections to ratification (e.g., see the December 1996 issue of *American Psychologist*). (See Appendix 8 for debate guidelines.)

11. At the beginning of this book, it was suggested that you collect articles for a current events (or What's in the News?) portfolio. To complete the portfolio, choose 12 of your collected articles that represent a variety of sources and give a complete citation for each article. Then write a reflection paper that answers the following questions:
    - Why did you select these 12 articles?
    - How do these articles relate to the class discussions?
    - How difficult was it to find these articles? Best source? Worst source?
    - If you used the Web, what were the best sites?
    - In newspaper and news magazines, in what sections were the articles generally found—for instance, lifestyles, front page (hard news section), education section, or editorial page?
    - What stories about young children attract the attention of reporters and editors of newspapers and newsmagazines?
    - What message(s) do these articles send to the general public about our society's stance toward young children and families?
    - What did you learn from this activity?
    - What would you like to see as the headline of tomorrow's regional newspaper? Give details to explain your response and write the first paragraph of the lead article.

■ References and Suggested Readings

Adams, G., & Schulman, K. (1998). *Child care challenges.* Washington, DC: Children's Defense Fund.

Allen, K. E. (1983, January). Public policy report: Children, the Congress, and you. *Young Children, 38,* 71–75.

Annie E. Casey Foundation. (1998). Child care you can count on: Model programs and policies. [Online]. Available: www.aecf.org/aecpub/child/qual.htm

Azer, S. L., Capraro, L., & Elliott, K. (1996). *Working toward making a career of it: A profile of career development initiatives in 1996.* Boston: Center for Career Development in Early Care and Education, Wheelock College.

Belsky, J. (1986, September). Infant day care: A cause for concern? *Zero to Three,* (5), 1–9.

Bredekamp, S., & Copple, C. (Eds.). (1997). *Developmentally appropriate practice in early childhood programs* (rev. ed.). Washington, DC: National Association for the Education of Young Children.

Bredekamp, S., & Willer, B. A. (Eds.). (1996). *NAEYC accreditation: A decade of learning and the years ahead.* Washington, DC: National Association for the Education of Young Children.

Burchinal, M. R., Roberts, J. E., Nabors, L. A., & Bryant, D. M. (1996). Quality of center child care and infant cognitive and language development. *Child Development, 67,* 606–620.

Bush, J., & Phillips, D. (1996). International approaches to defining quality. In S. Kagan & N. Cohen (Ed.), *Reinventing early care and education* (pp. 65–80). San Francisco: Jossey-Bass.

Bye, E. (1995, May). Why many child care providers are rated so low. *Young Children, 50* (4), 45.

Carnegie Task Force on Meeting the Needs of Young Children. (1994). *Starting points: Meeting the needs of our youngest children.* New York: Carnegie Corporation.

Carter, M. (1998, July/August). Revisiting quality, rekindling dreams. *Child Care Information Exchange, 122,* 81–83.

Chess, S. (1987, February). Comments: "Infant day care: A cause for concern." *Zero to Three, 7,* 24–25.

Children's Defense Fund. *The state of America's children* (Yearbook). Washington, DC: Author.

Cochran, M. (Ed.). (1993). *International handbook of child care policies and programs.* Westport, CT: Greenwood Press.

Collins, A., Jones. S., & Bloom, H. (1996). *Children and welfare reform: Highlights from recent research.* Columbia University: National Center for Children in Poverty.

Cost, Quality, and Child Outcomes in Child Care Centers Study Team. (1995, May). Cost, quality, and child outcomes in child care centers: Key findings and recommendations. *Young Children, 50* (4), 40–44.

Cryer, D., & Phillipsen, L. (1997, July). Quality details: A close-up look at child care program strengths and weaknesses. *Young Children, 53,* 51–60.

Deloria, D., & Brookins, G. K. (1982). The evaluation report: A weak link to policy. In J. R. Travers & R. J. Light (Eds.), *Learning from experience: Evaluating early childhood demonstration programs* (pp. 254–271). Washington, DC: National Academy Press.

Feeney, S., & Kipnis, K. (1992). *Code of ethical conduct and statement of professional commitment.* Washington, DC: National Association for the Education of Young Children.

Harms, T., Cryer, D., & Clifford, R. (1989). *Infant/toddler environment rating scale.* New York: Teachers College Press.

Harms, T., & Clifford, R. (1998). *Early childhood environment rating scale* (rev. ed.). New York: Teachers College Press.

Hendrie, C. (1998, May 27). High court in New Jersey ends funding suit. *Education Week, 17* (37), 1, 15.

Jalongo, M. R., & Hoot, J. (1997). Early childhood programs: International perspectives. In J. Isenberg & M. R. Jalongo (Eds.), *Major trends and issues in early childhood education* (pp. 172–187). New York: Teachers College Press.

Jorde-Bloom, P. (1997). *A great place to work: Improving conditions for staff in young children's programs.* Washington, DC: National Association for the Education of Young Children.

Kagan, S., & Bowman, B. (Eds.). (1997). *Leadership in early care and education.* Washington, DC: National Association for the Education of Young Children.

Kagan, S., & Cohen, N. (Eds.). (1996). *Reinventing early care and education.* San Francisco: Jossey-Bass.

Kagan, S., & Cohen, N. (1997). *Not by chance: Creating an early care and education system.* New Haven, CT: Bush Center for Child Development and Social Policy, Yale University.

Kamii, C. (1994, May). The six national goals: A road to disappointment. *Phi Delta Kappan, 75* (9), 672–677.

Katz, L. G. (1993). *Multiple perspectives on the quality of early childhood programs.* ERIC Digest. Champaign, IL: ERIC Clearinghouse on Elementary and Early Childhood Education. (ERIC Document Reproduction Service No. ED 355 041)

Kontos, S., & Wilcox-Herzog, A. (1997). Teachers' interactions with children: Why are they so important? *Young Children, 52* (2), 4–12.

Michel, S. (1998). The politics of child care in America's public/private welfare state. In K. Hansen & A. I. Garey (Eds.), *Families in the U.S.: Kinship and domestic politics* (pp. 837–848). Philadelphia: Temple University Press.

Mitchell, A., Stoney, L., & Dichter, H. (1997). *Financing child care in the United States: An illustrative catalog of current strategies.* Philadelphia: Pew Charitable Trusts.

National Association for the Education of Young Children. (1991). *Accreditation criteria and procedures of the National Academy of Early Childhood Programs* (rev. ed.). Washington, DC: Author.

National Association for the Education of Young Children. (1996a). *Guidelines for preparation of early childhood professionals.* Washington, DC: Author.

National Association for the Education of Young Children. (1996b). *Ten signs of a great preschool* (Brochure). Washington, DC: Author.

National Education Association. (1998). *Promoting quality in early care and education.* Washington, DC: Author.

National Institute of Child Health and Human Development Early Child Care Research Network. (1996). Characteristics of infant child care: Factors contributing to positive caregiving. *Early Childhood Research Quarterly, 11,* 269–306.

Neugebauer, R. (1998, July/August). Kids on campus: Status report of campus child care. *Child Care Information Exchange, 122,* 20–22.

Newberger, J. (1997, May). New brain development research—A wonderful window of opportunity to build public support for early childhood education. *Young Children, 52* (4), 4–9.

Peisner, E. S., & Burchinal, M. R. (1997). Relations between preschool children's child-care experiences and concurrent development: The cost, quality, and outcomes study. *Merrill-Palmer Quarterly, 43* (3), 451–477.

Phillips, D., McCartney, K., Scarr, S., & Howes, C. (1987, February). Selective review of infant day care research: a cause for concern! *Zero to Three, 7,* 18–21.

Rutter, M. (1981). *Maternal deprivation reassessed* (2nd ed.). Middlesex, England: Penguin Books.

Seligson, M. (1997, January–February). School-age child care comes of age. *ChildCare ActionNews, 14* (1).

Shore, R. (1997). *Rethinking the brain: New insights into early development.* New York: Families and Work Institute.

Topolnicki, D. (1994). The world's 5 best ideas. In K. Paciorek & J. Munro (Eds.), *Annual editions: Early childhood education* (pp. 6–11). Guilford, CT: Dushkin.

Whitebook, M., Sakai, L., & Howes, C. (1997). *NAEYC accreditation as a strategy for improving child care quality.* Washington, DC: National Center for the Early Childhood Work Force.

■ *A p p e n d i c e s*

■ *A p p e n d i x* 1 **Websites and Website Links**

■ *A p p e n d i x* 2 **Advocacy Tips**

■ *A p p e n d i x* 3 **Writing Advocacy Letters**

■ *A p p e n d i x* 4 **Working with the Media**

■ *A p p e n d i x* 5 **Visiting Public Officials**

■ *A p p e n d i x* 6 **Planning a Visit to Child Care Centers for Legislators**

■ *A p p e n d i x* 7 **Developing a Policy Briefing Paper**

■ *A p p e n d i x* 8 **Guidelines for an Informal Debate**

■ *A p p e n d i x* 9 **Four Steps to Selecting a Child Care Provider**

■ *A p p e n d i x* 10 **Facts about Child Care in America**

■ *A p p e n d i x* 11 **The Rights of the Child: Summary of the United Nations' Convention**

■ *A p p e n d i x* 12 **Are There Signs of Child Abuse and Neglect? (Are There Signs That a Family May Be in Trouble?)**

■ *A p p e n d i x* 13 **Diversity in the Classroom: A Checklist**

■ *A p p e n d i x* 14 **Books Related to Ethnic Diversity**

■ *Appendix 1*

Websites and Website Links

The Internet can be a valuable resource to advocates for young children and their families. Websites can provide information on current legislation and issues, advocacy organizations, as well as state, local, and federal government programs and resources. Listed below are selected sites that may be useful to advocates for young children. Many of these sites will provide links to a wide range of other sites. Be certain to verify with other sources any information you find on the Internet. The following sites were accurate at press time, but may have changed since then. If you are unable to access a site, try a search for the name of the organization.

American Academy of Pediatrics	www.aap.org
Carnegie Institute (Starting Points)	www.carnegie.org
Child Care Bureau	www.acf.dhhs.gov/programs
Child Trends, Inc.	www.childtrends.org
Child Welfare League of America	www.cwla.org
Children's Advocate	www.4children.org
Children's Defense Fund	www.childrensdefense.org
ERIC Clearinghouse on Early Childhood and Elementary Education	www.ericeece.org
Families USA	www.familiesusa.org
Families and Work Institute	www.familiesandworkinst.org
Family Education Network	www.familyeducation.com
IFAS (e-mail members of Congress)	www.ifas.org/activist/index.html
Kids Count	www.aecf.org/aeckids.htm
National Association for the Education of Young Children	www.naeyc.org/naeyc
National Child Care Information Center	www.nccic.org
National Coalition for Parent Involvement in Education	www.ncpie.org
National Resource Center for Health and Safety in Child Care (Links to state child-care licensure regulations)	nrc.uchsc.edu
Resources for Children, Youth and Family Professionals	www.cyfernet.mes.umn.edu
Stand for Children	www.stand.org
U.S. Department of Education	www.ed.gov
U.S. Department of Health and Human Services	www.os.dhhs.gov

■ *Appendix 2*

Advocacy Tips

The following are suggestions to help you become an effective advocate for young children and their families:

Be Aware

Notice what is happening, both in your area as well as nationally or globally, that affects the quality of life of young children and their families. Read newspapers and magazines; watch the local, national, and world news; and stay in touch with the current issues in the field of early childhood. Know your elected officials and their platforms. As issues are raised, or as you draw attention to injustices you have observed, ask yourself what you could do to help alleviate the problem or to raise the standards.

Be Avid

It is easier to begin, and maintain, your advocacy efforts if you are working on an issue about which you care deeply. Enlist the help of friends or join an organization that shares your concerns. Your resolve is less likely to wane if you are working with a group toward a common goal. Remember to focus your efforts on one issue at a time and you will be more successful.

Be Articulate

Present your issue to others in a reasonable and logical manner. Try to have them see its relevance to their lives. Research the history of the issue, know how others have solved the problem, anticipate obstacles, and be prepared with suggestions for solutions. Think about your approach, plan your strategies, and practice your presentation. If given only a short time to present your view, how can you best move others to join your efforts?

Be Adamant

Don't give up! If you have clearly defined an issue that negatively effects the lives of young children and their families, then be persistent until you see positive changes being made. Contact the media, local civic groups, and church organizations to recruit more support for your efforts. Write letters to law makers and newspapers, organize a campaign, and think of other positive steps you can take to effect change.

Be Appreciative

Don't forget to thank all those who helped make positive changes possible. Notes and accolades to policy makers, media personnel, and contributing individuals and organizations will lead to an advocacy network that will prove valuable in helping you improve the lives of young children.

FOR MORE INFORMATION

Goffin, S., & Lombardi J. (1988). *Speaking out: Early childhood advocacy*. Washington, DC: NAEYC.

Whitebook, M., & Ginsburg, G. (Eds.). (1984). *Beyond "just working with kids": Preparing early childhood teachers to advocate for themselves and others*. Berkeley, CA: Child Care Employee Project. (ERIC Document Reproduction Service No. ED 255 299)

■ *Appendix 3*
Writing Advocacy Letters

Whether advocating for new policy or raising awareness of the need for a change in policy, one of the most effective techniques to employ is letter writing. With a hard copy of your position statement in hand, the recipient can return to and refer to your letter frequently. Therefore, the content and tone of your letter needs careful consideration. As you compose a letter to the editor of a paper or magazine or to a local, state, or national policy maker, consider the following guidelines (Allen, 1983; Deloria & Brookins, 1982; Goffin & Lombardi, 1988):

1. *Remember your audience*. When writing a letter to the editor, your letter most likely will be published in the paper or magazine (if you follow established guidelines), so your audience is the readership who may lack awareness and knowledge of the issue. When writing to a policy maker, depending on the direct involvement of the policy maker in the issue, you may need first to explain the issue or identify a piece of legislation before proceeding with stating and supporting your position. Whenever possible, link the questions addressed in your letter to the real decisions the reader is or has been making.

2. *Use clear, vivid, concise language* devoid of educational or developmental jargon unfamiliar to the public. Avoid the use of acronyms. When quoting statistics, cite your source and be certain all facts contained in your letter are accurate. Sta-

tistics can be effective, but use them sparingly and limit their use to simple descriptive statistics such as actual numbers or percentages.

3. *Use the professional business-letter format.* When writing to public officials, use the correct salutation:

   U.S. Senator
   The Honorable _____
   U.S. Senate
   Washington, DC 20510
   Dear Senator _____

   Governor
   The Honorable _____
   Governor, State of ____
   State Capitol
   City, State ZIP
   Dear Governor _____

   U.S. Representative
   The Honorable _____
   U.S. House of Representatives
   Washington, DC 20515
   Dear Congressman / Congresswoman _____

   Mayor
   The Honorable _____
   City or Town Hall
   City, State ZIP
   Dear Mayor _____

4. *Stay focused.* Keep the central issue clear throughout your letter.

5. *Use real-life examples* to illustrate your point whenever possible.
6. *Take a positive stance,* opening and closing your letter with statements that will *establish rapport* with public readers. *Suggest viable alternatives* to plans you oppose rather than just lash out. Your letter should be respectful to the reader, stating honestly and clearly your position.
7. *Remember to write congratulatory letters,* too. When legislation has been passed, funding granted, or an issue resolved that you *affirm,* write and give the public officials who were responsible your support and plaudits.
8. *Save a copy* of all correspondence. Remember, you probably will have to write again (and again) before you feel that your advocacy efforts have reached a satisfactory conclusion.

REFERENCES

Allen, K. E. (1983, January). Public policy report: Children, the Congress, and you. *Young Children, 38,* 71–75.

Deloria, D., & Brookins, G. K. (1982). The evaluation report: A weak link to policy. In J. R. Travers & R. J. Light (Eds.), *Learning from experience: Evaluating early childhood demonstration programs* (pp. 254–271). Washington, DC: National Academy Press.

Goffin, S., & Lombardi J. (1988). *Speaking out: Early childhood advocacy.* Washington, DC: NAEYC.

■ *A p p e n d i x 4*

Working with the Media

The media can be an ally in your advocacy efforts on behalf of children and families. The following suggestions will help you establish a working relationship with media personnel and increase your effectiveness as a spokesperson on issues that have an impact on the lives of young children:

1. *Think of publicity as an integral part of your advocacy efforts.* Newspapers, TV, and radio will be effective in helping you get your message about an event or current advocacy effort to a wide audience. Calling in to radio talk shows, invit-

ing the media to cover events, writing letters to the editor, preparing public service announcements, and taking advantage of free advertising and publicity are all effective ways to take your message to the public arena.

2. *Cultivate a friend in the media.* Notice the by-lines in the local newspaper and identify the reporter who generally covers issues concerning families and children. Send information on an event or an advocacy issue to this reporter with a cover letter introducing yourself. Then follow this mailing with a brief visit to the newspaper office

and meet the reporter in person. Call this same person when you can offer a photo opportunity that would be of broad public interest, such as a fund-raising event or a special program at your child-care center. Television reporters and radio personnel could similarly be identified and contacted.

3. *Present yourself as a professional and an expert in your field.* When contacted by or meeting with media personnel, be prepared to discuss the issue or event by knowing all the details. Avoid the use of acronyms or professional jargon that would be unfamiliar to the general public. Remember to identify and acknowledge the efforts of others involved in the project.

4. *Think before you speak when contacted by the media to comment on an issue or event.* If you need time to collect your thoughts, tell the reporter you will call back shortly, gather the necessary information, and return the call as promised. When speaking, stay focused on your message; be positive, brief, and succinct; and present the information in an organized manner. McCall (1993) suggests the following strategies for dealing with difficult or antagonistic questions:
   a. Bridge to a topic of your liking.
   b. Redefine the question so you can answer it comfortably.
   c. Ask the questioner how he or she feels about the issue.
   d. Question the interviewer's assumptions.
   e. Avoid being forced to choose between extreme statements or to respond to a simplistic question.
   f. When badgered, do not respond in kind but remain calm, polite, and professional. Also, do not provide diagnostic or therapeutic prescriptions nor respond to personal questions from the interviewer. You can politely decline answering an inappropriate question by stating, "The ethics of my profession prevent me from answering that question directly, but I can talk about the topic in general terms."

5. *Stay well informed by reading newspapers and listening to the local and national news.* Be both proactive and reactive in your response to what you have seen and heard. Critique editorials, cartoons, and news coverage, and voice your reaction, be it positive or negative, as an early childhood professional and advocate for young children. Be proactive by suggesting stories to the media, such as a spin on a current news story that presents the impact it will have on the lives of children.

6. *Be persistent.* It may take several attempts before you get the attention you desire from the media. Also, realize that it is possible you will be misquoted or your words will be taken out of context at some point, but do not become discouraged. The benefits to be gained from involving the media in your advocacy efforts and having them help you take your message to the public will outweigh any negative aspects you may encounter.

7. *Submit articles to newsletters, magazines, and journals.* Contact the publisher of community and organization newsletters, local and national magazines, and professional journals to inquire about the guidelines for submitting articles for publication. Follow the guidelines carefully, and again, be persistent, as you may experience repeated rejections before being published.

REFERENCE

McCall, R. (1993). A guide to communicating through the media. In K. McCartney & D. Phillips (Eds.), *An insider's guide to providing expert testimony before Congress* (pp. 16–24). Washington, DC: Society for Research in Child Development.

Appendix 5

Visiting Public Officials

Child Care, Inc.

Talking directly to public officials about issues that concern you can be a very effective form of advocacy. It lets us present more material to them than a letter can, and counters their arguments immediately with our own arguments. In some cases, a visit may help to persuade ignorant public officials that we do in fact exist, live in their districts, vote, and do not have fangs and horns.

Step #1:   In this as in all activities, our first step must be to get clear information on what the problem is, what our position is, who is responsible for the problem, and how, when and where we should get to them.

Step #2:   Select one person to call on behalf of the group to make the appointment. The representative should tell the official's staff who we are, how many of us wish to see him/her, what we wish to see him/her about, and should give some kind of time frame. It often is a good idea to write a confirming letter to follow up on this. We should also decide whether we will accept a meeting with one of the offficial's assistants, or whether we want to meet with the official herself or himself. This is not an issue of principle—it is a practical question of who we think we need to get to at this time on this issue. Be persistent, since it may take several phone calls and a letter before we are able to pin down any kind of meeting.

Step #3:   Assemble the delegation to visit the official. It's a good idea to mix the delegation as much as possible, to show the range of interest in the issue. For instance, we want to include both workers and management, professionals and parents, ministers and business persons, day care and non-day care people, to show that our concern is a universal human concern, rather than a narrow "special interest."

Step #4:   Always caucus before meeting with the official to plan details of the meeting. Often we can simply meet an hour earlier, in a coffee shop or meeting room near the official's office. We need to agree on exactly who will say what, and in what order. This planning helps to overcome the tendency for one or two people to do all the talking, and helps people to overcome their shyness and their reluctance to be forceful with a public official. This planning also keeps us from wasting the official's time (or our own) in repetitions, and gives the official a vivid sense of our unity.

Step #5:   Be succinct and polite in the meeting, but don't give up the point. Avoid rhetoric as much as possible (there's little use these days in talking about how much we love children), and avoid begging or weeping. State the case and stick to it.

Step #6:   Caucus again immediately after the meeting, to evaluate it, and to agree on the follow-up steps. Again, this is something we can do in a coffee shop, a meeting room, or simply in the lobby after the meeting.

Step #7:   Write a thank-you letter on behalf of everyone who visited the official, and in the letter summarize clearly the points we made, and any agreements or disagreements, that we reached with the official.

Step #8:   In this, as in all activities, give the larger group that you represent feedback on what happened, through informal reports, meetings, memoranda, newsletters, or whatever.

Visiting public officials. (undated). New York: Child Care, Inc. Reprinted by permission of Child Care, Inc., New York City.

■ *Appendix 6*

Planning a Visit to Child Care Centers for Legislators

Children's Defense Fund

A legislative recess is a perfect opportunity to bring the message about child care to your congressman/[woman] or senator while they are visiting their home districts. While it is valuable to secure time on your representative's calendar for an office meeting, you can strengthen your case by inviting your representative to visit a local child care program.

The concept behind a site visit is a simple one: *seeing is believing*. Site visits (such as the Children's Defense Fund's *Child Watch Visitation Program*) allow elected officials and other community leaders to look into a child's eyes and see issues firsthand. They provide an opportunity for your elected officials to move out of their legislative chambers and into the world of the real children and families whose lives they affect every day with their decisions. The following are some tips and guiding principles that will help you to craft an effective visit.

Scheduling

Plan the visit to maximize attendance and attention. When home for a short recess, legislators are not likely to afford much more than an hour for such a visit, so plan according to their scheduling constraints. You may also find that the morning hours afford more scheduling flexibility for your representatives.

People who are not used to young children or child care can be helped to feel more comfortable if they have a specific focus for the visit. Trying to get adults to interact with children during free time is difficult, and the children may not be very welcoming if you are interrupting their "work." Send a letter from the children of the child care site inviting legislators to share 30 minutes with the children for a light breakfast. Legislators are likely to stay longer if they wish, but keep the official invitation to 30 minutes.

Site Selection

It is critical to select a site that *best illustrates* the core message you want to relay to your legislator. Avoid intrusiveness by selecting a site that can comfortably accommodate the size of your group.

What Makes a Good Site?

- *Programmatically sound services.* Select a site that is respected in the field so that it is beyond the reproach of a critical eye.
- *Opportunity to interact with children.* Seeing children's faces gives the greatest urgency to arguments for policies that can improve their lives.
- *Articulate, enthusiastic, personable directors.* An interesting site can quickly become an awful visit if the program director does not do a good job of explaining the program, answering questions, and addressing policy issues.
- *Programs serving a mix of children.* Make an effort to visit programs that serve a diverse group of children. This will avoid generalizations about services only being needed by "those people."

Activity

Attendees can be brought closer to the issue through interactive experiences. For example, sitting in little chairs with children in a structured time (such as breakfast) is more effective, and visitors can always start a conversation with children about the food.

If all visitors cannot be seated with the children at breakfast, take part of the group on a tour of the facility before bringing them back to interact with the children.

Message

All planning for a legislative site visit must be firmly rooted in a clear and concise message. It is critical to develop a uniform message that transcends any single site message so that your representative walks away with a greater understanding about local or state child care needs rather than a specific opinion about one child care center or program director.

Don't plan a big presentation or focus a lot of time talking. Instead, let visitors know you can answer any questions they have. Note that they are likely to ask questions when they arrive and when they leave.

Give legislators written materials as they leave or while taking them on a tour. Keep materials brief—i.e., a brochure about the program and a one-page fact sheet that highlights the message you want the legislator to understand.

What happens when issues are raised that you did not expect? Always neutralize potentially negative or distracting issues by connecting back to the message of the day. All written materials, briefers, and site directors must be prepared in advance to "be on page" with the central theme of the day in order to make sure the focus stays where it is most needed. Do your homework, and know your attendees and their concerns.

Thank participants for taking the time to visit and thank them for their past support, if appropriate.

Follow-Up

It is important to incorporate visits by local officials, business leaders, and community leaders as part of a regular routine. Children and staff can begin to get comfortable with "dignitaries" visiting, and you will learn how to make the visits less stressful for all.

The important element in visits with legislators is to establish a constructive connection with you and the program that will continue in the future. This should not be a one-time event.

In order to maximize effectiveness, there should be a plan as to how this site visit fits into a more extensive advocacy agenda. Impressions and experiences gleaned during a site visit should be revisited at a time when your representative is called upon to show leadership for child care that works for American families.

CDF, a children's advocacy organization, is located at 25 E. Street NW, Washington, DC 20001. For further information about planning a visit by legislators to a child care center, contact CDF, Child Care Division, 202-662-3547.

■ *A p p e n d i x   7*

Developing a Policy Briefing Paper

Karen B. Wiley

[*Note:* Here is an example of how to prepare and present a policy briefing paper. This example from another academic area translates well to the work of emerging and experienced early childhood advocates and leaders.]

Policy analysts and engineers have much in common. Both are practical problem solvers, distinct from their more theoretically oriented colleagues in the political and physical sciences. Both spend their professional lives designing solutions and comparing alternatives. In fact, in many settings, engineers are de facto policy analysts.

I teach public policy courses to engineers. Some of what I have learned in the process of tailoring these courses to the professional needs of engineers can be easily transferred to the teaching of policy analysts. Of particular value is the culminating exercise that I have used in several policy courses: *the policy briefing.* This is a term project that requires students to integrate skills and knowledge from humanities, social science, and technical courses in an exercise with clear practical applications. It is modeled on an activity in which most professionals en-

Karen B. Wiley. (1991). Teaching policy analysis using a briefing format. *PS: Political Science and Politics, 24,* 216–218. Reprinted by permission of the American Political Science Association.

gage frequently: briefing one's boss or a client. Because the practical value of persuading a boss or client is so obvious, students are willing to devote considerable energy to learning the relevant skills.

At the beginning of the semester, I give students four pages of "Briefing Instructions" describing what is expected of them. The first section of the Instructions reads as follows:

Briefing Instructions

One of the culminating activities for this seminar will be a briefing on a selected public policy issue. You will prepare a written briefing paper and give an oral briefing on a policy question selected in consultation with your professor. The briefing will be designed to give advice to a public official regarding:

- What courses of action are available to that official and his/her agency;
- The advantages and disadvantages of each course; and
- Your recommendation about the optimal course to follow.

You will take on the role of an aide or consultant to the public official in presenting your advice.

The earliest class meetings focus on laying out the range of possible issues from which students may choose their topics. This survey provides a good general introduction to the course in addition to suggesting topics to students. The guidelines for choosing a topic are laid out in the second part of the Briefing Instructions:

Selecting an Issue

The first step in your proposal is to select an issue. Keep in mind these constraints:

- Choose a topic that is a *real* issue—that is, there are two or more sides to the question. If everyone agrees, it's not an issue.
- Choose a topic that is a *live* issue—that is, it's not settled yet.
- Choose a topic for which there are some *people* in the local area whom *you can interview*. Why?
  — Interviewing real people on different sides of the issue will give you a vivid sense of how seriously the participants take the question (there are real winners and losers) and of how persuasive people can be when they have real stakes in an issue.
  — Interviewing people who are actively involved with the issue will uncover the most

up-to-date thinking and information relevant to the question.
  — Interviewing can save time. One interview can be worth days in a library, since interviewees have the relevant information right at their fingertips.
- Choose a topic on which *you* already *have some expertise*. For instance, if you are majoring in chemical engineering you might want to focus on a question related to fuel regulations to reduce air pollution.

The first assignment, usually due the second week of class, is for each student to write a one-page project proposal to his/her "boss" or "client." The specifications for this proposal are given in the third section of the Briefing Instructions:

Writing a Proposal

The second step in developing your briefing is to prepare a proposal on your topic. The proposal will be the basis for your consultation with your professor. It should be no longer than one page, typewritten, single-spaced. (Long-windedness is not a virtue.) Your proposal should include the following elements:

- Identify the *public official and agency* whom you are advising.
- Describe briefly the *public policy issue* you will tackle. The issue should be phrased as a question in the following form:
  What should Agency X do about Issue Y?
- Describe briefly the major *policy alternatives* (i.e., courses of action for the agency) you expect to examine.
- Describe briefly how you *plan to start getting information*. (To whom will you talk first? What written material will you read first?)

During your consultation, your professor will help you shape your topic more precisely, suggest kinds of questions to which your public official will demand answers, and suggest sources of information. The product of your consultation should be a thorough outline of your briefing paper.

The question, What should Agency X do about Issue Y?, forces students to target their attention clearly from the beginning on the question of *action*, so that their research efforts are not dissipated in wild goose chases.

Requiring them to brainstorm their own list of alternative courses of action *before* doing much research also helps focus their research efforts and, additionally, sets a salutary tone: students are expected to think on their own rather than copy down other people's ideas. I usually give them a couple of hints to get started: "There are always at least two possibilities: do nothing or do something. And, within the Do Something category, you can surely come up with at least two subdivisions, such as do something big or do something little."

Specifications for briefing papers are contained in the next section of the Briefing Instructions. The first portion offers guidelines regarding content and the second gives format guidance:

Writing the Briefing Paper—Content

The third step is preparing your briefing paper. In it you should cover the following items:

- Problem definition.
- Policy options for solving the problem, including the "do nothing" option.
- Analysis of the advantages and disadvantages of each option, in terms of categories specified by your professor. (For instance, for environmental problems, you should examine at minimum the costs and benefits in terms of technical efficiency, welfare/economic effects, health effects, and ecosystem effects.)
- Analysis of distributional and political effects of each option (who will gain and who will lose from each course of action).
- Recommendation: explanation of which option is best, which is second best, and which is worst—and why.

Writing the Briefing Paper—Format

Your paper should be neat and attractively formatted, organized so that a reader with little time can find things readily, and written in clear and concise prose. It should incorporate the following elements, which are designed to make life easier for your readers, thus inclining them to accept your message:

- Title page
- Executive summary (no more than one page)
- Table of contents
- Body of paper, with clear headings and subheadings
- Visual aids (graphs, tables, etc.) as needed
- Appendices if appropriate.

Use the "top-down" approach to organizing your findings: state your NEWS—that is, your recommendations and major reasons for them—first. Then discuss each major question in your outline, in order of importance to your "boss" or "client." You want to get the most important items on the table early, in case the reader loses interest or does not have time to finish the report.

How long should the briefing paper be? Long enough to present your recommendations, major supporting arguments, and evidence clearly and convincingly but not so long that the reader becomes bored. Remember: you can always relegate detailed supporting material to appendices.

Usually briefing papers are turned in at the time of the oral presentation, following common professional practice. However, this means they cannot be revised on the basis of feedback from the oral briefing. For pedagogical purposes, one might wish to deviate from this professional practice.

The Briefing Instructions also include guidelines for the oral briefing:

Preparing the Oral Briefing

The final step is to present your findings orally. Keep the following guidelines in mind:

- Your presentation should last no more than 3/4 of the total time available. The remaining quarter should be reserved for a Q&A (question and answer) period. NEVER exceed your time limit for presentation—it's rude. You may go overtime on Q&A if your audience wants to.
- Plan to get your main message across in the first five minutes of your presentation; your audience's attention may wander off to some other pressing matter after that. Use the rest of the time to present details of argument, evidence, and other material that you think important or interesting. Then give a short, snappy conclusion driving home your main message at the end.
- Use visual aids! They assist memory and comprehension (both your own and your audience's). Don't overcrowd your visuals. Can they be read from the back of the room?
- Check ahead of time to make sure the room you will be using has the proper equipment and that it works.
- Practice—at least by yourself in your room. Better yet in front of a friend or video recorder. Particularly, make sure that your timing is right.
- Dress professionally.
- Arrive ahead of time. Never keep a boss or client waiting!

Overall grades for the oral briefings are based on content and organization, communication skills, and overall persuasiveness. I write brief comments in each category on a half-page form, which is then given to the students marked with the overall grade.

Evaluation of the written briefing papers follows standard academic operating procedures for the most part. The major deviation concerns the matter of format. I am rather strict about employing special format features such as executive summaries, headings and subheadings, and copious graphics. Students often dismiss these requirements as "picky details," failing to recognize that good format frequently makes the difference between a report that gets read and acted upon and one that gets tossed into the file cabinet.

Certainly such an exercise takes a great deal of time, both in and out of class. What educational returns does this investment produce?

Students who participate in this exercise learn a variety of policy analysis skills:

- Analytical skills (e.g., cost-benefit analysis, risk assessment), which vary depending on the specific requirements of the issue chosen;
- Skill in use of evidence;
- Research skills;
- Oral communication skills; and
- Writing skills.

In addition, the students learn the specific content and methods of their own problem areas and are exposed to a wealth of information and methods in their fellow students' presentations. Further, in the process of attending each other's presentations, students develop a certain camaraderie and learn how to learn from each other. Most important, students come to see how seemingly disparate disciplines, skills, and perspectives can be integrated into meaningful endeavors with practical payoffs.

The major cost of using oral presentations is time. I normally allow each student at least 15 minutes—10 minutes for presentation and 5 minutes for Q&A. The larger the number of students in a class, the less feasible the exercise. To a point, this problem can be overcome by using a team approach. Teams of three or four students can work together on a single problem and jointly prepare the oral and written briefing. This does, however, introduce two new wrinkles: coaching the students in the fine arts of group work and assigning grades without knowing exactly which team members did which work. There are a variety of methods for handling such matters, but that's another story.

■ ***Karen B. Wiley*** *is an associate professor in the humanities and social sciences department of the Colorado School of Mines. Her teaching and research interests are in environmental politics and science, technology, and society.*

■ *A p p e n d i x   8*

Guidelines for an Informal Debate

Identifying a Significant Early Education Issue for Debate

By grappling with issues through public debate, we can better understand how to improve or to protect the welfare and future of children, families, or staff involved in early education. To assist you in selecting issues and developing questions for debate, this book offers assorted readings and references on current topics of concern in early education. An issue chosen for debate should represent a genuine dispute and a desire for change on the part of some people. Moreover, both sides of the issue to be debated should be able to present plausible arguments

and some sound evidence to support their position. Examples of issues that readers in the past have chosen to debate are as follows:

1. Is television viewing at home or in a child-care program detrimental to children's health or learning?
2. Are laws and programs for bilingual education effective?
3. Should preschool teachers encourage children's exploration of nontraditional gender roles in play?
4. Are formal parent education programs helpful in becoming an effective parent?

A Framework for Analyzing Issues and Developing Debate Positions

The following table offers a framework for analyzing issues and developing debate positions. Using this framework, each side of the debate can prepare its basic arguments, supporting points, and advocated actions.

To identify possible arguments to support a position, the main issue can be broken down into definition, verification, or prescription questions (Oliver & Newmann, 1969; Taylor, 1961). A *definition question* focuses on the meaning of a key concept, phrase, or problem. A *verification question* focuses on the true state of affairs or how the world actually operates. A *prescription question* focuses on actions that should or should not be taken based on identified values or ethical principles. Examples of definition, verification, and prescription questions to investigate in preparing for a debate are as follows:

1. What do we mean by child abuse?   (definition)
2. Is group care detrimental to infants and toddlers?   (verification)
3. If an investigation indicates that a parent has abused his or her child, should either that child

or that parent be removed immediately from the home?   (prescription)

When formulating questions to address, also consider what positions the opposing side will take, the possible delimitations or constraints that either side will claim, and the possible consequences and side effects for advocated actions. Specific strategies for justifying or clarifying a position or viewpoint include the following:

1. Elaborating terms or making distinctions
2. Citing authoritative (expert) definitions or opinions
3. Describing observational or clinical evidence such as personal experiences, anecdotes from others, or case study examples
4. Describing and evaluating empirical evidence such as research or evaluation results
5. Using an analogy or example of a comparable situation
6. Calling for logical reasoning
7. Appealing to common sense, common experience, or common emotions (Oliver & Newmann, 1969)

Framework for Identifying and Analyzing Child Advocacy/Early Education Issues

Step 1: Identification of a Significant Issue in Early Childhood Education Today	Step 2: Ways to Address This Issue	Step 3: Boundaries for Positions on This Issue	Step 4: Strategies to Justify or Clarify Your Position on This Issue
	1. Definition Questions: What is the meaning of a word, phrase, or problem?	1. The significance of the issue for early education	1. Elaborating terms making distinctions, or clarifying ecological context for the issue
	2. Verification Questions: What is the true state of affairs, or how does the world operate?	2. The opposing positions and proposals	2. Citing authoritative (expert) definitions or opinions, current legislation, or court rulings
	3. Prescription (Value) Questions: What should or should not be done?	3. The view of the nature of childhood assumed by the opposing positions	3. Describing observational/clinical evidence: (a) personal experience, (b) others' anecdotes, or (c) case studies
		4. The possible delimitations or constraints claimed by the opposing positions	4. Describing and evaluating empirical evidence: (a) research studies (reliable, valid, and representative), (b) evaluation studies, or (c) statistical surveys
			5. Using an analogy or comparable situation
			6. Calling for logical reasoning or common sense

For example, an issue can be approached with logical reasoning. In this case, arguments based on relationships between propositions are prepared. Consider the following argument:

With an increase in the number of single, working mothers with preschool children, the demand for day care services is increasing. If these preschool mothers cannot find adequate and affordable day care services, they can be neither productive workers nor effective parents. Therefore, the government should provide tax credit for building day care facilities and purchasing equipment in areas that serve low-income families and should refund the current tax credit for child care to low-income families using day care who otherwise might not benefit from this income tax credit. (H.R. 5966, 1982)

When both the propositions and the relationships have been verified, this type of argument can be very convincing.

When addressing an issue, use of an analogy can also be very persuasive. The following analogy might be used in the issue: Should the state regulate child-care homes in the same way it regulates child-care centers?

Let's consider Mrs. Conway who runs a day-care home for neighborhood children. Now suppose Mrs. Conway instead sewed clothing for others in her home. You probably would not say that the same regulations should apply to her as apply to the local clothing manufacturing firm. Likewise, it can be said that the state should not regulate Mrs. Conway's day-care home through licensing as it does day-care centers.

Appealing to your audience's concerns, common experiences, and emotions can sometimes sway their opinion dramatically. Melton (1983) reports an incident about a conservative senator who became an adoption advocate when a lobbyist admired family pictures in his office and then shared pictures of her large family, including adopted children, and discussed the problems of supporting them without public subsidy.

Research and evaluation data and expert opinion are often used selectively by policy makers and advocates to advance their positions (Forgione, 1980). For example, initiation of legislation for the Head Start program relied on the work of Hunt and Bloom (Melton, 1983). Likewise, debate arguments can be bolstered by reference to research, evaluation, and expert opinion.

The framework presented here will not eliminate challenges, but it can help us to predict them. With practice in debating and increased knowledge of issues, we can clarify our values and make better decisions about the issues and policies that affect early education practice. (See the table on the next page for an outline of how the framework can be applied to a sample issue.)

After developing ideas, supporting points and reasoning, and proposing actions for its position on an issue, each debate team should prepare four or five challenge questions for the team taking the opposing side of the issue. These questions are intended to stimulate discussion in the course of the debate. Effective challenge questions are often introduced with an example or a description of some evidence as a point of reference.

Orchestrating an Informal Debate

To prepare you for presenting an informal debate, the following guidelines are provided (Freeley, 1976; Guiliano, 1985; Williamson-Ige, 1984; Windes & O'Neil, 1964; Ziegelmueller & Dause, 1975).

How Can Teams Prepare for an Informal Debate?

1. Research relevant journal and magazine articles, books, ERIC documents, government documents, and newspaper articles published within the last 10 years. Visit the library and learn how to find information by using various resources such as the on-line catalog, Current Index to Journals in Education (CIJE), Resources in Education (ERIC), government document files, and newspaper databases. Also research appropriate websites (e.g., see Appendix 1).

2. Select an issue and develop a debate question. Consult with your instructor if you need assistance in phrasing your debate question.

3. Set up two teams (two or three people on each team). One team will take the *pro* side of the debate question and the other team the *con* side.

4. Search for relevant, specific, and credible evidence (i.e., expert definitions, expert opinions, statistics, research findings, evaluation findings, testimony, and case descriptions) to support key arguments or propositions. Record evidence entries with complete reference citations (author[s] and copyright date) on separate note cards. Use a marker to highlight key terms or figures for easy retrieval during the debate.

5. Each team gathers or develops personal experience examples and analogies related to key arguments or propositions and records these entries on evidence cards.

6. Organize the evidence cards by evidence type and/or topic.

7. Each team organizes arguments and propositions in terms of:

Application of Framework to Sample Issue

Step 1: Identification of a Significant Issue in Early Childhood Education Today	Step 2: Ways to Address This Issue	Step 3: Boundaries for Positions on This Issue	Step 4: Strategies to Justify or Clarify Your Position on This Issue
Does removing abused children from their homes protect the well-being of children and improve family functioning?	1. Definition: What is child abuse?	1. Teachers are required to report suspected cases of child abuse and are expected to support families in their task of nurturing children.	1. Describing types and indicators of child abuse
	2. Verification: Under what circumstances are abused children removed from the home? What percentage of abused children are removed?	2. The child's vulnerability must be the foremost consideration in these situations. Only by considering the functioning of the family unit can long-term solutions be found.	2. Citing definitions of child abuse found in state laws
	3. Prescription: Should abused children genenerally be removed from their homes?	3. Young children are vulnerable and exposure to abuse at this age has long-lasting effects. Children are part of an interactive family unit and only within that context can solutions to abusive relations be found.	3. Describing (a) own observations as a member of a foster-care family, (b) newspaper-magazine articles about failure to remove an abused child, or (c) examples given by a child protective services worker during an interview
		4. In situations where extreme physical evidence is evident, the child must be removed from the home.	4. Describing an evaluation study that documents recurrence or severe abuse in families during different treatment programs
			Describing findings from the New York State Senate Report on Child Protective Services that shows 32% of indicated abuse and maltreatment cases receive foster care
		5. If removed, the child: (a) may be safer, (b) will become more trusting of others, (c) will develop self-esteem and more positive coping strategies, (d) will become lonesome and withdrawn, (e) will be placed in foster care, or (f) will or will not be reunited with his or her family.	5. Compare child abuse to actions taken to prevent cruelty to animals.
			6. Call for need to consider how much responsibility governmental agencies can effectively assume for child rearing.
		If not removed, the child: (a) will be subjected to further harm, (b) will participate in family assistance programs to improve family functioning, or (c) will maintain contact with family members.	

a. Significance of the issue for early education (need)

b. Definitions of key concepts

c. Child advocacy actions or early childhood programs/services that have been initiated

d. Child advocacy actions or early childhood programs/services that could be initiated

e. Conclusions about the merit of various viewpoints, actions, programs, or services (advantages versus disadvantages or evidence of adequacy versus inadequacy)

8. Each team types a brief introductory statement, four or five challenge questions, a brief summary statement, and a reference list (10 to 20 selected references) with complete bibliographic information for all sources used.

What Is the Format of the Informal Debate?

1. The instructor serves as moderator and time-keeper.

2. Each team takes 3 minutes to present its introductory statements.

3. For the next 20 minutes, the teams take turns asking each other challenge questions.

4. During the next 25 minutes, the moderator solicits comments and questions from the audience.

5. Finally, each team is allowed 2 minutes to sum up and conclude its arguments.

6. Afterwards, each audience member responds to the debate practices questionnaire. (See the next page for the debate questionnaire used during the debates.)

7. From process notes and submitted materials, the instructor later analyzes and evaluates the performance of individual team members and records audience contributions.

What Strategies Are Helpful During Delivery of a Debate?

1. Maintain eye contact. (Do not bury your head and read from note cards.) Try to convince the audience of your point of view. Be animated.

2. Use your three-minute introduction as a springboard.

3. Address the significance of the issue for early education in your introduction and/or summary.

4. While listening to the other team, take notes for possible followup or rebuttal statements.

5. Repetition of key points during the debate can be persuasive. Visual aids (containing a limited amount of print) can be effective for this purpose. Refer to your visuals during the course of the debate.

The debate process presented here is only one way to incorporate advocacy preparation into professional development and teacher education programs, but it is a way that encourages you to find your own answers to current issues, to engage in critical thinking, and to be well prepared as advocates. Furthermore, presentations of debates can expand to include audience members not only from the campus student body and faculty but also from interested community or professional groups (Derryberry, 1997). Following issue debates, you can make an easy transition to other advocacy activities mentioned in the previous chapters and in the other appendices. As preparation for advocacy, these other activities also are important because they can help develop interpersonal relationship skills and other critical thinking processes needed for effective advocacy (Brookfield, 1997; Burnett & Olson, 1997). Becoming more effective as advocates for children, their families, and the early childhood profession is one of the biggest challenges facing early childhood teachers and administrators today.

REFERENCES

Brookfield, S. D. (1997, Fall). Assessing critical thinking. *New Directions for Adult and Continuing Education, 75,* 17–29.

Burnett, A., & Olson, C. D. (1997). *The dark side of debate: The downfall of interpersonal relationships.* Paper presented at the annual meeting of the National Communication Association, Chicago.

Derryberry, B. R. (1997). *Forensics as a cooperative agent: Building a tradition within an academic community.* Paper presented at the annual meeting of the National Communication Association, Chicago.

Forgione, P. D. (1980). Early childhood policy-making. *Education and Urban Society, 12,* 227–239.

Freeley, A. J. (1976). *Argumentation and debate: Rational decision making* (4th ed.). Belmont, CA: Wadsworth.

Guiliano, N. A. (1985, February). The identification of the most significant problems confronting high school novice debaters and recommended solutions. *Debate Issues, 18,* 9–13.

H. R. 5966. (1981, March). *Congressional Record, 128*(32), p. H 1145.

Melton, G. B. (1983). *Child advocacy: Psychological issues and interventions.* New York: Plenum.

Oliver, D. W., & Newmann, F. M. (1969). *Cases and controversies: Guide to teaching the Public Issues Series/Harvard Social Studies Project.* Middletown, CT: Xerox Corp.

Taylor, P. W. (1961). *Normative discourse.* Englewood Cliffs, NJ: Prentice-Hall.

Williamson-Ige, D. K. (1984, May). Debate in the junior high school. *Debate Issues, 17,* 11–16.

Windes, R. R., & O'Neil, R. M. (1964). *A guide to debate.* Portland, MD: J. Weston Walch, Publisher.

Ziegelmueller, G. W., & Dause, C. A. (1975). *Argumentation: Inquiry and advocacy.* Englewood Cliffs, NJ: Prentice-Hall.

Debate Questionnaire

Please respond to this short questionnaire to let us know how you feel about our debate. Just mark an X on the line that best expresses your opinion regarding each statement.

Team 1 Members: _____

_____

_____

Issue (Viewpoint Argued): _____

	SUPERIOR	STRONG	AVERAGE	WEAK	UNSATISFACTORY
1.					
2.					
3.					
4.					
5.					
6.					

1. *Arguments:* Major arguments/propositions clearly stated. Relationships drawn between evidence, arguments, and propositions. Organized.

2. *Supporting Material:* Variety of examples/testimony, statistics, expert opinion/definitions, comparisons/analogies, and visual aids. Appropriate, relevant, and credible evidence. Sufficient evidence.

3. *Strategies to Persuade:* Adjustment/responsiveness to audience comments/questions. Balanced use of logical, emotional, and ethical appeals.

4. *Delivery:* Effective voice quality, eye contact, gestures, and posture.

5. *Tone of Argumentation:* Positive attitude toward self and other team. Orderly, courteous, and fair.

6. *Overall rating:*

Comments:

Team 2 Members: _____

_____

_____

Issue (Viewpoint Argued): _____

	SUPERIOR	STRONG	AVERAGE	WEAK	UNSATISFACTORY
1.					
2.					
3.					
4.					
5.					
6.					

1. *Arguments:* Major arguments/propositions clearly stated. Relationships drawn between evidence, arguments, and propositions. Organized.

2. *Supporting Material:* Variety of examples/testimony, statistics, expert opinion/definitions, comparisons/analogies, and visual aids. Appropriate, relevant, and credible evidence. Sufficient evidence.

3. *Strategies to Persuade:* Adjustment/responsiveness to audience comments/questions. Balanced use of logical, emotional, and ethical appeals.

4. *Delivery:* Effective voice quality, eye contact, gestures, and posture.

5. *Tone of Argumentation:* Positive attitude toward self and other team. Orderly, courteous, and fair.

6. *Overall rating:*

Comments:

	SA	A	D	SD	NA
1.					
2.					

1. This activity made me think about points that I had not considered before.

2. My position on this issue most resembles that of Team 1.

SA: Strongly Agree
A: Agree
D: Disagree
SD: Strongly Disagree
NA: No Answer or Can't Decide

A p p e n d i x   9

Four Steps to Selecting a Child Care Provider

Child Care Bureau, Administration for Children and Families

1. Interview Caregivers

Call First

Ask . . .

- Is there an opening for my child?
- What hours and days are you open and where are you located?
- How much does care cost? Is financial assistance available?
- How many children are in your care?
- What age groups do you serve?
- Do you provide transportation?
- Do you provide meals (breakfast, lunch, dinner, snacks)?
- Do you have a license, accreditation, or other certification?
- When can I come to visit?

Visit Next (Visit more than once, stay as long as you can!)

Look for . . .

- Responsive, nurturing, warm interactions between caregiver and children.
- Children who are happily involved in daily activities and comfortable with their caregiver.
- A clean, safe, and healthy indoor and outdoor environment, especially napping, eating and toileting areas.
- A variety of toys and learning materials, such as books, puzzles, blocks, and climbing equipment, that your child will find interesting and which will contribute to growth and development.
- Children getting individual attention.

Ask . . .

- Can I visit at any time?
- How do you handle discipline?

- What do you do if a child is sick?
- What would you do in case of an emergency?
- Are all children and staff required to be immunized?
- Do you have a substitute or back-up caregiver?
- Where do children nap? Do you know that babies should go to sleep on their backs?
- What training have you (and other staff/substitutes) had?
- May I see a copy of your license or other certification?
- May I have a list of parents (current and former) who have used your care?

2. Check References

Ask Other Parents . . .

- Was the caregiver reliable on a daily basis?
- How did the caregiver discipline your child?
- Did your child enjoy the child care experience?
- How did the caregiver respond to you as a parent?
- Was the caregiver respectful of your values and culture?
- Would you recommend the caregiver without reservation?
- If your child is no longer with the caregiver, why did you leave?

Ask the Local Child Care Resource and Referral Program or Licensing Office . .

- What regulations should child care providers meet in my area?
- Is there a record of complaints about the child care provider I am considering and how do I find out about it?

Administration for Children and Families. (1998). *Four steps to selecting a child care provider.* Washington, DC: U.S. Department of Health and Human Services.

3. Make the Decision for Quality Care

From What You Heard and Saw,
Ask Yourself . . .

- Which child care should I choose so that my child will be happy and grow?
- Which caregiver can meet the special needs of my child?
- Are the caregiver's values compatible with my family's values?
- Is the child care available and affordable according to my family's needs and resources?
- Do I feel good about my decision?

4. Stay Involved

Ask Yourself . . .

- How can I arrange my schedule so that I can . . .
  — talk to my caregiver every day?
  — talk to my child every day about how the day went?
  — visit and observe my child in care at different times of the day?
  — be involved in my child's activities?
- How can I work with my caregiver to resolve issues and concerns that may arise?
- How do I keep informed about my child's growth and development while in care?
- How can I promote good working conditions for my child care provider?
- How can I network with other parents?

These steps are only the beginning. Gather as much information as possible to help you find the best care for your child. To find the Child Care Resource and Referral Program nearest you, call: (800) 424-2246. For more complete guidelines on health and safety in child care, call (800) 598-KIDS (5437).

■ *Appendix 10*

Facts about Child Care in America

Children's Defense Fund

Every Day, 13 Million Preschoolers—
Including 6 Million Babies and Toddlers—
Are in Child Care.[1]

- *This is three out of five young children.* Millions more school-age children are in after-school and summer activities, and nearly 5 million children are left home alone after school while their parents work.[2]
- Children enter care as early as 6 weeks of age and can be in care for as many as 40 hours per week until they reach school age.

Women Work Outside the Home in the
Overwhelming Majority of American Families.

- Sixty-five percent of mothers with children under age 6, and 78 percent of mothers with children ages 6–13 are in the labor force.[3] Even half of mothers with infants (under age 1) are in the labor force.[4]

- In 1996, only 23 percent of all families with children younger than age 6—and only one third of *married couple* families with young children—had one parent working and one parent who stayed at home.[5]
- The majority (55 percent) of working women in the United States bring home *half or more* of their family's earnings.[6]
- One out of three children of working mothers are either poor even though their mother works, or *would* be poor if their mother didn't work.[7]

Child Care Costs Are Unaffordable for Many
Families.

- Full-day child care easily costs $4,000 to $10,000 per year—at least as much as college tuition at a public university.[8] Yet, about half of America's families with young children earn less than $35,000 per year.[9] A family with both parents

Child Care Arrangements of Children Younger than Age 5 with Working Mothers in 1994[10]

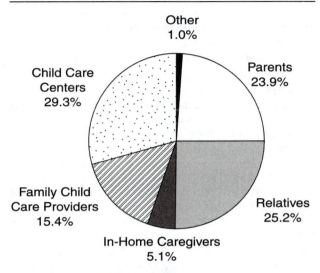

Definitions of Child Care Settings:

- *Child care centers:* care provided in nonresidential facilities, usually for 13 or more children
- *Family child care providers:* care provided in a private residence other than the child's home
- *In-home caregivers:* care provided within the child's home, by a person other than a parent or relative
- *Relative care:* care provided by a related person other than the parent, either in the child's or the relative's home

working full-time at minimum wage earns only $21,400 per year.

- Even though some subsidies are available for low-income families, funds are severely limited. *Currently, no state can afford to serve all families eligible under federal guidelines. Nationally, only one in 10 eligible children who need help are getting any assistance.*[11]
- The following are *average* child care costs for *one* 4-year-old child in a child care center; care for babies and toddlers costs more:[12]

Atlanta: $4,990	Kansas City: $5,200
Boston: $7,900	Los Angeles: $4,630
Columbus: $4,940	Raleigh: $5,070
Denver: $4,580	Seattle: $6,140

Child Care Helps Shape Children's Futures, Yet the Quality of Care for Many Children Is Inadequate.

- A recent Carnegie Corporation study confirmed that the quality of child care has a lasting impact on children's well-being and ability to learn.[13] Children in poor quality child care have been found to be delayed in language and reading

skills, and display more aggression toward other children and adults.[14]

- Recent studies have found that much of the child care in the United States is poor to mediocre. One study of four states found fully 40 percent of the rooms serving infants in child care centers to be of such poor quality as to jeopardize children's health, safety, or development.[15]
- Professional, quality child care is hard to find in a marketplace where child care teachers and providers do not earn as much as bus drivers ($20,150) or garbage collectors ($18,100)—and often earn less than bartenders ($14,450).[16] Child care workers earn an average of only $11,780 per year, and preschool teachers—many of whom are employed in the public schools—have an average annual salary of just $15,580.[17] In addition, child care workers tend to receive no benefits or paid leave.[18]
- Hairdressers and manicurists must attend 1,500 hours of training at an accredited school in order to get a license, yet 39 states and the District of Columbia do not require child care providers to have any early childhood training prior to serving children in their homes.[19]

Scarcity of After-School Programs Leaves School-Age Children Home Alone.

- Nearly 5 million children are home alone after school each week, during the afternoon hours when juvenile crime peaks.[20]
- A 1990 study found that eighth-graders left home alone after school reported greater use of cigarettes, alcohol, and marijuana than those who were in adult-supervised settings.[21]
- Good after-school activities for children and teens can be hard to find because options are inadequate in many communities. This problem is even more serious in low-income neighborhoods; in fact, only one-third of schools in low-income neighborhoods offered before- and after-school programs in 1993.[22]

CDF, a children's advocacy organization, is located at 25 E. Street NW, Washington, DC 20001. For further information about child care facts, contact CDF, Child Care Division, 202-662-547.

1. *Child Care and Early Education Program Participation of Infants, Toddlers, and Preschoolers.* (1996, Oct.). Washington, DC: National Center for Education Statistics.

2. *Factsheet on School-Age Children.* (1996, Sept.). Wellesley, MA: Center for Research on Women, Wellesley College.

3. The labor force includes mothers who are employed and mothers who are looking for work. Data from *Marital and Fam-*

ily Characteristics of the Labor Force from the March 1997 Current Population Survey, March 1997. Washington, DC: Bureau of Labor Statistics.

4. Most recent data available is from 1995. Data from *Fertility of American Women: June 1995 Update. Current Population Survey P20-499, October 1997.* Washington, DC: Census Bureau.

5. *Money Income in the United States, 1996. Report P60-197* (1997). Washington, DC: Census Bureau.

6. *Women: The New Providers. A Whirlpool Foundation Study.* (1995, May). New York: Families and Work Institute.

7. Calculations by CDF of data for 1996 from the *1997 Current Population Survey.* Washington, DC: Census Bureau.

8. Data on child care expenses from *Child Care Information Exchange.* (1996, July). Data collected from resource and referral agencies in each city. Data on average university costs cited in *Statistical Abstract of the United States.* (1994). Washington, DC: Census Bureau. Original data from the *Annual Survey of Colleges.* (1993). New York: College Board.

9. *Money and Income in the United States: 1996. Current Population Reports P60-197.* (1997). Washington, DC: Census Bureau.

10. Most recent data available is from 1994. CDF calculations of data from L. Casper (1997, March). *Who's Minding Our Preschoolers? Current Population Reports Household Economic Studies.* P70-62 Washington, DC: Census Bureau.

11. *Locked Doors: States Struggling to Meet the Child Care Needs of Low-Income Working Families.* (1998, March). Washington, DC: CDF.

12. Data from *Child Care Challenges.* (1998). Washington, DC: CDF. Also data from *The California Child Care Portfolio.* (1997). San Francisco: California Child Care Resource and Referral Network. Data collected from resource and referral agencies in each city.

13. *Starting Points: Meeting the Needs of Our Youngest Children.* (1994, Aug.). New York: Carnegie Corporation.

14. Testimony by Deborah Phillips before the Senate Committee on Labor and Human Resources, March 1, 1995.

15. Helburn et al. (1995). *Cost, Quality, and Child Outcomes Study: Executive Summary* (Denver: University of Colorado.

16. *Employment and Earnings.* (1994, Jan.). Washington, DC: Bureau of Labor Statistics.

17. *National employment and Wage Data from the Occupational and Employment Statistics survey, 1996.* (1997, Dec.). Washington, DC: Bureau of Labor Statistics. Annual wage calculated from hourly wage by CDF based on the assumption that child care staff work 35 hours per week, 50 weeks per year.

18. *Worthy Work, Unlivable Wages: The National Child Care Staffing Study, 1988–1997.* (1998). Washington, DC: Center for the Child Care Workforce; see also Helburn et al. (1995). *Cost, Quality, and Child Outcomes Study.* Denver: University of Colorado.

19. Azer & Capraro. (1997). *Data on Child Care Licensing.* Boston: Center for Career Development in Early Care and Education, Wheelock College.

20. *Factsheet on School-Age Children.* (1996, Sept.) Wellesley, MA: Center for Research on Women, Wellesley College.

21. Dwyer et al. (1990). Characteristics of Eighth-Grade Students Who Initiate Self-Care in Elementary and Junior High School, *Pediatrics, 86.*

22. *The Condition of Education: 1993.* (1993). Washington, DC: National Center for Education Statistics.

■ *Appendix 11*

The Rights of the Child: Summary of the United Nations' Convention

The Rights of the Child were adopted by the United Nations' General Assembly as a Convention on November 20, 1989. The Convention assumes that children have an inherent right to survival and development. Eleven basic rights that follow from this assumption are summarized below. These rights make the child's best interests the primary consideration but also take into account the rights and duties of parents (and where applicable the extended family or community), legal guardians, and others legally responsible for the child's care.

World Summit for Children. (1990). *First call for children.* New York: UNICEF.

1. Children have the right to be with their parents or with those who will care for them best.
2. Children have the rights to health care and to receiving enough food and clean water.
3. Children have the right to an adequate standard of living.
4. Children have the right to free and appropriate education.
5. Children with disabilities have the rights to special care and to access to developmental services.
6. Children have the rights to speak their own language and to practice their own religion and culture with other members of their group.
7. Children have the rights to be kept safe and not to be exploited, abused, neglected, or abducted.
8. Children have the right not be used as cheap labor or soldiers, or in the production or trafficking of drugs.
9. Children have the right to legal protection from injustice.
10. Children have the rights to express their own opinions, to meet together to express their views, and to privacy.
11. Children have the right to have access to information and material from a diversity of national and international sources.

■ *Appendix 12*

Are There Signs of Child Abuse and Neglect?
(Are There Signs That a Family May Be in Trouble?)

There are many indications that a family may be in trouble. Any one of them may not mean abuse or neglect and may have other explanations. If there are a number of them or if they occur frequently, child abuse or neglect may be suspected.

Type of Child Abuse/Neglect	Physical Indications/Child Appearance	Child Behavior	Parent/Caretaker Behavior
Physical Abuse 1. Assault with an implement 2. Assault without implement	Unexplained bruises and welts, especially in soft tissue area Unexplained burns Unexplained head or skeletal injuries Unexplained lacerations or abrasions	Wary of physical contact with adults Seeks affection from any adult Apprehensive when others cry Behavioral extremes (e.g., aggressiveness or withdrawal) Frightened of parents or little distress at separation Afraid to go home; hangs around school Reports injury by parents Exhibits anxiety about normal activities (e.g., napping) Wears concealing clothing	Harsh discipline, inappropriate for age and condition No explanation or offers explanation that doesn't make sense for child's injury Lack of concern about child Views child as "bad" Misuses alcohol or drugs Attempts to conceal child's injury History of abuse as a child Inappropriate expectations of the child to meet the adult's emotional needs

(continued)

Type of Child Abuse/Neglect	Physical Indications/ Child Appearance	Child Behavior	Parent/Caretaker Behavior
Physical Neglect 1. Abandonment 2. Refusal of custody 3. Failure to provide needed care for health condition 4. Inadequate physical supervision, including allowing excessive corporal punishment to be inflicted 5. Disregard of home hazards 6. Inadequate nutrition, clothing, or hygiene 7. Other (e.g., disregard for child's safety)	Consistent hunger, poor hygiene, inappropriate dress Consistent lack of supervision, especially in dangerous activities or for long periods Unattended physical problems or medical needs	Begging, stealing food Constant fatigue, listlessness, or falling asleep States there is no caretaker at home Frequent absence from school	Misuses alcohol or drugs Disorganized, unstable home life Apathetic Isolated socially Long-term chronic illness History of neglect as a child
Educational Neglect 1. Allowance of chronic truancy 2. Failure to enroll a child of mandatory school age in school 3. Failure to attend to a special educational need			
Sexual Abuse 1. Intrusion 2. Molestation with genital contact 3. Exhibitionism 4. Commercial exploitation through prostitution or the production of pornographic materials	Difficulty in walking or sitting Torn, stained, or bloody underclothing Pain or itching in genital area Bruises or bleeding in genital area Venereal disease	Unwilling to participate in some physical activities Withdrawal; fantasy or unusual infantile behavior Bizarre, sophisticated, or unusual sexual behavior or knowledge Poor peer relations Reports sexual assault by caretaker	Very protective or jealous of child Encourages child to engage in prostitution or sexual acts Misuses alcohol or drugs Frequently absent from home
Emotional Maltreatment 1. Verbal or emotional assault 2. Close confinement 3. Inadequate nurturance/ affection 4. Knowingly "permitted" drug or alcohol abuse or delinquency 5. Refusal of or failure to provide needed psychological care 6. Spousal abuse in the child's presence	Speech disorders Lags in physical development Failure-to-thrive	Habit disorders (sucking, biting, rocking, etc.) Conduct disorders (antisocial, self-destructive, defiant, etc.) Neurotic traits (sleep disorders, inhibition of play) Psychoneurotic reactions (hysteria, obsession, compulsion, phobias, hypochondria) Behavior extremes (e.g., compliant, passive, apathetic, aggressive, demanding) Overly adaptive behavior (e.g., inappropriately adult or inappropriately infant) Developmental lags (mental, emotional)	Blames or belittles child Cold and rejecting; withholds love Treats children in the family unequally Indifferent about child's problems Habitual scapegoating

Source: Based on Broadhurst, D. D. (1979). *The educator's role in the prevention and treatment of child abuse and neglect* (DHEW Publication No. OHDS 79-30172). Washington, DC: National Center on Child Abuse and Neglect; Broadhurst, D. D., Edmunds, M., & MacDicken, R. A. (1979). *Early childhood programs and the prevention and treatment of child abuse and neglect* (DHEW Publication No. OHDS 79-30198). Washington, DC: National Center on Child Abuse and Neglect; and National Clearinghouse on Child Abuse and Neglect Information (1998). What is child maltreatment? [Online]. Available: www.calib.com/nccanch/pubs/whatis.htm

Appendix 13

Diversity in the Classroom: A Checklist

Karen Matsumoto-Grah

This checklist is designed to help teachers and other educators to effectively identify and respond to diversity in the classroom. It focuses on various aspects of the classroom environment, including curriculum materials, teaching strategies and teacher/student behaviors.

Teaching Materials

_____ Are contributions and perspectives of women and cultures other than EuroAmericans integrated into textbooks and other curriculum materials?

_____ Are women, ethnic minorities and people of diverse socioeconomic classes and religions portrayed in a nonstereotypical manner?

_____ Do the resource materials include appropriate information about religion when religion is integral to the context of the subject?

_____ Do textbooks or curriculum materials focus on "famous people," usually those of privileged class status; or are the accomplishments and hard work of poor and working class people given equal focus and respect?

_____ Do the resource materials include cultures represented by families in your school and community?

_____ Are there resource materials available for limited-English-proficient students in their native languages?

_____ Are teaching materials selected that allow all students to participate and feel challenged and successful?

Teacher as Role Model—Questions to Ask Yourself

_____ Am I knowledgeable about the religious, cultural, linguistic and socioeconomic backgrounds of my students and people in my community?

_____ In my own life, do I model respect for, and inclusion of, people who are different (religion, race, language, abilities, socioeconomic class)?

_____ Do students perceive me as sincerely interested in, and respectful of, contributions made by women and the many ethnic, religious, racial and socioeconomic groups that make up the country?

_____ Do I know where to find resources regarding:
- Multicultural studies?
- Disabled students/specific handicaps?
- Religion?
- Other languages?
- Gender bias?

_____ Do I respectfully accommodate differently abled students in my classroom?

_____ Do I recognize and acknowledge the value of languages other than standard English?

_____ Can I recognize and constructively address value conflicts based on race, religion or socioeconomic class?

Teacher/Student Interactions

_____ Am I careful not to prejudge a student's performance based on cultural differences, socioeconomic status or gender?

_____ Do I promote high self-esteem for all children in my classroom? Do I help each child to feel good about who he/she is?

_____ Do I encourage students to understand and respect the feelings of others who are different from them?

Karen Matsumoto-Grah. (1992). Diversity in the classroom: A checklist. In D. A. Brynes & G. Kiger (Eds.), *Common bonds: Anti-bias teaching in a diverse society* (pp. 105–108). Reprinted by permission of Karen Matsumoto-Grah and the Association for Childhood Education International. Copyright © 1992 by the Association.

_____ Do my students see me as actively confronting instances of stereotyping, bias and discrimination when they occur?

_____ Given what I ask students to talk or write about, do I avoid placing value on having money, spending money or major consumer products?

_____ Do I put myself in the place of the limited-English-proficient student and ask, "How would I feel in this classroom?"

_____ Do I make an effort to learn some words in the home languages that my limited-English-proficient students speak?

_____ Am I conscious of the degree and type of attention I am giving to members of each gender in classroom interactions? Do I have an equitable system for calling on students?

_____ Do I use gender-neutral language?

_____ Do I teach about religion, rather than teaching religion or ignoring religion altogether?

_____ When teaching about religion, do I:

- Place religion within historical and cultural context?
- Use opportunities to include religion in history, literature and music?
- Avoid making qualitative comparisons among religions?
- Avoid soliciting information about the religious affiliations or beliefs of my students?

Teaching Children to Be Proactive

_____ Do I teach children to identify instances of prejudice and discrimination?

_____ Do I help my students develop proper responses to instances of prejudice and discrimination?

General Strategies

_____ Do I involve parents and other community members to help children develop greater understanding of the benefits and challenges of living in a culturally diverse society?

_____ Do I inform parents of my multicultural, anti-bias curriculum?

_____ Do I support and encourage the hiring of minority teachers and staff?

_____ Do I build a secure and supportive atmosphere by creating a noncompetitive classroom environment?

_____ Do I use opportunities such as current events to discuss different cultures and religions?

_____ Do I provide students with opportunities to problem-solve issues of inclusiveness?

_____ Do I use activities that demonstrate how the privilege of groups of higher economic status is directly connected to the lack of privilege of lower socioeconomic status people?

_____ Do I have students examine and analyze the representation of class, race, gender, ability and language differences in media and their community?

_____ Do I recognize that tracking reinforces "classism" and is counterproductive to student learning at all ability levels?

_____ Do I utilize children's literature to help students understand and empathize with individuals who have experienced prejudice and discrimination and to discuss important social issues?

Appendix 14

Books Related to Ethnic Diversity

EXAMPLES OF BOOKS THAT CONVEY UNDISTORTED OR ANTIRACIST MESSAGES

Ancona, G. (1994). *The pinata maker*. San Diego, CA: Harcourt Brace.

Ashley, B. (1992). *Cleversticks*. New York: Crown.

Ata, T. (1989). *Baby rattlesnake*. San Francisco: Children's Book Press.

Bryan, A. (1995). *What a wonderful world*. New York: Atheneum.

Chocolate, D. M. N. (1996). *A very special Kwanzaa*. New York: Scholastic.

Crews, D. (1991). *Bigmama's*. New York: Greenwillow.

Dorros, A. (1991). *Abuela*. New York: Dutton.

Heo, Y. (1994). *One afternoon*. New York: Orchard.

Hoffman, M. (1991). *Amazing Grace*. New York: Dial.

Hru, D. (1996). *The magic moonberry jump ropes*. New York: Dial.

Joosse, B. (1991). *Mama, do you love me?* San Francisco: Chronicle.

King, S. M. (1995). *A special kind of love*. New York: Scholastic.

McKissack, P. C. (1989). *Nettie Jo's friends*. New York: Knopf.

McKissack, P. C. (1997). *Ma Dear's aprons*. New York: Atheneum.

Mitsui Brown, J. (1994). *Thanksgiving at Obaachan's*. Chicago: Polychrome.

Munsch, R., & Kusugak, M. (1988). *A promise is a promise*. Toronto: Annick Press.

Nikola-Lisa, W. (1994). *Bein' with you this way*. New York: Lee & Low.

Norman, H. (1987). *Who-Paddled-Backward-With-Trout*. Boston: Little, Brown.

Osofsky, A. (1992). *Dreamcatcher*. New York: Orchard.

Say, A. (1990). *El Chino*. Boston: Houghton Mifflin.

Soto, G. (1995). *Chato's kitchen*. New York: G. P. Putnam's Sons.

Steptoe, J. (1988). *Baby says*. New York: Lothrop.

Swamp, J. (1995). *Giving thanks: A Native American good morning message*. New York: Lee & Low.

Wheeler, B. (1986). *Where did you get your moccasins?* Winnipeg, CAN: Peguis.

Williams, V. B. (1990). *More, more, more, said the baby*. New York: Greenwillow.

Wood, D. (1996). *Northwoods cradle song from a Menominee lullaby*. New York: Simon & Schuster.

EXAMPLES OF BOOKS THAT CONVEY STEREOTYPES OR RACIST MESSAGES

Baker, B. (1975). *Three fools and a horse*. New York: Macmillan.

Bierhorst, J. (1987). *Doctor Coyote*. New York: Macmillan.

Eastman, P. D. (1964). *The cat in the hat beginner book dictionary*. New York: Random House.

Friskey, M. (1959). *Indian Two Feet and his horse*. Chicago: Children's Press.

Fritz, J. (1982). *The good giants and the bad Pukwudgies*. New York: G. P. Putnam's Sons.

Hoff, S. (1961). *Little chief*. New York: Harper.

Martin, B., & Archambault, J. (1987). *Knots on a counting rope*. New York: Holt.

McGovern, A. (1976). *If you lived with Sioux Indians*. New York: Scholastic.

Paterson, D. (1983). *Hey, cowboy!* New York: Knopf.

Roth, S. L (1988). *Kenahéna, a Cherokee story*. New York: St. Martin's Press.

Sendak, M. (1962). *Alligators all around*. New York: Harper & Row.

■ *Index*

Aber, L., and Palmer, J., 62, 63–65
Advocacy (*see also* Legislation and regulations; Policy formation):
  attributes and skills needed for, 6–7, 94–97, 220–221, 222–223
  early childhood personnel and:
    needs of, 3–4, 71–72, 101–102, 106, 109–110, 209–211
    role of, 3–7, 67–69, 70–72, 93–97, 98, 106, 109–110, 193–194, 210
  families and:
    needs of, 1–3, 70–72, 74–78, 88, 92–93, 156–158, 159–160
    role of, 3–4, 50–51, 52, 54–55, 56, 68–69, 151–155, 157, 178–185
  strategies, 7–11, 39–42, 56–59, 73, 79–80, 82–84, 89, 100–102, 110–112, 133–136, 159–162, 188–189, 212–216
    coalitions, 7, 46, 55, 68, 73, 101, 157, 221
    court actions, 73, 76, 117
    debates, 7, 59, 135, 187, 229–234
    hearings, 7, 54, 75, 210
    information pamphlets and displays, 7, 41–42, 56, 83, 100–101, 160–161, 189, 226
    legislative initiatives, 7, 73, 83, 193–194, 210, 212–213, 224, 225–226, 231
    letter writing, 7, 46, 54, 56, 57, 73, 82, 210, 215, 221–222
    media coverage, 7, 57, 73–76, 135, 188, 221, 222–223
    position statements, 7, 33, 36, 48, 54, 62, 70–72, 88, 146–147, 165, 167, 171, 173, 226–229
    speakers and panel discussions, 7, 59, 83, 161, 188–189, 212–213
Aggression, 37, 88, 91, 143, 158, 239–240 (*see also* Violence)
Aidman, A., 45, 49–51
American Academy of Pediatrics, 45, 48, 220
Antibias curriculum, 17, 24, 28–30, 106, 107–113, 114, 115, 134
Assessment, 185, 186, 195–196 (*see also* Evaluation of early childhood programs; Screening)
Axelrod, L., 45, 46–47

Bilingual education, 117–120, 130, 131, 134–135, 173
Brain development, 3, 48, 62, 63–65, 75, 81, 144, 172–173, 186–187, 188–189, 199
Bredekamp, S., 4, 9, 25, 135, 136, 165, 167, 168, 170, 171, 174, 185, 187, 188
Bronfenbrenner, U., 3, 121, 122

Center for Media Education, 46, 53–54, 56, 57
Charlesworth, R., 58, 165, 170–177
Charren, P., 45, 46–47
Child care (*see also* Evaluation of early childhood programs; On-site program study; Policy formation):
  accreditation of, 8–9, 197, 200, 210, 213
  attachment, effects of, 64, 211–212
  costs and funding for, 2–3, 29, 193–194, 199–200, 201, 203, 206, 207, 210, 212, 237
  enrollment in, 2, 151, 203, 236
  ethnic diversity and, 2–3, 104–106, 134, 173–174, 206
  kinds of, 1, 28, 29, 121–130, 132, 160, 184, 195–196, 202–203, 236–237
  need for, 1–3, 151, 194, 195, 202, 212, 225, 236–237
  in other countries, 179, 184, 201–208, 213–214
  quality of, 2–3, 64, 68, 72, 194, 195–198, 202–203, 207, 210, 211, 213, 214–215, 237
  regulations, 97, 121, 197, 199, 202, 207, 212, 213
  selection of, 70, 132, 197, 211, 212, 235–236
Child Care Bureau, 220, 235–236
Child Care, Inc., 224
Child development, 22–27, 37, 48, 50, 63–64, 66–67, 148–149, 153, 165, 166–168, 173, 174, 186, 187, 189, 197, 211
  gender identity and, 14–15, 23–24, 42, 109
  racial identify and, 107–109
Children's Defense Fund, 82, 212, 220, 225–226, 236–238
Children's rights, 4, 88, 238–239
  access to information and, 25, 37–38, 59, 239
  child abuse and, 3, 64, 88, 91, 98, 239
  early intervention services and, 68, 72, 91, 121, 131, 132, 239
  environmental hazards and, 63–64, 66–69, 81, 88, 239
  health care and, 70–71, 82, 88, 201, 239
  nutrition and, 63, 88, 239
  privacy and, 23, 25, 38, 53–55, 91, 204, 239
  quality child care, appropriate education and, 64, 70, 82, 88, 120, 132, 173, 202, 239
Comer, J. P., 173–174
Computers, 53–56, 187, 188
Concerned Educators Allied for a Safe Environment (CEASE), 87, 88, 101
Coontz, S., 161
Copple, C., 4, 9, 135, 165, 170, 171, 185, 187, 188
Cost, Quality, and Child Outcomes Study, 64, 195, 196, 207
Coucheour, D., and Chrisman, K., 15, 22–27
Creaser, B., and Dau, E., 133

Cultural values (*see also* Violence):
  child abuse and, 3, 88, 89–91, 94–95, 97, 98
  diversity of, 3, 28–29, 36–37, 39, 90–91, 94–95, 98,
     104–106, 114–115, 133–134, 144, 157, 173–174
  early childhood programs and, 2, 73, 77, 173, 174,
     178, 201, 205, 207
  economic, 4, 52, 53–55, 64, 74–75, 145, 206–207
  environment and, 63–64, 66–69, 81, 168–169
  gender roles and, 15, 16, 20, 22, 23, 24, 37–42
  media and, 24, 25, 39, 49–50, 52, 54, 57–59, 74–76,
     77, 88–90, 99, 101, 105, 108, 114, 216
Current events portfolio, 7–8, 216

Derman-Sparks, L., 17, 18, 24, 32, 33, 36, 38, 106, 107–
     113, 114, 116, 133, 134
Developmentally appropriate curricula, 8–9, 25–26, 30,
     37–38, 41, 99, 135, 143, 165, 166–169, 170–177,
     178–185, 187, 188, 189, 196, 206
Discussion of issues:
  with children, 20, 24–25, 95–96, 111
  with parents, 25, 26, 30–37, 95, 96–97, 112, 174
Disease prevention, 67, 70–71, 83–84
Division of Early Childhood/Council on Exceptional
     Children, 132, 174

Elkind, D., 140, 141–145, 158, 161, 168, 187
Environmental Protection Agency (EPA), 66, 84
Erikson, E., 144, 173
Ethics, 27, 96–97, 223
  codes of, 4, 211
Evaluation of early childhood programs (*see also* On-site
     program study):
  bilingual, 117–120, 131
  computer, 45, 53–55, 56
  developmentally appropriate practice and, 171–172
  nutrition, 75–78
  in other countries, 55, 184, 201–208
  parenting, 157
  television, 45, 47, 48–51, 55–59

Families (*see also* Parents):
  changes in, 1–2, 4, 39, 52, 140, 141–145, 148,
     156, 161
  child-rearing practices in, 2, 22–23, 24–25, 89, 91, 92–
     93, 139–140, 148, 153–155, 158, 197
  incomes of, 1–2, 52, 63–65, 66–67, 196, 197
  influences of, 3, 22, 38, 142, 144, 148–149, 156,
     158–159
  relationships in, 3, 41, 91, 92–93, 98, 141–142, 148,
     151–152, 159
  values of, 22, 23, 27, 29–36, 38, 39, 112, 141–
     145, 197
Family Involvement Partnership for Learning, 140,
     146–147

Garbarino, J., 87, 89–91
Gilligan, J., 101

Hauser-Cram, P., 140, 153–155
Head Start, 1, 121, 122, 148–149, 151–152, 174,
     199, 207
Healy, J., 55, 187

Jacobson, L., 186, 188, 194, 199–200
Jensen, M. A., 1–13, 62, 73–80

Kagan, S. L., 2, 136, 140, 156–158, 173
Kindergarten, 1, 143, 165, 171, 172, 173, 178–185
Koralek, D., 87, 92–98

Lakey, J., 15, 28–37
Leadership, 3–7, 11, 35, 46–47
  strategies, 39–42, 56–59, 82–84, 100–102, 133–136,
     159–162, 188–189, 212–216
Legislation and regulations (*see also* Advocacy; Policy
     formation):
  bilingual education, 117
  child-care programs, 1, 197, 207, 210, 212–213, 214
  child nutrition programs, 70–71, 73–80
  child protection, 3, 50, 68, 81, 88, 94
  parenting and family support programs, 157–158, 159,
     160, 161
  programs for children with disabilities, 68, 72, 121,
     132, 135, 136, 174
  television programming for children, 46, 50, 55,
     56, 88
Levin, D. E., 55, 57, 100
Lieber, J., Beckman, P. J., Hanson, M. J., and others,
     106, 121–130
Louv, R., 45, 52

Matsumoto-Grah, K., 241–242
McBride, B., and Rane, T. R., 140, 148–150, 158
Mental health, 4, 17, 22, 23, 29, 63–64, 72, 82, 102,
     143, 151–152, 173, 179, 180, 183–184, 185, 204,
     239–240

National Association for the Education of Young
     Children (NAEYC), 8–9, 38, 130, 131, 165, 167,
     170, 171, 173, 197, 200, 210, 213, 215, 220
National Center for Early Development and Care, 194,
     195–198
National Education Goals, 3, 4, 82, 136, 146, 162, 185–
     186, 211, 215
Nutrition, 63, 72, 73–86, 139–140, 204, 205, 240

On-site program study, 8–11, 39–41, 55, 83–84, 101–
     102, 134, 161, 188, 211, 213, 214–125

Paley, V. G., 24, 180
Parents (*see also* Families):
  conferences with teachers, 25, 96–97, 139–140,
     154–155
  education of, 140, 144, 154–155, 156–158, 161–162
     antibias curriculum, 28–29, 112, 133
     child-care choices, 70, 197, 236–236

Parents *(continued)*
  developmentally appropriate practices, 144, 180, 189
  general health and nutrition, 70–72, 83
  media, 56
  sexuality development, 25–26, 39, 41
  expectations of, 22–23, 30, 31, 33, 118, 135, 140, 153, 158, 159, 172, 182, 183, 188
  guidelines for, 50–51, 54–55, 56, 235–236
  involvement in education, 25–26, 29, 36, 111–112, 140, 146–147, 148–150, 151–152, 158, 159, 161, 162, 174, 178–179, 211
  rights of, 33, 97, 131, 207, 238
  as teachers, 144, 152, 184, 189
Pelzer, D. J., 101
Phillips, C. B., 133
Phillips, L., 37, 42
Piaget, J., 24, 25, 166, 170, 173
Pipher, M., 56
Play, 23, 38, 48, 55, 179, 180, 181, 182, 184, 204, 205–206
Poinsett, N., and Burns, V., 133
Polakow, V., 99, 194, 201–208
Policy formation *(see also* Advocacy; Child care, regulations; Legislation and regulations):
  bilingual education, 117–120
  books for children, 17–18, 37–38, 39–41, 41–42, 115–116, 134, 241, 242
  child-care funding, 193–194, 197, 201, 207, 213–214
  child health, 25, 27, 64, 67–69, 70–72, 81–86, 201
  child nutrition programs, 73–80
  child protection, 89–91, 98, 99, 239–240
  children with disabilities, 68, 82, 121–122, 132
  early childhood personnel, 72, 121–130, 197, 202, 206, 208, 210–211, 214–215
  family involvement and parenting, 146–147, 148–150, 157–158, 201
  goals for early childhood programs, 26, 29, 36, 109, 167–168, 170–171, 241–242
  media for children, 45, 46–47, 48, 50, 53, 54, 55
Pollack, W., 37, 42
Poverty, 1, 63–65, 66–67, 73, 88, 156, 201 *(see also* Families, incomes of; Welfare reform; Working parents):
Professional relationships, 27, 96–97, 106, 121–130, 223
Professionalization, 4–5, 67–69, 93–97, 106, 109–110, 151–152, 153–155, 183 *(see also* Ethics, codes of)
Program field study *(see* On-site program study)

Reddy, M. T., 131, 133
Reese, D., 106, 114–116
Resource and referral agencies, 92, 197, 212, 236
Richards, K. N., 101
Ruenzel, D., 165, 178–185

Scherer, M., 140, 141–145
Screening, 68, 71, 136, 181
Sex education, 15, 22–27, 38, 39, 41–42

Shioshita, J., 194, 209–211
Slapin, B., and Seale, D., 115, 133
Social change, 1–2, 4, 52, 89–90, 110, 112, 121–122, 140, 141–145, 148, 156–158, 179–180, 183, 195
Staff:
  morale, 3–4, 204, 206
  preparation and professional development, 3, 4, 71, 72, 101–102, 112, 115–116, 129, 135, 174, 195, 197, 199, 202, 210, 214–215, 233, 237
  skills needed *(see also* Advocacy):
    for child guidance, 20, 24–25, 95–96, 111, 182, 203–204, 205–206, 209
    for curriculum planning, 104–106, 110–111, 115, 165, 166–169, 173
    for working with children with disabilities, 106, 121–130, 132, 135, 174
    for working with children from diverse cultural backgrounds, 104–106, 107–113, 114–116, 144, 170–174, 241–242
    for working with parents, 25, 27, 35–36, 96–97, 115, 146–147, 149–150, 151–152, 153–155, 158, 159
  wages and benefits, 3, 194, 195–196, 197, 200, 202, 204, 209–211, 215, 237
Stereotyping:
  disability, 58, 109, 132
  gender, 14–15, 16–21, 23, 37–38, 39–41, 42, 57–58, 109
  race and ethnicity, 58, 108–109, 114–116, 131, 134, 172
  socioeconomic class, 148, 172

Tatum, B. D., 133
Television, 25, 39, 44–45, 46–52, 55, 143

United Nations' Convention on the Rights of the Child, 59, 98, 131, 216, 238–239
U.S. Department of Health and Human Services, 2, 62, 70–72, 81, 84, 220

Violence, 59, 90, 100–101, 151–152 *(see also* Aggression)
  guns and, 88, 99
  television and, 49–51, 55, 59, 87, 88, 100

Walters, L. S., 106, 117–120
Welfare reform, 4, 161, 193–194, 195, 207
Wellhousen, K., 15, 16–21, 39
Whitebook, M., 3–4, 7, 196, 197, 213, 221
Wiley, K. B., 226–229
Wilson, R. A., 62, 66–69, 165, 166–169
Women, Infants and Children (WIC), Special Supplemental Food Program for, 61–62, 70–71, 73–80, 83, 160
Working parents, 2, 141, 183, 193, 195, 202, 206, 236–237
World Summit for Children, 238–239

Zeak, G., 140, 151–155